Short Cuts to Great Gardens

A PRACTICAL GUIDE TO
LOW-MAINTENANCE GARDENING

PUBLISHED BY THE READER'S DIGEST ASSOCIATION LIMITED
LONDON • NEW YORK • SYDNEY • MONTREAL

www.readersdigest.co.uk

Paperback edition 2001

Origination: Colourscan, Singapore
Printing and binding: Milanostampa, Italy

ISBN 0 276 42568 5

Contents

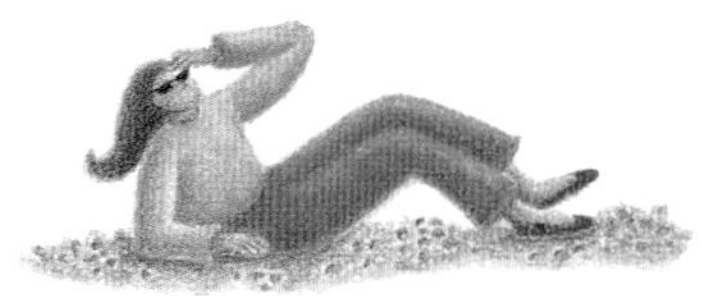

SHORT CUTS TO GREAT GARDENS
was created and produced by Carroll & Brown Limited,
20 Lonsdale Road, London NW6 6RD
for The Reader's Digest Association Limited, London

CARROLL & BROWN

Publishing Director Denis Kennedy
Art Director Chrissie Lloyd

Managing Editor Laura Price

Editor Jonathan Edwards
Assistant Editor Georgina Power

Senior Art Editor Anne Fisher
Art Editor Gilda Pacitti

Photographers David Murray, Jules Selmes
Photographic assistants Sheryllin Cutler, M-A Hugo, Colin Tathan

Picture research Sandra Schneider

Production Wendy Rogers

Computer Management John Clifford, Elisa Merino, Paul Stradling

HORTICULTURAL CONSULTANT

Sue Phillips

CONTRIBUTORS

Jane Courtier Lisa Davis Liz Dobbs Martin Fish Jenny Hendy
Daphne Ledward Sue Phillips Philip Swindells

SPECIALIST CONSULTANTS

Guy Barter Matthew Biggs Ruth Chivers Fred Downham Jo Wells Sarah Wilson

ILLUSTRATORS

Sharon Beedon Tony Graham Valerie Hill Vanessa Luff
Gill Tomblin Sue Williams John Woodcock

FOR THE READER'S DIGEST

Editor Henrietta Heald
Art Editors Julie Busby, Joanna Walker

READER'S DIGEST GENERAL BOOKS

Editorial Director Cortina Butler
Art Director Nick Clark
Executive Editor Julian Browne
Editorial Group Heads Ruth Binney, Noel Buchanan
Style Editor Ron Pankhurst

Foreword

Life gets busier and busier and it is harder than ever to fit in all the things you have to do, let alone what you'd like to do. It isn't just working people and parents of young children who are short of time; people are retiring younger and keeping fitter, and they soon find their new-found freedom swallowed up by a host of tasks, social events and leisure activities.

Finding time to look after your garden might not be easy, but the rewards are great. The right garden has a beneficial effect – an oasis of calm to recharge your batteries – and it is also one that is tailored to suit your lifestyle, and your gardening aspirations.

To cope with a busy life, you will need to organise your garden to give you more of what you want for less effort – whether it is the desire to have well-kept surroundings, to enjoy the creative satisfaction of designing with plants or to relax and entertain family and friends out of doors.

Being busy doesn't mean you have to make do with a boring garden. It means taking advantage of the latest labour-saving products and techniques, and using easy-care plants that allow you to cut down on chores so that you have more time to spend doing what you enjoy most.

This book helps you to tip the balance back in favour of gardening for enjoyment. It shows you how you can have the garden of your dreams in the time you can afford. It tells you how to make a garden that suits the way you want to use it; where you can cut corners and still achieve acceptable results. It explains which jobs will save you time in the long run; how to choose the right plants, products or equipment for best results; and when it's worth getting someone in to tackle a specific task.

However much or little of a gardener you are, you'll find something in here that will help you to make more of your time in the garden. You can 'dip in' at your leisure, and do anything from find a quick solution to a nagging problem to treating yourself to a completely new, easy-care garden.

Enjoy your gardening.

Sue Phillips
Horticultural consultant

High interest, low upkeep

BY ELIMINATING TIME-HUNGRY TASKS YOU WILL BE ABLE TO CREATE A DELIGHTFUL GARDEN AND STILL HAVE TIME TO LEAD A BUSY LIFE

The successful gardener who leads a busy life knows that a garden must be designed for beauty and pleasure without being a burden. To achieve this, you must decide exactly what you want from your garden, what you like and dislike as well as how much time and money you can afford to spend achieving it. This book helps you to sort out your priorities and, like a good gardening friend, explains how you can reduce the workload without sacrificing results or missing out on gardening activities you enjoy. It tells you when it is worth spending money instead of time to get a job done and why it sometimes pays to put in a little effort now to gain an enormous benefit later.

The book shows you how, by making simple design changes and choosing attractive yet trouble-free plants, you can create a garden that is high on interest but low on maintenance. By taking advantage of new time-saving products and techniques you can even indulge in activities that are traditionally high-maintenance, such as growing lots of plants in containers or having a productive fruit and vegetable plot, without becoming a slave to your garden. Above all, this book helps you to eliminate the chores so that you can spend your time doing what you love most in the garden.

Reflections on an easy-care garden With the right tips at hand, you can create a beautiful garden with the minimum of effort. Even a feature such as this formal pond with fountain can be set up to require hardly any routine care.

How much time do you waste in your garden?

If you find that gardening is one long battle against the clock and the calendar, take a look at the way you have designed your garden, the plants you have chosen and how you organise the work. Consider the 12 top time-wasters on these pages and decide how you could achieve the garden that you really want and also leave yourself time to enjoy it.

Identifying the time-wasters
Use the two gardens illustrated to help you pinpoint where you can save time in your garden.

❶ = time-hungry features
① = time-saving features

1 TRAINING – select climbers that need no tying to their supports. Avoid trained forms of plants that require pruning and tying in every year. Also avoid climbers that need regular pruning to keep them healthy, productive and under control.

2 HEDGING – instead of a formal hedge that needs trimming twice a year, use an informal border of compact evergreen shrubs which don't need pruning. If you want a hedge, choose one that is not too vigorous for the chosen position and that is trouble free.

3 EQUIPMENT – use the right tools, garden products and equipment to get the job done fast. If a task is easy to do, don't leave it to become a problem. For occasional big tasks, consider hiring specialist tools or employing a contractor to do the job for you.

4 WATERING – to reduce watering time grow drought-tolerant plants, apply a layer of mulch to prevent evaporation from the soil and water only those plants that really need it. Install an automatic watering system, especially where regular watering is needed, such as for container plants and in the greenhouse.

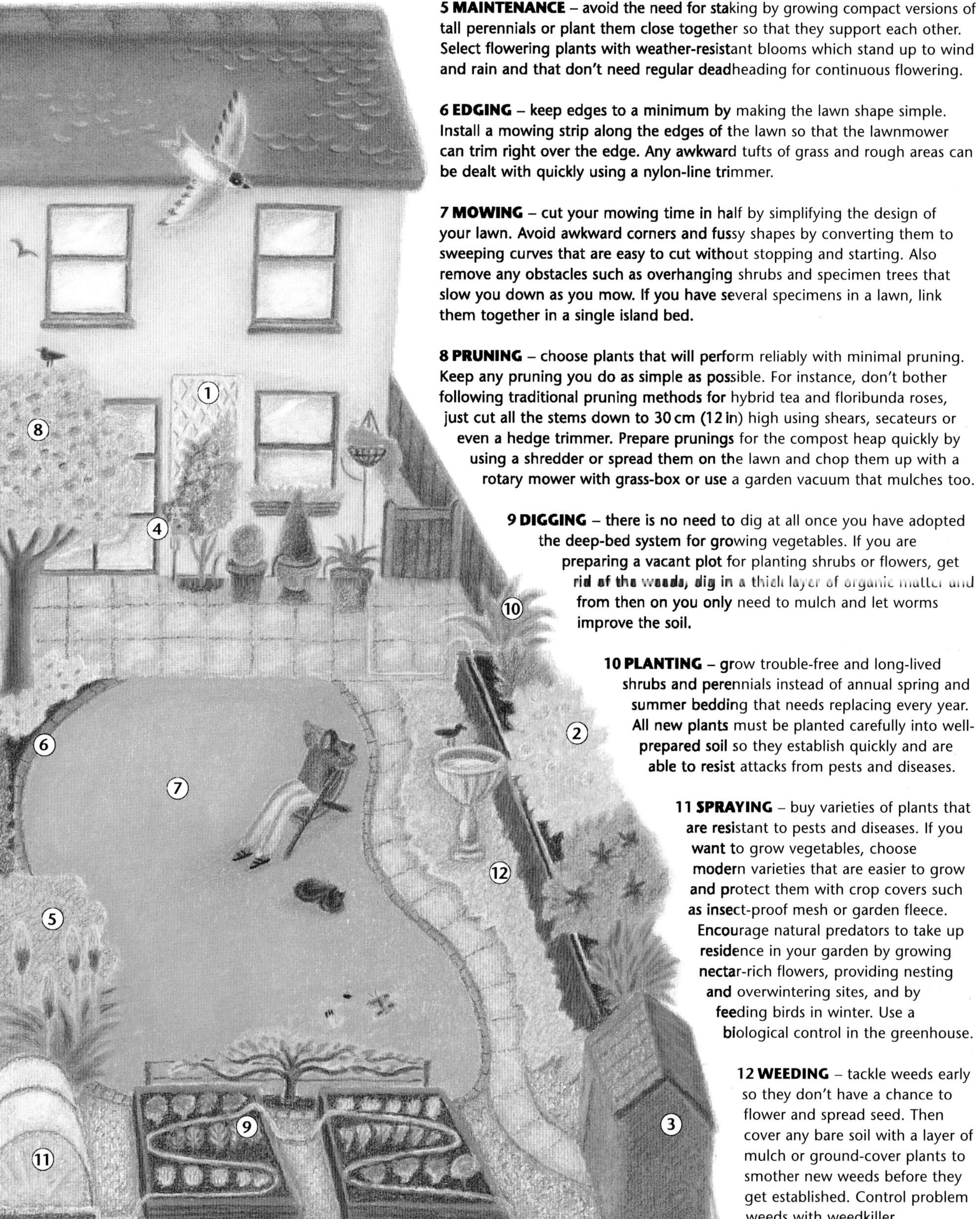

5 MAINTENANCE – avoid the need for staking by growing compact versions of tall perennials or plant them close together so that they support each other. Select flowering plants with weather-resistant blooms which stand up to wind and rain and that don't need regular deadheading for continuous flowering.

6 EDGING – keep edges to a minimum by making the lawn shape simple. Install a mowing strip along the edges of the lawn so that the lawnmower can trim right over the edge. Any awkward tufts of grass and rough areas can be dealt with quickly using a nylon-line trimmer.

7 MOWING – cut your mowing time in half by simplifying the design of your lawn. Avoid awkward corners and fussy shapes by converting them to sweeping curves that are easy to cut without stopping and starting. Also remove any obstacles such as overhanging shrubs and specimen trees that slow you down as you mow. If you have several specimens in a lawn, link them together in a single island bed.

8 PRUNING – choose plants that will perform reliably with minimal pruning. Keep any pruning you do as simple as possible. For instance, don't bother following traditional pruning methods for hybrid tea and floribunda roses, just cut all the stems down to 30 cm (12 in) high using shears, secateurs or even a hedge trimmer. Prepare prunings for the compost heap quickly by using a shredder or spread them on the lawn and chop them up with a rotary mower with grass-box or use a garden vacuum that mulches too.

9 DIGGING – there is no need to dig at all once you have adopted the deep-bed system for growing vegetables. If you are preparing a vacant plot for planting shrubs or flowers, get rid of the weeds, dig in a thick layer of organic matter and from then on you only need to mulch and let worms improve the soil.

10 PLANTING – grow trouble-free and long-lived shrubs and perennials instead of annual spring and summer bedding that needs replacing every year. All new plants must be planted carefully into well-prepared soil so they establish quickly and are able to resist attacks from pests and diseases.

11 SPRAYING – buy varieties of plants that are resistant to pests and diseases. If you want to grow vegetables, choose modern varieties that are easier to grow and protect them with crop covers such as insect-proof mesh or garden fleece. Encourage natural predators to take up residence in your garden by growing nectar-rich flowers, providing nesting and overwintering sites, and by feeding birds in winter. Use a biological control in the greenhouse.

12 WEEDING – tackle weeds early so they don't have a chance to flower and spread seed. Then cover any bare soil with a layer of mulch or ground-cover plants to smother new weeds before they get established. Control problem weeds with weedkiller.

The garden you want in the time you've got

Whatever stage you are at in your gardening career, there is never enough time. At first there is a garden to create, whether from scratch or by adapting an existing one. The garden will have to be functional and easy to look after, yet attractive to look at. As time goes by and your gardening knowledge increases, more ambitious plans may take root. Time may be even more precious but finances are often not so restrictive, presenting a whole new set of gardening opportunities. Later on, changes in responsibilities and the way you live often require a complete rethink in the garden.

Here we summarise ten case studies of gardeners that appear elsewhere in this book. They are typical of the lifestyles of many gardeners, each with varying amounts of time to spend in the garden and with very different requirements. Look for the case study that corresponds most closely to your own needs and then follow the signposts to the most appropriate parts of the book. There you will receive straightforward advice on how to achieve the garden you want in the time you have available.

PROFESSIONAL COUPLE, NEW HOUSE
Joanna and Richard Robinson both work full-time and wanted an attractive outdoor living space (page 210).

Time available An average of 2 hours a week.

Features wanted Patio for eating and entertaining; formal pool and fountains.

► **Go to** Summer colour (page 130); patios (page 170); garden lighting (page 197); water gardening (page 204); buying plants in flower (page 260); using a hired contractor (page 302).

PROFESSIONAL COUPLE, TWO CATS
Alison and Denis Kennedy have full-time jobs in the city. They wanted a garden where they can relax at weekends, and on fine spring and summer evenings (page 183).

Time available An average of 1 hour a week.

Features wanted A private patio filled with climbers, and plants in containers to give colour all the year round.

◄ **Go to** An evergreen garden (page 92); boundaries and walls (page 145); patios and containers (page 171).

COUPLE WORKING FROM HOME, YORKSHIRE TERRIER
Karen and Phill Lloyd work from the loft of their Edwardian house. They want to give a greater feeling of space to their garden (page 148).

Time available An average of 4 hours a week.

Features wanted Low-maintenance, economical features, robust plants.

► **Go to** Boundaries and walls (page 144); using trellis as a screen and plant support (page 154); easy-care planting for boundaries (page 156); quick lawncare (page 59).

PROFESSIONAL COUPLE, PLANT LOVERS
Mhairi and Simon Clutson have full-time jobs and two children. They are avid plant collectors and wanted an ordered, easy-care garden (page 14).

Time available An average of 3 hours a week.

Features wanted Low-maintenance but adaptable garden design that shows their plants at their best.

► **Go to** Automatic watering (page 188); potager (page 238); mulching (page 264); hiring contractors (page 302); flower shows (page 304).

TEACHING DUO
Dan and Kath James are teachers and wanted a garden to enjoy at weekends and in school holidays (page 123).

Time available Irregular: 2 hours a week in term-time, more in the holidays.

Features wanted Sitting area; all-year colour, especially in summer; water feature.

▶ **Go to** Giving up the lawn (page 50); easy-care shrubs (page 79); providing colour in hot spots (page 122); trellis (page 159); plants for containers (page 180); moving water (page 222).

MIDDLE AGED COUPLE
Louise and Phil Pankhurst are in their early fifties, and they both work. They wanted to redesign their garden to make it suitable for entertaining and easy to look after (page 76).

Time available An average of 4 hours a week.

Features wanted Easy-care borders with year-round interest; terrace with barbecue.

▶ **Go to** No-prune shrubs (page 88); evergreens (page 92); easy-care trees (page 106); climbers (page 156); garden furniture (page 196); mulching (page 264).

GROWING FAMILY
Sarah Deal has two children, aged 3 and 7. They wanted to grow their own food organically (page 230).

Time available An average of 4 hours a week.

Features wanted Herbs, fruit and vegetables that are low-maintenance; easy-care borders and boundaries.

◀ **Go to** Improving poor soil (page 22); kitchen garden (page 229); no-dig bed for vegetables (page 239); fruit trees (page 246); beneficial creatures (page 272); getting rid of rubbish (page 276).

OLDER CHILDREN
Anne and David Fenwick are in their forties with a 12-year-old son. They like to relax in the garden at weekends, and their son uses it to practise cricket and observe wildlife (page 18).

Time available An average of 4 hours a week.

Features wanted Easy-care borders with year-round interest and robust plants; secluded patio; wildlife pond.

◀ **Go to** Lawn mowing strip (page 53); garden for all the family (page 64); improving an existing border (page 76); wildlife pond (page 220).

PLANNING FOR RETIREMENT
Madeleine and Edward Lambert moved to a newly built house just before retiring, which meant they were creating their garden on virgin territory (page 17).

Time available An average of 6 hours a week.

Features wanted Above all, a garden which was easy to maintain, with no heavy tasks.

▶ **Go to** Choosing ground cover (page 50); paving (page 66); easy-care climbers (page 156); containers (page 170); hiring contractors (page 302).

RETIRED COUPLE
Barbara and James Heythorpe wanted their front garden to cope with a minimal amount of care. They also wanted to open up the views (page 36).

Time available An average of 2-3 hours a week.

Features wanted Easy-care garden design; succession of flowers; foliage interest.

▶ **Go to** Easy-care front gardens (page 42); designing a rockery (page 40); space for the car in the front garden (page 46); covering up eyesores (page 159); non-organic mulches (page 264).

Deciding your priorities

Gardening gets you out in the fresh air and is a good way to keep fit, as well as an excellent way to relax. It is one of the most popular pastimes, probably because it is easy to adapt to suit your interests and lifestyle. For some, gardening is a labour of love, and time is invested in nurturing treasured plants. For others, the garden is a design statement, and is treated as another room to the house. Most garden lovers, however, agree that gardening is made up of a mixture of pleasurable activities that they would like to do more often and chores to be got out of the way.

A busy gardener must be an effective gardener. So, even if you are dissatisfied with the garden you have, do not rush out to try to put everything right at once, but spend some time thinking and planning. What you want to get out of your garden determines what you have to put into it. Not just in terms of the plants, hard landscaping and other features, but your time and the way you spend it.

Try keeping a 'garden diary' for a couple of months. In it, log how many hours you spend in the garden, and what you do when you are there. Note how long you spend on different tasks as well as the time you spend relaxing in it. Then tot up the hours spent 'enjoying' your

Creating a plant paradise

Mhairi and Simon Clutson work full-time, and they don't get home until late most evenings. They are gardening enthusiasts, but their work and family commitments – they have two young children – mean they have little time for regular garden upkeep.

The Clutsons prefer the creative side of gardening, especially designing new features and planning new planting, rather than more mundane tasks, such as mowing and weeding. They enjoy spending time at weekends combining walks in the countryside with their children with visits to specialist nurseries and plant fairs. They also attend the big flower shows in order to absorb new ideas and find unusual plants. Mhairi and Simon have a small garden so they needed to make maximum use of the space available, but they still wanted an area where they could sit and relax. They are environmentally aware, so avoid using chemical sprays in the garden.

THE OLD GARDEN Mhairi and Simon Clutson wanted to transform this small 10x5 m (11x6 yd) plot to make an interesting garden filled with their favourite plants, but without creating more work than they could handle. They did not want to keep the lawn, which was full of weeds and had bare patches.

DECIDING THEIR PRIORITIES

How much time?
Only 3 hours a week on average. Some weeks no time at all.

Essential ingredients?
A flexible design that can be easily adapted to accommodate new plants. An attractive but easy-care area for eating and relaxing in the garden.

Likes and dislikes?
Both like scented plants and colourful flowers, especially purple ones. Mhairi also wanted some plants that she could cut and use in indoor arrangements. Chores include mowing, weeding and watering.

garden – doing pleasurable tasks or relaxing – and the hours spent 'working' in the garden. Compare the two totals in order to find out the ratio of pleasure to work that your garden offers.

Next, list the features that you like about your garden and those that you dislike. Then list the things you must have and the things you would like to have. Take your time assembling the lists and number the items in order of importance. Keep your lists and go back to them periodically in order to make changes and to add new things.

The results of your research may surprise you. The information will help you to decide on your gardening priorities and to arrive at an action plan, which may cover the next six months or the next 10 years – and which doesn't have to be followed to the letter. Whether you are wavering over impulse purchases at the garden centre or planning to stagger the cost of expensive improvements, it will act as an on-going reminder of your personal goals, and help you to use your most valuable asset – your spare time – the way you want to.

It is essential that you design your garden to suit your needs, but do it with style. Here, a family garden successfully integrates a large climbing frame and tree house into a low-maintenance design.

THE NEW GARDEN They have reduced the workload by getting rid of the lawn and replacing it with low-maintenance materials and by mulching borders to prevent weeds.

Outdoor living *A semi-circular gravel area in front of the french doors is used for relaxing on warm evenings and at weekends. Containers filled with scented, creeping herbs add to the atmosphere.*

Easy access *An attractive stepped path made from a variety of low-maintenance paving materials sweeps up and around the edge of the patio and disappears invitingly out of sight behind the lush borders.*

Boundaries *A range of colourful easy-care climbers, including seven varieties of clematis and an ornamental vine, mask the fencing, making the garden seem bigger than it really is.*

Borders *Densely planted shrubs, bulbs and herbaceous plants, and a generous layer of organic mulch keep the soil moist and prevent weeds from growing.*

Designing out the workload

Most gardens are never designed at all. Instead, they evolve over many years, as their owners add new ideas – or find room for impulse buys of anything from plants and planters to ponds and gazebos. Many people buying a house 'inherit' someone else's garden which, though ideal for the previous owners, is not right for their lifestyle. Whether you want to create a totally new garden, or simply to adapt your existing one, good design can appreciably lighten the workload.

Your 'garden diary' (see page 14) will probably highlight several areas where a minor design 'tweak' could save hours in the long run. For instance, if you have an average-size lawn which takes more than an hour to mow and trim round the edges, something as simple as smoothing out sharply curved borders could knock 15 minutes or more off your weekly schedule straightaway. Over an entire gardening season this is the equivalent of reducing the workload by a whole day.

It can take a lot of time to make design changes. To decide if a change is worth making, you will need to balance the time spent on setting up the design change against the time saved by implementing it. Work that can be done in winter, when mainstream gardening jobs dry up, is particularly worth while. For instance, if each autumn you have to reseed bare patches in the lawn where people wear a path to get to the shed or back gate, a few hours spent in winter sinking stepping stones a stride apart into the grass will mean that you never need to reseed the patches again.

Not all time-saving design tips are cheap. For instance, converting a fiddly small front lawn to ground-cover plants grown through mulch matting under gravel will be an expensive, though attractive, way to eliminate the need to mow. But if the alternative is to pay someone to keep the garden tidy or to spend large amounts of time and money on controlling weeds, the initial outlay may look like better value.

The biggest time-saving, however, comes by careful planning when adding a new feature. For instance, when building a pond, you can save hours of clearing out fallen leaves in future years by positioning it away from deciduous trees. Also, the correct siting of a greenhouse will mean the plants in it grow better and are easier to look after. For additional ideas, visit libraries, watch TV programmes, read books and look through magazines. By planning carefully from the start you will be able to avoid problems later on.

Quick results

Installing an outdoor tap is one of the most effective changes that you can make on moving to a new house with a garden. This saves time clearing up the mess walked into the house when filling watering cans or threading hosepipes through windows, as well as reducing the number of hours spent on watering. Special kits are available from DIY stores or get a plumber to install a tap for you.

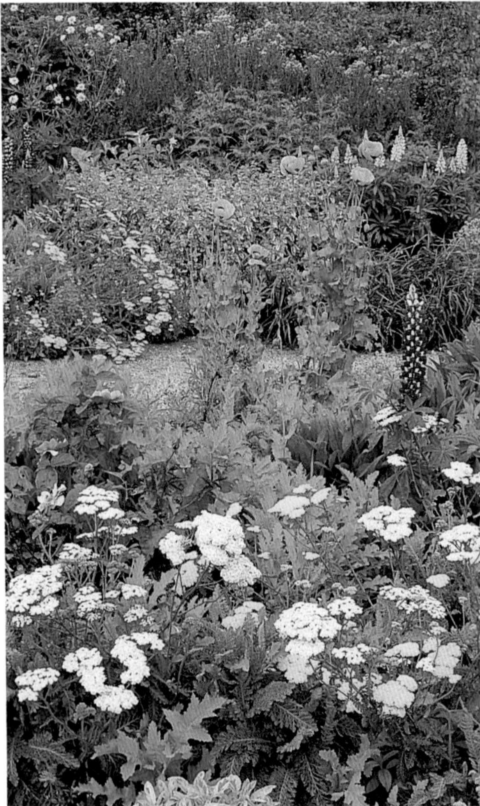

Combine non-invasive, low-growing perennials and grasses with a gravel mulch to create a weed-free meadow-style planting that provides an eye-catching display all summer.

Planning a garden for retirement

Madeleine and Edward Lambert were coming up to retirement age, so they decided to move to a new, smaller house that would be easier to maintain. They wanted a garden for use as an all-year, outdoor 'living-space' that was fully integrated with the indoor rooms.

This was a new house, so the Lamberts were lucky in not having to work within the confines of an existing design. The garden was much smaller than their previous one, so they wanted to maximise the use of space. They had always enjoyed gardening as a hobby, but had taken up so many new interests since their children had left home that their retirement days looked as if they were going to be as busy as when they were working. Both of them were fit and active, but they were aware that they would not want to cope with so much bending or heavy work as they advanced in age. The aim, therefore, was to make their new garden as low maintenance as possible.

THE OLD GARDEN Given that the house was a brand-new development, the first job was to check on the quality and depth of the topsoil, and to make sure that no builders' rubble had been dumped in the garden. And, like so many gardens in urban areas, they had to find ways of contending with a long, narrow space with strong vertical boundaries.

DECIDING THEIR PRIORITIES

How much time?
Around 6 hours a week on average between them, more if necessary during the peak months.

Essential ingredients?
Patio; a seating area in dappled shade at the end of the garden; space for storage.

Likes and dislikes?
They want to be able to enjoy their garden while sitting in the living room. They like scented climbers and plants that offer autumn colour.
They dislike labour-intensive tasks, such as mowing, and heavy tasks, such as digging.

THE NEW GARDEN The diagonal lines make the most of the plot's narrow shape. Maintenance-free paving materials and easy-care plants keep down the workload.

Easy-care plants *The shrubby amelanchier works as a focal point, providing spring flowers and autumn colour. Other plants provide a mixture of heights.*

Gravel *Pea gravel is laid to a depth of about 2.5 cm (1 in), with a layer of membrane underneath to suppress weeds.*

Paving and edging *Concrete slabs are laid at a 45 degree angle to make the garden appear wider. They are brightened up by using edging bricks, which also serve to stop gravel from creeping into the beds.*

Stained woodwork *The blue-grey stain on the closeboard fencing provides a good, low-maintenance backdrop for plants, while the grey of the arch, arbour and trelliswork shows off the climbers to their best.*

Vertical structures *An arch and pergola clothed with climbers, provide shelter from the hot summer sun.*

Using modern techniques

Gardening techniques are constantly evolving. Each year dozens of new developments make it possible to garden more efficiently or with better results. The easiest way to keep up to date is by subscribing to a gardening magazine. Choose one that regularly features new products and techniques, and that has an extensive small ads section at the back. This is the best place to find manufacturers of new or specialised products, which are often only available by mail order.

Many new products and techniques can save hours. For example, mini-plants called 'plugs', or the slightly larger 'tots', will allow you to raise the latest and best plant varieties without having to grow them from seed. This saves not only time and avoids the expense of having to buy specialised facilities, such as a greenhouse or heated propagator, to raise seedlings.

Vegetables can also be bought as small plants, and you can eliminate a lot of hard work by growing them using the no-dig bed system (see page 239). Instead of spending time spraying with pesticides, you can protect your crops from pests by covering them with insect-proof mesh or horticultural fleece, or by using biological control.

Letting in the light

Anne and David Fenwick are in their forties with one son aged 12. They like to spend time in the garden at weekends, and their son and his friends spend a lot of their free time in the warmer months playing outside.

David Fenwick works in the sales department of a local manufacturing company and often works late in the evenings. Anne works part-time at a bank and is home by mid afternoon. Although their medium-sized 9x21 m (10x23 yd) plot faces south, the sun was kept off the garden for most of the day by large neighbouring trees. Apart from the trees, the garden consisted mainly of overgrown flowerbeds around the edges and a patchy lawn in the middle. The Fenwicks' wanted a garden that was easy to keep tidy and able to withstand ball games, because their son likes to practise cricket on the lawn. They also wanted somewhere private and pleasant to sit and relax and an informal pond that attracted wildlife in order to keep their son occupied.

THE OLD GARDEN Overgrown trees and shrubs, and a threadbare lawn make this garden look neglected and uninviting. The trees also keep the sun off the garden for most of the day, making it difficult for other, non-shade loving plants to flourish.

DECIDING THEIR PRIORITIES

How much time?
4 hours on average each week.

Essential ingredients?
Easy-care borders with year-round interest; a water feature to attract wildlife; a secluded patio; and a low-maintenance, hard-wearing lawn.

Likes and dislikes?
They like relaxing in the garden and using the patio area on warm summer evenings. Anne is also interested in the creative use of plants. Dislikes include anything that steals a lot of time at weekends, such as lawn mowing and weeding.

Elsewhere in the garden, you can almost eliminate weeding by planting through mulch matting covered with gravel or bark chippings for a decorative, low-maintenance finish. You can also avoid hand watering, one of the most time-consuming summer tasks, by investing in an irrigation system that waters plants automatically (see page 188). Power equipment makes light of heavy work, such as digging. You don't even need to buy and look after machinery – hire it when you need it, or pay a professional to do the job for you.

Even shopping for the garden has been made more convenient. Garden centres offer a basic range of plants, but you will have to buy from a specialist nursery if you want something a little unusual. Nurseries are increasingly selling by mail order and going 'on-line' so that you can order via the Internet. Instead of reading lots of nursery catalogues, look up suppliers of unusual plants in *The RHS Plant Finder* – also available on CD-ROM. Garden accessories can be bought by mail order or via a TV satellite shopping channel.

Reduce the workload by using low-maintenance materials, such as gravel and paving, to cover the ground and mulch borders to prevent weeds.

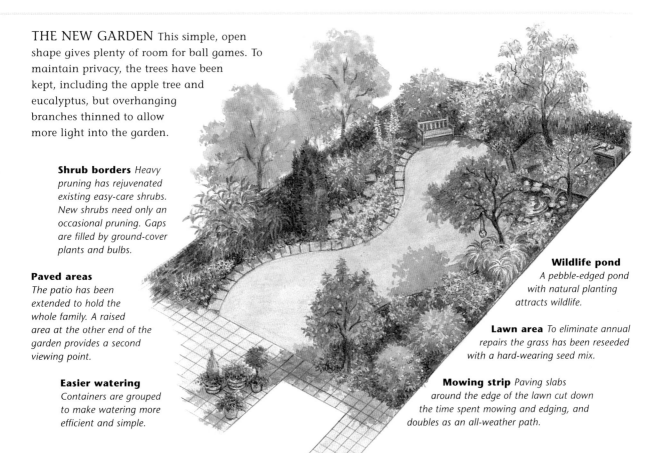

THE NEW GARDEN This simple, open shape gives plenty of room for ball games. To maintain privacy, the trees have been kept, including the apple tree and eucalyptus, but overhanging branches thinned to allow more light into the garden.

Shrub borders *Heavy pruning has rejuvenated existing easy-care shrubs. New shrubs need only an occasional pruning. Gaps are filled by ground-cover plants and bulbs.*

Paved areas *The patio has been extended to hold the whole family. A raised area at the other end of the garden provides a second viewing point.*

Easier watering *Containers are grouped to make watering more efficient and simple.*

Wildlife pond *A pebble-edged pond with natural planting attracts wildlife.*

Lawn area *To eliminate annual repairs the grass has been reseeded with a hard-wearing seed mix.*

Mowing strip *Paving slabs around the edge of the lawn cut down the time spent mowing and edging, and doubles as an all-weather path.*

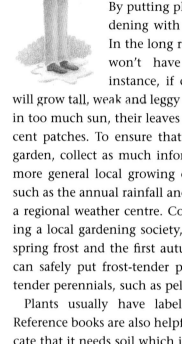

How to get to know your own garden

By putting plants in the right place, you will be gardening with nature rather than fighting against it. In the long run, this saves a lot of time because you won't have to replace unsuitable plants. For instance, if conditions are too shady, some plants will grow tall, weak and leggy and may refuse to flower. Or, if they are in too much sun, their leaves will scorch and develop brown translucent patches. To ensure that you choose the right plants for your garden, collect as much information as you can about the soil and more general local growing conditions. Get details of the climate, such as the annual rainfall and the number of days of sunshine, from a regional weather centre. Contact local gardeners, perhaps by joining a local gardening society, to find out when they expect the last spring frost and the first autumn frost. This will tell you when you can safely put frost-tender plants outside – and when to bring in tender perennials, such as pelargoniums and fuchsias, for winter.

Plants usually have labels indicating where they grow best. Reference books are also helpful. For example, a plant label may indicate that it needs soil which is 'moisture-retentive, but well-drained'. This means that it needs ground containing plenty of humus (decomposed organic matter) but which is never waterlogged. If your soil has little humus, you can dig in well-rotted organic matter, such as manure or compost. To make clay soil more free-draining, dig in well-rotted organic matter and grit (see 'Improving clay soil', page 27).

To help you to decide what to plant where, draw up a rough plan of the garden and mark in the position of the house, any large trees and buildings, and which direction is north. Then mark which parts of the garden are in sun or shade, and are dry or damp (see illustration, left).

Once you have drawn the plan, use the descriptions opposite to identify the type of soil you have and choose plants which flourish in these conditions. Look around your area to see what is growing

What type of soil?

Look at your soil carefully. It can vary greatly within a small area.

Clay soil Sticky when wet, and puddles take a long time to vanish after rain. It dries out into rock-hard clods, and you may find cracks in the lawn and borders.

Sandy and gravelly soil Feels gritty when rubbed between your fingers. Puddles of water disappear quickly – the soil is usually dry.

Loamy soil Crumbly dark earth. The more humus the soil contains the darker it will be.

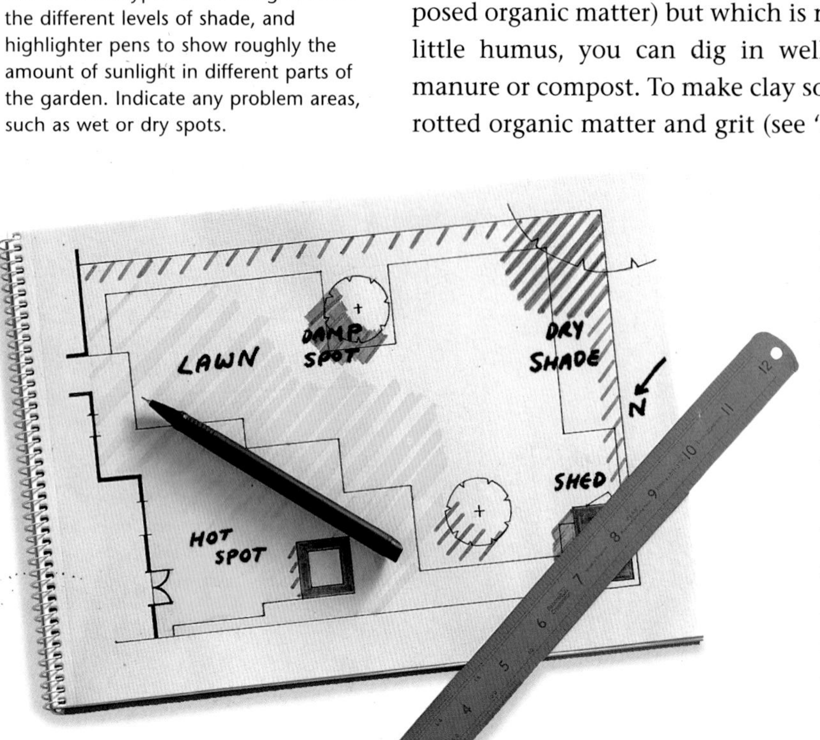

On your plan, mark areas of your garden that are in sun and shade during the day. Use different types of hatching to show the different levels of shade, and highlighter pens to show roughly the amount of sunlight in different parts of the garden. Indicate any problem areas, such as wet or dry spots.

in neighbouring gardens. If acid-loving plants, such as rhododendrons, heathers, camellias and pieris, are growing well, the soil is probably acidic. Also check the surroundings. If you are near chalk downs or cliffs, or the soil looks pale to white, it is probably chalky (alkaline). To be sure, use a soil-testing kit to do a pH test.

Acid soil Woodland plants tend to like moist, humus-rich soil combined with light, dappled shade. Many, including camellias, rhododendrons and pieris, are ericaceous, requiring acid conditions (pH5-6). Slightly less acid conditions (pH5.5-6.5) are liked by some vegetables, including beans, brassicas, potatoes, rhubarb and tomatoes, as well as some fruit, such as red, white and blackcurrants, and raspberries. The majority of garden plants thrive in neutral soil or in ground that is slightly acid or slightly alkaline.

Alkaline soil Usually based on chalk or limestone, alkaline soils are often described as 'hungry' since microbes break down organic matter faster than under neutral or acid conditions. This means that you will need to add more organic matter to alkaline soils than other soil types to improve their water-holding capacity and nutrient content. There is no quick or cheap method to make alkaline soils more acidic.

Trillium, azalea and ornamental grasses *(above)* mulched with bark chippings make an easy-care combination in this acid border.

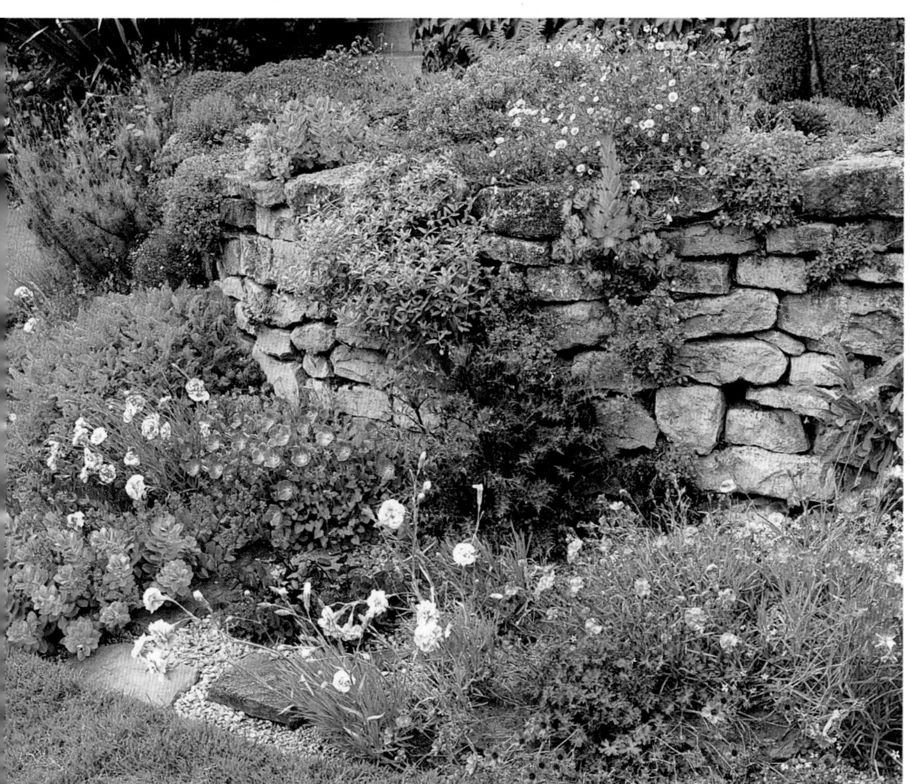

All but acid-loving plants grow reasonably well on slightly alkaline soils. However, for very alkaline gardens, such as the one shown left, select plants that tolerate lime, such as campanula and pinks.

PLANTS FOR ALKALINE SOIL

Most plants will grow in alkaline soil, but the following are particularly tolerant of high levels of alkalinity.

Anemone
Campanula
Dianthus (pinks)
Gypsophila
Iris
Pulsatilla
Scabious
Thyme
Verbascum

Hot and sunny gardens

Sun-loving plants need exposure to direct sunlight to keep growth compact and to ensure good flowering. Insufficient light makes them grow weak and spindly, and may stop them from flowering. Check the label on the plant before you buy it for advice about the correct growing position, or consult reference books for further detail.

Some plants will grow in a wide variety of situations. Their label may say, 'grows in sun or light shade'. When a label says 'for a sunny situation', for example, on conifers and fruit trees, the plant must be in sun for at least half the day. Plants which prefer to have sun all day long will have 'full sun' on the label, such as herbs, rock plants, grasses and ceanothus, which need to be in a south-facing position, away from shade-casting trees, walls or other features.

Some plants will scorch if the weather is very hot, so the label may indicate full sun is needed except at midday, when the sun is at its hottest. Shade only at midday is not easy to find – ideally place the plant where a rock, container or tree trunk provides temporary shade at this time of the day. Alternatively, though not for golden-leaved plant varieties, take a chance and plant in a spot with all-day sun, but make sure that the soil stays moist.

It is easier to choose plants that suit a particular site, but you could, if necessary, alter the site to suit particular plants. To provide shade, you could plant trees or shrubs, or put up a structure such as a

Improving poor soil

Dry soil beside a wall Dig out the soil and any rubble, making a trench at least 60 cm (24 in) wide. Lay a seep hose along the length of the trench in order to make watering easier. Fill the trench with well-rotted organic matter, such as compost or horse manure, to create suitable conditions for growing climbers or wall shrubs. Alternatively, use topsoil, available from garden centres or commercial suppliers, but you will need to check the quality. Finish off with a 5 cm (2 in) layer of loose organic mulch (see page 264) in order to help retain moisture and cut down on weeding.

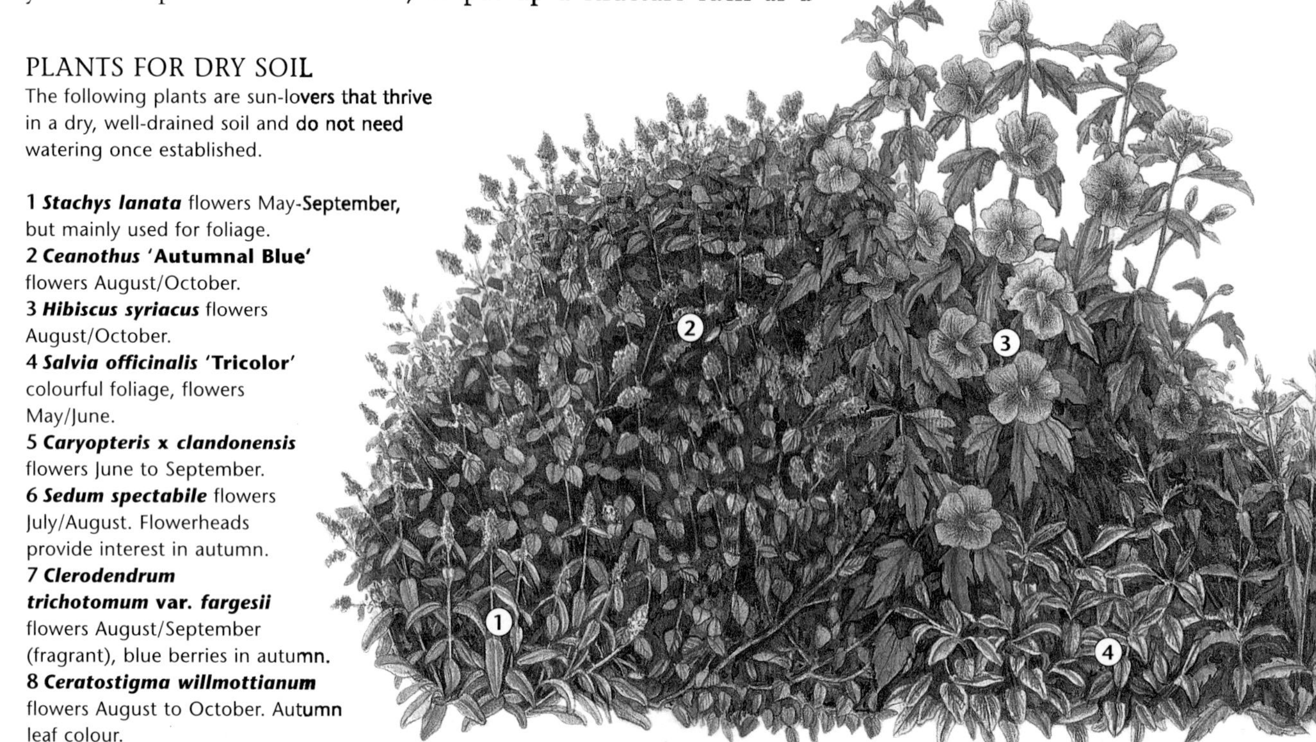

PLANTS FOR DRY SOIL

The following plants are sun-lovers that thrive in a dry, well-drained soil and do not need watering once established.

1 ***Stachys lanata*** flowers May-September, but mainly used for foliage.
2 ***Ceanothus* 'Autumnal Blue'** flowers August/October.
3 ***Hibiscus syriacus*** flowers August/October.
4 ***Salvia officinalis* 'Tricolor'** colourful foliage, flowers May/June.
5 ***Caryopteris* x *clandonensis*** flowers June to September.
6 ***Sedum spectabile*** flowers July/August. Flowerheads provide interest in autumn.
7 ***Clerodendrum trichotomum* var. *fargesii*** flowers August/September (fragrant), blue berries in autumn.
8 ***Ceratostigma willmottianum*** flowers August to October. Autumn leaf colour.

bamboo screen or a pergola with climbers trained over the top to filter the light. A few plants – lilies, honeysuckle and clematis, for example – grow best with their roots in cool shade, and their stems and flowers in sun. Create shade at the base of the plant either by growing shorter, ground-cover plants, or by putting large pebbles over the soil surface or clustering planted pots around the base.

The soil at the base of a sunny wall is often dry and impoverished, but some plants flourish here, such as *Amaryllis belladonna,* winter iris (*Iris unguicularis*) and *Nerine bowdenii*. Also try other drought-tolerant plants, such as acaena, *Helichrysum angustifolium,* sempervirum or many of the euphorbias, including *Euphorbia dulcis* 'Chameleon' and *Euphorbia characias* ssp. *wulfenii*. To grow a wider range of plants you will need to improve the soil by adding well-rotted organic matter (see box, left). You will then be able to use the bed to grow climbers or wall shrubs, and sun-loving tender perennials or bedding plants less tolerant of poor, dry conditions. For spring bedding, tulips and wallflowers will enjoy this situation.

In a hot spot a lawn is difficult and time-consuming to maintain. Here, a wooden deck provides a low-maintenance alternative, surrounded by drought-tolerant easy-care plants, such as coreopsis, lady's mantle, red-hot poker, lavender and euphorbia.

PLANTS FOR MOIST SOIL IN THE SUN

Pick from the following easy-care plants for a sunny spot that stays moist in summer.

Agapanthus
Aubrieta
Buddleja
Heather
Iris
Malus (crab apple)
Nepeta
Passionflower
Rose
Wisteria

EASY-CARE PLANTS FOR DAPPLED SHADE

This collection of trouble-free plants for light shade would be ideal for growing under a deciduous garden tree, such as this *Malus* 'John Downie', which casts dappled shade from late spring to autumn.

1 ***Brunnera macrophylla*** flowers April/May.
2 ***Dicentra spectabilis*** (bleeding heart) flowers April/May.
3 ***Hyacinthoides hispanica*** (Spanish bluebell) flowers May.
4 ***Narcissus* 'Bell Song'** flowers March/April.
5 ***Pulmonaria saccharata*** flowers January to April. White-spotted evergreen leaves.
6 ***Polygonatum x hybridum*** (Solomon's seal) flowers May/June.
7 ***Bergenia* Ballawley Hybrids** (elephant's ears) flowers April/May. Leaves are red-tinged in winter.

Cool and shady gardens

In deep shade, where even weak shafts of sunlight do not penetrate, very few plants will grow. As a general rule, if the shade is too deep for you to read comfortably, then it is too dark for plants. However, a certain amount of shade provides ideal conditions for some plants that will not grow happily elsewhere. Ferns, hostas, ivies and periwinkles (vinca) are all shade lovers. If they are grown in too much light, their leaves will scorch and their flowers fade fast, or the whole plant may shrivel up and die. However, not all shade-loving plants need the same degree of shade – some need full shade, others only shade from strong, midday sun and others dappled shade – and many of them grow in more than one type of shade.

On a plant label, 'shade' can mean good light but no direct sun, except weak evening, early morning or winter sun – hardy ferns will flourish in this position. 'Light shade' means that the plant likes light, but not direct sun. 'Partial shade' usually means that the plant needs sun for part of the day; for example, bleeding heart (*Dicentra spectabilis*), which grows well in borders between other plants. Japanese maple (*Acer palmatum*), epimedium, lily-of-the-valley, rhododendrons and violets prefer the dappled shade found under a light tree canopy – such as that of a silver birch – where rays of weak sunshine are able to break through. Although few flowering plants thrive in this situation, add a splash of colour by growing hydrangea, busy lizzies (impatiens) and fuchsias in containers.

Adding light to shade

There are ways of making even dense shade attractive to look at and suitable for growing plants.

Painting walls Make best use of all available light by painting walls white. Also lay light-coloured paving, stain trelliswork white, and use seats and containers which are either white or pastel.

Mirrors You can create the illusion of space and brighten up dark corners by putting up a mirror to reflect light onto the plants.

Water features The reflected light and the gentle sound of a water feature with a fountain will help to lift a dark corner.

PLANTS FOR CONSTANT MOIST SHADE

The following tolerate deep, damp shade, for example, in a north-facing corner of a building.

Ajuga
Alexandrian laurel (*Danae racemosa*)
Box (*Buxus sempervirens*)
Hardy fern
Hellebore
Hosta
Hydrangea
Ivy
Mahonia aquifolium
Snowdrop

Escape the heat of a summer's day by creating a shady retreat. Variegated periwinkle helps brighten even the darkest corner, while the delicate fronds of the royal fern (*Osmunda regalis*) shimmer in the dappled sunlight.

Beneath big deciduous trees, shade is very deep in summer and the soil is dry and impoverished because the tree takes up all the moisture and nutrients. The ground will also be full of tree roots so there is virtually no soil in which to plant. Here, the best solution is to mulch the ground deeply and to plant spring bulbs – such as the short-stemmed, early daffodil 'February Gold' – that flower and complete their life cycle early, before the trees come into leaf.

Another testing type of shade is the year-round deep shade with dry soil found along a passageway, for example. Plants that tolerate these conditions include *Euphorbia amygdaloides* var. *robbiae* and *Iris foetidissima*. In deep shade with damp or wet soil, grow Alexandrian laurel (*Danae racemosa*).

On the shady side of a boundary, go for *Aucuba japonica*, euonymus or ivy, and to cover the ground and suppress weeds, lamium, Indian strawberry (*Duchesnea indica*), *Geranium phaeum* or periwinkle (vinca).

Wet, sticky soil

In soil that stays wet, the roots cannot take in air because the air spaces within the soil are filled with water. The roots then 'drown' and rot, causing plants to die. Some plants, however, are specially adapted to life in wet soil, particularly bog-garden plants and those that grow in shallow water along pond margins. Some border plants are also happy in permanently moist soil that is not waterlogged, such as astilbe, hosta, *Iris sibirica*, lysimachia, lythrum, monarda, rodgersia and schizostylis.

In a garden with a problem wet area, a common solution is to use the site to build a pond. However, the wet spot will often dry up in hot weather: adding a liner does not help since in very wet weather ground water will rise up under the liner to make it balloon up, pushing out planting baskets. The best solution for a naturally damp spot is to use it for moisture-loving perennials, digging in lots of well-rotted organic matter to help it stay moist even in dry spells.

Plants for clay soil Once established, many trees and shrubs like clay soil, but they can suffer from waterlogging in winter so plant them on a slight mound. The best trees for clay soil include birch, *Crataegus* 'Paul's Scarlet', ornamental elders, wild cherry (*Prunus avium*) and *Sorbus aucuparia*. Clay-loving

To grow plants such as the hosta, mimulus, myosotis and rodgersia featured in this garden, incorporate plenty of organic matter so that the soil doesn't dry out, even in summer.

DAMP SOIL IN THE SUN

A mid-summer scheme for a damp corner, with flowers of contrasting colours. The lysimachia provides an evergreen, golden-yellow carpet of foliage.

1 ***Lysimachia nummularia* 'Aurea'** bright yellow flowers June.
2 ***Iris ensata*** purple flowers late June.
3 ***Ligularia* 'The Rocket'** yellow flowers July to August.
4 ***Mimulus* 'Wisley Red'** blood-red flowers June to August.

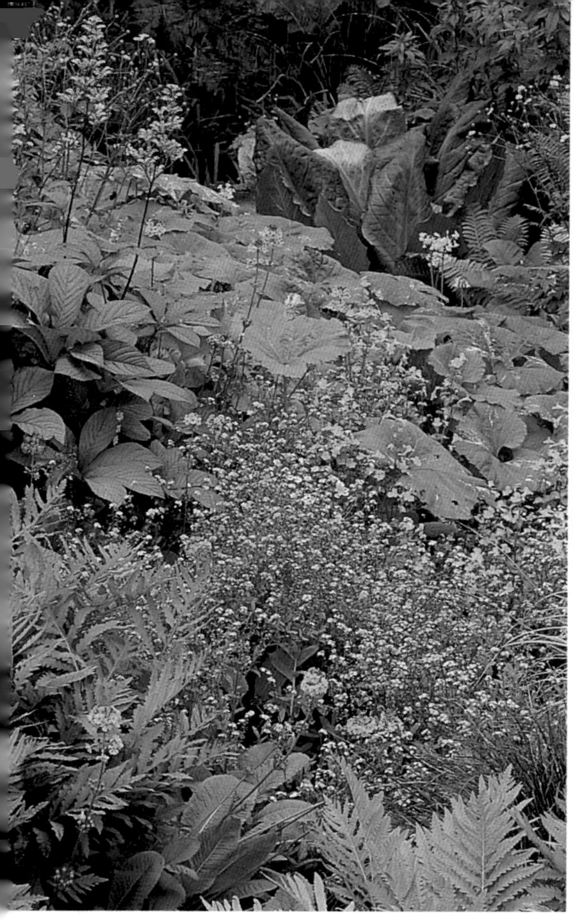

shrubs include aucuba, chaenomeles, dogwood (cornus), *Corylus avellana* 'Contorta', elaeagnus, hydrangea, philadelphus, pyracantha, ribes, shrub roses, *Rubus cockburnianus*, salix and viburnum. On improved clay, many perennials will also do well, including *Arum italicum* 'Pictum', astilbe, euphorbia, hellebores, hosta, *Iris foetidissima*, Solomon's seal (polygonatum) and *Symphytum* 'Rubrum'. For planting under deciduous trees, daffodils, snowdrops and primula are good partners. Annuals and tender perennials are slow to get away on cold, clay soils, so they need to be confined to containers.

Improving clay soil Clay can make a good garden soil if it is improved, which need not be hard work. Don't dig deeply because this can bring to the surface infertile, yellow or blue subsoil. Improve the soil by digging in a barrowful of well-rotted organic matter for each square metre and a 5 cm (2 in) layer of grit, sharp sand, pea shingle or fine gravel (lime-free, if possible) to one spade's depth. Don't use building sand because the particles are too small and it contains too much lime. Each spring, mulch with organic matter.

If you have wet soil but you want to grow plants that need good drainage, such as herbs, rock plants and some perennials, you will need to build a raised bed (see page 192).

DAMP SOIL IN THE SHADE
The shade is lifted using golden and variegated foliage, and white and yellow flowers. Slugs love these moist, cool conditions, so you will need to protect emerging growth in spring.

1 ***Cornus alba* 'Spaethii'** white flowers March to May and red stems in winter.
2 ***Zantedeschia aethiopica* 'Crowborough'** succession of white spathes from April to June.
3 ***Aruncus dioicus*** plumes of creamy white flowers in June and July.
4 ***Primula prolifera*** pale yellow flowers in June.
5 ***Hosta* 'Zounds'** puckered leaves, pale lavender flowers in May and June.

Dry, free-draining soil

On free-draining soils you can grow a range of plants that are not happy in moist conditions. Since rain soaks through fast, you can dig and cultivate the soil almost at any time – even in winter, when most gardens are too boggy to work on. However, on excessively free-draining soils, such as sand, gravel and chalk, it can be a time-consuming chore to keep plants moist. There are several solutions – choose naturally drought-resistant plants, improve the soil so that it retains more moisture or install an automatic watering system. Free-draining soils can run short of certain nutrients because they are soluble and are literally washed away.

Choosing drought-tolerant plants When drawing up a planting scheme for dry soil in sun, include plenty of drought-proof self-seeding flowers, such as California poppy, *Eryngium giganteum*, *Euphorbia dulcis* 'Chameleon', *E. characias* ssp. *wulfenii*, evening primrose (*Oenothera biennis*), *Linaria purpurea*, nasturtium, *Onopordum arabicum* and *Verbascum bombyciferum*. If you leave self-sown seedlings to grow where they come up, you will not have to water them. If you transplant seedlings, no matter how carefully, the roots will be disturbed so they must be kept watered until they are established. Even pot-grown, drought-tolerant plants need to be watered for the first few weeks after transplanting.

Many tender perennials are drought-tolerant, such as gazania, mesembryanthemum, osteospermum and pelargonium. If

Coping with dry soil

Do choose drought-proof plants.

Do conserve moisture by mulching in spring when the soil is moist.

Do mulch problem soils – too dry, sandy or chalky – twice a year, in spring and autumn.

Do build a deep, no-dig bed if you want to grow fruit and vegetables (see page 239).

Don't try to grow a conventional grass lawn. Instead, create patches of green with a herb lawn using thyme or camomile (see page 62).

PLANTS FOR DRY SHADE

All these plants are tough customers, able to survive under the canopy of a mature tree. To maximise growth, plant them in a deep layer of well-rotted compost.

1 ***Mahonia aquifolium*** yellow flowers in February and May.
2 ***Symphytum* 'Hidcote Pink'** pink flowers in March and April.
3 ***Iris foetidissima* 'Variegata'** scarlet berries from September until November.
4 ***Geranium* x *oxonianum* 'Wargrave Pink'** flowers from May to September.
5 ***Dryopteris filix-mas*** a deciduous fern.
6 ***Euphorbia amygdaloides* var. *robbiae*** green cymes in March and April.

you want to grow non-drought tolerant bedding plants on dry soil, dig into the soil well-rotted organic matter or water-retaining gel crystals – usually used in hanging baskets – to help the soil to hold water. To grow fruit and vegetables on dry soil, build a deep bed filled with compost (see page 239) and install a watering system (see page 188).

Improving dry soils When preparing a dry border for planting, add organic matter to improve the water-holding capacity and nutrient content of the soil. On problem sandy or chalky soils, which are particularly 'hungry', dig in organic matter in autumn, and then each spring apply 140 g per m^2 (4 oz per sq yd) of general fertiliser such as growmore – or use a rose fertiliser – and mix it into the soil.

On very thin soils, like those sometimes found over chalk, mix good-quality topsoil with the top few centimetres of garden soil, incorporating well-rotted organic matter as you go, to increase the soil's depth. Plant in autumn so that winter rains keep new plants watered. Before planting, soak the rootball of each plant. After planting, apply a 5 cm (2 in) mulch of well-rotted organic matter. If you do not have time for regular soil improvement, restrict your choice of plants to the more drought-tolerant types.

On a free-draining soil, cut down the workload by choosing naturally drought-tolerant plants such as allium, salvia and penstemon and by applying a mulch to prevent evaporation from the soil.

DRY SUNNY SCHEME

A Mediterranean-style scheme to site next to the house, where architectural forms work best. The muted colours would go well against pale gravel.

1 *Verbascum* 'Gainsborough' flowers from June until August.
2 *Helictotrichon sempervirens* (blue oat grass) an evergreen, blue-grey grass.
3 *Sedum* 'Vera Jameson' flowers in August/September.
4 *Acanthus spinosus* white flowers with purple bracts from April to July.
5 *Oenothera speciosa* 'Rosea' white-and-pink flowers from June until September.

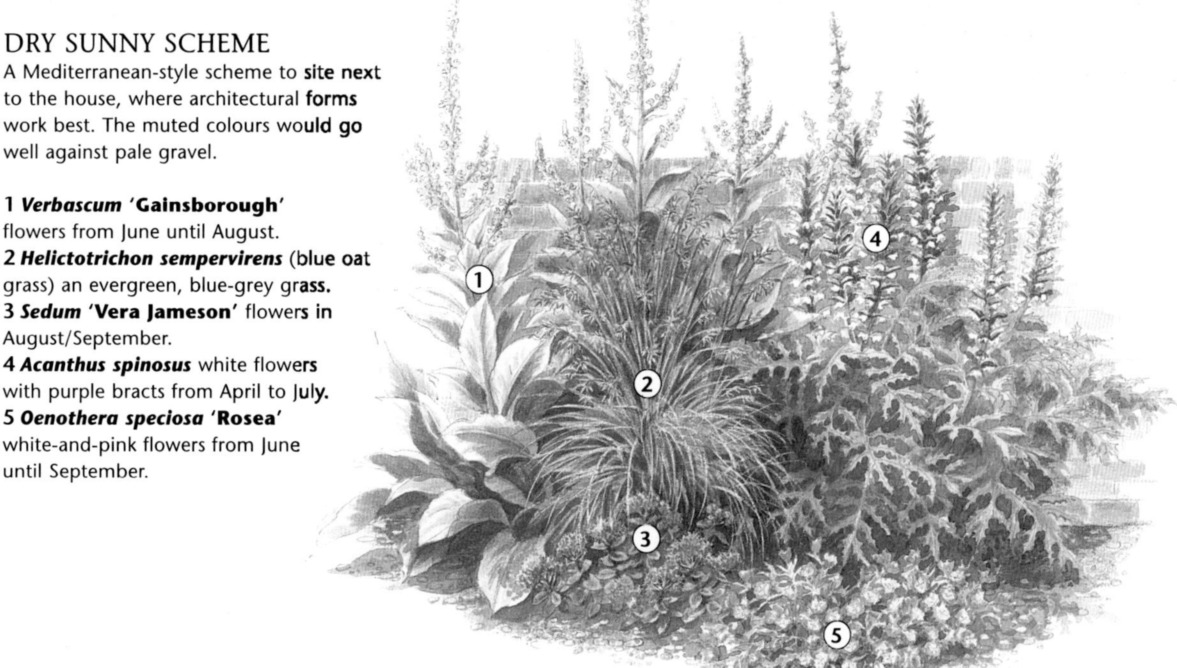

Exposed gardens

On an exposed site, such as a hillside or coastal garden, wind can cause more damage than frost and cold. The first step in a windswept location is to provide some shelter. A solid barrier such as a wall or fence will make the wind eddy over the top and can cause strong back-draughts on the leeward side. Instead, filter the wind to slow it down with a hedge or an artificial windbreak, which will give useful shelter for a distance of about ten times its height to the leeward side.

If you have the space, plant a mixture of trees as a shelter belt (see below). For a country-style hedge, elder trees (sambucus) growing up through a trimmed row of hawthorn (crataegus) serves as a good windbreak. You can achieve a similar effect by training blackberries over chain-link or post-and-wire fencing. Plant small specimens of trees and shrubs to avoid the difficulty of having to stake in a windy spot; they will also shelter each other as they grow.

Alternatively, construct an artificial windbreak. First, check local planning restrictions for any limitations enforceable on the height. Although an artificial windbreak doesn't necessarily look attractive, it can serve as a quick fix or a temporary measure until a natural barrier becomes established. Use firmly anchored stout poles to support green, woven plastic mesh or the more durable type made from wide,

Windy solutions

Reduced growth Wind slows plant growth by increasing water loss through evaporation. This can significantly reduce the yields of vegetables so protect the vegetable plot with windbreak netting.

Poor pollination Pollinating insects avoid windy areas, so to get good pollination of fruit crops grow them against sheltered walls.

Vulnerable plants Avoid plants with big leaves and those that come into flower early in the season because they are more vulnerable to damage from the wind.

New plants It is essential to protect new plants, especially evergreens, because they are particularly susceptible to wind damage. Protect them with temporary windbreak netting until well established. Keep all new plants well watered.

SEASIDE GARDEN
A shelter belt of pines and shrubs protects more decorative salt-resistant plants from the prevailing wind in this coastal garden. 'Windows' in the planting have been left on either side of the stooled eucalyptus, to guide the eye towards sea views.

1 ***Tamarix ramosissima***
2 ***Eucalyptus gunnii***
3 ***Genista lydia***
4 ***Atriplex halimus***
5 ***Pinus nigra ssp. laricio***
6 ***Eryngium maritimum*** (sea holly)
7 ***Olearia x haastii*** (daisy bush)
8 ***Elaeagnus x ebbingei* 'Limelight'**
9 ***Sambucus racemosa* 'Sutherland Gold'**
10 ***Pinus radiata*** (Monterey pine)
11 ***Sorbus aria*** (whitebeam)
12 ***Rosa rugosa* 'Fru Dagmar Hastrup'**
13 ***Amelanchier canadensis***
14 ***Arbutus unedo*** (strawberry tree)
15 ***Hebe pinguifolia* 'Pagei'**
16 ***Dianthus alpinus*** (alpine pink)
17 ***Rosmarinus officinalis*** (rosemary)
18 ***Catananche caerulea*** (Cupid's dart)
19 ***Brachyglottis compacta* 'Sunshine'**
20 ***Buddleja davidii* 'Black Knight'**

Plants have to be tough to grow on a coastal site. Here, a raised parapet and a windbelt of plants give protection.

black plastic strips. Sheep hurdles and willow wattles – barriers hand-woven from hazel twigs or willow – are more attractive than windbreak mesh, but the wood becomes brittle and breaks after only about five years if erected in a very exposed situation.

Once effective shelter has been established round the edges of the garden, other plants can then be expected to thrive in the protected areas. If a garden has wonderful views that you don't want to block out with a continuous shelter belt or hedge, create 'windows' by staggering the planting so that you can still appreciate parts of the view. In exposed areas of the garden, use only wind-resistant trees and shrubs. Using shelter belts will also protect the house and serve to keep your heating bills lower.

In a coastal garden, the light is intense, winds can be strong and the plants need to be tolerant of salt. For an effective barrier of trees and shrubs, you will need to 'layer' the planting away from the direction of the prevailing winds (see illustration, left). First, create an outer perimeter of large trees, such as maritime pine (*Pinus nigra* ssp. *laricio*) and *Pinus radiata* (Monterey pine), or whitebeam (*Sorbus aria*) for a native, deciduous tree. Fill gaps with smaller, more ornamental trees, such as the strawberry tree (*Arbutus unedo*) or tamarisk (tamarix), with its fine, feathery foliage. To complete the windbreak, add large shrubs, evergreen or deciduous, in the lee of the trees, such as ornamental forms of elder (sambucus), elaeagnus or large varieties of hebe. This barrier will then provide you with the shelter needed to plant borders of smaller shrubs and tough perennials.

Front Gardens

A FRONT GARDEN IS ON VIEW TO ALL, SO MUST LOOK GOOD ALL YEAR. BY PLANNING PROPERLY YOU CAN HAVE AN IMPRESSIVE PLOT THAT REQUIRES THE MINIMUM OF MAINTENANCE

First impressions count most – and it is the front garden that gives the first impression of your home. It is what welcomes you home at night and sends you on your way in the morning. And it plays the dual roles of greeting welcomed visitors, while keeping out intruders; letting you see the surrounding neighbourhood, while maintaining privacy.

Front gardens vary tremendously in size: from pocket handkerchief plots squeezed under the front window to a sweeping landscape where the house is set well back. Most front gardens have to be functional as well as attractive, because they may need to accommodate a car and rubbish bins, as well as provide easy access to and from the house and garage.

A well-designed front garden should look good all year round with the minimum of maintenance. The design should be simple, using plants with bold features that have immediate impact and that can be appreciated both close up and from a distance. Remember that tools are often located at trudging distance – in a shed in the back garden – so avoid features that need specialist equipment or regular attention.

1 FOCAL POINT – *box topiary spheres provide a permanent feature and are easy to maintain.*
2 PAVING STYLES – *a mixture of brick and stone creates extra interest with little maintenance work.*
3 CLOSE PLANTING – *drought-tolerant plants, such as hebe and choisya, squeeze out weeds.*
4 SMART DESIGN – *an illusion of depth is created by laying the path at a diagonal across the plot.*

EASY-CARE CALENDAR

EARLY SPRING
Remove any weeds and tidy away debris before the herbaceous plants emerge. Top up the mulch so that it is at least 5 cm (2 in) deep. Sweep paving and treat with a path weedkiller to prevent weeds all season. Apply slug pellets around susceptible perennials.

MID SPRING
Sprinkle rose fertiliser evenly between the shrubs. Spot treat any established perennial weeds.

LATE SPRING
Check shrubs such as hebe and choisya for frost damage and snip off any black shoot tips. If necessary, prune straggly shoots to improve plant shape.

EARLY SUMMER
Remove dead flowerheads from shrubs and perennials. Trim box in containers with shears to maintain shape.

MID SUMMER
Sprinkle a high-potash feed to promote flowering the following year.

AUTUMN
Tidy up any debris before winter. Fallen leaves can be left on borders as a mulch.

STARTING FROM SCRATCH
You could plant this front garden in half a day, with the help of a planting plan. Choose a fine day to dig over the soil, incorporating well-rotted organic matter, and after planting apply a mulch to keep down annual weeds. A builder would take about three days to lay the paving on a bed of firmed hardcore and to point the cracks.

Making an entrance A stone path weaves an entrance through the brick paving and planting. Trouble-free perennials, shrubs and evergreens combine to produce an all-year, ever-changing display.

Formal entrances needn't require high maintenance. An impressive pair of golden yews frames the doorway, with a row of lavender for added interest.

Design options that make an entrance

Most front gardens need to be functional and easy to look after. All too often, however, this leads to a stark, uninviting area that is low on interest for much of the year. A well-designed front garden combines the practical considerations, such as easy access and space for a car, while being pleasing to the eye. Many people make the mistake of treating the front garden like a miniature version of the back garden, with a small area of grass, narrow borders and high boundaries. All these features require a lot of maintenance, which is inconvenient and unnecessary.

Covering the ground The traditional way of filling space in a front garden is to grass it over. However, this is not necessarily the best or most attractive way of covering the ground. Mowing a small area of lawn is inefficient because a lot of time is wasted turning and cutting awkward shapes. A front lawn also usually means having to manoeuvre the mower and other tools through a narrow access from the back of the house to the front – or even through the house itself. Many

front-garden lawns are very close to the house and can get heavily shaded if not south-facing, a problem compounded by high boundaries. This means they do not grow well and are easily colonised by shade-loving weeds and moss which are time-consuming to control. Some front gardens are on a slope, making mowing difficult or even dangerous. There are easy-maintenance alternatives to a lawn such as massed ground cover plants or attractive combinations of paving materials. Use the ideas on page 48 to help you to decide which low-maintenance options best suit your circumstances.

Paved areas A properly laid hard surface, such as pavers or bricks, will need only an occasional sweep and maybe an annual treatment for moss and algae. Gravel, although cheaper and easier to lay at the outset, will demand periodic weed control, unless laid over a permeable membrane, and raking every now and again to level the surface.

Mix together different finishes so that the paved area doesn't look too stark, but keep the number of finishes to no more than three otherwise the design will look bitty and complicated. Or use different finishes to demarcate different areas. For example, hard-wearing, blue engineering bricks for the parking area and lighter-coloured paving slabs for the path to the front door, or paving slabs placed as stepping stones in gravel to show visitors the way to the main entrance.

Paving within planted areas can be used to give access for pruning and weeding, as well as creating the illusion of space among evergreen plants that would otherwise merge into one amorphous blob.

Making plans

Do draw a scaled plan on graph paper to decide the positioning of essential features.

Do use fences, walls, trellis or hedges to screen the garden from neighbouring properties or the road.

Do check your house deeds before erecting a new boundary because many properties are subject to restrictions.

Do use bold plantings, strong focal points and sweeping curves to create the best impression.

Don't have a complicated design. A simple layout is usually the most effective and the easiest to achieve.

A dense planting of tough, easy-care evergreens are used to disguise and soften the expanse of paving and prevent weed growth for a maintenance-free display.

A small basement area *(left)*, with white-painted walls to reflect light, is planted with shade-tolerant *Fatsia japonica*, ivy and pyracantha. Pots of colourful flowers are added as they come into bloom.

Creative use of gravel, setts and slabs means this entrance looks attractive even when the planting is not at its peak.

Adding plants For impact, use only a few varieties of shrubs and perennials and mass them together. This works better and is easier to look after than having a single specimen of lots of different varieties. Block-like architectural plantings of trimmed evergreens, such as box that needs clipping once a year, or a specimen tree or shrub with a strong, sculptural shape (see panel, page 39) are among the simplest features and can be planted in gravel. Planting close together will provide you with instant ground cover, suppressing weeds. Make sure to use easy-care plants (see page 268). Choose varieties that need no regular pruning or cutting back and that give all-year interest, such as bergenia, heuchera, skimmia and *Viburnum davidii*. Avoid annuals and bedding plants that need regular watering, feeding, weeding, deadheading and then replacing twice a year.

Combine plants so they produce bold areas of colour in simple patterns that are easy on the eye. Make sure that different plants have complementary periods of interest so that the garden has something to offer all year round. Front gardens are a good place to use plants with a striking appearance, such as yucca and phormium or lush

Improving the outlook of a front garden

Barbara and James Heythorpe are a couple in their fifties with many interests. James had recently retired from the RAF so this is the first home that they have owned. They were interested in gardening, but their knowledge was limited and they wanted to concentrate their available time on the back garden.

The property was built in the Seventies on the site of a former farmyard. The developers did not remove a lot of rubble before adding topsoil so the soil is shallow. The plot slopes towards the house; the gradient is not pronounced, but potential exists to create more interest. A terraced feature could be constructed and planted with many of the more unusual rockery plants in which Barbara and James are interested. Apart from opening up the views of the village green from the downstairs windows and letting in more light, the couple wanted to screen the narrow passageways on either side of the house that stored the dustbins and an oil tank. At that time, they were camouflaged by lilac bushes, which were untidy, overgrown and of interest only when in flower.

THE OLD GARDEN The front garden was entirely lawn, with a narrow concrete drive and inadequate paths. A beech hedge obscured the view of the village green. Along one side was a screen of *Rosa rugosa*. The lawn was thin and weedy, and full of moss and algae because of the shade cast by the hedges. A narrow bed ran along the front of the house, with dingy perennials, a rampant *Clematis montana* and out-of-hand pyracantha.

DECIDING THEIR PRIORITIES

How much time?
On average 2-3 hours a week, most of which they want to devote to the back garden.

Essential ingredients?
To open up the front garden to allow light in and create unobstructed views out; easy access; extra parking space.

Likes and dislikes?
They like plants used for foliage and year-round colour, as well as rockery plants with unusual forms – and not too many evergreens. They don't mind basic pruning, but dislike deadheading and weeding. They don't like organic mulches, because birds can throw them around.

foliage such as the *Fatsia japonica*. Keep the maintenance minimal by planting through mulch matting (see page 264), which will suppress weeds and help retain moisture in the soil. Loose organic mulches are not so practical in a front garden because they can attract cats and cocoa shells can appeal to dogs because they like the smell.

Secure boundaries The boundary is an important feature in most front gardens. It defines the edge of the property, as well as providing security and privacy. There are many low-maintenance options, depending on the style of garden and how much time you can afford to spend looking after them (see page 146). Security is an important issue when planning a front garden. Apart from removing tall screens, behind which burglars can hide, good lighting puts the spotlight on loiterers and the crunching of gravel provides advance warning of visitors arriving. Even a garden gate will psychologically cause a burglar to think twice about entering the garden, especially if it is kept closed or has spikes on it. Garden furniture and statues should never be put in the front garden unless fixed securely (see page 296).

Front garden paths

Functional paths Paths from garden gate to front door should take the shortest route if they are going to be used by casual visitors. However, they can be made to look more attractive by introducing gentle curves or by using a variety of paving materials (see picture opposite).

Decorative paths In large gardens a second path can be used to meander through the garden and provide easy access to each area. It can be a continuous 'snake' of paving or stepping stones, or a combination of both.

THE NEW GARDEN Taking out the beech hedge and *Rosa rugosa* screen removed the two most time-consuming features. It also allowed more light into the garden and opened up a vista of the village green.

Lawn *The old lawn, the existing topsoil and rubble were removed and new topsoil was brought in. This was left to settle for a few months during which time emerging weeds were treated with a glyphosate-based weedkiller.*

Planting *Mixed flowerbeds were filled with slow-growing, easy-care plants interplanted with spring bulbs.*

Mulching *The area between the plants was covered with a 5 cm (2 in) mulch of stone chippings for decoration and to suppress weeds.*

Paving *The paths were widened and lengthened to allow easy access. Brick pavers of a colour to complement the house bricks were used, with a defining edge in a contrasting colour.*

Terraces *The slope was recontoured by creating two flat terraces retained by low limestone walls, and planted with a range of unusual rockery plants.*

Easy maintenance *Each terrace was ringed with stepping stones for clear access to the areas for maintenance.*

Climbers *The* Clematis montana *was removed and replaced with self-clinging climbers, including variegated ivy, and the wall shrub* Euonymus fortunei *'Variegatus'.*

Self-supporting trouble-free perennials, some of which have been allowed to self-seed and colonise the gravel ground cover, combine effectively in this cottage-style front garden *(above, left)*.

Simple designs can be the most striking in appearance. In this oriental-style garden *(above)*, clipped box is combined with gravel and paving for an effective yet genuinely low-maintenance finish.

Gravel gardens

A simple design is the key to keeping down the workload in your front garden. Gravel gardens can provide the ideal solution – growing easy-care plants through mulch matting topped by a 5 cm (2 in) layer of gravel. The natural colour and texture of a gravel garden not only help to set off plants to their best effect, but the 'fluid' nature of the loose materials used is ideal for covering an area of an irregular shape. And don't stop at just plants in gravel; also consider non-living items with an intriguing nature, such as large stones, rocks, empty containers, pieces of slate or driftwood.

Gravel garden care Several materials are available for gravel gardens. The most usual are: water-worn shingle – called pea shingle if particles are small; true gravel, which is stone crushed to a gravel size; or more jagged stone chippings, which are available in a wider choice of colours – in tones of grey, yellow and red, and even in white.

A gravel garden will need regular raking, however, to restore an even spread of the material used, and to remove dead leaves and other plant debris collected on the surface. If mulch matting is not used, apply a path weedkiller as a once-a-year treatment to kill weeds and prevent weed seeds from germinating, but use with care because it can 'creep', to affect nearby ornamental plants as well. Avoid sweeping down the debris from paved areas onto the gravel because this will only contaminate it and encourage weeds. A gravel garden will also need topping up every few years. Make sure that the new material blends with the existing one.

What to include

Do plant groups of the same plant to create a series of 'green' focal points.

Do choose a few big, bold plants, with a strong shape, to use as focal points or special features – but remember to use them sparingly.

Do plant creeping plants near the edge of the gravel garden to create a natural appearance.

Don't underlay gravel with different-coloured or shaped stone chippings because they will rise to the surface with time and look ugly.

The best plants provide all-year interest and don't shed lots of leaves or petals. In a sunny site, select a Mediterranean-style planting of grey or blue-leaved plants that thrive in hot, dry situations. Choose colours that contrast and complement those of the gravel. For example, a gravel with strong yellows would go well with green or orange, as provided by a red-hot poker or *Euphorbia mellifera*, or with the purplish green stems of the bamboo *Pleioblastus auricomus*. Grey stone chippings, on the other hand, suit white, vivid green and steely blue plantings, with a dab of crimson red.

A gravel garden in a shady spot will have a completely different ambience. Easy-care plants for such a location could include bergenia, box and ferns with different textures and colours, as well as larger, architectural plants such as *Mahonia* x *media* and *Fatsia japonica*. Allow moss to creep over the gravel to give a natural look.

Creating impact Focal points are best lined up from main viewing points, such as the front door or a downstairs window. For a corner of a larger area or in a small, urban front garden, a tall bamboo, a bushy evergreen, a small tree or an empty decorative container could form a central attraction. For contrast, mulch with pebbles or stones – possibly adding a meandering 'river' of larger pebbles or slate of a contrasting colour for extra interest – and plant with pockets of easy-care bulbs, such as *Iris reticulata* and daffodils, for an early display.

This low-maintenance gravel courtyard with deep borders is filled with deciduous and evergreen foliage plants chosen for their texture, colour and shape.

FOCAL PLANTS TO LOOK GOOD ON THEIR OWN

For a simple, yet aesthetic front garden, choose plants that look good from inside and out. Here are some easy-care varieties. The trees can be used singly, while most of the other plants need to be grouped to create impact.

Small trees *Acer davidii* 'George Forrest', *A. palmatum* 'Bloodgood' (pictured), *Betula pendula* 'Youngii', *Pyrus salicifolia* 'Pendula', *Prunus incisa* 'Kojo-no-mai', *Robinia pseudoacacia* 'Frisia' and *Salix caprea* var. 'Pendula'.

Easy-care shrubs *Berberis darwinii*, *Chaenomeles* x *superba*, *Cotoneaster* x *watereri* (pictured), *Ilex cornuta*, *Olearia* x *haastii*, *Osmanthus delavayi*, *Photinia* x *fraserii* 'Red Robin' and *Weigela florida* 'Variegata'.

Herbaceous plants Bergenia, including *Bergenia* 'Sunningdale' (pink flowers in spring and bronzed leaves in winter), *Euphorbia characias* ssp. *wulfenii* 'Lambrook Gold' or 'John Tomlinson', *Iris pallida* 'Variegata' (pictured).

Grasses, sedges and bamboos *Carex oshimensis* 'Evergold' (sedge, pictured), *Fargesia murieliae* 'Simba' (bamboo, yellowish stems), *Pleioblastus auricomus* (bamboo, yellow-striped leaves) *Stipa gigantea* (grass).

Coping with a sloping site

Many front gardens have a gradient, which makes mowing a lawn impractical. A low-maintenance alternative is to carpet the slope with easy-care ground-cover plants (see page 62). Alternatively, you can create a rockery on the gradient. Embed rocks into the slope or, especially if the gradient is steep, terrace the slope by creating a series of low retaining walls with planting in between. A terraced garden may be expensive and time-consuming to have built, but it allows easy access for maintenance and can be linked by shallow steps. Terracing can also create the illusion of space by combining open areas, for example of gravel, with planting beds.

When building a terrace, make sure that the retaining walls are secure: they should be able to support at least the weight of a person. For ideas on how to make an easy-care retaining wall, see 'Making a planting wall' on page 150 and 'Raised beds made easy' on page 192. Clear all weeds by using glyphosate-based weedkiller, then allow any new soil added to the terraces to settle for a few weeks. Before planting, top up the beds with extra soil to form a gentle backwards slope to the bottom of the terrace above.

This combination of low-growing evergreens and mat-forming rock plants makes the most of a sloping front garden. Seen here in spring, it provides a succession of colour all year round.

Making a rockery Rockery plants need an open, sunny site and good drainage, although the soil should not be particularly rich. If your soil is 'heavy', with a high clay or silt content, improve it by digging in grit or sharp sand (see page 27). If the subsoil has poor drainage, dig out the top 30 cm (12 in) of soil, put in a 15 cm (6 in) base of rubble or hard core, and then a 5 cm (2 in) layer of sharp sand followed by 10 cm (4 in) of topsoil – hard work, but your efforts will be rewarded.

When choosing stones to embed in a rockery slope, first contact quarries in your area because they may be able to provide you with a local stone that blends with the surrounding landscape. Otherwise, common stones for rock gardens include limestone, which weathers quickly but is not liked by acid-loving plants, and sandstone, which comes in attractive colours. Other materials include driftwood and slate, which comes in grey, green and purple, and tufa, which is lightweight and good for a small rockery.

Choosing rockery plants Choose plants that are easy to establish, but not invasive. Along the top edges of the wall, plant prostrate alpines so that they tumble over to soften the hard structure (see page 151). To prevent alpines rotting at the base, plant shallowly with 2.5 cm (1 in) of the rootball above soil level and mulch with about 5 cm (2 in) of pea shingle or stone chippings. This will also conserve moisture during dry spells, control weeds and look attractive.

Time saver

Use a leaf blower to blow leaves and other plant debris into a pile, leaving the gravel or stone chippings undisturbed. The pile can be easily scooped up and put in a barrow using two small wooden boards, one in each hand.

Design tips

Stones Use the same type of stone for the whole rock garden, with a range of sizes from 10 kg (22 lb) to 100 kg (220 lb). For the best effect, the stones should be embedded, with a third of their mass visible above the soil and the grooves and fissures all running in the same direction, so they look like a natural outcrop. Make sure you have help lifting heavy stones.

Verticals Use columnar conifers to add vertical interest to the rockery.

Shade For a shady rockery, use evergreen foliage plants such as *Euonymous fortunei,* fern, hellebore, ground-cover ivy and mahonia.

Quick interest To enliven a gravelled or paved area, use a rocky outcrop planted with alpines.

A sloping site can be terraced to provide extra space. Here, a low-labour raised bed is filled with easy-care plants so that all the work is concentrated into one area.

TROUBLE-FREE ROCK GARDEN PLANTS

The following easy-care plants like free-draining, open conditions provided by a well-built rockery. They will look good against gravel or stone chippings.

Alpines *Aster alpinus, Aurinia saxatilis, Dianthus deltoides,* iberis, sagina, mossy saxifrages, *Sedum spathulifolium,* sempervivums (house leeks – pictured), *Thymus serpyllum.*

For hanging over walls Arabis, modern aubrieta varieties, *Lysimachia nummularia* 'Aurea', *Nierembergia repens, Oenothera macrocarpa* (pictured), saponaria, *Veronica prostrata.*

Dwarf shrubs Heathers, dwarf hebes, *Lavandula angustifolia* 'Munstead', *Potentilla fruticosa* 'Beesii', *Salix* 'Boydii', *Spiraea japonica* 'Goldflame' (pictured).

Dwarf conifers *Cryptomeria japonica* 'Vilmoriniana', *Juniperus communis* 'Compressa', *J. squamata* 'Blue Star', *Pinus mugo* 'Gnom' (pictured), *Thuja orientalis* 'Aurea Nana'.

Bulbs *Allium moly* (pictured), *Anemone blanda,* species crocus, *Cyclamen hederifolium, C. coum, Iris reticulata,* dwarf narcissi, scilla, kaufmanniana and species tulips.

Designing a low-labour front garden

Most people concentrate their gardening time on looking after areas at the back, where they sit out, entertain friends and relax. But a front garden has an important role to play – it is the gateway to your home, it is viewed from both the inside and the outside. As is shown by this example, work can be kept to an absolute minimum without compromising on impact. In fact, often the simpler the design, the more aesthetic it can be.

Rust protection Prevent rust by treating ironwork, such as gates and hanging-basket brackets, with a rust-inhibiting primer before it is painted.

Watering and feeding can be fully automated with timers, drip irrigation, porous hose and In-line feeders (see page 188).

Pressure-treated softwood will remove the necessity for frequent applications of wood preservative.

Mulches can keep borders and beds weed-free for a whole year. Alternatively, plant through mulch matting.

A pressure washer keeps paving pristine, while a path cleaner, with moss and algae controls, has a lasting effect.

Electric or petrol shredders will rapidly reduce garden rubbish into a mulch that can be spread on beds and borders.

Leaves and similar debris on paths, lawns and flowerbeds can be cleared up with a garden vacuum or leaf blower.

Abiding by the law

You should contact your local authority when planning to modify your front garden. You may need permission for:

Walls and fences To build a wall, fence or non-living plant support adjoining a public road higher than 90 cm (36 in). No restrictions are placed on hedges, but you may be asked to cut back vegetation that gets in the way of a road.

Terracing You will need to submit plans and specifications for terracing which has a retaining wall more than 1.2 m (4 ft) high and which is to be built within 3.5 m (12 ft) of the road.

Roadside verges You will need a licence to cultivate the verge outside your house. The council may limit what you can grow.

Creating a 'crossover' If you are building a new driveway, ask the council to flatten the curb outside your house to allow for easy access. You will have to pay.

Make sure that any **ornaments or containers in the front garden are secured to prevent theft.**

Security lights On the front of the house or above the garage, lighting with an infra-red sensor will switch on automatically.

Make the access to your front door direct, because meandering paths will be ignored by visitors.

Gravel is quickly and easily kept free of weeds by applying a path weedkiller in spring, or by raking occasionally to disturb and kill weed seedlings.

EASY-CARE PLANT SELECTOR

Combine a selection of the following low-maintenance plants to create a front garden that is easy to look after and full of interest throughout the year.

Tall shrubs
Cotoneaster franchetii, Elaeagnus x *ebbingei, Hibiscus syriacus* (pictured), *Mahonia* x *media, Prunus laurocerasus, Rosa moyesii, Viburnum opulus.*

Medium shrubs
Berberis verruculosa, chaenomeles, *Cotinus coggygria* 'Royal Purple', forsythia (dwarf varieties), osmanthus, *Viburnum carlesii* (pictured), *Weigela* 'Bristol Ruby'.

Low shrubs
Cotoneaster microphyllus (pictured), *Euonymus fortunei,* hebe (dwarf varieties), *Potentilla fruticosa, Salix lanata,* senecio, *Viburnum davidii.*

Perennials for sun
Eryngium, euphorbia, *Festuca glauca,* geranium (cranesbill), heuchera, kniphofia, *Liriope muscari,* nepeta, *Sedum spectabile* (pictured), sisyrinchium.

Perennials for shade *Arum italicum* ssp. *italicum* 'Marmoratum' (pictured), bergenia, epimedium, *Euphorbia amygdaloides* 'Purpurea', helleborus, lamium, pulmonaria.

Good companions – *Rosa* 'Golden Jubilee' and *Clematis* 'Vyvyan Pennell' – add colour to this house wall in early spring.

Trouble-free plants for a front garden

The need for no-work planting is greater in the front garden than in the back garden. The front is a place of passage and viewing, and not for relaxing while you trim or prune – and more often than not, the garden tools will be located in a shed in the back garden.

Plants also need to be tough, and capable of recovering quickly from damage. Delivery people will take short cuts over the beds; cars and lorries may pass by, belching their fumes; dogs will trample on beds; and pedestrians will throw their litter into hedges.

The most suitable plant candidates are also those that need no regular pruning – they must thrive without pampering. And remember that plants with prickly stems or leaves, such as holly, may help to deter intruders, but they make picking out rubbish more difficult.

For the design of a front garden to work well, the plants need to have additional functions. Some are needed to guide visitors up to the main access to the house, and possibly to and from a side garage

PLANTS FOR A HOT WALL

A colourful display, especially in summer and autumn. Winter-flowering pansies will extend the scheme's interest through winter.

1 *Ceanothus* 'Autumnal Blue' evergreen shrub with blue flowers Aug-Oct.
2 *Nerine bowdenii* pink flowers Sep-Oct.
3 *Romarinus* 'Miss Jessopp's Upright' main flush of mauve-blue flowers Apr-June.
4 *Potentilla fruticosa* 'Abbotswood' white flowers from May until October.
5 *Agapanthus* 'Lilliput' a dwarf variety with blue flowers in July-Aug followed by decorative seed heads.
6 *Rosa* 'Compassion' compact, repeat-flowering climber with apricot-tinged pink, scented flowers.
7 *Hebe* 'Youngii' Violet-blue flowers, fading to white, May-Sep.

or a car parked in a driveway. Possible candidates are a low evergreen hedge of *Lavandula angustifolia* 'Hidcote' for a sunny site or sarcococca, with its floral winter perfumes, for a more shady location.

Scented shrubs are also well-placed to mark the main entrance, to greet people before the doorbell is answered. An easy-care shrub rose, such as the deep yellow *Rosa* 'Graham Thomas', or the compact mock orange, *Philadelphus* 'Manteau d'Hermine', would be ideal.

Choose a style of planting that fits in with the message that you want to give the world. Include easy-care plants already featured in the back garden to provide a design unity to your plot. The dramatic forms of architectural planting, such as phormium or *Fatsia japonica*, are particularly suitable for town gardens. Cottage-style planting may be better for a rural location, using easy-to-grow, self-seeding perennials, such as *Alchemilla mollis*, aquilegia and geranium (cranesbill).

Don't forget to add a vertical element for privacy and interest. Choose a small tree with a strong burst of spring flowers, or autumn colour or berries, such as *Sorbus cashmiriana*, which has rose-tinged, white berries that are the last to be eaten by the birds in winter, or *Acer palmatum* 'Sango-kaku'. Avoid trees with water-seeking roots, such as eucalyptus or willow, especially near to the house.

Quick results

Regular care of some shrubs, including *Elaeagnus* x *ebbingei* and the red-leaved *Berberis thunbergii* 'Bagatelle', involves no more than an all-over trim with shears or a hedgetrimmer when necessary. Alternatively, some easy-care shrubs that can be kept under control by cutting to near ground level each spring, include lavatera, ornamental elders (sambucus) and dogwood (cornus).

PLANTS FOR SHADE
An all-year display of tough, undemanding plants with particularly attractive foliage. Upkeep is minimal.
1
2
3
4
5
6
7
8

1 *Hydrangea anomala* ssp. *petiolaris* white flowerheads June/July. Self-clinging.
2 *Viburnum davidii* blue fruits follow white flowers in July. Evergreen foliage.
3 *Polystichum setiferum* evergreen fern.
4 *Chaenomeles* x *superba* 'Crimson and Gold' red flowers Mar-June and fruits.
5 *Bergenia purpurascens* Evergreen foliage turns purplish-red in winter.
6 *Galanthus nivalis* (snowdrop)
7 *Euonymus fortunei* 'Emerald Gaiety' bright green leaves with white edges. Foliage becomes tinged pink in winter.
8 *Garrya elliptica* winter catkins that last well into spring.

Time saver

A quick way to improve the look of a garden is to paint the garage doors a subtle colour, such as deep green or blue. Then use a brighter shade for the front door, and use complementary colours in the planting.

Easy-care front gardens with space for cars

A car parking space doesn't have to be purely functional: it can also look attractive. The golden rule is that the larger the parking area, the greater the need will be to break up the monotonous appearance of paving. This can be done in several ways: by introducing a variety of textures and colours by using more than one paving material; by creating a single central bed, either circular or elliptical, which is positioned so that cars can easily drive right round it; or by adding ornamental edging, or clusters of containers.

Easy-care drives Solid construction is vital for an area regularly driven over by vehicles. You will need at least 15 cm (6 in) of well-compacted hardcore for the foundations. The surface material you choose depends on the look you want to achieve and how much time is available for maintenance. Because of its soft appearance and versatility, gravel is good for large areas and those that are curved or have an irregular shape. It is cheap and easy to lay, and its natural colour and texture blend well with most building materials, architectural styles and surroundings. The crunching sound made by walking

Use planting pockets to break up hard areas. The undercarriage of a car can easily pass over these low-growing plants.

Gravel gives a naturally soft appearance to a drive. Use a path weedkiller in spring to keep the gravel clear of weeds all season.

A variety of paving materials helps to break up the appearance of this driveway. A curved raised bed filled with evergreens and mulched with gravel keeps the workload to a minimum and makes access straightforward.

Weed control

A properly laid driveway should have had all weeds removed during excavation for the foundations, and additionally may incorporate a weedproof membrane. It is much better to deal with weeds in driveways as they appear so they don't have time to set seed. Most seedling weeds can be pulled out easily. More established ones respond well to suitable weedkillers, or can be controlled organically with a fatty acid spray, boiling water, or a flame gun – though these treatments will need repeating regularly. Weedkillers with a lasting effect are the most labour-saving (see page 270).

on it also acts as a good burglar deterrent. However, to look smart, gravel needs occasional raking and weed control (see above). It also needs a firm edge to stop stones from 'creeping' into other areas.

Unlike gravel, which has naturally good drainage, hard paving materials must be laid with a slight slope to allow efficient drainage. Pavers are durable, clean and practical. Hard wearing setts – small, cube-like, usually granite blocks – provide a traditional appearance. Concrete is comparatively inexpensive, but may look austere, although firms specialising in pattern imprinting can produce a decorative finish. Other options include asphalt and resin-bonded gravel.

Planting in drives At the edges of the drive, plant tough plants, such as heathers and creeping thymes, which will survive an occasional clipping by a car tyre. Many ornamental grasses and sedges are suitable for this position, too; the bronze-coloured *Carex comans* and the yellow-striped *Carex oshimensis* 'Evergold' both add evergreen foliage that cascades over the edge of the paving. For a shady drive, choose tough hardy ferns such as *Dryopteris erythrosora* or *D. affinis* 'Crispa Gracilis'. In a central bed choose robust, low-growing plants, such as *Aubrieta* 'Alix Brett' or *Ajuga reptans* 'Pink Surprise'. All are easy care.

Covering the Ground

BY SIMPLIFYING THE SHAPE OF YOUR LAWN, REMOVING OBSTACLES AND ADDING EASY-CARE FEATURES YOU CAN CUT THE HOURS SPENT MOWING. A MORE RADICAL SOLUTION IS TO CHOOSE A NON-GRASS SURFACE THAT REQUIRES VERY LITTLE MAINTENANCE

The traditional ideal of a lawn is a manicured close-cropped expanse of grass that covers the 'floor' of the garden. Its big drawback from the busy gardener's point of view is the time that such a lawn takes to maintain. Even in a small garden it is easy to spend an hour or more each week from spring to autumn cutting grass, emptying the grass-box, disposing of clippings and trimming lawn edges. And even in winter the jobs may still need doing occasionally.

By simplifying your garden's design and using the right lawn products and equipment it is possible to reduce the workload. But there are some exciting alternatives to traditionally cropped grass. A different kind of ground covering can mean far less work and yet still look good, particularly in places where grass does not grow well, such as in shade or dry sunny sites. For areas that suffer heavy wear, hard surfaces of gravel or paving would be a better option, while in isolated parts of the garden which are rarely walked on you could lay a decorative flowering feature which will not need cutting.

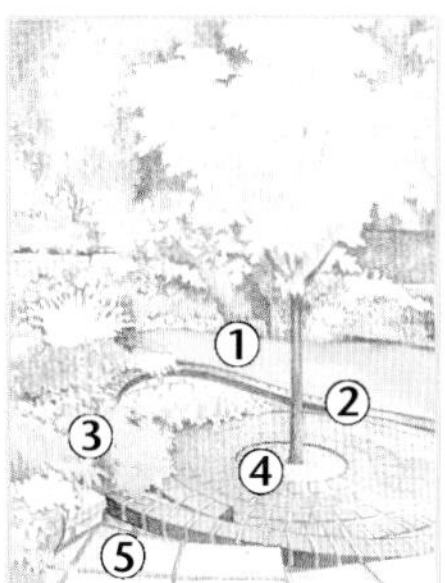

1 DESIGN – *make your lawn a less important garden feature and reduce the area to mow.*
2 SWEEPING CURVES – *lawns with gentle curves mean less stopping and turning when mowing.*
3 GROUND-COVER PLANTS – *suppress weeds and give a softer appearance to hard surfaces.*
4 GRAVEL – *attractive and low-maintenance.*
5 PAVING – *ideal for areas that suffer heavy wear.*

EASY-CARE CALENDAR

EARLY SPRING
Set the blades of your mower at their maximum height and mow the lawn when the weather is mild and the grass is dry. Then mow weekly. Apply a mosskiller, if needed, as a short-term cure. For long-term prevention, tackle the root causes, such as shade, compaction or waterlogged soil.

MID SPRING
After a few cuts, lower the cutting height of your mower to 4 cm (1½ in). Apply a combined weedkiller and fertiliser, or use an autumn preparation so as not to encourage too much lush growth and to improve root growth.

LATE SPRING
Mow regularly. Do not use a grass-box. Leave clippings on the lawn to act as an organic mulch.

SUMMER
Mow and edge as necessary. There is no need to water even in a drought because the lawn will recover with the next rains.

EARLY AUTUMN
Aerate compacted areas (see page 61). Rake out thatch using a powered lawn rake. Re-seed bare patches.

STARTING FROM SCRATCH
For an average-sized lawn of 50 m^2 (60 sq yd), allow a weekend to prepare the ground and a day to lay the turf. Lawns grown from seed require the same preparation, but sowing takes just a couple of hours. Paving will take an additional day to lay and is a heavier job. Gravel and ground-cover plants take the least time to set up.

Hard and soft options A lawn requires regular maintenance throughout the growing season, gravel needs to be raked and weeded occasionally, whereas paving is almost maintenance-free.

HOW MUCH TIME?

Do not skimp on preparations or materials when covering the ground because this may lead to problems that are time-consuming and costly to put right. If you cannot spare the start-up time, consider employing a contractor (see page 302).

Type	Start-up	Maintenance	Cost
Grass	••	•••	£
Plants	•••	••	££
Gravel	•	••	£
Paving	••	•	££
Bricks	•••	•	££
Cobbles	•••	•	££
Decking	••	••	£££

Key to ratings
• (quick and easy) to
••• (time-consuming/hard work)
£ (cheap) to £££ (expensive)

Choosing your ground cover

A lawn may seem the perfect way of covering most of the ground in your garden, but if you want to reduce the time spent on garden maintenance there are various options to consider. For example, where a well-kept 'bowling green'-style lawn might require 100 hours of maintenance a year, a similar area covered by a tough family lawn which contains hard-wearing, drought-tolerant rye grass would claim about 50 hours of your time. If the area were covered in ground-cover plants or a wild-flower meadow, however, you would need to allow only about 10 hours to maintain it. Gravel would take less than 5 hours of raking and weeding each year, while paving could cut maintenance time to almost nothing.

Although a completely paved garden would be very stark, you can achieve a satisfying overall effect by combining paving with a small, carefully designed lawn, and low-maintenance borders, beds and ground-cover plants. Or combine paving with a range of other surfaces and containers to construct an easy-care courtyard-style garden.

The main benefits of grass are that, if kept trim, it looks good for much of the year, requires little skill to maintain and is an all-purpose covering for most situations. Paving, bricks and gravel do not need so much maintenance, but may be less appealing than a well-kept lawn. Cobbles and decking are more interesting, but are more expensive.

Grass is troublesome when growing conditions are not ideal. Even if you put in many hours of extra work maintaining the lawn, the result is likely to be disappointing. In deep shade, for example, the grass will struggle to compete with shade-loving weeds and moss, especially if the ground remains wet for long periods. Either replace the lawn with a hard surface or plant the area with a mixture of shade-tolerant wild flowers and grasses, including naturalised bluebells (hyacinthoides), or a carpet of moss or mind-your-own-business (soleirolia). Where the grass does not thrive in a hot, sunny spot, a

GROUND-COVER OPTIONS

Grass is attractive, versatile and adaptable. Ground-cover plants are useful in sites where grass struggles, such as under trees. Gravel is the easiest type of hard surface to lay, but slabs, bricks and cobbles need less maintenance. Wooden decking looks good, but is expensive.

Combine split-level decking with borders of easy-care shrubs, such as *Acer palmatum* and bamboo underplanted with hostas, to create a low-labour garden. Cover bare soil with a mulch of bark chippings or stones.

herb or alpine lawn is a low-maintenance alternative (see page 62), although it must not be an area that is often walked on.

Heavy wear is a common reason for a poor-quality lawn. If constant trampling is the problem, you could put up a barrier, such as a small, linear shrub bed, to prevent people taking short cuts across the lawn. If the route between the back door and a washing line is creating worn tracks that need regular repair, install a hard path or sink a row of stepping stones. Protect the turf from rough treatment by children or pets by reinforcing it with stiff, plastic mesh with 2.5 cm (1 in) holes or by creating a special hard-wearing play area.

On banks and slopes that are tricky to mow, use evergreen ground-cover plants. They can be either low, spreading plants, such as periwinkle (vinca) or ivy (hedera), or taller evergreens, such as cistus or euonymus, that are planted in sufficient density to smother out the weeds. For extra weed protection, grow through mulch matting.

Once established, a gravel garden featuring drought-tolerant plants such as phormium, blue grass (helictotrichon), iris, alpine pinks and sempervivum needs almost no maintenance.

Paving slabs *Wire-cut bricks* *Pebbles* *Decking*

Sweeping curves and a mowing strip reduce mowing time. Ground-cover plants around the specimen tree keep weeds under control.

For family lawns that get very heavy wear, choose a tough ornamental ryegass. Feed it in late spring and consider reinforcing worn patches with mesh.

Design tips for easy-care lawns

A grass lawn is easy to establish, but keeping it in top condition demands a lot of commitment. If you want a lawn, but don't have time for mowing and edging every week in spring and summer, a few simple changes will reduce the workload.

Two or more small lawns take a lot more maintenance than a single larger lawn. Not only do you have more edges to trim, but corners on smaller lawns will be tighter, making manoeuvring the lawnmower more awkward. If you have a large lawn in the back garden and a small one in the front, you could ease the burden by replacing the front lawn with a non-grass surface such as gravel or paving (see page 66).

The shape of a lawn influences the amount of time needed each week to keep it looking tidy. The most efficient lawn shape for mowing is a circle. You can start at the outside and keep mowing in ever-decreasing circles until you reach the centre, without having to stop and turn at all. A large,

Lawncare

Do buy the right mower for your size and type of lawn (see page 60).

Do cut the grass by less than 2 cm (¾ in). Then you will not need to use a grassbox, and the clippings can be left on the lawn to act as a mulch.

Don't cut grass shorter than 4 cm (1½ in) because if you do it will grow faster and not be as drought-resistant as grass that is longer.

Don't feed your lawn unless there is good reason, such as heavy wear; it will only grow faster and need cutting more often.

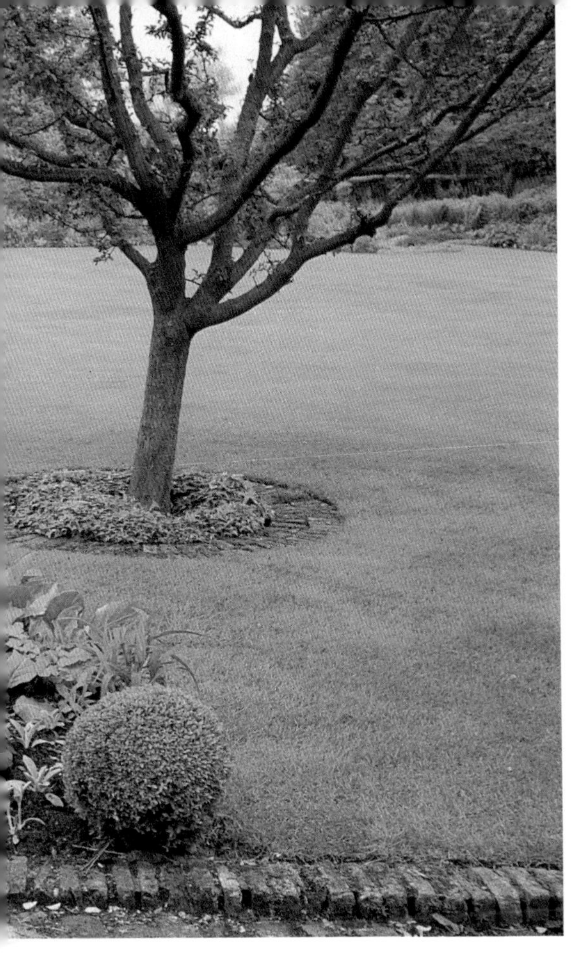

kidney-shaped lawn has sweeping curves that can also be mowed without the need to stop and turn, but avoid complicated curves, which are fiddly to trim. A square lawn is less time-efficient, but is the best choice for a formal garden.

The more obstacles in a lawn, such as beds and trees, the longer it will take to mow. Having to duck under an overhanging tree or mow round a shrub will slow you down. Do not use a nylon-line trimmer around a young tree, however, because the line may cut into the bark and injure the tree. If plants cascade over the edge of the lawn, put a row of bricks along the edge of the grass to make a 'mowing strip', which reduces the need to tidy the lawn edges.

If you have several trees in the lawn, incorporate them into a single island bed to reduce the amount of edging. Discourage weeds by underplanting with ground-cover plants and mulch any bare soil. If you want a specimen tree, you can also lay a bed of gravel round it or leave a drift of long grass to grow underneath.

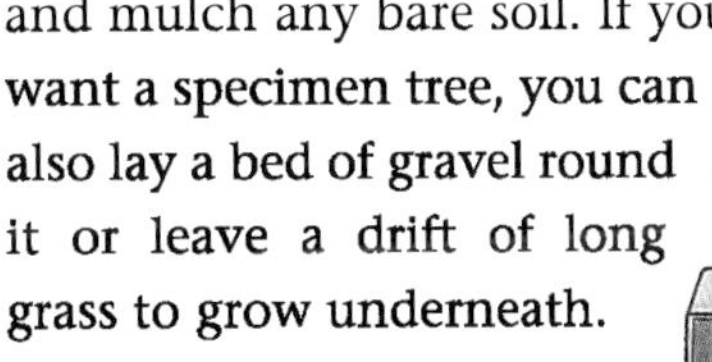

Laying a mowing strip

By adding a mowing strip of paving or brick round the edge of a lawn, you can eliminate the need for frequent trimming apart from tidying up the odd grass tuft once every couple of months. When you mow, push the mower right onto the mowing strip.

Mark the edge Use a plank as a guide for straight edges or a hosepipe for curves. Dig a trench deep and wide enough for the edging bricks and foundations.

Wet the mix Brush dry mortar mix into the cracks between the bricks, then water thoroughly.

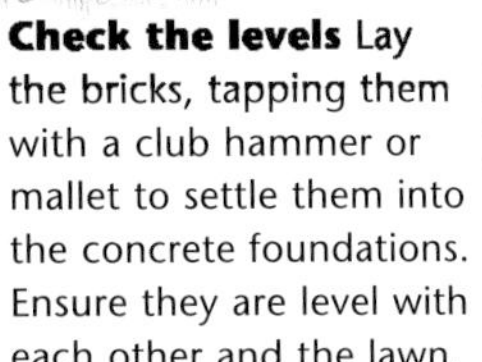

Lay the foundations Cover the bottom of the trench with a 7.5 cm (3 in) layer of dry concrete mix and spread it fairly level.

Check the levels Lay the bricks, tapping them with a club hammer or mallet to settle them into the concrete foundations. Ensure they are level with each other and the lawn.

Time saver

A lawn of white clover stays green all summer, needs no feeding and mowing only once to remove dead flowerheads. It grows up to 7.5 cm (3 in). Sow away from sunbathing areas because clover attracts bees.

The wild-flower alternative

A flowering meadow, with tall grass and meadow-type wild flowers, is the lowest-maintenance wild-flower option because it needs cutting only twice a year with a nylon-line trimmer or powered scythe – once in early spring and then again when the flowers have set seed. But for a shorter, flowering lawn, use low-growing wild flowers or bulbs planted in drifts or groups.

Wild-flower-and-grass seed mixes to suit particular sites and soil types are available for flowering meadows and lawns. Sow as you would an ordinary lawn (see page 58) or, to convert an existing lawn into a wild-flower lawn, plant pot-grown species, such as bird's-foot trefoil, sweet violet, celandine and speedwell. These creeping plants withstand mowing as long as the lawn is not cut shorter than 5 cm (2 in), but avoid cutting altogether when flowers are setting seed. Do not feed a wild-flower lawn, because you will

Use clover for a longer 'rough' lawn which needs much less maintenance than an ordinary grass-only lawn. Unlike a conventional lawn, clover will stay green through a drought.

Crocuses are ideal for naturalising in lawns because they flower early and their grass-like foliage does not become an eyesore.

encourage the grass at the expense of the wild flowers, or use lawn weedkiller, because this will kill the wild flowers.

Bulbs should be grouped under trees or planted in drifts so that they are easier to mow around. Plant the bulbs in existing turf in autumn. Suitable species for an open lawn include crocuses and daffodils. In areas of dappled shade, try wood anemones (*Anemone nemorosa*), snowdrops (galanthus) or bluebells (hyacinthoides), and in moist, light shade, snake's head fritillary (*Fritillaria meleagris*).

Do not mow a lawn planted with bulbs until at least six weeks after the bulbs have finished flowering, or once their foliage has turned yellow, otherwise they may not flower the following year. While waiting for the bulb foliage to die down, feed with an autumn lawn fertiliser, which is lower in nitrogen than spring lawn fertiliser and, therefore, does not encourage the same lush growth of grass. Do not use lawn weedkiller until the bulbs have died down completely.

CREATING A WILD-FLOWER MEADOW

A wild-flower meadow can provide flowers from May to September, depending on the varieties planted. Choose wild flowers according to the soil type and site conditions, as well as the effect that you want to create.

Old-fashioned cornfield species They suit an open, sunny site – similar to conditions in a cornfield. They include corn cockle (pictured), corn marigold, mayweed, field poppy, and oxeye daisy.

Grassland plants For colonising damp grassy places try buttercup, cowslip, harebell and knapweed. For dry grassland, use field scabious, *Pulsatilla vulgaris*, speedwell and yarrow (pictured).

Early-flowering species To create a meadow that looks at its best in spring, include cow parsley, cowslip (pictured), hawkbit, lady's smock, lesser stitchwort and the daffodil *Narcissus pseudonarcissus*.

Shade-tolerant plants Primroses (pictured) can be planted under trees for a spring display. For long grass in an orchard or under trees, snake's head fritillary and wild orchid provide a pleasing effect.

Shallow steps, bordered by cranesbill and golden sedge, provide easy access between different levels of the lawn. A slab sunk into the grass prevents wear at the base of the steps.

Rescuing a neglected grass lawn

Regular mowing keeps grass growing thickly and prevents weeds from getting established. To rescue an overgrown lawn colonised by weeds, cut back the long grass either in spring or autumn using a nylon-line trimmer or a rotary lawnmower (see page 60) with blades set high, at 5-7.5 cm (2-3 in). For a large area, hire a powered scythe or get in a contractor for the first cut. Then feed the neglected lawn with a lawn fertiliser.

Mow regularly, deciding what height you want your lawn and mowing each time it grows 1-2 cm (½-¾ in) more than this. By cutting the lawn by less than 2 cm (¾ in), you won't need a grass-box because these short trimmings will sink into the lawn quickly, returning nutrients to the soil. Longer trimmings will tend to stay on the surface longer and look messy, although they won't do any intrinsic harm. In autumn, use a lawn rake to remove dead stems and moss, aerate with a spiker (see page 61) to allow air in to the soil for better root growth, and apply an autumn lawn fertiliser.

Weeds Regular mowing kills upright weeds. Rosette-forming weeds, such as daisies and dandelions, and creeping weeds, such as speedwell and selfheal, go unharmed under the mower. The fastest remedy is a combined liquid weedkiller and lawn feed in May. Remove individual rosette-forming weeds by applying a spot weedkiller for lawns.

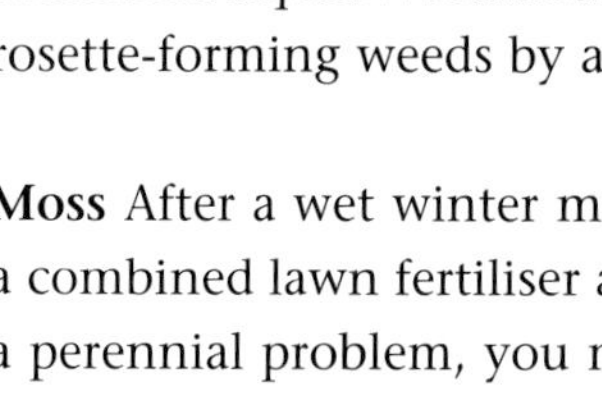

Moss After a wet winter moss can be a problem on any lawn. Apply a combined lawn fertiliser and mosskiller in May. However, if moss is a perennial problem, you must tackle the conditions that encourage it. In shade, thin out the branches of overhanging trees or replace the lawn with shade-tolerant ground-cover plants. On waterlogged soils,

TACKLING LAWN WEEDS

Most weeds can be controlled quickly by applying a lawn weedkiller in May. On heavily infested lawns, several applications may be needed, plus another the following spring.

Clover *To control this spreading weed use a liquid lawn weedkiller containing 2,4-D in May or rake before mowing to lift its stems, and use a grass-box. (See page 54 for ornamental use.)*

Moss *Apply mosskiller in spring to gain quick control. For a long-term solution, deal with the underlying causes of moss, such as dense shade and compacted or waterlogged soil.*

Daisy *Rosette-forming lawn weed that is most prolific on neutral and alkaline soils. Flowers from January until October. Self-seeds. Use lawn weedkiller in spring or spot treatment.*

Plantain *This rosette-forming weed spreads by seed. It likes to colonise lawns suffering from drought, and flowers all summer. Use spot weedkiller during growing season.*

Dandelion *Spreads by wind-dispersed seeds from dandelion 'clocks'. Destroy this rosette-forming weed with a spot weedkiller at any time during the growing season.*

Repairing a ragged lawn edge

A lawn edge is easier to trim if it is neat. A ragged or broken edge can be repaired by cutting out the damaged area in spring with a garden spade or a half-moon edging iron. Use a plank of wood as a guide to cut a straight edge, or a length of hose to cut a neat curve.

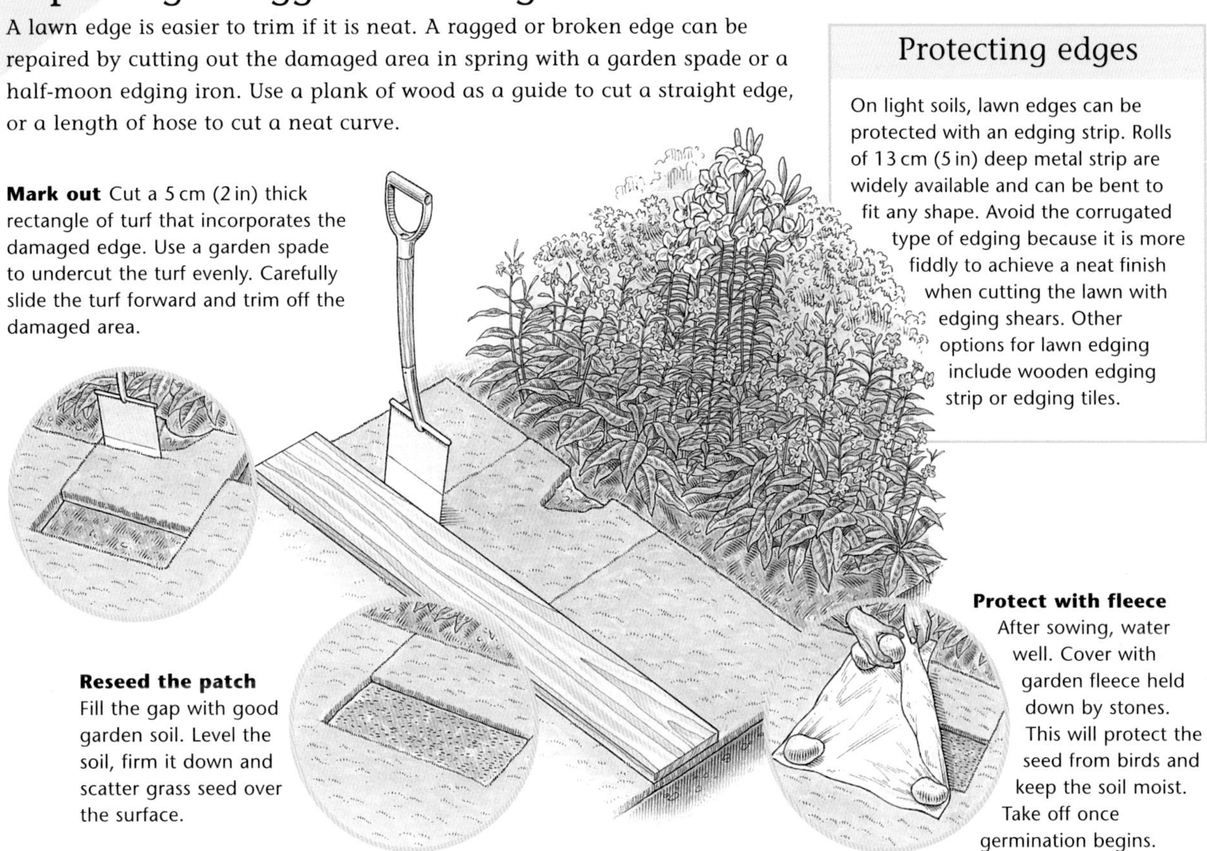

Mark out Cut a 5 cm (2 in) thick rectangle of turf that incorporates the damaged edge. Use a garden spade to undercut the turf evenly. Carefully slide the turf forward and trim off the damaged area.

Reseed the patch Fill the gap with good garden soil. Level the soil, firm it down and scatter grass seed over the surface.

Protect with fleece After sowing, water well. Cover with garden fleece held down by stones. This will protect the seed from birds and keep the soil moist. Take off once germination begins.

Protecting edges

On light soils, lawn edges can be protected with an edging strip. Rolls of 13 cm (5 in) deep metal strip are widely available and can be bent to fit any shape. Avoid the corrugated type of edging because it is more fiddly to achieve a neat finish when cutting the lawn with edging shears. Other options for lawn edging include wooden edging strip or edging tiles.

and old or heavily used lawns, scarify and aerate the turf in autumn. Then brush in two bucketfuls of sharp sand per square metre without burying the grass. This treatment may need repeating every few years.

Bare patches On poor, thin grass or a lawn that gets heavy wear, apply a dose of slow-release feed in spring and an autumn lawn feed in September or October. Repair any bare patches in spring or autumn. Prick the soil with a fork to loosen it and sprinkle on seeds from a lawn repair kit, or returf the area (see page 58).

Other lawn problems Slimy patches or liverwort, which look like overlapping green platelets, colonise bare patches in winter. Control in spring with a liquid mosskiller, but check the product is suitable.

Ignore occasional toadstools in autumn because they are a seasonal symptom and will disappear with the first frosts. Fairy rings – rings of small toadstools around a yellow circle of grass – persist all year. Like other toadstools, fairy rings don't harm the lawn. Hire a contractor to inject a chemical through the turf if you want to eradicate them.

Quick results

To make sure that lawn weedkillers and mosskillers work in one 'hit', apply them when the soil is moist and the grass is growing, but when rain is not expected for at least 12 hours. The products act on the leaves and may fail if washed into the soil too soon. Use lawn weedkillers before weeds start flowering – after that they become more resistant and several treatments may be needed.

Holiday tips

Do cut the grass shortly before you leave home.

Do arrange for your grass to be cut while you are away, especially if you are gone for more than two weeks.

Do 'top' long grass on your return with a nylon-line trimmer or powerful rotary mower. If cut short, long grass turns yellow, so make sure that you set the blades as high as possible for the first cut, then mow again a few days later.

Don't apply fertiliser for six weeks before you go on holiday.

Don't water the lawn in summer because it will suffer even more if the weather is dry when you are away.

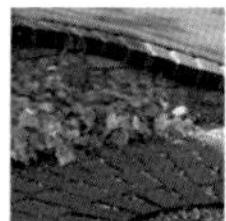

Creating an easy-care lawn

No matter how weed-infested or bald an existing lawn has become, it will take less effort to improve it than to create a new lawn altogether. However, if you prefer quick results, or if you have no lawn to begin with, you will have to start from scratch.

Laying cultivated turf is the quickest way to create a lawn, but it is expensive. Turf will thrive anywhere except in heavy shade or on poor soil. The two main grades are the cheaper meadow turf – likely to contain weeds and bare patches – or the better quality, but more expensive, custom-grown turf. Lay turf in autumn, during a mild winter or in spring when the soil is warm and moist.

The cheapest and easiest way to create a new lawn is to sow seed. But you will have to wait several months after sowing before you can use it. Autumn sowings require least work, and will be established and ready to use by the following summer. Choose the type of seed to suit your situation. Modern ornamental rye grasses, such as 'Hunter' or 'Barclay', make a good-quality, hard-wearing lawn. Special mixes also exist for shade or dry soil.

Laying turf

Before the turf is delivered, prepare the ground as described in steps 1, 2 and 3 (see illustration, left). Lay the turfs in a bonded pattern like bricks in a wall so that the lawn knits together quickly. Leave turfs at the edges as whole as possible with offcuts used as filler pieces further in. This reduces the risk of the newly laid turf drying out. Water well after laying and keep moist until the turf roots into the soil – test by peeling back a piece of turf.

Sowing or laying a new lawn

Good preparation is the key to success when creating a new lawn, but this is the most time-consuming and labour-intensive part of the process, so it may be worth employing a contractor (see page 302).

1 Clear the ground Use a flame gun or spray with a glyphosate-based weedkiller.

2 Break up the soil Use a powered rotavator and then remove any perennial weeds and other debris.

3 Level the soil Rake level, scatter growmore at the rate of 75 g per m^2 (2 oz per sq yd) and tread down.

4 Sowing seed Buy or hire a spreader to make it easy to sow evenly. Check in advance that the spreader can be set to sow grass seed. After sowing, rake to partly bury seed.

5 Protect the seed After sowing, cover with bird-proof netting or fleece.

6 Make the first cut Remove the fleece when the seedlings are growing stongly. Once the grass is more than 7.5 cm (3 in) long, trim it lightly.

MAKING LIGHT WORK OF LAWNCARE

Use the following chart to minimise the workload while keeping your lawn looking good

SPRING
(March and April)

▲ Start mowing Make the first cut as soon as grass begins to grow in spring. Adjust blades to cut the lawn at a height of 4 cm (1½ in). Mow whenever grass is 1-2 cm (½-¾ in) higher than desired.

Leave clippings Do not use a grass-box if cuttings are shorter than 2 cm (¾ in). Leave them as a mulch to return nutrients to soil.

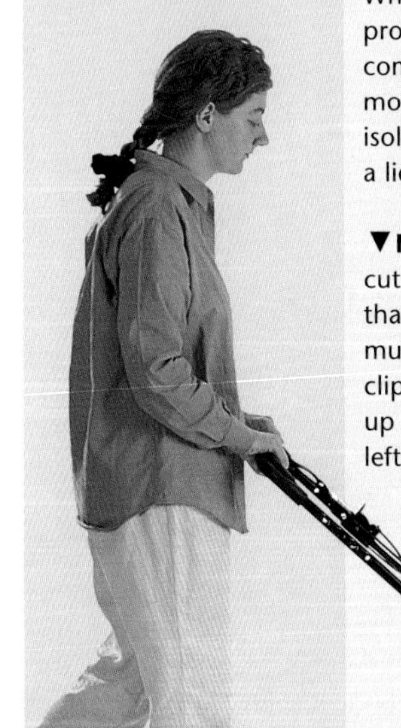

EARLY SUMMER
(May)

Mowing Continue mowing as necessary.

Feeding Feed lawns that get a lot of wear. Apply a slow-release lawn feed to give nutrients over the rest of the season, but don't apply any other feed.

Lightly used lawns Use an autumn lawn feed, which will thicken and toughen grass, but not encourage it to grow faster.

Weed control Use a combined lawn feed and weedkiller, or spot-treat individual weeds.

Moss treatment Where moss is a problem, use a combined feed and moss treatment. Treat isolated patches with a liquid mosskiller.

▼ Mulch mowers To cut the lawn by more than 2 cm (¾ in), use a mulch mower so that clippings are chopped up fine enough to be left as a mulch.

SUMMER
(June to early Sept)

Mowing Continue cutting the lawn regularly in order to prevent weeds. Even though grass stops growing in dry conditions, weeds do not. If they are left to grow unchecked, they spread and take over.

Do not water It is not necessary to water lawns during a dry summer. Even if the grass turns brown, it is rarely killed by summer drought and recovers naturally with autumn rains. Do not use lawn feeds, even liquid ones, to make a brown lawn turn green – it will only worsen the problem.

Bare patches Move children's play equipment around the lawn regularly to prevent excessive wear in one place.

Let grass grow Avoid mowing too closely – close cutting puts grass under stress. Cut to 4 cm (1½ in) to keep grass green during droughts, help it to withstand wear and smother out weeds.

AUTUMN
(Mid Sept to Oct)

Brown grass Gently rake out the worst of the dead material (a powered lawn rake does this quickly) and wait for rains to revive the grass. Do not feed, even after new grass appears – the grass will be suffering from stress and a late feed will leave the grass too soft to thrive during winter.

▲ Fallen leaves If they are left on a lawn for more than a few weeks, leaves will turn the grass yellow. Gather up the leaves and compost them or make them into leaf-mould (see page 276). Collect leaves spread out over the lawn by running over them with a rotary mower with grass-box attached. Alternatively, use a garden vacuum (pictured).

Continue mowing Cut as necessary to keep weeds under control. If the grass is growing well, apply an autumn lawn feed in September or October.

WINTER
(Nov to Feb)

Keep off the grass Save yourself a lot of repair work in spring by keeping off the grass when the ground is soft, otherwise it will soon become muddy and rutted. Also keep off the lawn when it is frozen because this encourages moss, algae, moulds and lichens.

Protect the grass When the ground is soft, unroll a temporary path of heavy-duty plastic mesh to avoid damaging the grass, for example, if you need to push a wheelbarrow across it. If you need to work on beds adjacent to the lawn, lay down planks or a sheet of exterior plywood temporarily to protect it.

Continue mowing In mild weather grass will continue growing, so do not stop cutting it completely otherwise it will be too long to tackle by spring. If the grass is dry enough, mow once every four to six weeks.

EFFICIENT MOWING

A wide cutting width is best for big lawns because you will cover the area quicker. For small lawns, stick to a small mower to tackle tight curves.

Lawn size	Small	Medium	Large
Cutting width	25 cm (10 in)	30 cm (12 in)	+35 cm (+14 in)
Ride-on			•
Hover	•		
Rotary	•	•	•
Cylinder	•	•	•

Small = Up to 50 m² (60 sq yd)
Medium = 50-200 m² (60-240 sq yd)
Large = 200-300 m² (240-360 sq yd)

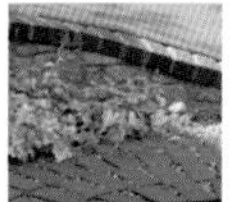

Time-saving tools for your lawn

You can save time on regular jobs, such as lawn edging, by investing in the right equipment. Occasional jobs, such as spiking the lawn, can be made easier by hiring equipment or employing a contractor.

Cutting the grass If you have a small lawn and want a fine finish, and don't mind a little gentle exercise, then consider a hand-push mower. Electric machines are an easier option, but their range is limited by the length of cable. Battery-powered mowers are suitable for small and medium-sized lawns, but are not powerful enough to cut a large lawn without recharging. Petrol-driven machines are more powerful, but expensive. They are the time-saver's choice for tackling longer grass and for medium to large lawns. If you allow the grass to grow by more than 2 cm (¾ in) between mowings, a mulch mower will save time. It has no grass-box to empty, and the blades chop the grass fine enough to be left on the lawn.

Raking and scarifying Raking by hand takes time and is hard work, so it is worth hiring or buying a powered lawn rake in order to 'scarify' the lawn. The rotating teeth remove moss and dead grass from the lawn, collecting it in a grass-box. Do this every autumn to achieve a high-quality lawn.

MOWER OPTIONS

Investing in the right equipment is the easiest way for the busy gardener to reduce the time spent on lawncare. Mowing is the most time-consuming task, so make sure you choose a mower that suits the type and size of your lawn.

Ride-on *The time-saver's choice for a very large garden. Ride-on mowers have an extra-wide cutting width and move faster than you can walk with a powered mower. They are not suitable for fine lawns.*

Hover *A good solution for small or fiddly lawns and banks. The mower can be moved sideways as well as back and forth and the blades glide over the lawn edges, speeding up mowing around beds and borders.*

Rotary *A large area of unobstructed grass suits the rotary mower best. Rotary mowers are ideal for longer grass, but their wheels make it difficult to get right up to lawn edges. Petrol models are the most powerful.*

Cylinder *Necessary only if you want a top-quality lawn. It is the only mower to make well-defined stripes in grass. It needs a level surface and dry grass. Small electric and large petrol versions are sold.*

Clearing leaves Fallen leaves that are left on the ground smother the grass and turn the lawn yellow. In small gardens a garden vacuum is handy for leaf collection. Vacuums are also useful for removing leaves from awkward corners. To clear up leaves on a larger lawn, use a leaf sweeper or a rotary mower with a grass-box attached and the blades set high.

Spreading fertiliser Save time feeding large lawns by buying or hiring a lawn fertiliser spreader. For fast, easy application to a small area, choose a fertiliser that comes in a shaker pack. For an even spread, mark the lawn into strips with canes or string to work out how much fertiliser to use in each strip.

Improving drainage Aerating the soil will improve growing conditions by allowing air, food and water to get in and improve surface drainage. This is especially important for soil compacted at the surface of a lawn that gets heavy wear. For quick results, hire a powered spiker (which makes holes), or use a slitting attachment (which cuts narrow channels) that can be towed behind a powerful mower. If you are doing the job by hand, use a spiker (shown below) or a hollow-tined fork. Small areas can be aerated by pushing in a garden fork about 7.5 cm (3 in) into the turf, spacing holes 5 cm (2 in) apart, but this is very time-consuming.

Edging made easy

Neat lawn edges improve the look of your lawn; and if you use a half-moon edging tool to create sharp edges they will be easy to trim.

Powered edger A powered edger is the most efficient way of keeping edges neat. But you need a firm, horizontal surface at the edge of your lawn over which to guide the trimmer.

Nylon-line trimmer This can save you hours of tidying tufts of grass growing against walls or around patios. Do not use close to trees or shrubs because it can damage trunks and stems. Choose a model with an automatic line feed so you don't have to keep stopping to adjust the length of the nylon line.

Hand-pushed mower *Light and manoeuvrable, so worth considering for a small lawn that is mowed regularly. It will not tackle long or wet grass and the wheels make it difficult to mow right up to the edges.*

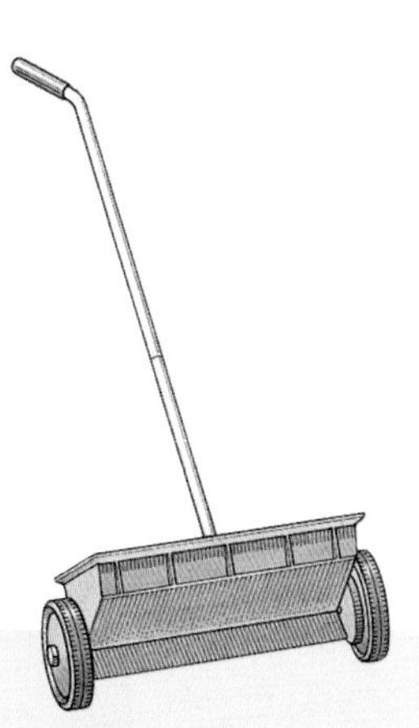

Fertiliser spreader *Ideal for scattering fertiliser evenly over a lawn. Garden centres sometimes lend or hire them to customers who are buying lawn feed. Some spreaders can be adjusted to spread lawn seed.*

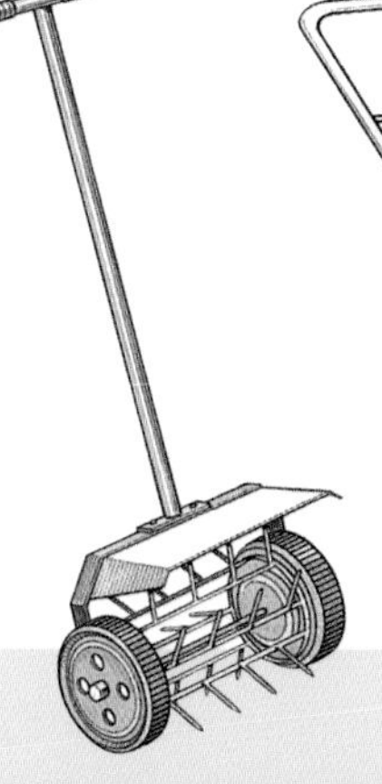

Spiker *A spiker aerates and improves surface drainage of a compacted lawn by making holes in the turf. This is time-consuming, so for large areas hire or buy a powered version.*

Leaf sweeper *A leaf sweeper collects leaves in a flexible container and is useful in gardens with large lawns surrounded by deciduous trees. Powered versions are also available for hire.*

Grass-free 'lawns' sown with colour

Herb lawns and ground-cover plants are easier to maintain than a grass lawn because they do not require regular mowing. They are often more successful than traditional lawns in difficult situations, such as dry sunny sites, on steep banks or in shade under trees. But non-grass lawns are not a perfect substitute for grass: they won't stand hard wear, so would not survive long in a child's play area. If you need to walk through a herb lawn regularly, cut a path or put in a series of stepping stones.

Ground-cover plants A quick-care alternative to grass on a steep bank, which can be difficult to cut, are ground-cover plants (see page 268), such as *Hypericum calycinum*. Alternatively, use taller, knee-high plants that if planted tightly will also stop weeds from taking hold. For even more effective weed control, especially if the ground harbours perennial weeds, cover the bank with mulch matting before planting (see page 264). Plant the bank thickly with evergreens to hide the sheet mulch and smother out germinating weeds.

Steep banks dry out quickly, so choose drought-tolerant plants to avoid having to water in summer, such as hebe, potentilla or cistus in sun, and ivy or euonymus in shade. For a sunny bank with acid, slightly moist but well-drained soil, a dense carpet of mixed heathers, some with coloured foliage, will look good all year round. It will also cope well with an exposed location.

Plants used as ground cover generally require little routine maintenance. In spring, after the last frosts, cut back frost-damaged shoots as well as untidy stems, and then feed with a general fertiliser. Clip heathers lightly after flowering to keep them tidy; for extra fast work, use a nylon-line trimmer. Keep hypericum neat by running a rotary mower over it in autumn, if the bank is not too steep.

Herb lawns A well-drained sunny site is vital for a successful herb lawn. To suppress weeds, spread mulch matting over the prepared soil and plant through it. Hide the matting with a 5 cm (2 in) layer of gravel. Plant with a mixture of creeping thymes or the non-flowering camomile, *Chamaemelum nobile* 'Treneague', spaced 25 cm (10 in) apart. Little maintenance is necessary. Trim thyme lawns lightly after flowering to tidy up deadheads. Or, clip the camomile in summer to keep compact, but no shorter than 10 cm (4 in). Feed with a general fertiliser in early summer. Once established, there is no need to water.

Low-growing conifers, hebes and heathers, underplanted with tulips and daffodils, form an easy-care evergreen ground cover over a bank.

Make a path of stepping stones where you need to walk across a flowering lawn because plants, such as these thymes, will not stand regular wear.

In sun or partial shade, spreading pratia *(above)* forms a continuous mat of evergreen foliage that is covered in pale blue flowers from late spring.

Alpine lawn A decorative alpine lawn is ideal for a low-maintenance front garden. A mixture of low, creeping or spreading rock plants, such as New Zealand burr (acaena), thrift (*Armeria maritima*), rockery pinks (dianthus), *Sedum spathulifolium* and sempervivum, require little weeding if the beds are mulched with 5 cm (2 in) of stone chippings. An alpine lawn is most successful when naturally drought-tolerant species can be planted in a reasonably sunny spot with very good drainage. To keep the lawn looking good, top up the chippings in spring and remove any weeds.

Bulb carpets In woodland or under large trees, a carpet of bluebells or daffodils requires virtually no maintenance. The bulb foliage smothers early weeds, and shade from the trees combined with dry soil conditions in summer makes it impossible for most weeds to survive. To encourage flowering year after year, feed the bulbs with a general fertiliser or a special bulb feed after they have flowered but before the foliage dies down. Remove any problem weeds, such as brambles, by cutting them back and spot-treating any regrowth with a glyphosate-based weedkiller. Do not remove fallen leaves during the autumn because they form a weed-suppressing mulch and help to improve the soil.

Problem solver

Shady lawns Achieve a cool green look in a shady area with soleirolia (mind-your-own-business). Plant it 25 cm (10 in) apart and mulch with pebbles or gravel. To remove any weeds without killing the plant, use spot weedkiller or a hand fork.

A garden for all the family

Families make many conflicting demands on a garden. Children need space to play and keep pets, while adults want an attractive environment in which to relax and to entertain friends. The design of a family garden needs to reflect these different requirements and be flexible enough to evolve as the family grows up. Try to look at your garden as a whole, and go for features that are either dual-purpose or easily adapted to take on a new use with time.

Nature area Children and adults can enjoy a 'wild' area of trees, long grass and wild flowers. Put up nestboxes to attract birds.

A playhouse can be used for storage when the children grow up.

Build a brick barbecue with storage space. It can be used as a stand for plants in winter.

Wildlife pond For older children, you could include a shallow pond to encourage frogs and other wildlife.

A gate and log fence keep smaller children away from the wildlife pond area.

An arch can double as a swing support – the swing is easily removed in order to keep the path clear.

The garden bench doubles as storage space for toys or tools.

Use cheap slabs for the patio. But add a brick mowing strip to minimise lawn maintenance.

Safety first

Poisonous plants In gardens used by children, avoid plants with toxic or irritant leaves, fruit or berries, such as daphne, foxglove, hellebore, juniper, laburnum and yew. Hazardous plants sold at garden centres are now marked, so always check the labels before buying.

Pet problems If animals have access to the lawn, clean up after them regularly. To avoid exposing children to the risk of parasites, such as *Toxocara canis,* worm dogs and cats frequently – consult your vet.

Lawn protection Reinforce heavily used areas of lawn with heavy-duty plastic mesh to help to prevent muddy patches forming.

Safe play surfaces

Impact-absorbing surfaces Made from recycled tyres they come in two forms: either tiles (1) that can be laid on firmed ground; or wet pour (2 and 3) laid in situ on an existing hard surface or hardcore.

Loose surfaces Materials such as bark chippings (4) or cocoa shells (5) can also make safe play surfaces. They need to be at least 15 cm (6 in) deep within a timber frame.

Jungle zone A dense thicket of shrubs where children can play. To add humour, make stepping stones out of cement moulded in the shape of giant footprints.

An arbour can also make a practice goal if you add a net to the top which rolls down.

Help your children to carve their initials on an immature marrow and they can watch their letters grow.

Children's garden Give children their own patch of garden where they can raise quick-growing plants, such as sunflowers, gourds, nasturtiums and radishes.

Fit the children's sandbox with a bamboo roller blind to protect it from the weather and cats. When it is outgrown, convert the sandbox into a raised herb bed.

CHILD-FRIENDLY PLANTS

There are many easily grown non-toxic plants soft enough to do no harm if children fall against them, yet resilient enough to withstand the effects of garden games.

Shrubs for sun
Buddleja, ceanothus, cistus, hardy fuchsia, hazelnut (*Corylus avellana*), hebe, lavender, potentilla (pictured), rosemary, santolina, senecio and spiraea.

Shrubs for shade
Camellia, cornus, evergreen euonymus, hamamelis (witch hazel), hydrangea, kerria, *Lonicera pileata*, ribes, viburnum, vinca (pictured).

Perennials for sun
Achillea, *Alyssum saxatile*, artemisia, calamintha, geranium (cranesbill), helianthemum, *Iberis sempervirens* (pictured) and catmint (nepeta).

Perennials for shade Ajuga (pictured), *Alchemilla mollis*, Japanese anemone, bergenia, brunnera, doronicum, epimedium, *Geranium phaeum*, lamium, *Viola odorata*.

Cuddly plants
Phlomis fruticosa (Jerusalem sage), *Salix lanata*, *Salvia argentea*, *Stachys byzantina* (bunny's ears – pictured), *Verbascum olympicum* and *V. bombyciferum*.

Paving and gravel for work-free surfaces

Hard surfaces need virtually no maintenance. They can be used in all sorts of creative ways in place of a lawn. For instance, you can create a courtyard garden enclosed by walls, a Mediterranean-style garden surrounded by evergreens, a minimalist Japanese-style garden, a walk-through rock garden, a modern patio or a traditional, formal terrace.

Gravel The quickest and easiest surface to lay yourself is gravel (see page 68). It is also very versatile, making it ideal for use in a garden that you may want to alter later. You can plant through gravel that has been laid over mulch matting to make a gravel garden. Gravel also makes an ideal surface for a courtyard. Several sizes and colours are available from builders' merchants and garden centres.

Paving slabs Once good foundations have been established (see box), slabs are quick to lay. Point the cracks between the slabs with mortar to prevent weeds getting a foothold. Paving need not be dull. Slabs are available in various shapes, sizes, colours and surface finishes, including some that resemble old brick. The slabs can be laid in

Good foundations

Laying hard surfaces Paving work takes time and skill so unless you are keen on DIY, it is advisable to employ a contractor (see page 302). Surfaces that take the weight of garden furniture or equipment, or are frequently walked over, need proper foundations – at least 10 cm (4 in) of hardcore well firmed down (best done with a hired plate vibrator). Patios should slope slightly so that rainwater runs off them away from the house.

This cottage garden combines cobbles with slabs of various sizes, shapes and colours to give a pleasing informal effect.

different patterns and combinations of types of finish for an unusual effect. Textured finishes are naturally non-slip. But avoid deeply textured patterns because they trap soil, are difficult to clean, and encourage moss and algae.

Cobbles Although time-consuming to lay, cobbles are good for decorative detail in small areas – between paving slabs or around a formal feature, such as a fountain. They are also useful for filling awkward corners and, because they are difficult to walk on, for discouraging people from areas where you don't want them to go. For a low-upkeep finish, bed the stones in cement so that weeds can't grow between them. Pebbles, which are smaller than cobbles, can also be used.

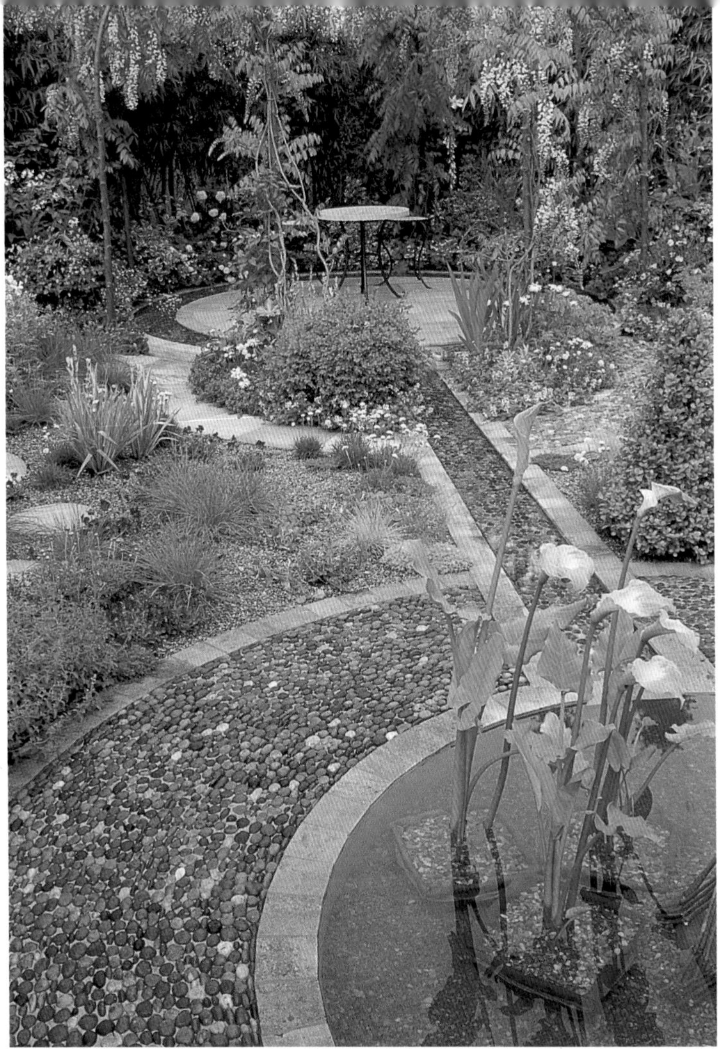

A variety of hard surfaces including pebbles, slabs and gravel irregularly planted with drought-tolerant plants make this garden practical to use and quick to maintain.

Bricks and concrete blocks These take longer to lay than slabs because they are smaller, but a wide range of effects can be achieved from the variety of colours and styles available. Old bricks look irregular and give a rustic appearance; engineering bricks – a particularly weather-resistant type of brick available in blue or red – are good for modern schemes. Bricks can be laid in traditional patterns, in a basket-weave or herringbone style, for example, or in more adventurous designs, such as a sweeping arc. Concrete-block paving, available in a range of colours, is easy to lay on a 7.5 cm (3 in) layer of sharp sand over a firm base.

Decorative finishes Coloured, moulded surfaces can be cast by specialist contractors who re-create traditional finishes, such as those of cobbles or York stone. No cracks are left for weeds to colonise. The surface can be laid over existing paving.

Timber decking Wood will blend in naturally with any garden design, and is easier on the eye and more forgiving underfoot than paved surfaces. Either pressure-treated softwood or hardwood is used. Hardwood will last longer but costs at least three times as much. Timber decking is available in self-assembly kits, or you can hire a specialist contractor to do the job for you.

Manhole covers are often sited awkwardly in the middle of patios and drives. Do not pave over them. Recessed and inset covers are available, into which bricks or slabs can be cut to fit.

Keeping in step

Do clean slabs with a pressure washer or a stiff brush and patio cleaner in late autumn to remove algae and soil.

Do remove dead leaves and weeds.

Do spray path or patio cleaner over paving slabs in winter to prevent moss and algae growth.

Do provide grip by stapling small mesh wire netting over wooden steps and plank bridges.

Do install a handrail beside steps.

Do sprinkle paving and steps with salt in icy conditions – but avoid sprinkling your plants.

Don't choose slate or York stone because they are slippery when wet; textured modern paving is safer.

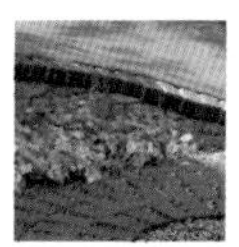

Making garden paths and steps

Building paths and steps requires a great deal of advance preparation so it is probably best left to a contractor (see page 302). Point the cracks between slabs with mortar to prevent weeds taking hold. Heavily used paths need proper foundations, but paths that are used infrequently, such as an informal path in a border, can be built relatively easily. Set paving slabs or bricks to half their depth in firmed soil. Or, to set bricks or slabs lightly in place, fork dry mortar mix into the top few centimetres of soil, set paving units in place, and then water them.

Stepping stones If a strip of lawn is becoming worn from frequent use, lay stepping stones as an informal path along the line where you need to walk. Cut out patches of turf about a stride's length apart and deep enough for the stones to sit just below the level of the lawn, so that the mower is able to glide cleanly over the top of them. Tread down the soil to make a firm, level base and drop the stepping stones into place. If the stones are not steady or if they are set too low, lift them and sprinkle a little sand underneath.

How to make a simple path

A cottage-garden path leading between rock features, raised beds or shrub borders is quick to make. Fork the soil over, then tread it down firmly, rake it level and spread at least 5 cm (2 in) of loose-laid gravel or bark chippings over the top. For a more permanent path that is easy to keep tidy, install edging boards and lay gravel over mulch matting (as illustrated).

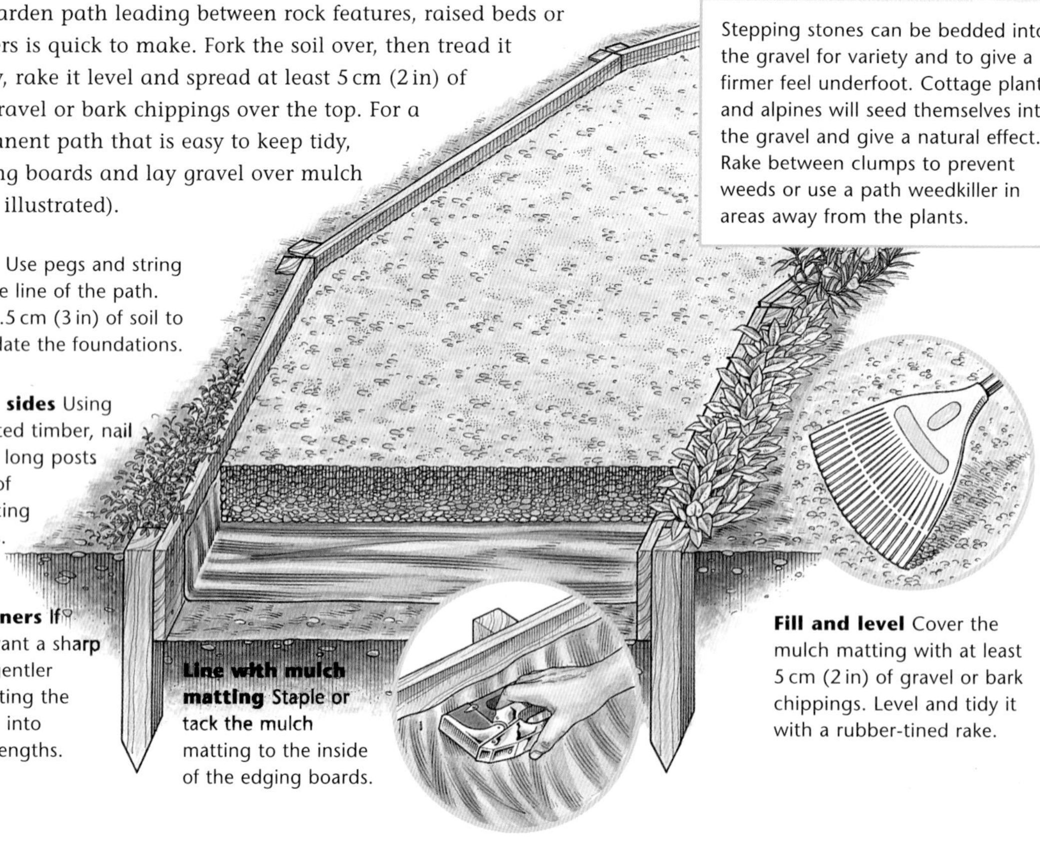

Mark out Use pegs and string to mark the line of the path. Excavate 7.5 cm (3 in) of soil to accommodate the foundations.

Making the sides Using pressure-treated timber, nail 30 cm (12 in) long posts to each end of standard fencing gravel boards.

Turning corners If you do not want a sharp turn, create gentler curves by cutting the gravel boards into 60 cm (2 ft) lengths.

Line with mulch matting Staple or tack the mulch matting to the inside of the edging boards.

Fill and level Cover the mulch matting with at least 5 cm (2 in) of gravel or bark chippings. Level and tidy it with a rubber-tined rake.

Finishing touches

Stepping stones can be bedded into the gravel for variety and to give a firmer feel underfoot. Cottage plants and alpines will seed themselves into the gravel and give a natural effect. Rake between clumps to prevent weeds or use a path weedkiller in areas away from the plants.

Time saver

On paths which have cracks that weeds can grow through use a path weedkiller in spring. This will kill existing weeds and prevent any further weed growth for the rest of the season.

Old railway sleepers bedded into gravel make an attractive informal path. For a woodland effect in a shady area, encourage moss to grow by watering plant-free areas with a weedkiller based on paraquat and diquat. This will kill the weeds, but keeps the moss.

In a wild garden, a path of bark chippings combined with a simple step gives a natural look. To reduce maintenance further, the bark path could be extended right through the wild-flower area.

Wild and woodland paths For rustic 'stepping stones' through a wild or woodland garden, use 10 cm (4 in) thick wooden 'slices' cut from fallen trees; alternatively, buy look-alike paving slabs. For a more formal effect, excavate a level channel (about the same depth as the wooden slices) through the soil. Edge it with pressure-treated gravel boards nailed to wooden pegs that are driven into the ground. Lay out the tree slices about a stride length apart and fill the rest of the channel with bark chippings.

Bridge feature Make a quick and easy 'bridge' over a narrow ditch or a stream by laying two thick, parallel wooden planks or secondhand railway sleepers across the gap. Ensure that the planks are long enough to allow at least 90 cm (36 in) either side of the gap. Sink the ends 15 cm (6 in) or more into the soil with a layer of bricks underneath to make a firm foundation.

Simple steps For gentle inclines where the soil is very firm and stable, steps can be cut into the slope. Make them shallow and wide for maximum stability. Cut out the shape of the steps with a spade. Then set in railway sleepers to form the risers, angling them slightly backwards and held in place by sturdy stakes at each end. Fill the 'treads' with rammed rubble and top-up with gravel. To ensure that steps are safe, check them regularly and reset loose or uneven areas straightaway.

Shrubs, Roses and Trees

CREATE LOW-UPKEEP BORDERS THAT LOOK GOOD ALL YEAR BY GROWING TROUBLE-FREE PLANTS THAT HAVE A LONG SEASON OF INTEREST

Trees and shrubs form the ideal basis for an easy-care garden because they need less routine maintenance than any other group of plants. Combining the right plants from this group will provide interest all-year round, giving a long sequence of flowers, fruits or berries, winter bark and stems, as well as variegated and evergreen foliage. A simple way to extend seasonal interest is to mix deciduous, seasonal-flowering shrubs with evergreens. Ideally, you should combine two-thirds compact evergreens with a third deciduous shrubs and add ground-cover plants to smother weeds.

Trees and shrubs provide the backbone of a garden's design. Whether as a group or as individual specimens, their size and shape, and colour and texture of their bark and foliage can be used to great effect. Go for reliable flowerers not susceptible to pests and diseases. For instance, choose trouble-free *Weigela* 'Florida Variegata' rather than the similar-looking, blackfly-prone *Philadelphus coronarius* 'Variegatus'. And if you choose to grow quick-growing shrubs, such as forsythia or buddleja, be prepared to prune them each year.

1 *LILAC (*Syringa vulgaris*) – very fragrant flowers May/June.*
2 CLEMATIS MONTANA – *flowers May/June.*
3 LABURNUM ANAGYROIDES – *flowers May/June followed by seedpods. All parts are poisonous.*
4 ROSA *'Frühlingsgold' – flowers June/July.*
5 ROSA *'Roseraie de l'Haÿ' – flowers June/July.*
6 *BOX (*Buxus sempervirens*) – evergreen foliage. Good for shade.*

EASY-CARE CALENDAR

EARLY SPRING
Remove any weeds and tidy away debris. Top up the mulch to at least 5 cm (2 in) deep.

MID SPRING
Sprinkle rose fertiliser evenly between the shrubs. Spot treat established perennial weeds with a glyphosate-based weedkiller.

LATE SPRING
Snip off black, frost-damaged shoot tips of hebes. If necessary, prune back straggly shoots to improve plant shape.

EARLY SUMMER
Use a contact weedkiller to destroy young suckers of plants such as roses, lilac and prunus before they become woody.

MID SUMMER
Deadhead shrub roses not grown for hips by removing old flowerheads with 15 cm (6 in) of stem, cutting just above a leaf joint. Cut back over-long shoots to keep bushes tidy. Sprinkle a high-potash feed to promote flowering the following year.

AUTUMN
Tidy up any debris before winter. Fallen leaves can be left as a mulch on beds.

STARTING FROM SCRATCH
You could assemble this border in under half a day by planning ahead. Draw a planting plan and order your plants in advance. Dig the soil thoroughly, incorporating well-rotted organic matter and fertiliser. When the plants arrive, try to choose a fine day for planting them out. Then apply a mulch to keep down weeds.

Planting for year-round interest
Once the bed is established, you will need to spend only a few hours each year topping up the mulch, spot-treating persistent weeds and pruning unruly shrubs.

Easy-care borders using shrubs and trees

Trees and shrubs are an easy and effective way of adding long-lasting colour and interest to a border, but to keep down the workload you will need to choose plants that need minimum pruning (see page 88). Shrubs and trees can provide the border with a framework – some structure on which to build seasonal displays – or they can be used individually to create a particular effect, such as a focal point. For the ultimate easy-care garden, add only as many perennials and annuals as you have time to look after because they generally need more upkeep.

Spend plenty of time planning what to put where, so you don't have to move plants around later. Walk around your neighbourhood to see which trees and shrubs grow well in other gardens and which plants are invasive; and seek advice from your local garden centre or nursery as to which plants are suitable for the area. To decide on where to place a tree or shrub in the garden, especially one chosen to give height, use a tripod of canes – or, even quicker, just a single cane – which can be moved around the garden to give you an idea of where the new addition will fit in best.

When choosing a tree, give particular consideration to its rate of growth and ultimate size, because a tree can survive for many decades, easily dominating a garden. A fast-growing plant may have the advantage of filling up empty spaces quickly, but it will need extra maintenance to keep it within bounds later on.

Decide first on the effect that you want to create – either using trees and shrubs in groups or singly – and then choose plants that suit your needs. If you want

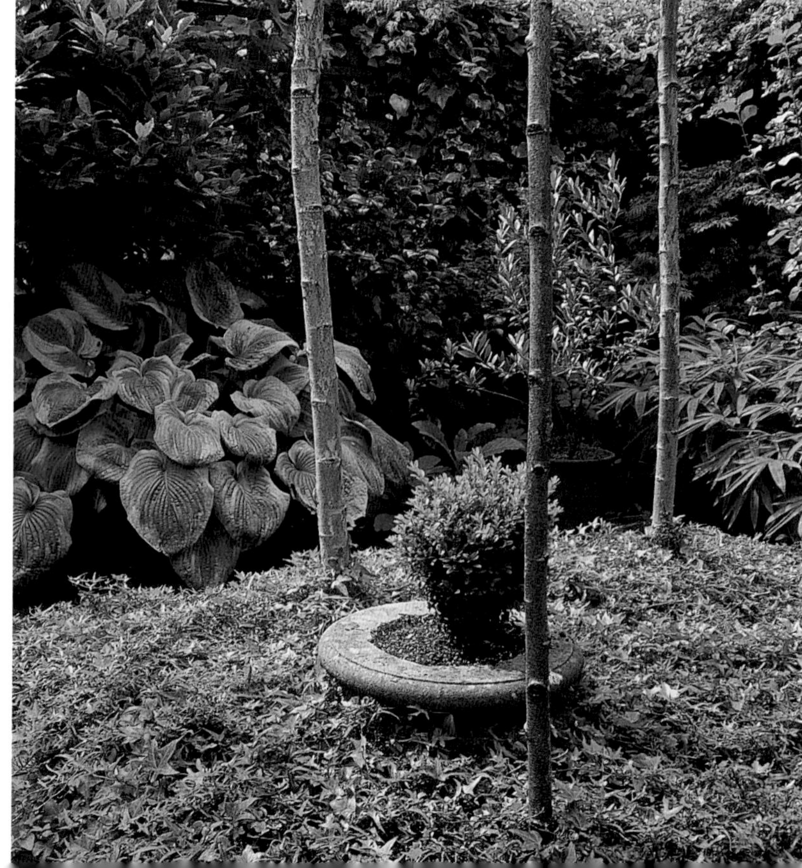

The upright trunks of three silver birches provide a perfect focal point to catch the eye. Surrounded by a ground cover of ivy, this grouping is the ultimate in easy care.

Time saver

Look for plant combinations that work well together when visiting other gardens. Don't be afraid to copy tried and tested ideas from books and magazines as this will save you time experimenting by trial and error.

An all-year framework of evergreens serves to set off deciduous foliage shrubs and perennials such as the red-flowered *Rheum palmatum* in the foreground.

to focus the eye on the end of a border to create a 'full stop', use an upright, columnar shape, such as the Irish yew (*Taxus baccata* 'Fastigiata') or the upright flowering cherry, *Prunus* 'Amanogawa'. To lead the eye across the garden, go for a low, spreading plant that gives a horizontal effect, such as a Japanese maple (*Acer palmatum*). And for a good focal point, consider a compact, weeping tree, such as *Salix caprea* 'Pendula'. For greater impact, combine two different effects. For example, use the prostrate, horizontal *Juniperus* x *pfitzeriana* with an upright group of three silver birches.

Colour and texture should also be considered. Trees with golden or variegated foliage, such as *Robinia pseudoacacia* 'Frisia' or the wedding-cake tree (*Cornus controversa* 'Variegata'), can brighten up a dark part of the garden or contrast well against a dark background. Colour can be used to create an illusion of space. Cool blues and purples, which fade into the background, can be used at the end of a small garden to make it look longer (see page 98).

Several other design implications arise when choosing and planting trees and shrubs for the border. For a cascading effect, plant the tallest plants at the back, graduating to the lowest in the front, while shrubs with scented foliage or flowers, such as a fragrant rose or *Choisya ternata*, should be placed near a path or doorway for full effect.

Creating interest

Do find out the ultimate size of the plant and its rate of growth before buying. A tree that grows to 1.8 m (6 ft) in ten years is slow-growing.

Do select compact plants that require little or no pruning.

Do use a few large, architectural plants, such as phormiums or fatsia, to create a dramatic effect, rather than lots of fussy, small plants.

Don't select large, vigorous plants for a small garden. They will need regular pruning to restrict their size.

Don't plant all evergreens in one part of the garden. Go for a contrast of foliage, shape and texture in the border to provide visual interest.

Don't plant winter-interest shrubs in a part of the garden used only in summer. Think of your needs.

Year-round interest

For a sequence of interest throughout the year, shrubs are the ideal easy option. With some careful planning, flowers in spring and summer can be followed by fruit or berries in autumn, and attractive bark or coloured stems in winter, as well as evergreen foliage for a year-round backdrop. For the smaller garden, create areas in different parts that come into their own in different seasons. In large gardens, a mixture of trees and shrubs can be laid out to give all-year interest in one area.

Often a garden and its design is inherited when moving to a new house, or it has evolved without much thought given to the time needed for upkeep. A garden with a traditional herbaceous border, for example, will look leafy and colourful in spring and summer, but bare and dull in winter. The border will need weeding, and plants staking, tying and cutting down in autumn. To provide all-year interest, and to save time spent on maintenance, replace some of the herbaceous perennials with a selection of easy-care shrubs that offer autumn and winter interest, such as *Hibiscus syriacus*, which has white, pink or blue flowers until mid autumn, or the winter-flowering *Viburnum tinus*. Also introduce shrubs that offer all-year foliage, such as the spotted *Aucuba japonica* or a variegated euonymus, such as *Euonymus fortunei* 'Emerald 'n' Gold' or *E. fortunei* Emerald Gaiety.

Likewise, beds of annuals can be replaced by shrubs to reduce the amount of time spent planting out each year. Go for compact shrubs that have a long flowering season, as well as easy maintenance, such as hebes, low-growing cistus and potentilla, or patio roses.

Under taller shrubs and roses, use low-growing plants to extend the seasonal interest, improve the visual balance, and to suppress weed growth. These could include perennials, such as geranium (cranesbill) or *Alchemilla mollis,* or shrubs, such as hebes, variegated euonymus, sarcococca, or gaultheria on acid soil.

Choose colour schemes according to the effect you want to create: hot colours, reds and oranges, will bring warmth, while cooler colours, whites, greys and blues, will cool down a hot spot.

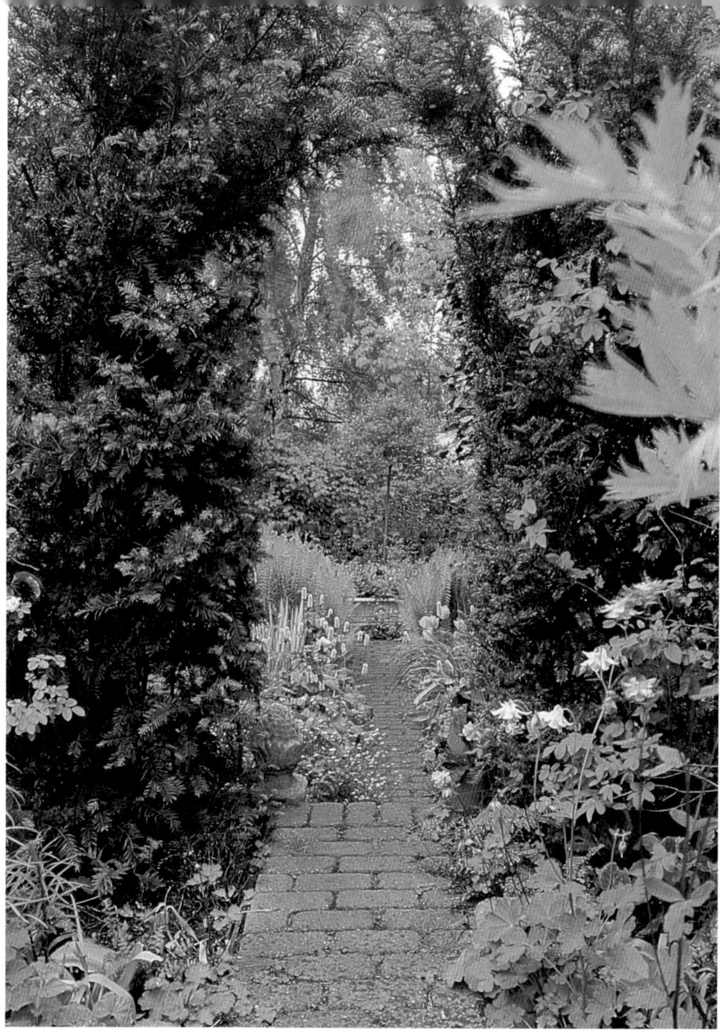

A yew arch provides a perfect frame for the view leading down the path. It will need clipping only once a year, in August.

Quick results

Shrubs offering interest over two seasons are doubly good value. They include *Mahonia* x *media*, which has yellow winter flowers and architectural, evergreen foliage, and *Cotinus coggygria* 'Royal Purple', with purple leaves that turn red in autumn. For extra-intensive interest, plant around a tree that casts light shade, such as the upright *Pyrus calleryana* 'Chanticleer'.

Framing a view When choosing shrubs, take into account the views. If you have a lovely open view, it is a shame to block it with tall trees or shrubs, use them instead to frame it. You can also use plants to frame a particularly eye-catching element within the garden. For example, a statue at the end of a path. An ugly building, on the other hand, can be obscured by a quick-growing evergreen shrub, such as *Ceanothus* 'A. T. Johnson', that bears blue flowers in the spring.

Specimen plants An easy way to transform the look of a garden, and to keep upkeep low, is to position a few 'specimen' plants to act as focal points. A specimen plant can be any plant that you find attractive. Usually they are plants that are striking to the eye and that look good standing on their own. Consider plants with a good shape (such as *Phormium tenax*, with its sword-like leaves), sculptural foliage (*Fatsia japonica*), attractive flowers (shrub rose, camellia or hibiscus – *Hibiscus syriacus*), colourful berries (callicarpa, cotoneaster, malus, pyracantha), or attractive looking bark on trees (*Acer griseum*, *A. pensylvanicum* or *Betula utilis* var. *jacquemontii*).

The shiny bark of *Prunus serrula* is the focal point for this colourful grouping. The azalea blooms will be followed by those of the cherry, while the variegated holly makes for a lively backdrop.

Planting an easy-care shrub border

This simple design uses five evergreens for all-year interest: *Ceanothus thrysiflorus* var. *repens*, *Euonymus fortunei* 'Emerald 'n' Gold', *Hebe rakaiensis*, *Photinia* x *fraseri* 'Red Robin' and *Lonicera nitida* 'Baggesen's Gold'. The young red photinia leaves and blue ceanothus flowers lend spring colour. The hebe has white flowers in summer.

Decide on a shape Use a hosepipe to decide on the shape of your new bed or border. You can then modify the curves until you are happy with the result.

Combining shrubs Position the shrubs, still in their pots, so that you can stand back and view the effect from several angles.

Improve the soil Dig over the soil and remove weeds. Incorporate well-rotted manure to improve the soil. Add grit too if the soil is heavy (see page 26).

Planting Plant each shrub at the same depth as it is in the pot through mulch matting or cover the soil between shrubs with a 5 cm (2 in) thick loose organic mulch to keep the soil moist and prevent weeds (see page 264).

Aftercare

Shrubs require little maintenance once they are in the ground.

First season Water sufficiently to keep soil damp in dry weather. Top up loose mulches from time to time, and rake over to keep tidy. Prune and trim evergreens and summer-flowering shrubs, if needed, in early spring, and spring-flowering shrubs immediately after flowering.

Improving an existing border

Sometimes old borders lack interest, especially if some of the shrubs are past their best. One option is to replace all the shrubs and start again, but this will leave you with an empty border until the new shrubs begin to grow. A quicker method is to keep some of the existing plants to provide the overall structure for the new border as well as shrubs that offer more than one season of interest, then replace the rest – in particular, short-lived shrubs such as lavender, santolina and broom – with healthier or more interesting plants. Using this method, the height and structure of the border is maintained while the new shrubs become established.

Once the border has been thinned, the old shrubs that are being kept may look misshapen or bald at the base. You can transform their appearance by simple pruning, taking out a few of the oldest stems each spring (see page 88), but don't prune them back hard because many shrubs may not regrow or may take years to flower again.

To fill the gaps in the border quickly, buy a few larger specimens rather than several smaller plants. If the old shrubs are dominated by green, brighten up the display by introducing shrubs with golden,

Making time for gardening

Louise and Phil Pankhurst are in their early fifties. They both work full time, but like to spend time in the garden at weekends and on summer evenings. They wanted a garden that reminded them of their holidays in the Mediterranean, in particular in the Aegean.

Phil Pankhurst is an information technology specialist and works at the local university. Louise is the director of a charity. They wanted a garden with exotic-looking evergreens, and light, airy foliage – and to get rid of the leyland cypress trees. The garden needed to be easy to keep because of their busy working lives; they wanted to avoid time-wasters, such as shrubs that needed regular pruning. Their young grandchildren often come to stay, so the garden had to be safe for them to play in. Most importantly, they wanted somewhere pleasant to sit and relax, and where they could entertain their friends – possibly upgrading the existing terrace, giving it more privacy from the neighbouring properties.

THE OLD GARDEN Most of it was under grass, with a few overgrown flowerbeds. The terrace next to the house had no balustrade or railings, making it dangerous for their grandchildren to play there. The boundaries were sharply defined by rickety fencing and leyland cypress trees, which took a lot of light off the garden.

DECIDING THEIR PRIORITIES

How much time?
4 hours on average each week.

Essential ingredients?
Easy-care borders with year-round interest; a secluded area for entertaining, with built-in barbecue; child-friendly plants.

Likes and dislikes?
They like relaxing in the garden and using the terrace on summer evenings. Any garden tasks where the grandchildren can help are enjoyed. Dislikes include anything that steals a lot of time at weekends, such as watering lots of containers and weeding.

purple or variegated foliage. For example, to lighten up a border display add the golden-leaved *Spiraea japonica* 'Goldflame' or *Choisya ternata* Sundance; to add interest try the variegated *Aucuba japonica* 'Crotonifolia', *Elaeagnus pungens* 'Maculata' or *Euonymus fortunei* 'Emerald 'n' Gold'; and for purple foliage either *Berberis thunbergii* f. *atropurpurea* or *Cotinus coggygria* 'Royal Purple'.

Before planting, improve the soil by forking into each planting hole a bucketful of well-rotted organic matter, and applying a general or rose fertiliser. Once the new shrubs are in the ground, water them regularly to help them grow faster and to compete against older plants with more established root systems. Cover the ground between the plants with mulch matting or an organic mulch to help to retain soil moisture and prevent weed growth. For the first few seasons, while the new plants are filling out, plant flowering perennials or annuals between them to provide extra colour (see page 263).

The variegated foliage of the cornus provides a backcloth for this white, purple and silver border. In autumn, the foliage will fall to reveal the shrub's red stems.

THE NEW GARDEN Easy-care climbers on trelliswork and exotic potted plants create an arbour of tranquillity on the terrace. The lawn is curved, making mowing easier, while an automatic watering system helps keep down the workload in the borders.

Intimate terrace *Siting the terrace next to the house makes for easy entertaining. Climbers bring greater intimacy.*

Lush pots *Exotic plants, such as the palm* Trachycarpus fortunei, *recall balmy climates and need little water.*

Easy pruning *The wisteria is easy to reach over the balustrade. Cut back whippy stems to 20 cm (8 in) in August.*

Boundary *Waney-edge fencing is easy to erect and forms an instant visual barrier. To give a greater feeling of space, it has been mostly obscured by planting.*

Effective planting *Evergreens help to suppress weeds, and give borders an all-year structure. A sweet gum tree (liquidambar) provides dappled shade in summer and brilliant autumn colours.*

Sweeping lawn *The gentle curve of the lawn makes maintenance easier and helps to set off the rest of the garden design.*

Stone focal points *The pineapple finials provide an instant focal point and they mark the top of the flight of steps.*

Planting singly or in groups

The way a border is designed and planted can play an important part in reducing the amount of time needed for maintenance. Once you have decided what to plant, you then have to decide whether to plant the shrubs or trees singly or in groups of the same variety. One advantage of planting in groups is the instant impact of each plant type due to the greater area covered. Instead of a single flowering shrub, there is a mass of colourful flowers, stems or evergreen foliage. However, planting in groups will reduce the number of different varieties that you can fit into a border.

There are no set rules, but in a small garden it is often better to plant a mixture of single specimens than groups for more seasonal variety. In a larger garden with more space, planting in groups creates a sense of scale which is more in proportion to the surroundings.

Quick results

For a new border to look established in just one season, plant a selection of quick-growing shrubs. Choose large shrubs such as buddleja, lavatera and ceanothus for the back of the border and the smaller spiraea and hebe at the front. Keep them watered and fed in their first season so that they make good growth, achieving the height and interest needed for the border.

Wide planting If you want to see each plant's individual shape, you need to give them ample space to develop, so plant at the distances recommended on the plant labels or in gardening books. It will also save you the work of thinning out overcrowded borders later on. However, you will have to wait several years for the border to establish fully and this method of planting exposes more bare soil, which allows weeds to grow. To save time weeding the border, plant the shrubs through mulch matting (see page 264), or fill the gaps with relatively short-lived shrubs. Use silver-leaved lavender, santolina and

YEAR-ROUND INTEREST

Planting shrubs singly makes good use of a small space. However, make sure that you draw up a planting scheme that has something to offer all year round, such as the grouping shown here of shrubs that will need only minimal pruning.

1 ***Chaenomeles* x *superba* 'Crimson and Gold'**
2 ***Mahonia aquifolium* 'Apollo'**
3 ***Nandina domestica* 'Firepower'**
4 ***Hamamelis* x *intermedia***
5 ***Acer palmatum* 'Osakazuki'**

Winter into spring *The red flowers of the chaenomeles and the yellow mahonia blooms take over in spring from the spider-like, fragrant flowers of the hamamelis.*

Cytisus x *praecox* in sun, or try euonymus and skimmia in moist shade. The temporary fillers can be removed when they are past their best and the main shrub planting has established (see also page 263).

Close planting For the busy gardener, closer planting than normally recommended achieves a more instant effect because the garden looks full from the start, and it means that the plants cover the ground, smothering weeds more effectively. But it is more expensive, and later on shrubs will need pruning and thinning out to keep the border display balanced. To prevent this type of planting looking dull and uninspiring, choose a selection of shrubs.

Easy maintenance Whichever planting method you choose, make sure that you have variety in your scheme. Many flowering shrubs are easy to look after. Mix in a few between evergreens, plus some shrubs chosen for their stem colour or coloured foliage. This ensures that your border always looks attractive, but is also easy to look after.

Clearing the ground for planting can be time consuming. Spray perennial weeds such as dandelions, docks, bindweed or brambles with a glyphosate-based weedkiller. Dig over the border to loosen the soil, then position your shrubs and prepare a generous planting hole for each one. Fork over the base of the hole and add planting-mix compost and general fertiliser. After planting, mulch the areas of the border between the plants with bark chippings.

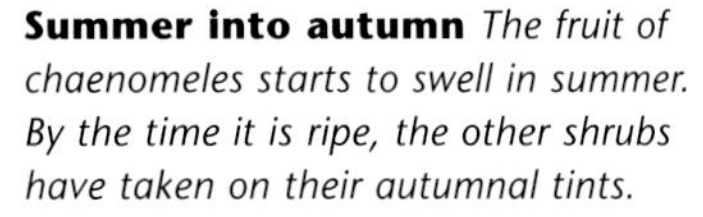

Summer into autumn *The fruit of chaenomeles starts to swell in summer. By the time it is ripe, the other shrubs have taken on their autumnal tints.*

COMBINING SHRUBS FOR YEAR-ROUND COLOUR

Keep your garden looking good all year by planting a selection of easy-care shrubs, each with different attractions, making sure their flowering times vary.

Deciduous flowering *Ceanothus* x *delileanus* 'Gloire de Versailles', *Chaenomeles* x *superba* 'Crimson and Gold' (pictured), *Deutzia gracilis*, *Lonicera* x *purpusii*.

Evergreen flowering *Ceanothus* 'A. T. Johnson', *Choisya ternata*, *Cistus* x *corbariensis*, *Escallonia* 'Apple Blossom', *Lavandula angustifolia* 'Hidcote' (pictured).

Coloured foliage *Aucuba japonica* 'Crotonifolia' (pictured), *Cotinus coggygria* 'Royal Purple', *Euonymus fortunei* 'Emerald Gaiety', *Photinia* x *fraseri* 'Red Robin'.

Fruits and berries *Callicarpa bodinieri* var. *giraldii*, *Ilex aquifolium* 'J C van Tol', *Pyracantha* 'Orange Glow' (pictured), *Skimmia japonica*, *Viburnum opulus* 'Compactum'.

Autumn foliage and stem colour *Acer palmatum* 'Osakazuki' (pictured), *Cornus alba* 'Sibirica', *Nandina domestica* 'Firepower', *Rubus thibetanus*.

The woodland garden

A woodland garden will provide conditions for growing a wide range of plants that would normally struggle in bright conditions. Its cool, dappled shade creates a completely different environment to other areas of the garden, such as a sunny mixed border. It is sheltered and peaceful. With careful planning, a woodland garden can provide colour and interest through the seasons – even in winter, using flowering bulbs and trees and shrubs with attractive bark and stems. And it is easy to maintain, although you will need to keep brambles and self-sown saplings at bay.

Underplant with easy-care shade lovers, such as *Acer palmatum*, bergenia, box, ferns, foxgloves, holly, lamium, lilies, lily-of-the-valley, mahonia, sarcococca, sanguinaria.

Recycling prunings
All woodland prunings can be shredded on the spot and used as path material or to mulch around trees and shrubs.

Extra spring colour is provided by bright, young foliage, catkins on willow and hazel, as well as spring-flowering plants, such as hellebore, honesty, pulmonaria, Solomon's seal and violets.

LOOKING AFTER A WOODLAND GARDEN

SPRING & SUMMER

Paths Start to mow grass paths once every two weeks or so in spring. Bark paths may need topping-up with fresh bark chippings.

Watering Any newly planted trees, shrubs and perennials should be kept watered to help them to become established.

Weeding Keep a 1 m (3 ft) diameter circle free of weeds and grass around newly planted trees and shrubs.

AUTUMN

▲Grass clippings Cut long grass with a nylon-line trimmer or rotary scythe. Rake off the clippings so they don't rot down and make the grass grow faster next year.

Clear leaves Rake off fallen leaves, but use some as a natural mulch under shrubs and trees. Do not overmulch as this could rot young stems.

Planting Plant bulbs for naturalising. This is also the best time to plant new woodland trees and shrubs.

Weeding Clear brambles and saplings, especially those of sycamore (*Acer pseudoplatanus*), which self-seeds prolifically.

WINTER

▲Pruning Cut out any damaged branches or those that show signs of disease. Also cut back branches that overhang paths in order to keep access to the woodland open.

In areas with spring bulbs, use a nylon-line trimmer in autumn to cut long grass to 5 cm (2 in) so that the spring flowers are easy to see.
A rustic seat at the end of a path will create a focal point as well as a place to relax in the shade on a sunny day.
In autumn, fruits and berries will give colour as well as provide food for wildlife.
To keep bases of shrubs and trees weed-free, spray round them twice a year with a weedkiller based on glyphosate.
Rough-mow woodland pathways. To save time, cut the rest of the grass only once a year in late summer or autumn with a rotary scythe or nylon-line trimmer.

Flowering bulbs For colour from January till May, plant snowdrops, winter aconites, crocuses, species daffodils and wood anemones.

The horizontal stems of *Cornus controversa* 'Variegata' are underplanted with a dense group of euphorbia, catmint, phlomis and geranium that will suppress weed growth.

Mix plant types to provide more seasonal colour. Here, the hakonechloa grass and the fuchsia provide late-summer interest.

Choosing and caring for your shrubs

The choice of easy-care shrubs is vast. Most shrubs are hardy and need either no pruning or a simple pruning once a year (see page 88), and many require no specific soil type or position in the garden. Even if they do require some upkeep, sometimes it is possible to cut out one or two of the normal tasks to save time, keeping the end result just as pleasing. Dogwoods, for example, are grown for their coloured winter stems. Normally they are pruned nearly to ground level each spring to encourage strong new shoots that produce the brightest colours. To save time, this can be done every other year. Alternatively, for the plant to retain its shape, remove half of the shoots each year.

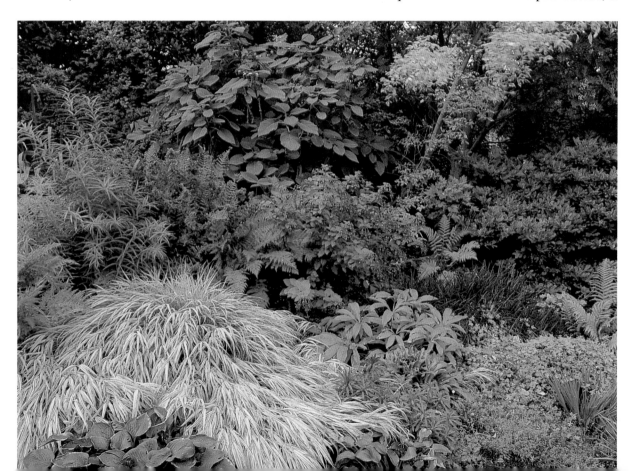

Soil and position Shrubs that require special soils or positions can take up time if planted in the wrong conditions. For example, for an acid-loving plant to thrive in an alkaline soil, a lot of work will be required to alter the soil's pH. Instead, if you want to include a plant not naturally suited to the soil in your garden, grow it in a large container or a raised bed using suitable compost (see page 192). Some shrubs need particular amounts of shade or sun; if you cannot provide this, it is better not to include them in your scheme.

Mature size Before buying a plant, consider its eventual size. There is no point planting a shrub that grows to 3 m (10 ft) in a position where you only want it to reach 90 cm (36 in). Most evergreens can be pruned to size, but vigorous varieties will need pruning two or three times a year to keep them under control. Planting a smaller variety in the first place saves time.

Pruning Consider when shrubs need to be pruned, and the number of other tasks that need doing at the same time. You may have more time to prune in early spring, for example, because there is no lawn mowing or weeding to be done. But if lots of shrubs are planted that need summer pruning, it can be a drain on your gardening time as other jobs may need doing. Avoid this by planting a mixture of shrubs that need spring or summer pruning, or, better still, no pruning at all.

MOVING ESTABLISHED SHRUBS

Deciduous shrubs should be moved while dormant, and evergreens in September/October, or March/April. Dig a small trench around the shrub so that you can get your spade underneath, and lift out a good-sized rootball. To compensate for the damage to the roots, prune back the top growth of deciduous shrubs by 25 per cent to reduce transpiration from the leaves. Evergreens should not be cut back, but they will benefit from protection from cold, drying winds. Spray with an antitranspirant spray, sold as Christmas tree spray.

Heavy rootballs *Place the well-wrapped rootball onto an old compost sack or other heavy-duty sheet in order to drag the shrub to its new planting site.*

EASY-CARE SHRUBS

For a low-maintenance border, plant a backbone of easy-to-grow shrubs that can be relied on to give a good display every year without much attention.

***Spiraea japonica* 'Goldflame'** Young red tips turn a brassy colour, then green. Foliage is best if hard-pruned each spring. Grows to 75x75 cm (30x30 in). Sun lover.

Cytisus x kewensis Deciduous, low-growing with arching habit. Grows to 30 cmx1.5 m (1x5 ft). Creamy-white flowers in late spring. Grow in well-drained soil in full sun.

***Cornus alba* 'Elegantissima'** Deciduous. Red winter stems and variegated leaves. Grows to 1.8x1.8 m (6x6 ft). Prune hard in spring for bright stems and to restrict growth.

***Mahonia x media* 'Charity'** Evergreen, upright shrub with large glossy leaves and fragrant yellow flowers from early winter to spring. Grows to 3x3 m (10x10 ft) in time.

Kalmia latifolia Evergreen shrub with clusters of pink flowers from May to July. Grows to 3x3 m (10x10 ft). Likes rich, acid soil in full sun.

Continued on p. 84

EASY-CARE SHRUBS

Continued from p. 83

***Viburnum tinus* 'Eve Price'** A compact form of this evergreen shrub. Flowers pink in bud opening to white from mid autumn to spring, followed by deep blue berries. Grows to 2.4x2.4 m (8x8 ft). Sun or shade.

***Berberis* x *ottawensis* 'Superba'** Round, red-purple leaves that turn crimson in autumn. Produces yellow flowers in late spring. If this deciduous shrub is left unpruned, it grows to 2.4x2.4 m (8x8ft).

***Lonicera nitida* 'Baggesen's Gold'** Evergreen with small, bright yellow leaves that take on a bronzed effect in winter. Grows to 1.5x1.5 m (5x5 ft). It prefers a sunny position.

***Abelia* 'Edward Goucher'** Deciduous or semi-evergreen. Foliage is bronzed when young. Grows to 1.5x1.5 m (5x5 ft). Lilac-pink flowers from mid-summer. It prefers a sheltered, sunny position.

***Hebe* 'Autumn Glory'** Evergreen, rounded leaves. Purple-blue flowers from mid summer until well into autumn. Grows to 75x75 cm (30x30 in). It likes a sunny position.

How and when to buy plants

Most plants are bought at garden centres, nurseries and DIY superstores. The range varies according to the time of the year, and the largest selection is available in spring. Many plants are sold container-grown and can be bought and planted all through the year, but the best times to plant are in spring or autumn when the soil is warm and moist, and the plants become established quickly. Summer planting requires more aftercare because you have to ensure that the plants are well watered – many also need shading.

Some nurseries and mail-order companies supply bare-root plants – grown in the soil and then dug up to sell. Bare-root plants, mostly hedging plants or roses, should be planted during the dormant season, between November and March.

Avoid the temptation to buy all your plants in one go in spring. Instead, visit your local nursery or garden centre several times during the year so that you can see a wide range of different plants at their best. Staggering your purchases will also make for a more varied selection of plants.

What to look for Buy a tree or shrub only if it looks healthy; the leaves should be in good condition, and the overall shape compact and bushy. It should have plenty of good, strong, evenly spaced branches, especially towards the base. Ideally, there should be no weeds growing in the pot, but the odd one or two is an indication that the plant is established. The plant should be clearly labelled and the compost moist.

A plant that has pale, yellowing leaves is possibly pot-bound, and its compost lacking in fertiliser. Knock it out of the pot to see if the roots are a tangled mass or if they are growing thickly through the drainage holes, in which case do not buy. However, the roots need to be established and should fill the pot. Avoid dry or wilted plants; ones with signs of pests or diseases; or those that are lopsided or have only a few shoots, because they will need remedial pruning to put right (see page 260).

Quick results

A small shrub will fill a big gap in half the time if the outside stems are layered into the surrounding soil. Bend down a vigorous young stem and where it touches the soil make a slanted cut on its underside. Cover the wounded section with soil and hold in position with wire loops (see page 91). Good shrubs to layer include rhododendron and camellia on acid soil, and cornus and weigela elsewhere.

Grow Japanese maples, such as this purple-leaved variety *(right),* in a raised bed or container if your soil is limy.

A good garden centre *(below)* will display plants in groups to show associations of shapes, colours and textures.

Plant size The largest plants are not always the best ones to choose. Often the taller ones will have started to lose leaves lower down, so pick one that has a bushy, symmetrical shape and strong growth with foliage down to the base.

The size of the plant will also affect the time that it takes to establish. A larger plant will take longer for its roots to establish in the surrounding soil than a smaller specimen, which will catch up with the larger one in a couple of seasons. However, some slower-growing shrubs, such as magnolia and *Acer palmatum* var. *dissectum,* are worth buying as large specimens because they will take many years to reach a decent size and, in the case of the magnolia, to flower. Larger specimens are also ideal for creating an instant effect (see page 287).

Routine shrub care

Maintenance tasks will need to be carried out regularly in order to help your garden to become established, and to keep it neat and tidy. If time is short, concentrate on weeding and watering new shrubs and trees. To ease the task of deadheading flowering shrubs, gather together the flowering stems once they are past their best and trim them with a pair of secateurs. Alternatively, cut them back with garden shears if their stems are thin, such as for lavender and santolina.

Weeding The demands for weeding are highest in spring and summer. You will need to keep on top of the task otherwise, once the weeds flower and produce seeds, you will have a weed problem for years to come. When creating a new border, try to start with clean, weed-free ground (see page 270). If you are not in a hurry, leave the area fallow for a season. As weeds appear, either hoe them out or spray them with a weedkiller. Weeds can also be controlled by growing plants through mulch matting, or by using an organic mulch, such as well-rotted compost or bark chippings (see page 264).

To save time weeding around established shrubs, use a dichlobenil-based weedkiller each spring to create a chemical barrier in the top layer of the soil, killing weed seeds, including those of pernicious perennial weeds such as bindweed, as they germinate. This chemical also kills herbaceous plants and bulbs, so in a mixed border use a

WATERING AND FEEDING

It makes sense to water and feed plants at the same time. Soluble fertilisers can be applied through a hosepipe or watering can, and are available to the plant straight away. If, on the other hand, you rarely need to water the plants, a granular, slow-release fertiliser, can be applied once a year, in spring, round the base of the plant.

Hose-end feeder *Water and feed in one go using a hose-end feeder fitted to the end of your hosepipe. As the water rushes through the feeder, it dilutes the feed automatically at the correct rate, saving you time and effort.*

Watering a new shrub *To make watering a new plant quicker and more effective, make a ridge of soil around each plant to form a moat when it is watered. The ridge of soil will hold the water until it soaks into the rooting zone below.*

Permanent hosepipe *Avoid having to drag a hose down a long garden by fitting a multiple snap-lock connector part-way down the garden, such as next to the greenhouse or vegetable bed, and then using a shorter hose to do the watering.*

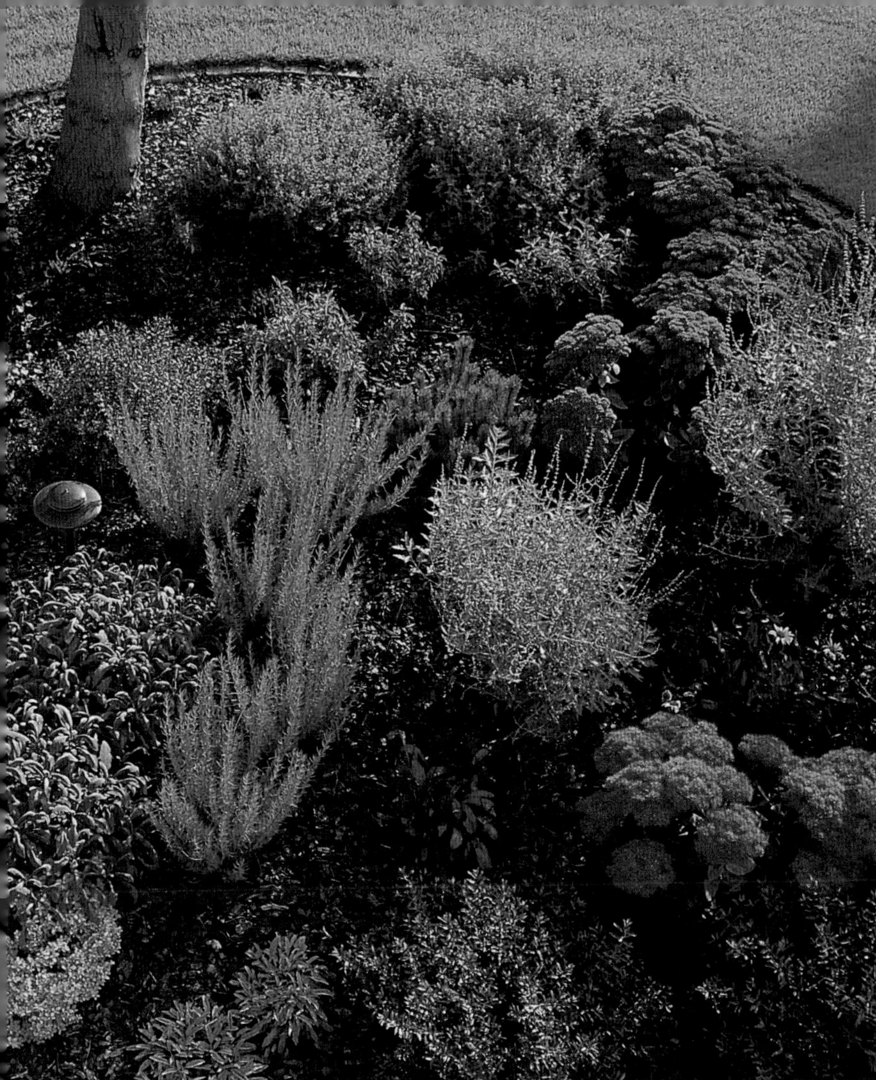

Time saver

To destroy young, green suckers of plants such as roses, lilac, prunus and rhus, spray them with a weedkiller based on paraquat and diquat. This will destroy the suckers without harming the bark of the parent plant.

Laying an attractive organic mulch, such as cocoa shells, in a newly planted border helps to suppress weeds, retain moisture, and sets off the foliage of young plants.

Jobs calendar

Spring Just before growth starts, prune shrubs that flower from mid June onwards and those that have coloured stems (see page 89). Prune shrubs that flower before mid June immediately after flowering. In late spring, prune evergreen foliage plants, including shoots damaged by frost. Feed borders with fertiliser and top up organic mulch.

Summer Water newly planted shrubs regularly and keep weeds under control. Deadhead.

Autumn Rake off any leaves smothering small plants or ground cover. Let the rest form a mulch, rotting down into the soil.

Winter Make sure that the borders are weed-free before spring. Have a general tidy up.

glyphosate-based weedkiller, which is absorbed through the leaves and transferred to the rest of the plant. Apply this once or twice during the growing season to kill annual and perennial weeds, but you will need to protect other plants from the chemical by covering them with a polythene sheet before spraying. Glyphosate is biodegradable, leaving no residue in the soil, enabling you to add new plants after only a week. Hand hoeing is an effective way to kill annual weeds. Do not waste time raking off small weeds after hoeing, unless the soil is wet. They will soon rot down.

Watering and feeding New plants need watering and feeding in order to develop a strong root system and to grow, while established plants may need watering in dry weather. To save time, lay a seep hose around the shrubs and connect it to a tap with a time switch, set it to turn on the water at night when it is cooler and evaporation lower. If you have to use a hose, concentrate the water on the root area of the plants. To water the roots of shrubs and trees directly, sink a plastic pipe or a plastic bottle with its tops cut off into the soil.

NO-PRUNE SHRUBS

Most shrubs benefit from some trimming or pruning occasionally, but some can be left unpruned without getting too large or out of hand. The following can be planted and left almost entirely alone.

Aucuba japonica
Ceanothus thyrsiflorus* var. *repens
***Choisya ternata* Sundance**
Cotoneaster microphyllus
Euonymus fortunei
Genista lydia
Prunus laurocerasus
'Otto Luyken'
***Skimmia japonica* 'Rubella'**

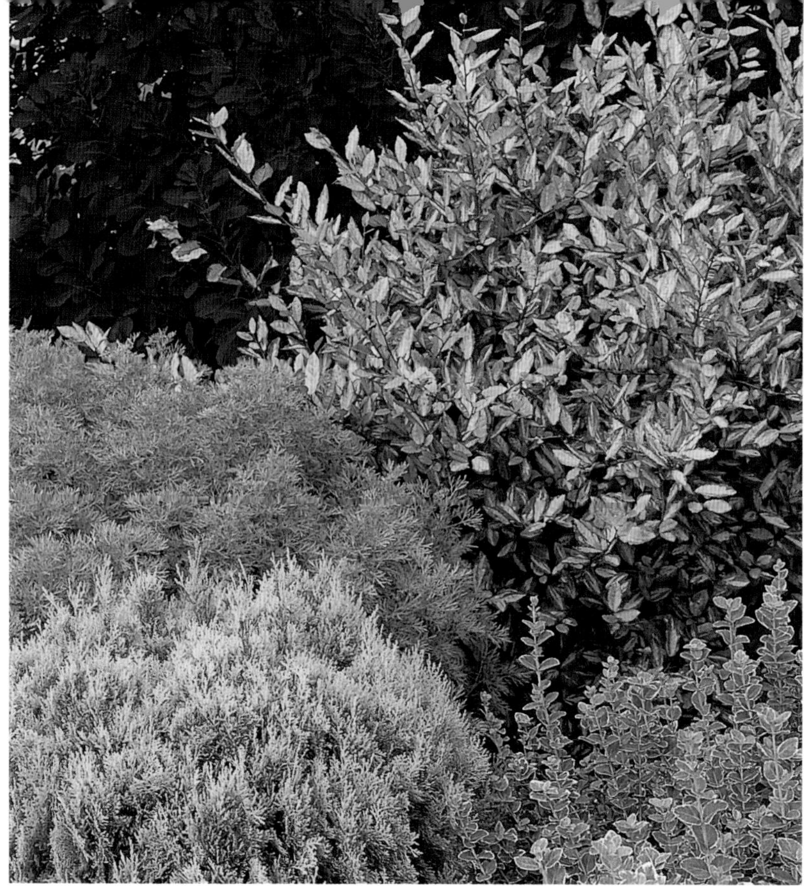

This foliage border provides all-year colour with no regular pruning. From top right, clockwise: elaeagnus, *Euonymous fortunei*, a dwarf thuja and artemisia.

Pruning for better results

As long as you keep to a few basic rules, pruning is not complicated – it can even be enjoyable. Prune little and often to keep your plants under control and in good health; if left for years, it will build up into a massive task. Not all shrubs have to be pruned each year, but they should certainly be checked and lightly pruned when they get untidy. It is important to know a little about the shrubs that you grow to determine when and how to prune them.

When pruning, make as clean a cut as possible to avoid damaging the plant. Try to prune to an outward-facing bud or pair of buds. On shrubs with lots of thin stems, such as *Lonicera nitida*, *Spiraea japonica* and *Potentilla fruticosa*, it is not easy or practical to make such a precise cut, so to save time prune them with garden shears. After a few weeks of growth, they will lose their stark appearance.

Rejuvenating an old shrub Old, overgrown shrubs can be rejuvenated by pruning them over several seasons. In the first year, in early spring, cut out a quarter to one-third of the old wood as low down in the plant as possible. This will encourage strong new shoots to grow. When the new growth is at its maximum – probably in mid summer – trim it back by one-third to make the plant bushier. In the second year, cut back the remaining old wood to leave only the new growth from the previous season.

Pruning tips

Do make as clean a cut as possible.

Do prune out all dead, diseased or damaged wood before starting to prune a shrub to shape.

Do cut out any frost-damaged shoots once frost-free weather has arrived.

Do remove any all-green shoots on variegated shrubs as soon as you see them. If not, they take over.

Do cut down eucalyptus to near ground level each spring, once frosts are over, to give a constant supply of fresh, young foliage.

Don't worry about pruning to a bud if the plant has thin, wiry stems.

Don't prune on wet, cold days, because wet foliage makes the job unpleasant. Choose a fine, dry day.

Don't prune if in doubt or unless the shrub really needs it.

PRUNING MADE EASY

As a general rule, pruning to remove any dead, damaged or diseased wood – the three Ds – can be done at any time of year, and if you buy well-shaped shrubs you should not need to prune them for the first three to five years.

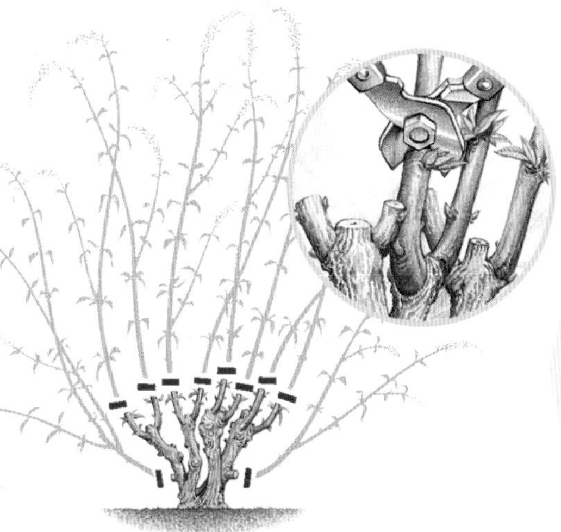

Shrubs flowering after mid summer *Plants that produce flowers on the current year's growth tend to bloom from mid summer and into autumn. Prune them in early spring, just before the new growth starts. Cut back last season's flowering stems and any weak shoots* (inset). *The harder you prune, the more new growth will be made. Flowers will develop on this new growth.*

Which shrubs?
Buddleja davidii, Caryopteris x *clandonesis, Ceanothus* x *delileanus* 'Gloire de Versailles', *Ceratostigma willmottianum,* hebes (large-leaved types), *Hydrangea paniculata,* lavatera, *Potentilla fruticosa, Spiraea japonica.*

Shrubs flowering before mid summer *Plants that produce flowers on the previous year's growth bloom mainly in spring and early summer. Prune as soon as the flowers fade. Cut out a quarter to one-third of older flowering shoots, cutting back to the highest new shoot or bud* (inset). *The plant will then make new growth in the summer that will produce flowers the following spring.*

Which shrubs?
Deutzia, escallonia, exochorda, such as *E.* x *macrantha* 'The Bride', *Forsythia* x *intermedia,* such as *F.* x *intermedia* 'Lynwood', *Kerria japonica, Kolkwitzia amabilis,* philadelphus, *Prunus triloba, Ribes sanguineum, Spiraea* 'Arguta', weigela.

Young foliage or coloured stems *Some shrubs are grown for their attractive new foliage or coloured stems. Prune these in early spring to encourage lush new growth for the summer and brighter stems for the winter. Prune back all of the previous year's growth to near ground level or back to an established framework of branches* (inset).

Which shrubs?
Cornus alba and *C. stolonifera, Rubus cockburnianus, Salix alba* and *S. daphnoides.* Also shrubs with attractive young foliage, such as varieties of *Sambucus nigra, Philadelphus coronarius* 'Aureus' and *Spiraea japonica* 'Goldflame'.

Evergreen foliage *Prune shrubs that are grown mainly for their evergreen foliage when they need to be kept in shape. Best times to prune are late spring and summer. Avoid pruning in frosty weather because this can cause frost damage. Cut out unwanted shoots to maintain shape and size* (inset). *Shorten over-long shoots and thin congested plants.*

Which shrubs?
Elaeagnus pungens, such as *E. pungens* 'Maculata' and *E.* x *ebbingei, Griselinia littoralis, Lonicera nitida, Photinia* x *fraseri, such as P.* x *fraseri* 'Red Robin', *Prunus laurocerasus, Prunus lusitanica, Viburnum tinus* (some flowers may be lost).

Problem solving and propagation

Most shrubs are generally trouble free, but from time to time they may be attacked by pests and diseases. If there is not much damage, or not many pests, it may not be worth taking action. Instead, let birds and other natural predators clear up the problem. For example, leave greenfly that appear on shrubs and trees in spring, in particular on roses, for breeding bluetits, which will clear them quickly to feed to their chicks. However, you will still need to monitor any signs of attack to ensure that they stay under control. As a general rule, do not spray routinely against pests. Instead, try to encourage a balance between pests and natural predators.

Keep your plants healthy. Plant the right plant for the right position and soil conditions in your garden. Ensure that newly planted shrubs are sufficiently watered and fed until they become established. A plant under stress because of lack of water is more susceptible to fungal diseases. Remove any dead or diseased foliage or stems to stop problems spreading to other plants.

Tonic for sick plants

If a plant lacks certain nutrients, it will look unhealthy – with pale or yellowing leaves, stunted growth or withering stems. In general, sick-looking plants are suffering from more than one nutrient deficiency. However, it can be difficult to identify which deficiencies a plant is suffering from, because there are so many different types and symptoms can vary from plant to plant.

As a quick and easy solution to reviving a plant that you suspect is lacking nutrients, give it a liquid feed that contains a good mix of trace elements or a foliar feed for faster uptake. Always follow the manufacturer's instructions. Some liquid feeds can also be used at half strength as a foliar feed.

HOW TO DEAL WITH COMMON PROBLEMS

▲ FROSTED LEAVES
Container plants and evergreens are most at risk. Plants tend to recover and make new growth in spring. If a late frost is forecast, drape plants with garden fleece.

WIND DAMAGE
Some plants, such as *Acer palmatum*, can be disfigured by warm, dry winds, while cold north or east winds can damage evergreen foliage in winter. Protect susceptible plants with windbreak netting or fleece.

CATERPILLARS
Caterpillars can cause a lot of damage in late spring and summer. Spray them with insecticide as soon as damage is spotted or pick them off by hand.

▲ BROWN FLOWERS
A late frost can damage blossom in spring. Avoid planting tender or very early-flowering plants, such as camellia, in low-lying frost pockets or areas facing the full, early morning sun, which could cause frost-thaw damage.

APHIDS
Aphids feeding on tender new growth will cause leaves to twist and distort. Use a strong jet of water to wash off small colonies. Control larger outbreaks with an insecticide.

SOOTY MOULD
A black fungus grows on the sticky honey-dew excreted by aphids. A fungicide will kill the fungus or it can be washed off with a jet of water. But keep aphids under control.

POWDERY MILDEW
This fungal growth often attacks plants short of water or nutrients. A general fungicide will stop the white powdery patches spreading. Water well, mulch and feed each spring in order to reduce attacks.

▲ LEAF MINER GRUBS
This pest tunnels between the upper and lower leaf surface. Control with a systemic insecticide.

SHOT HOLE
Small brown spots on the leaves develop into holes. Remove any damaged foliage. This disease tends to attack unhealthy plants, especially of the prunus family, so feed with a general fertiliser.

SCALE INSECTS
Sticky leaves and black, sooty mould are the first signs. The small brown scales are usually under the leaves and on stems. Pick off by hand or spray with systemic insecticide.

▲ VINE WEEVILS
Adult beetles eat notches in leaf edges from mid spring to mid autumn, while the larvae eat the roots of plants. Use compost impregnated with insecticide or introduce predatory nematodes.

Raising your own shrubs A good way to stock a new garden with shrubs is to propagate your own. Not only does it save money, but growing a healthy plant from a cutting can bring a great sense of satisfaction. If you want to plant a large area using one type of plant, it is well worth propagating your own from one bought plant. (See page 280 for how to take cuttings and plant lists of suitable subjects.)

Not all shrubs are suitable for raising from cuttings. In general, those more expensive to buy are more difficult to propagate, and are best bought from the garden centre or nursery as plants. These include *Acer palmatum* var. *dissectum*, *Cotinus coggygria*, daphne, *Elaeagnus pungens* 'Maculata', *Fremontodendron californicum*, *Garrya elliptica*, hollies, *Mahonia* x *media* 'Charity', lilacs, rhododendrons and azaleas, and *Viburnum carlesii*.

Ground-cover shrubs can be easily propagated from cuttings, as well as certain types of hedging, such as privet and box. Euonymus, cotoneaster, senecio and *Lonicera pileata* can be taken as semi-ripe cuttings in July and August and inserted into trays filled with a mixture of equal quantities of compost and perlite, or vermiculite. Place the cuttings under a simple propagator made from garden wire bent into hoops and covered with polythene (see page 281). Alternatively, insert the cuttings into the soil in a sheltered part of the garden and cover with the propagator frame. The young plants can be lifted the following spring and potted before planting out.

Time saver

To grow a hedge of box, *Lonicera nitida* or privet, insert hardwood cuttings directly where you want the hedge to grow. This will save time having to plant them out at a later date.

TWO EASY TECHNIQUES

Take cuttings to propagate easy-to-root plants or those needed in larger numbers, such as for ground cover. Alternatively, many shrubs, such as camellia, can be layered, but this produces few new plants at a time. (See also page 280.)

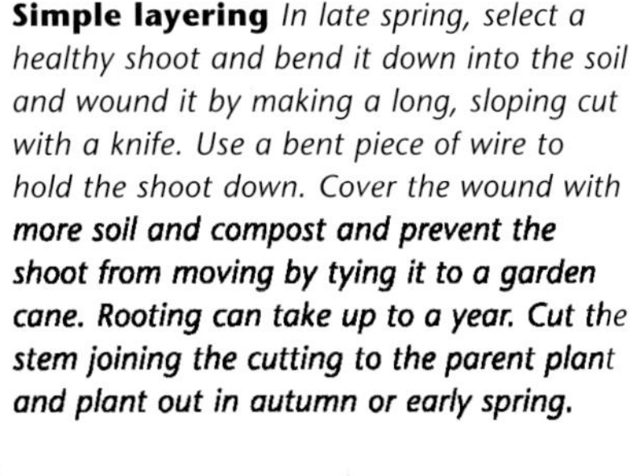

Simple layering *In late spring, select a healthy shoot and bend it down into the soil and wound it by making a long, sloping cut with a knife. Use a bent piece of wire to hold the shoot down. Cover the wound with* ***more soil and compost and prevent the shoot from moving by tying it to a garden cane. Rooting can take up to a year. Cut the stem joining the cutting to the parent plant and plant out in autumn or early spring.***

Easy hardwood cuttings *In early autumn, cut off and trim pencil-thick shoots to 25 cm (10 in) long with a leaf joint at each end. For evergreens, remove all but the top four leaves. Push cuttings through black polythene into prepared soil in a sheltered, sunny spot, leaving one-third above ground. The polythene keeps the soil warm and moist, and prevents weed growth. Plant out rooted cuttings the following autumn.*

The role of evergreens in a time-saving garden

Evergreens are an important feature for any garden because they provide all-year interest and are easy to look after. By choosing a mixture of silver, gold and variegated evergreens as well as different shades of green you can reduce the amount of additional seasonal colour that is needed.

For an easy formula, a maximum of 85 per cent of plants in a time-saving garden should be evergreen, with at least 15 per cent deciduous shrubs, perennials and bulbs. This will give you a colourful, all-year evergreen backdrop that sets off a limited amount of seasonal colour, while keeping the workload low.

Evergreens also have other uses. They can be used for screening unsightly views and giving extra privacy. An ugly shed or fence can be hidden very quickly by tall, dense evergreens. They can be used in a shelter belt, reducing wind speed and traffic noise, and trapping

The natural tones and varied textures of the brick, gravel and timber add interest to the easy-care, mainly shrub planting.

A mixture of different evergreen shrubs and conifers makes this low-maintenance garden interesting throughout the year.

dust and litter from a busy road. By planting evergreens a little closer together than recommended on the label, you can produce a total ground cover, blocking the sun from reaching the ground. This will suppress weed growth all year round – unlike herbaceous or deciduous ground cover, which allows weeds to establish until they cover the soil in late spring. Since evergreens don't shed all their leaves at once, the gardener will have fewer leaves to rake up in autumn.

There are evergreens for most situations. Some are not fussy, tolerating sun or shade, such as *Viburnum tinus* and pyracantha, while those with golden foliage, including *Choisya ternata* Sundance, will turn green if they receive no sun. Plants that tolerate heavy shade include *Prunus laurocerasus* and *Aucuba japonica*.

Many evergreens produce a colourful display of flowers, such as the sun-loving cistus and the easy-care hebes. Others have aromatic flowers, such as *Elaeagnus* x *ebbingei*, which bears small, white blooms that fill the autumn air with fragrance, and aromatic leaves, such as those of *Choisya ternata*.

When planting evergreens, especially in dry shade, improve the soil by digging in lots of well-rotted organic matter. Until they establish, feed and water the plants regularly. Some evergreens, including camellias, rhododendrons and pieris, need acid soil, so if you intend to grow them test the soil first to make sure it is suitable. If not, grow them in containers of ericaceous compost. To develop their full colour, all coloured evergreens and conifers benefit from a general feed in spring, such as growmore or blood, fish and bone fertiliser.

TRIMMING MADE EASY

Low-growing and ground-cover shrubs planted near to a path will need occasional trimming. An easy technique to prune them while maintaining their natural shape is to lift the growth off the path and cut out the lower shoots back to near the centre of the plant. When the existing stems are lowered back onto the ground, they will cover the cuts made beneath.

Keep in shape
Cut back the remaining top shoots by shortening them slightly to keep the overall shape of the plant.

TROUBLE-FREE EVERGREEN SHRUBS

Evergreens are useful for adding year-round interest. The following are easy to grow on most soils.

***Elaeagnus* x *ebbingei* 'Limelight'** Up to 3 m (10 ft) tall. The glossy, variegated leaves are silver-grey beneath. Prune in spring to control size, and remove any all-green shoots. *E.* x *ebbingei* 'Gilt Edge' has yellow, variegated margins.

Choisya ternata A compact, rounded shrub that can grow to 2.4 m (8 ft). The glossy green leaves are aromatic when crushed. Fragrant white flowers in May and June, often with a second flush in August and September.

Cistus* x *hybridus A low, spreading shrub up to 75 cm (30 in) tall. Coarse, wrinkled, dark green leaves, paler underneath. Masses of white flowers with yellow centres from May onwards. Good for a sunny spot with light, poor soil.

***Camellia* x *williamsii* 'Donation'** A robust, upright evergreen growing to 3 m (10 ft) tall. Rose pink, semi-double flowers from late winter to early summer. Grow on well-drained, acid soil. Best in partial shade. Avoid east-facing aspect.

Cedrus deodara provides a sculptural focus for this grouping, but it is a large conifer so is suitable only for a sizeable garden.

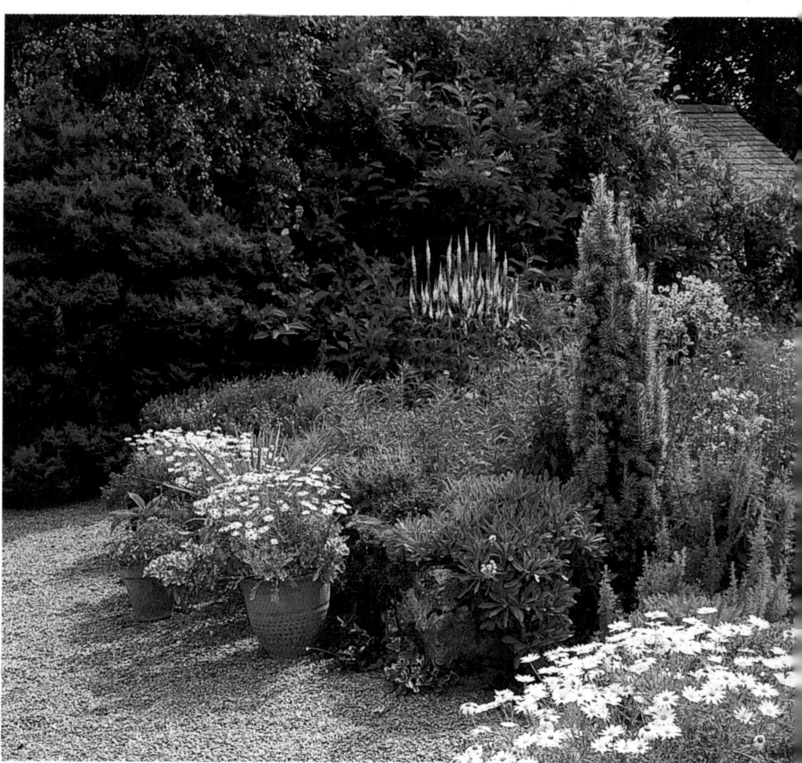

Rejuvenating a conifer

Save time removing old, browning conifers by transforming them into a new garden feature by pruning.

Brown in the centre Remove the small dead branches, especially those from the centre, to reveal the shape of the main branches. Cut off a few of the lower larger branches so that you can underplant the conifer with ground-cover plants that tolerate dry shade, including vinca, geranium (cranesbill) and lamium.

Brown at the base Variegated ivy or periwinkle (vinca) planted at the base of the tree will use the brown, lower branches as a climbing frame.

Standard conifers Transform a conifer into a standard by removing all branches up to 1.5 m (5 ft) – or lower if desired – and then lightly trimming the top to shape.

Spoilt for choice with conifers

Conifers are ideal for a busy gardener, because they require little attention. Most need no pruning and grow happily for many years, providing an all-year display. Many also come in striking, architectural shapes – upright and columnar, or horizontal and spreading – which make them good for grouping with other plants.

Buying conifers Spend a little time making the right choice of conifer in order to save overcrowding and having to dig up and replant a tree later. You may be tempted to buy an attractive small conifer, but it could become enormous after a few years. Some conifers are sold as dwarf varieties, but this may indicate only a slow growth rate and they may still grow very large. Labels should show their ultimate size.

Look for plants that have a good, bright colour. The tree should be compact with healthy foliage. Avoid tall and lanky plants that are bare at the base. Dead foliage indicate that the plant is pot-bound or that it has not had enough water, and most conifers will not regrow from old brown stems. Most importantly, make sure the conifer is labelled, because many look very similar while still young.

Choose conifers for their natural shape. *Taxus baccata* 'Fastigiata Aurea' makes a beautifully natural, golden pillar to mark an entrance.

Planting Traditional planting times for conifers are in late spring or early autumn, but you can plant at most times of the year as long as the plants are kept watered and the soil is not waterlogged. In cold areas, avoid planting in mid winter because of likely frost or wind damage.

Taller trees may need a stout cane or stake to prevent rocking (see page 262). On very windy sites, protect the conifer by erecting windbreak netting around it for the first month or so (see page 99). Because conifers lose water through their leaves all year round, keep their roots moist at all times until established. Pot-grown plants are generally fairly easy to establish. When planting, mix some compost and fertiliser into the base of the hole and use soil to infill. Field-grown plants for hedging need planting as soon as possible after purchase; they also need more care to help them to establish because their roots will have been damaged during lifting.

Using hedging conifers Leyland cypress (x *Cupressocyparis leylandii*) is a popular hedge. It also has a golden form, 'Castlewellan', and a variegated form, 'Harlequin'. It makes an excellent screen, and helps to reduce road noise and filter pollution. Its main disadvantage is size. If left unpruned, it will reach up to 30 m (100 ft) and have many enemies. A Leyland cypress hedge grows very fast, but doesn't need a lot of maintenance once established. Allow it to grow a little taller than the desired height, and then cut it back a little lower than required. Once established, trimming once a year in August will keep the hedge neat and tidy. Never cut back the sides into old brown stems, because they will not regrow. Other good hedging conifers include *Chamaecyparis lawsoniana* 'Green Hedger' and 'Golden Wonder', *Cupressus macrocarpa*, and *Thuja occidentalis* 'Smaragd', Western red cedar (*Thuja plicata*) or yew for hedging 1.2-1.5 m (4-5 ft) high.

EASY-CARE CONIFERS

Conifers come in shapes, colours and sizes to suit all garden situations. Choose a selection from the following easy-care varieties.

Columnar conifers
Chamaecyparis lawsoniana 'Ellwood's Gold', 'Fletcheri', 'Pottenii' and 'Lane' (pictured), *Cupressus sempervirens* 'Stricta', *Juniperus chinensis* 'Pyramidalis', *J. scopulorum* 'Skyrocket', *Taxus baccata* 'Fastigiata'.

Dwarf conifers
Chamaecyparis lawsoniana 'Minima Aurea' and 'Minima Glauca', *Juniperus communis* 'Compressa', *Picea abies* 'Little Gem' (pictured), *Pinus mugo* 'Gnom', *Thuja orientalis* 'Aurea Nana'.

Prostrate conifers
Cedrus deodara 'Golden Horizon', *Juniperus communis* 'Hornibrookii', *J.* x *pfitzeriana* 'Pfitzeriana' (pictured), *J. sabina* 'Tamariscifolia', *J. virginiana* 'Grey Owl', *Taxus baccata* 'Repandens'.

Blue conifers
Cedrus libani ssp. *atlantica* Glauca Group, *Chamaecyparis lawsoniana* 'Ellwoodii' and 'Pembury Blue', *C. pisifera* 'Boulevard', *Juniperus squamata* 'Blue Star' (pictured), *Picea pungens* 'Koster', *Pseudotsuga menziesii* var. *glauca*.

Topiary shrubs

Bay (*Laurus nobilis*) Ideal for globes and cones, but not so good for small, intricate designs because of its large leaves. Trim once or twice a season between May and September.

Box (*Buxus sempervirens*) Small, round leaves and compact growth make it best suited to smaller topiary features. Trim twice a year between May and September.

Box-leaved honeysuckle (*Lonicera nitida*) A small-leaved, fast-growing evergreen. Green, golden and variegated forms available. Trim two or three times a year, in April, July and September.

Holly (*Ilex aquifolium*) A good specimen feature. Several forms available with green or variegated leaves. Trim once a year, in April.

Yew (*Taxus baccata*) Its stiff, compact growth is easily clipped into a shape. Green and gold forms available. Trim once in August.

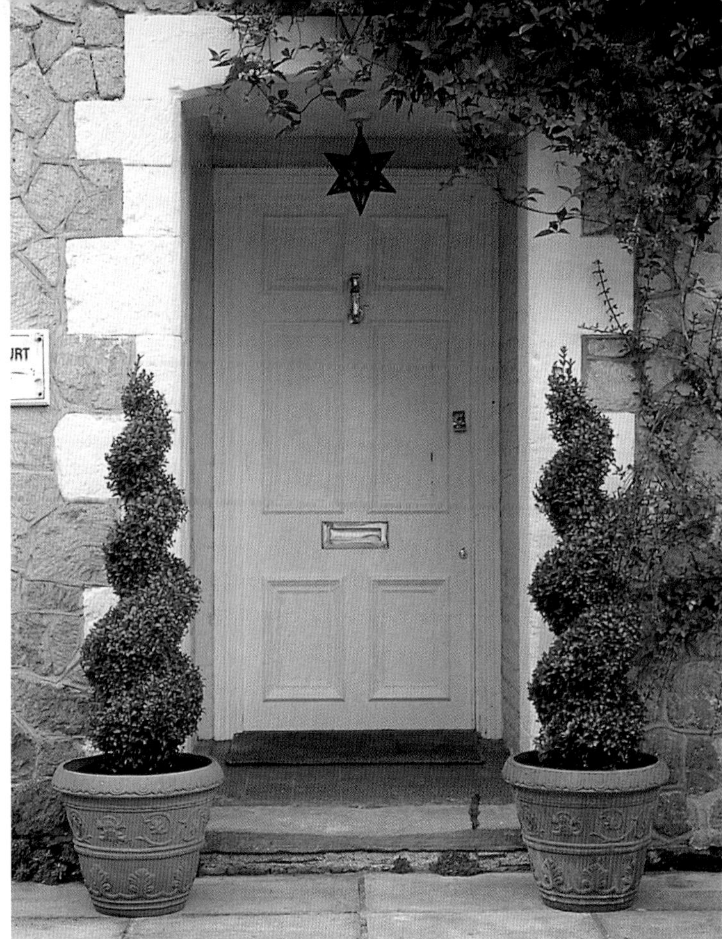

These spiral box topiaries provide a perfect finishing touch to this formal entrance; they are easy to create, and should take about five years to grow to their full height.

Using evergreens as display plants

The striking form of many evergreens makes them ideal specimen plants, positioned so that they stand out from other plants. You will also be able to reduce your workload because fewer plants will be needed to produce an eye-catching display. Use them as focal points, either in a large container or in the garden.

In a small border, a selection of evergreens with different coloured foliage and flowers can be used to create a screen or to break the view down the garden. Give the plants space to develop fully. You can also plant a specimen evergreen among herbaceous perennials to maintain interest once the perennials have died down, although don't let the perennials shade the foliage of the evergreen. Choose a shrub that looks good throughout winter, such as a colourful variegated holly, which can be easily kept to size.

Alternatively, evergreens can be planted as specimens in containers (see page 186). They look particularly effective when positioned on paved areas or around buildings. When choosing the type of shrub to plant in the container, do not worry too much about the eventual size because the container will limit the plant's growth, rather like a large bonsai. If you intend to keep the shrubs in the container as a permanent feature, use a John Innes compost because it will retain its

Time saver

Before trimming or shaping a plant growing in a container, stand it in a wheelbarrow. This not only saves you from having to bend over to cut it, but the wheelbarrow also collects the trimmings as you work.

physical structure for longer than soil-free composts, and is also less likely to blow over in breezy weather because of its weight. Evergreens in pots can be allowed to grow to their normal shape for an informal look or shaped to give a more formal appearance. To change the look of your garden, move the containers around.

Shaping evergreens Evergreens are the most common type of plant used for topiary, the shaping and training of trees and shrubs into geometric designs or animal shapes. Some shapes are complicated and intricate, but you can easily create simple and interesting topiary designs in a short time. Position specimens in borders or in pots by entrances to the garden or doorway to add extra interest.

You can buy topiary from a garden centre; pyramids, spirals and spheres are the most popular shapes. You may wish, however, to create your own. Either buy a frame or make one yourself out of wire or canes. As a short cut, use ivy to make a topiary lookalike in a couple of seasons (see below). Growth will be even speedier if the topiary is placed in a greenhouse, even an unheated one, over winter.

Quick results

Several berrying evergreens need a male plant to get berries on the females. To be sure of getting berries on a holly, choose the hermaphrodite *Ilex* 'J C van Tol'; it also has fewer spines. With *Skimmia japonica*, plant a male and female form in the same planting hole, such as 'Veitchii' with 'Rubella', to have what looks like a single plant with winter berries and flower buds.

Creating a quick topiary

An easy way to make a topiary shape is to grow ivy over a wire frame. Frames of many shapes are available from garden centres or you could make your own with strong garden wire.

Plant the ivy Start by planting two or three small-leaved ivies with long trailing stems around the edge of a big pot filled with John Innes compost.

Train the ivy Insert the wire frame around the plants, making sure it is secure. Wind several long, trailing stems of ivy around each piece of wire, tying them into position with green garden ties. Pinch out the tips of long stems to encourage the plants to bush out.

Keep the shape Once the form is established, pinch out the tips of shoots regularly to maintain the shape.

Tie in new shoots As the ivies grow, keep twisting and tying in shoots to the frame, cutting off sideshoots that grow out beyond it.

Aftercare

By growing topiary in pots, you can move them around – a focal point in a bed, indoors as an ornament or in a sheltered spot for winter. Ivy tolerates dry conditions, but for best growth water daily in hot weather and feed regularly (see page 266). Pot on if pot bound. Alternatively, remove the topiary from its pot each spring, and carefully replace loose compost and put the plant back in the same pot.

How to care for evergreens

Most problems tend to occur shortly after planting, while the evergreen is establishing itself in a new position. The main reason for failure is lack of water. Evergreens continue to lose water through the underside of their leaves all year round. Water lost through the leaves has to be replaced by water taken in by the roots, otherwise the plant dehydrates. To encourage quick establishment and so save time in the long run, keep the rootball moist, even when planting in autumn or early winter. Soak the rootball for a few hours in the pot before planting. If the rootball is a solid mass of roots and pot-bound, tease out some of the roots with your fingers, doing as little damage as possible, and spread them out in the planting hole.

Give the plant a thorough soaking every week or two, letting the water soak down to the roots, rather than just dampening the surface, to encourage deep rooting. Speed up watering by laying a seep hose beside new plants so they can be watered all in one go. To prevent evaporation from the soil, apply a loose organic material such as bark chippings (see page 264). Do not water if the ground is already moist.

Check the rootball occasionally after planting to make sure that it has not dried out. Even if the soil around the newly planted evergreen is moist, the rootball may not have sufficient water. To check, disturb the surface of the compost near the base of the plant. If it feels dry,

USING EVERGREENS TO DECEIVE THE EYE

Evergreens are ideal for adding instant structure to a garden because they retain the same shape all year round. You can also use them as a quick way of hiding an eyesore, framing a view or creating the illusion of space in a small garden.

Screening an eyesore or framing a view *Evergreens can be used to screen an eyesore all-year round or to frame an attractive view inside or outside the garden. As shown in the illustration, it is easier to hide an eyesore by planting a smaller evergreen – which is faster to reach its desired height – nearer the viewing point than by planting at the boundary, which would require a much taller evergreen to do the same job.*

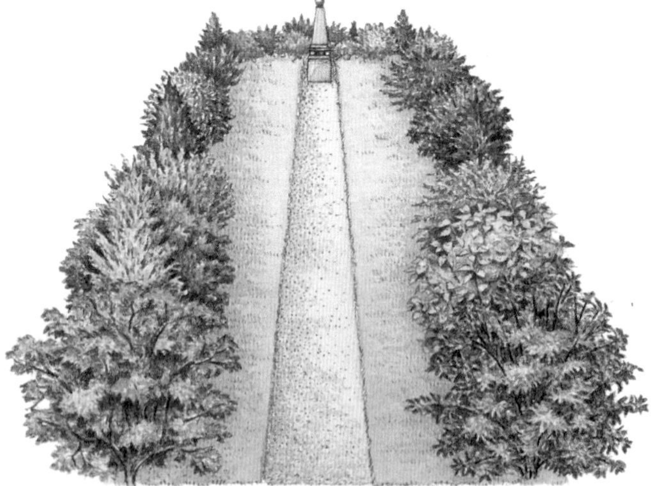

Altering perspective *Make your garden look longer by using the shape, texture and colour of evergreens to alter the perspective. This can be done by planting progressively smaller plants as you go down the garden. Similarly, plants with larger leaves will seem closer, and those with smaller leaves more distant. Emphasise this effect by using colours; pale blues and mauves will recede into the distance, while bright oranges and reds will appear closer.*

EVERGREENS FOR CONTAINERS

The following evergreens are ideal for growing in containers. Use a pot at least 45 cm (18 in) wide and deep filled with John Innes compost.

***Aucuba japonica* 'Variegata'**
Eucalyptus gunnii
***Euonymus japonicus* 'Aureus'**
***Fatsia japonica* 'Variegata'**
Hebe
***Laurus nobilis* (sweet bay)**
***Lonicera nitida* 'Baggessen's Gold'**
***Pittosporum tenuifolium* 'Tom Thumb'**

Combine upright and ground-hugging conifers to make a low-upkeep border. Keep spreading plants within bounds by pruning once every two or three years.

water thoroughly around the base. If the compost is very dry, especially if it is peat based, it may be difficult to wet again. To help to rewet the compost quickly, add a few drops of washing-up liquid to the water. This reduces the surface tension of the water, allowing it to soak into the compost more easily.

Newly planted shrubs can suffer in strong drying winds which draw moisture out of the plant faster than the roots can take it in. The plants may wilt despite the soil around the roots being moist. In these circumstances, erect a temporary windbreak of netting around the plant (see left), or mist it over from time to time with cool water.

Evergreens suffer more from waterlogging in winter than deciduous shrubs, because deciduous plants go into a state of dormancy for the winter while evergreens continue to grow slowly. Waterlogged soil causes a shortage of air around the roots and after a period of several weeks plants can suffer. If a part of your garden is wet for most of the winter, try to improve the drainage before planting (see page 26). Large, newly planted evergreens may need supporting with canes or stakes to prevent them from blowing over in strong winds. This is normally necessary for the first season only, by which time the roots will have become well enough established to anchor the plant.

Problem solver

Windbreak netting Protect newly planted evergreens and those exposed to cold winds in winter with a barrier of windbreak netting. Either put up a temporary screen, attaching the netting to stout posts, or create a more permanent shelter if the garden is exposed (see page 30).

Advice on buying

Do buy from a reputable grower. Ask for disease-resitant varieties.

Do look for roses with at least three or four strong shoots.

Do check the flower is the same as on the label if buying in summer.

Don't buy roses that have been allowed to dry out. They will have dull, wrinkled stems.

Don't buy cheap, pre-packed, bare-root roses dipped in wax or starting to make long, pale growths.

Don't buy old, pot-bound roses.

Don't buy roses with pests or diseases, including aphids, blackspot, mildew or rust.

Easy-care techniques give new bloom to roses

Roses are one of the most popular garden plants. They have beautiful flowers in a wide range of colours, shapes and sizes. They mix well with other shrubs and herbaceous perennials and, unlike many flowering shrubs, repeat-flowerers carry their blooms for much of the summer, and often into the autumn. As well as flowers, many roses produce eye-catching hips in late summer to give a colourful display well into the winter. Some also have attractive foliage, adding extra interest in summer. Leaves vary from the smooth, dark green and glossy, through bright green and wrinkled, to rich blue-green.

Traditional methods of growing roses can be time consuming, with much time spent on spraying against pests and diseases, and on adopting the right pruning technique. To a busy gardener this is not encouraging. However, much of this can be avoided by choosing disease-resistant varieties and the right type of rose for the right place and function. Most roses are easy to grow and will thrive in almost any soil, although light soils may need improving with well-rotted

Bushy shrub roses, such as this repeat-flowering *Rosa* 'Ballerina', also look good spilling over the edges of large containers.

organic matter to prevent the plants suffering in dry weather. Like most other plants, roses are more prone to disease if under stress from lack of water or nutrients. For lots of flowers and healthy foliage, it is best to apply a rose fertiliser in spring, before the leaves are fully open, and again in June or July, to encourage further blooms.

To reduce pruning, plant shrub roses because they need only minimal shaping. Even hybrid teas and floribundas can be more simply pruned to save time. To get the most from your roses, choose varieties that have a long flowering season and those that flower reliably in poor weather. Most hybrid teas and floribundas will flower throughout the summer, but varieties with large, double flowers can be ruined in wet weather as well as many old-fashioned roses, which in addition have a short flowering season.

Miniature and patio roses are good for small gardens and containers. Their heights vary between 20 cm (8 in) and 60 cm (24 in), with patio roses being at the taller end of the scale. If grown in a container, though, they need regular watering and feeding; to encourage flowering use a liquid tomato feed. General upkeep is similar to most other roses, and they can be attacked by the same pests and diseases. Pruning is simple and most often consists of a little thinning and trimming, making them very easy and quick to look after.

Repeat-flowering roses provide continuous colour all summer. Pick a variety with blooms that withstand heavy rain.

Time saver

For containers, patio roses make a good low-maintenance alternative to summer bedding plants. They have the same long flowering season, lots of colour, and they can stay in the same pot for several years.

HYBRID TEAS AND FLORIBUNDAS

The most popular types of roses are hybrid teas and floribundas. The following are easy to grow, offering good disease resistance and a long flowering season.

'Alec's Red' A strong, healthy hybrid tea growing up to 90 cm (36 in). Gives an abundance of crimson flowers all summer. The blooms hold themselves well against the rain.

'Amber Queen' Compact floribunda, only growing up to 60 cm (24 in). Free-flowering, with large, fragrant amber-yellow blooms with contrasting young, bronze foliage.

'Grandpa Dickson' Hybrid tea with glossy, dark green foliage and large, blooms that are slightly fragrant. Good rain resistance. Upright habit up to 90 cm (36 in) tall.

'Just Joey' A free-flowering hybrid tea rose with attractive buds and coppery orange blooms with ruffled edges. Good resistance to rain. This variety grows up to 75 cm (30 in).

'Southampton' An upright floribunda with slightly fragrant flowers which are almost the colour of marmalade. Dark green, semi-glossy leaves. It grows to about 90 cm (36 in).

Choosing the best shrub roses

Shrub roses cover a wide range of types, and it is easy to become confused when trying to choose one from a catalogue. Names that you are likely to come across include alba, bourbon, centifolia, China, damask, English, gallica, ground cover, hybrid musk, modern, moss, musk, rugosa and species. Many of these types are very old, but others are recent introductions.

Busy gardeners are often put off by shrub roses because of their size. The name shrub rose makes them sound large, and indeed many do grow to 2.4 m (8 ft). However, some do not grow any larger than a hybrid tea or floribunda, making them suitable for gardens of all sizes. Modern shrub, rugosa and ground-cover roses usually flower repeatedly, adding colour to the garden all summer; it is the old garden roses that tend to flower only once, such as alba, damask, gallica and musk roses, albeit that often their blooms appear in one spectacular burst for about six weeks in early or mid summer.

When choosing a shrub rose, take time to select a variety that will not grow too large for the planting site – needing pruning and maintenance time – and choose one that repeat flowers (see panel, opposite) for interest throughout the summer, and possibly into autumn. Once planted, shrub roses require little attention. To ensure a good supply of flowers and healthy growth, feed in spring and again in mid summer. Mulching will help to control weed growth and conserve

Quick results

An easy method of propagating roses is to take hardwood cuttings in late summer. This will produce plants that do not sucker. Select a healthy, well-ripened shoot and trim it to 25 cm (10 in), making a cut above and below a bud. Dip in rooting powder and insert two-thirds directly into the soil in a sheltered part of the garden. Lift and plant the following autumn.

GROUND-COVER ROSES

Many of the following newer ground-cover roses are ideal garden plants, being compact and repeat flowering from early summer to autumn.

'Flower Carpet'
'Kent'
'Hertfordshire'
'Northamptonshire'
'Nozomi'
'Partridge'
'Sussex'
'Suffolk'
'The Fairy'

Shrub roses are easy to slot into a mixed border. Here, 'Fritz Nobis' mingles with poppies and a fig in the background.

Geranium (cranesbill) is an ideal partner for a shrub rose. It suppresses weeds, prolongs flowering interest and covers any bare rose stems at the base.

soil moisture. Check foliage regularly for signs of pests or diseases and take necessary action straightaway (see page 105).

For the first few years after planting, shrub roses need little pruning except for the removal of dead or damaged shoots. After that, for best flowering results, prune modern shrub, rugosa and ground-cover roses in winter or early spring, just before growth begins (see page 104), although some long deadheading – removing about 15-20 cm (6-8 in) of the flowering stem – can be done in summer to keep the roses tidy. Old garden roses can be pruned by 'long deadheading' as soon as blooms are over. Species roses need no special pruning at all.

Renovate old shrub roses – of whatever type – by cutting out between a quarter and a third of old wood close to ground level each year in winter or early spring over several years. If you cut out any more wood than this, you will be encouraging the plant to produce suckers from the rootstock.

TROUBLE-FREE SHRUB ROSES

The following shrub roses offer superb displays of flowers, many with attractive foliage, and some have colourful hips in autumn as well. All are resistant to diseases.

'Ballerina' Large sprays of small, single flowers are produced on a healthy plant that grows to about 1.2 m (4 ft). The pink flowers have a slight musk-like scent. Repeat flowering.

'Fru Dagmar Hastrup' A compact plant up to 1.2 m (4 ft). Single, rose-pink, scented flowers are followed by large, attractive crimson hips. Repeat flowering.

'Graham Thomas' Double, deep yellow, fragrant flowers are produced from early summer to late autumn. Pale foliage. Grows to about 1.2 m (4 ft) and has an arching habit.

'Harhero' Large clusters of cupped, red flowers with white centres in summer and autumn. An abundance of glossy, light green foliage. Grows to about 1.2 m (4 ft).

'Golden Wings' Regular flushes of large, pale yellow flowers with amber stamens from June onwards. Fragrant. Freely branching. Weather-resistant. Up to 1.5 m (5 ft).

Routine care of roses

Roses are often thought of as being high-maintenance plants, but pruning can be simplified by adopting several quick techniques, and pests and diseases kept at bay by selecting disease-resistant varieties and by prompt action as soon as signs of a pest or disease attack are noticed (see opposite).

Pruning Hybrid teas and floribundas need 'proper' pruning only once a year, the time depending on your garden's exposure. If you have a sheltered garden, prune just before growth starts in late February or early March. If your garden is exposed to strong winter winds, shorten long stems in early winter to prevent the roses being damaged by rocking. Then prune properly in late March.

You can use the same technique to prune both hybrid tea and floribunda roses (see below). Established shrub roses need to be pruned only once a year, and in the first year or two, a few of the longest shoots may be shortened by a third to encourage new, bushy growth. And miniature and patio roses are best pruned in late spring, once the frosty season is over, using secateurs or scissors to snip off any dead or frost-damaged shoots and if necessary thin crowded stems. Of all types of roses, though, ground-cover ones are the easiest to maintain because they need pruning only if straggly.

ROSE PRUNING MADE EASY

In the past, a lot was made of pruning roses, but it needn't be hard work or difficult. As for other woody plants, cut out all dead and diseased wood, and open up the centre of the bush; but this does not have to be done every year.

Trim ground-cover roses *If they become straggly or out of control, cut back ground-cover roses with a pair of shears in early spring, removing upward-growing stems and thinning overcrowded growth.*

Quick prune floribundas/hybrid teas *Cut across at a height of 15-20 cm (6-8 in) with a hedge trimmer in early spring. Every few years, use secateurs to clear away weak and dead shoots in the base.*

Keep shrub roses in shape *Once established, pruning need be done only every two years – in early winter or spring. Thin out a few old shoots and trim back untidy growth to maintain a good shape.*

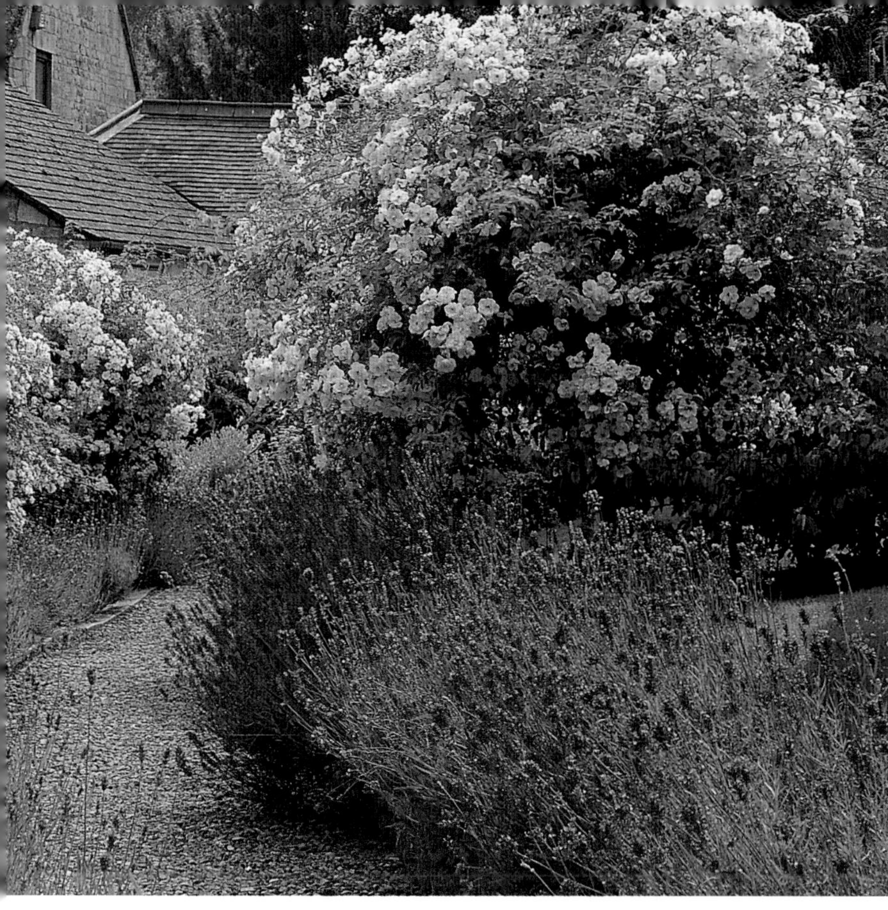

Buying roses

You can buy roses as either bare-root plants between October and March or as container plants all year round.

Bare-root plants These are grown in the soil and lifted in autumn to be sold by March, when they start growing. They need to be planted out immediately – temporarily or in their permanent position – so that the bare roots do not dry out.

Container roses Usually grown in the soil, lifted and potted into containers. Their main advantage is that you can see the rose growing and flowering when you buy it. They tend to be more expensive, but the planting season is all year round.

Growing roses as standards brings flowers to eye level, making pruning easier and allowing you to underplant with weed-smothering ground-cover plants.

ROSE PESTS AND DISEASES

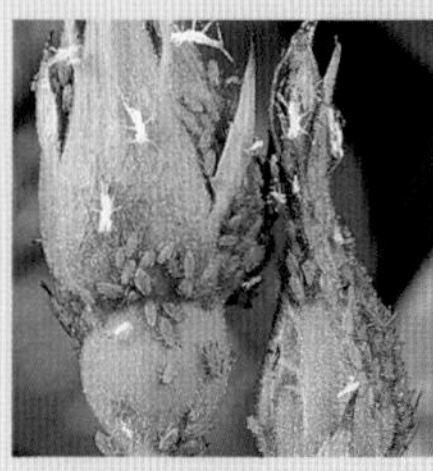

▲APHIDS
Feed on new growth and around flower buds. Severe attacks can cause distorted growth. Control is easy with a general insecticide or an organic soft-soap spray. For small numbers of aphids, it is quicker to wipe them off by hand or to leave them for the birds.

FROGHOPPERS
Cuckoo spit, a characteristic white frothy substance, is left by sap-feeding frog-hoppers on stems and leaves of plants in late summer. They secrete the froth to protect themselves. The easiest control is to wash them off with a hose.

▲BLACK SPOT
A common rose fungal disease that causes leaves to pale and dark spots to develop. To stop the fungus spreading, burn all prunings and spray roses in winter with a tar-oil wash. Also spray with a rose fungicide or with sulphur in early spring and mulch around the roses with garden compost in late winter.

SPIDER MITES
They cause leaves to turn a bronze colour, with fine webbing underneath. They are more of a problem in hot, dry weather. Control with a systemic insecticide or spray the foliage with water daily in dry weather because the mites don't like damp conditions.

CATERPILLARS
Irregular-shaped holes in leaves can be the work of caterpillars. Control by picking them off by hand or with an insecticide.

▲MILDEW
A grey-white powder on leaves and buds. Severe attacks can cause leaves to fall. Mildew is often a sign that the roots are dry or the plant is lacking nutrients. Spray with a rose fungicide or with sulphur at the first signs of attack, and water and feed. Mulch well in spring.

DIE-BACK
Shoots die back for no apparent reason. Causes can be frost damage, waterlogging or nutrient deficiency. Cut affected shoots back to healthy wood. Then feed plants in spring and summer and mulch well the following spring.

▲RUST
A problem in mild, wet summers. Orange pustules develop on the underside of the leaves and can cause premature defoliation. Spray with a rose fungicide containing myclobutanil.

Easy-care trees for your garden

Trees are probably one of the easiest ways to create a permanent feature in the garden. They last a long time, add an element of height and are virtually maintenance free, making them an ideal plant for the busy gardener. They come in all shapes and sizes, and there is a tree for every situation.

Trees do not provide just foliage; a large choice of flowering trees is available, including ornamental cherry, crab apple or ornamental thorn (crataegus). For bark effect, plant birch (betula) or a maple, such as *Acer pensylvanicum*, with its green and white-striped bark; for golden foliage, false acacia (*Robinia pseudoacacia* 'Frisia'); and for evergreen foliage and berries, a tree cotoneaster, such as *C. salicifolius* 'Pendulus'.

Select a tree for your garden with care. Planting a large tree in a small garden will lead to problems in years to come. The tree will dominate the garden and put it in shade. So, unless you have a large garden, avoid big ornamentals, such as

The trees provide this border with a vertical dimension needing little work. They include *Catalpa bignonioides* 'Aurea' and columnar *Juniperus chinensis* 'Stricta'.

Avoiding problems

Restricting root spread If tree roots are a potential problem, restrict their growth by using thick polythene or a polypropylene membrane, which can be trenched into the soil to act as a physical barrier and will prevent the roots growing where they are not wanted. New pipes and drains can also be wrapped in the material to prevent roots seeking moisture from them.

Trees near paving Trees planted in areas that are paved or covered in tarmac can cause the surface to lift with time. To combat this, use a membrane (polypropylene or thick polythene) to line the sides of the hole at planting time in order to encourage the roots to grow down, and not along the surface.

cedars, tulip tree (*Liriodendron tulipifera*) or *Prunus* 'Kanzan', and woodland trees, such as oak, beech and horse-chestnut, because they will all eventually grow to at least 20 m (66 ft).

Some trees can be kept smaller by regular lopping and pruning, but this is time consuming and the tree will lose its natural shape. Often it is better to remove the tree and start again with a more suitable, ornamental variety.

When planting a tree, you will also have to make sure that the roots cause no structural damage to nearby buildings, drains and foundations – and remember that planting on a boundary may not affect your property, but it could affect a neighbour's. As a rough guide, do not plant a tree closer to the house than its ultimate height because the roots will grow out to at least the same as the spread of the branches. And avoid water-seeking trees, such as willows and poplars, especially on clay soils, which shrink when they dry out.

Like other plants, it is important to choose the right tree for the situation. Consider whether it has any special soil requirements – acid or alkaline, for example – and the amount of maintenance needed, if any. If choosing several trees, go for a selection that will provide interest all year.

Cotinus coggygria is normally grown as a shrub, but it can also makes a good small tree when grown on a single stem, providing interest from spring to autumn.

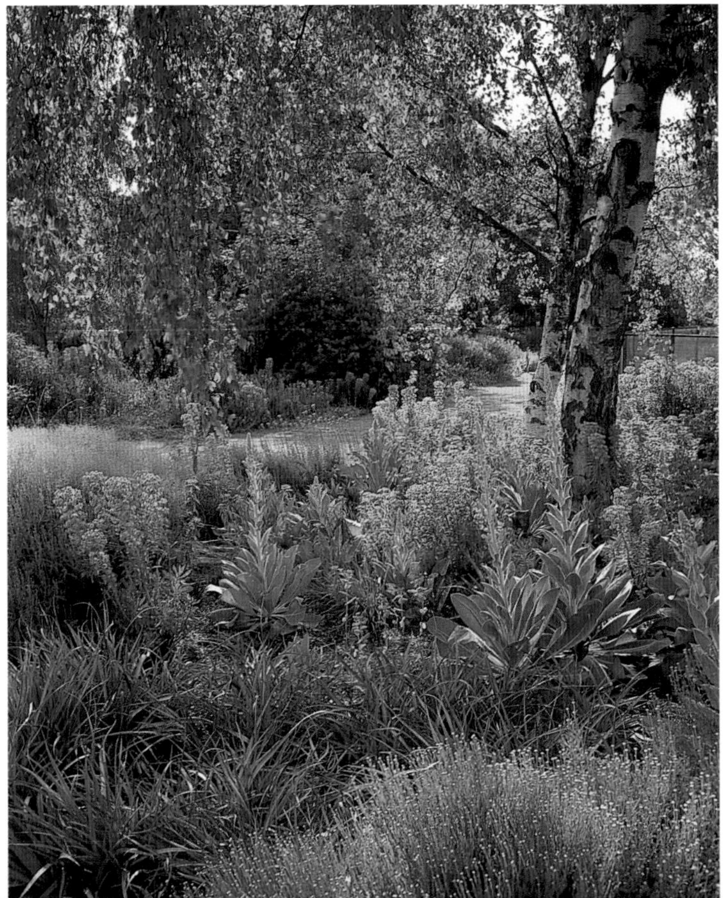

In a small garden *(left)*, avoid trees that cast too much shade. Verbascum, santolina and euphorbia are all thriving under the open canopy of a silver birch.

TREES WITH GREAT BARK

The following trees are trouble-free and have attractive bark, adding colour when most needed – in winter.

Acer capillipes
Acer davidii
Acer griseum
Acer pensylvanicum
Betula utilis* var. *jacquemontii
***Betula nigra* 'Heritage'**
Eucalyptus dalrympleana
Prunus serrula
Stewartia pseudocamellia

Trees for small gardens

The first rule in choosing a tree for a small garden is to check its ultimate size – a small tree bought today could eventually turn into a 30 m (100 ft) giant, blocking out all sun and making it difficult to enjoy your garden let alone to grow an interesting choice of plants. A small garden also means growing fewer plants because only limited space is available, so the plants chosen need to work harder to give you as much all-year seasonal interest as possible in terms of foliage, flowers, berries or fruit, and bark.

For a long season of interest, consider an ornamental tree, such as the thorn *Crataegus persimilis* 'Prunifolia', which produces white flowers in early summer followed by dark red berries, as well as orange and scarlet tints in autumn; or a sorbus, such as *Sorbus cashmiriana*, with pink-flushed white flowers in summer, followed by large white berries in autumn, which are usually the last to be eaten by the birds.

To provide your garden with a consistent, all-year backbone, you will need to use evergreen trees, such as a small-sized conifer or *Cotoneaster* x *watereri* 'John Waterer'. For architectural features, consider a fig tree (*Ficus* 'Brown Turkey') or Korean fir (*Abies koreana*), a conical conifer with striking, violet-blue cones.

Particular shapes of trees are also more suited to the small garden than others. Weeping trees make good focal points and grow not

Robinia pseudoacacia 'Frisia' may be a tall tree, but its fine foliage and narrow shape allows through plenty of light.

TREES CHOSEN FOR THEIR SIZE

Choose the right tree and it will give you decades of pleasure. The following are trouble-free varieties that offer more than one season's interest.

1 ***Prunus* 'Accolade'** Deciduous, semi-double pale pink blossom in early spring.
2 ***Acer pseudoplatanus* 'Brilliantissimum'** Deciduous, salmon-pink leaves in spring turning to yellow-green.
3 ***Cotoneaster* x *watereri* 'John Waterer'** Dark green evergreen or semi-evergreen foliage. White flowers in early summer and red berries in autumn.
4 ***Pyrus salicifolia* 'Pendula'**. Deciduous, white flowers in spring, silver-grey leaves.
5 ***Arbutus unedo*** Evergreen, white flowers and red strawberry-like fruits in autumn. Cinnamon coloured bark.
6 ***Crataegus laevigata* 'Paul's Scarlet'**. Deciduous, with double red blossom in spring.
7 ***Amelanchier canadensis*** Deciduous, star-shaped white flowers in spring. Orange-red autumn tints.
8 ***Malus* 'Royalty'** Deciduous, crimson-purple blossom in spring and purple foliage. Dark red crab apples in autumn.

much higher than the trunk on which they are grafted. For a very small area, *Salix caprea* 'Kilmarnock', grows to about 1.5 m (5 ft), with a similar spread. For a larger weeping tree, try *Betula pendula* 'Youngii' or a weeping cherry. To avoid mowing underneath, surround them in gravel planted with spring bulbs or low ground-cover plants (see page 268). You can also cut an entrance through the branches to create a living arbour. The compact shape of upright trees, such as *Pyrus calleryana* 'Chanticleer' or the fastigiate *Prunus* 'Amanogawa', also make them an ideal candidate for a small garden.

Many trees may ultimately grow big, but can be coppiced – cut to near ground level – to keep them small or shrub-like. Larger and more eye-catching foliage compensates for lopping off flowering shoots. Trees you can treat this way include the golden-leaved Indian bean tree (*Catalpa bignonioides* 'Aurea'), tree of heaven (*Ailanthus altissima*) and the more tender foxglove tree (*Paulownia tomentosa*). Let them establish for a few years first, and then cut down to ground level every year or two in early or mid spring once the main frosts are over. Alternatively, cut to a 60-90 cm (24-36 in) 'leg' every three or four years. Other, hardier trees to coppice for more pronounced foliage, include *Acer negundo* 'Flamingo' (for pink-edged leaves), *Robinia pseudoacacia* 'Frisia' (yellow foliage), *Liquidambar styraciflua* 'Variegata' (variegation) and eucalyptus (young, round leaves).

Time saver

To save time waiting for trees to grow, plant a few semi-mature specimens in with the smaller ones to give an instant effect. Use the larger trees in prominent positions or as the focal point in a collection.

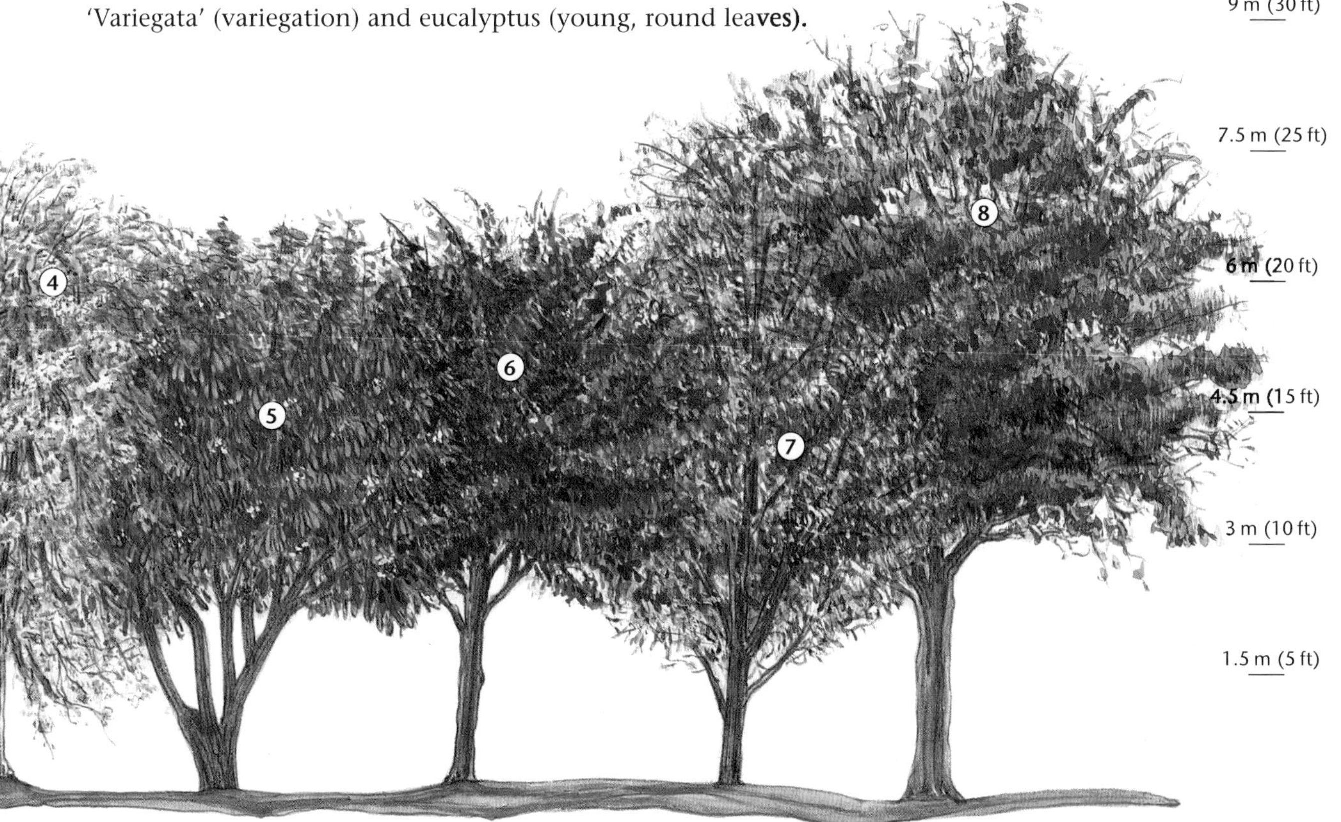

TREES FOR A SMALL WOODLAND GARDEN

Choose native trees that offer more than one season's worth of interest to create a natural-looking woodland. A few ornamentals, though, including Acer griseum, *can be added to create colourful focus points.*

Mountain ash (*Sorbus aucuparia*) Attractive pinnate foliage, cream flowers in late spring, and red berries and coppery foliage in autumn. Grows to 5x2 m (16x6½ ft) after 20 years. Finally to 12 m (40 ft).

Hazelnut (*Corylus avellana*) Multi-stemmed shrub or small tree. Coppice for new growth. Catkins, hazelnuts, autumn colour. Also, yellow and purple-leaved varieties. After 5 years, 3x2.4 m (10x8 ft).

Paper-bark maple (*Acer griseum*) Cinnamon-coloured, peeling bark. Leaves turn brilliant red in autumn. Needs sheltered site with protection from midday sun. After 20 years, 5x2 m (16x6½ ft).

Bird cherry (*Prunus padus*) Fragrant white spring blossoms followed by black cherries and yellow autumn foliage. 'Watereri' (pictured) has 20 cm (8 in) slender racemes of flowers. Final height of 9 m (30 ft).

Silver birches are good for woodland gardens of any size. They are trouble-free and provide only light shade, enabling other plants to grow underneath.

Woodland trees for smaller gardens A woodland garden does not have to cover acres of ground; it can even be part of a small garden. But it is best positioned away from the house so that the trees – their roots and the shade that they cast – do not interfere with the house.

To create a woodland effect from scratch, plant a group of three or five small trees, such as *Sorbus aucuparia*, about 3 m (10 ft) apart, while silver birch (*Betula pendula*) is best planted even closer for greatest effect, at a maximum 1.8 m (6 ft), because they have a light canopy. In gardens where trees already exist, you can easily add to them to create a woodland garden, but any new trees must be able to cope with dappled shade.

Keep plantings of ornamental trees to just a couple; they may give you more colour, and link in better with the rest of the garden and the surrounding area, but if they tip the balance towards ornamentals rather than natives, your woodland will start to look unnatural. Whichever trees you choose, it is the underplanting that gives the natural woodland feel. Leave enough dappled shade to create sweeps and pockets of spring and autumn bulbs, ground-cover foliage and the climbing growth of wild roses, clematis and honeysuckle. Use the canopy of an existing mature tree as a quick way to create a woodland scene. Choose a spreading, deciduous tree, such as an old fruit tree, either in your garden or overhanging from a neighbouring one. If there is lawn under the canopy, let the grass grow longer and plant groups of bulbs, perennials and wild flowers. If there is a bed, replace formal plants with the likes of anemone, crocus, cyclamen, hellebore and foxglove. Use natural bark chippings as a mulch.

Trees for containers If you don't have the space for a woodland, trees can also be planted in pots. The simplest method is to use the tree as a single plant, such as a clipped laurel outside the front door or on the patio. Or, it can be part of a larger scheme, linking in to plants behind or around the container, or in the same pot. For ease of care, it is best to go for trees with shallow roots, junipers and pines are best.

You will need to repot your tree every three to five years. To see if the tree is pot-bound, look out for roots growing through drainage holes, quick-drying compost or unusually slow growth. If you want to keep your tree at a certain size for a bonsai effect, or in a certain container, remove your pot-bound plant from its pot during the dormant season. Tease out some old compost from the rootball with a hand-fork and trim the root tips by no more than a quarter, then repot.

Quick results

Create an instant woodland in miniature using a multi-stemmed tree, which has several small trunks instead of a single large one. Many have colourful winter bark. Trees that can be grown in such a way include birches (*Betula pendula* and *B. utilis* 'Jacquemontii'), snake-bark maples (*Acer capillipes* and *A. pensylvanicum*), eucalyptus and *Prunus sargentii*.

PATIO TREES

By growing trees in pots you can try types that would not normally thrive in your garden or would grow too big if grown in the border soil.

1 *Acer palmatum* 'Bloodgood' Needs non-alkaline soil. Leaves turn bright red in autumn. Here, it is underplanted with the ivy *Hedera helix* 'Glacier'.
2 *Eucalyptus gunnii* One of the hardiest eucalyptus. Its vigorous growth can be cut back hard in early spring. Here, it is with *Euonymous fortunei* 'Silver Queen'.
3 *Pinus mugo* 'Gnom' A naturally dwarf variety of pine with shallow, fibrous roots. Here with *Acaena saccaticupula* 'Blue Haze'.

Flowers and Foliage

CHOOSE TROUBLE-FREE ANNUALS, PERENNIALS AND BULBS TO PROVIDE A COLOURFUL INFILL BETWEEN STRUCTURAL PLANTS AND TO GIVE SEASONAL VARIETY TO BORDERS THROUGH THE YEAR

Seasonal flowers and foliage can provide a tapestry of vibrant colours and scents that changes as the year rolls by. Select easy-care annuals, perennials and bulbs that combine to provide a seamless continuity of colour through the seasons. To keep the workload light, the secret is to grow them in a site for which they are suited, otherwise they will become vulnerable to pests and diseases.

Choose plants carefully; almost every plant family has good and bad members. For instance, for an early summer display from the pea family, plant the white or blue-flowered wild indigo (baptisia) or yellow or purple-flowered thermopsis instead of lupin, which is prone to aphids. Most Michaelmas daisies (*Aster novi-belgii*) are plagued by powdery mildew, but varieties of *Aster amellus* and *A.* x *frikartii* are practically trouble free. Some plants are more work because they are short-lived. For example, if planting scabious, the newer *Scabiosa* 'Butterfly Blue' or 'Pink Mist' need frequent replacing, which takes time, so select longer-living older varieties, such as 'Clive Greaves' or 'Miss Willmott'.

1 ALL-YEAR INTEREST – *evergreen ornamental grasses add year-round texture and interest.*

2 DROUGHT-RESISTANT – *day lilies, red-hot poker and penstemon (hardy in mild areas).*

3 RELIABLE PERFORMERS – *globe thistle is tough and long lived so it will flower for many years.*

4 EASY CARE – *plants in this selection do not need supporting and are naturally disease free.*

Easy-care borders Combine trouble-free perennials such as day lily, globe thistle, penstemon and ornamental grasses. Once established, this bed will need only a few minutes' maintenance each week – mainly deadheading.

EASY-CARE CALENDAR

EARLY SPRING
Remove any weeds and sprinkle a general fertiliser, such as balanced blood, fish and bone, around plants and mulch with a 2.5-5 cm (1-2 in) layer of bark chippings or well-rotted compost.

LATE SPRING
Plant dahlia tubers. Remove rogue weeds. Leave the foliage of spring bulbs; it will be quickly hidden by the fast growing new foliage of perennials. Clump-forming perennials, such as alchemilla, day lily, globe thistle, helenium, hosta and red-hot poker, cover the ground by early summer, smothering out annual weeds for the rest of the season.

SUMMER
Deadhead fading flowers.

AUTUMN
Cut back perennials as the foliage starts to wither. Leave plants with decorative seed heads, such as globe thistle, for winter decoration. In a mild region, dahlias can be left in the ground if the soil is well drained and they are covered by a 5 cm (2 in) layer of bark chippings for insulation. Elsewhere, dig them up, dry off the tubers and store in a frost-free place to replant the following spring.

STARTING FROM SCRATCH

With a planting plan to work to, this mixed border of flowers and foliage *(left)* could be planted in about half a day. Dig over the ground thoroughly and mix in well-rotted organic matter and add a slow-release fertiliser. Group plants in odd numbers to create the best effect. Water well and mulch after planting. Keep the plants watered until they are established.

Foliage and flowers are combined to dramatic effect *(above)* in this low-maintenance border. Pink-flowered rodgersia with its crinkled green leaves contrast with the silver artemisia and purple berberis in the foreground and the spiky silver-leaved cardoon behind.

An easy-care mixed border overflowing with colour *(above, right)*, includes pink *Geranium endressii* in the foreground with globes of purple allium. Behind, purple salvia and lime-green alchemilla contrast well with the silver foliage of artemisia. Sugar-pink linaria completes the scene.

A patchwork of colour in the mixed border

The easiest way to achieve an attractive, continuous display is to create a mixed flower border. You can plant a whole range of flowering perennials, bulbs and annuals around a framework of shrubs, roses and small ornamental trees. The different kinds of plants will help to support each other visually, making a rich patchwork of colour and texture. To keep the workload to a minimum, choose long-lived, hardy perennials and bulbs that will perform reliably year after year. Also, suppress weeds by mulching (see page 264) and by close planting. To top up the flowering display, add annuals, biennials and tender perennials, but only as many as you have time for.

A huge selection of perennials exists from which to choose, but some need more work than others (see page 117). They can be used to create a multitude of effects – and all without much bother. Plant tall and mound-forming perennials between shrubs to create more seasonal interest. Use low-growing perennials, such as ajuga, London pride (*Saxifraga* x *urbium*) and heuchera, as ground cover or near the

front of the border, where they will make a low-maintenance alternative to annual bedding. To extend the season of interest of herbaceous perennials, underplant deciduous shrubs in autumn with dwarf spring bulbs, such as snowdrops, crocuses and scillas, and daffodils, hyacinths and tulips. While a dense carpet of permanent, naturalised bulbs will serve to smother weeds. Autumn is also the best time of year to plant biennials, such as polyanthus, sweet william and wallflowers, for spring and early summer blooms. Others, such as forget-me-nots, honesty and foxgloves, will self-seed prolifically, so you won't have to buy new plants, only remove unwanted seedlings.

Fill gaps in borders with trouble-free bedding plants that will flower all summer and into autumn without being deadheaded (see page 138). Many hardy annuals, such as love-in-a-mist (nigella), pot marigold and nasturtium, are easy to grow from seed sown direct in the ground. They are quick to flower and make useful gap fillers.

One or two tender perennials, such as bidens, marguerite daisies and pelargoniums, can be a valuable asset to a mixed border. They are free-flowering over a long period and reasonably drought tolerant. In a hot, dry summer they often outperform traditional bedding plants. But do not plant too many because they are not hardy and have to be planted out each year afresh.

Problem solver

Instant colour More and more plants are available from garden centres in flower. If bought in bud, potted bulbs, such as dwarf daffodils, crocuses, hyacinths and tulips, allow you to instantly transform an otherwise dull border into a colourful, early spring centrepiece. This is particularly useful for adding colour to prominent beds near to the house.

Combining flowers and foliage

Perennials are much less work than annual bedding plants: even if they do not bloom for as long, their foliage can provide a textured background for growing other plants, and they do not need replacing every year. Most of them tolerate a range of conditions, but it is still safer to grow those that are suitable for the spot that you have in mind. As a general rule, lush large-leaved plants will not tolerate a hot, dry position, and grey or silver-leaved plants, especially those with finely cut foliage, will not thrive in shade or heavy, waterlogged soil.

Luckily, there are perennials to suit every situation. For an easy-care border, choose trouble-free varieties that can be left largely to their own devices once planted. Most herbaceous perennials will need dividing every three to five years, depending on the growing conditions, or even more frequently in the case of golden rod (solidago), unless they have room to spread. For a low-labour border, choose plants that can be left for years undisturbed, such as agapanthus, hostas and peonies. If you want a tall perennial to fill a gap in a border, either make sure it doesn't need staking (see page 127) or increase the planting density so that the plants support each other.

Leaves last far longer than blooms, so select plants that have attractive foliage as well as flowers. Some are striped, marbled or speckled, while others range from purple, silver and blue, to butter-yellow or

A mixed border of plants for flowers and foliage is easier to plan than one for just flowers *(above)*. Aim to include plants with contrasting forms, colours and texture.

To reduce the workload, grow together plants with similar needs. In this dry border *(left)*, the pairing of the mauve perennial wallflower *Erysimum* 'Bowles' Mauve' with the acid-green *Euphorbia polychroma* will require little attention once established.

PERMANENT EDGING

Some perennials make excellent permanent edging. Choose neat, compact plants with attractive evergreen foliage or a long-flowering period.

Alchemilla mollis
***Bergenia cordifolia* 'Purpurea'**
Geranium* x *oxonianum
***Heuchera micrantha* var. *diversifolia* 'Palace Purple'**
Liriope muscari
Saxifraga* x *urbium
***Ophiopogon planiscapus* 'Nigrescens'**

Perfect combinations

Do blend foliage plants with flowering ones to keep the border looking at its best over the longest possible time.

Do combine foliage and flowers that contrast with each other in colour, shape and texture.

Do use plants with ornamental seedpods, such as agapanthus, feathery grass heads, such as pampas grass (*Cortaderia selloana*), and evergreen foliage (see list, right).

Do use plants with variegated leaves, such as striped, blotched and marbled, to their full advantage.

Do choose flowering plants that have attractive foliage, such as *Alchemilla mollis* and geranium (cranesbill) so that they add interest to the border over several months.

lime-green. Geranium (cranesbill) and succulent-leaved sedum are good examples, while several perennials, including hostas and lamium, are grown mainly for their leaves.

To create a soft, billowing effect, use plants with feathery foliage, such as bronze fennel, or those with masses of leaflets, such as aquilegia and many of the ferns. Ornamental grasses can also be used to soften displays; many are particularly useful because they are drought tolerant. For instance, blue grasses, such as *Festuca glauca* and *F. valesiaca* 'Silbersee', form dense spiky tufts and are excellent edging plants. On the other hand, the more lax habit of *Helictotrichon sempervirens,* with its attractive arching flower stems, or the purple-tinged *Molinia caerulea* look good almost anywhere. Light up a shady corner with the yellow-striped sedge *Carex oshimensis* 'Evergold'.

The foliage of some perennials is dramatic and sculptural. For example, *Acanthus spinosus* throws up bold, jagged leaves up to 60 cm (24 in) long and is ideal for growing as a specimen or in the middle of a border. It also has spectacular flowers. In a damp spot, *Rodgersia aesculifolia* looks effective – it has large spiky bronze-tinged leaves up to 30 cm (12 in) across. Some perennials are evergreen, so they will provide foliage interest throughout the year; for example, *Bergenia cordifolia* 'Purpurea' has rounded, dark green leaves that turn an attractive shade of red in winter.

CAREFREE PERENNIALS

There is a huge range of perennials available. Use the following lists of trouble-free types to help you choose plants that suit your tastes and the conditions offered by your garden.

Long flowering
Acanthus, achillea (pictured), Japanese anemone, astrantia, centranthus, coreopsis, dicentra, erysimum, linaria, lythrum, malva, nepeta, rudbeckia, scabiosa, sedum.

Drought resistant
Alchemilla, armeria, artemisia, bergenia, echinacea, eryngium, gaillardia, geranium (cranesbill), heliopsis, penstemon (pictured), sedum, verbascum, waldsteinia.

Evergreen Ajuga, bergenia, carex, dianthus, euphorbia, fargesia, festuca, hellebore (pictured), heuchera, kniphofia, liriope, morina, ophiopogon, *Sisyrinchium striatum.*

Windy gardens
Alchemilla, *Anthemis cupaniana,* Japanese anemone, aquilegia, astrantia, centranthus (pictured), cerastium, geranium (cranesbill), euphorbia, lychnis, persicaria, stachys.

Seaside gardens
Achillea, agapanthus, armeria (pictured), aruncus, bergenia, centaurea, crocosmia, erigeron, gaillardia, geum, heuchera, kniphofia, nepeta, oenothera.

Adding colour with hardy bulbs

Hardy bulbs can usually be left in the ground to naturalise, flowering year after year, and needing little maintenance. Cultivars and species are available to create a splash of colour in a variety of situations – from sunny rock gardens to wild areas under trees. Bulbs that flower in the second half of summer, such as lilies, make good fillers for gaps left by faded early flowering perennials; taller lilies may need staking, but not the smaller, self-supporting hybrids, such as orange-flowered 'Enchantment'. And bulbs with decorative seed heads, such as alliums, don't need deadheading.

For planting in a mixed border, dwarf daffodil varieties, such as 'Tête-à-tête', 'Jack Snipe' and 'Jenny', are a good easy-care choice. Their foliage is much shorter than normal-sized daffodils and dies away unobtrusively after flowering. They are also relatively weather-resistant. The best tulips for permanent planting are early flowering, dwarf varieties, such as 'Red Riding Hood' and 'Heart's Delight'. Tulips do best in soil with good winter drainage (see page 20).

Buying To get the best choice and quality, buy bulbs as soon as they become available. If you are using a mail-order catalogue, order spring-flowering bulbs from August. The largest bulbs tend to flower well in the first year. With the exception of tulips and hyacinths, which are liable to rot if they are planted earlier than late October, plant the bulbs as soon as they arrive. If you have to store bulbs, unpack them and keep them in a cool, dark place for as short a time as possible, in order to prevent dehydration. If you

DEPTH GUIDE FOR BULBS

Fork over the soil and dig a hole deep enough for the bulbs. Make the hole wide enough to take a cluster of bulbs of the same variety, but make sure they don't touch. Fork over the base so that the roots can penetrate the soil easily. Very small bulbs need to be planted in large numbers (20 or 30) to give a good display in the first year.

1 *Chionodoxa luciliae*
2 *Crocus vernus*
3 *Cyclamen coum*
4 Snowdrop
5 Hyacinth
6 *Muscari armeniacum*
7 Dwarf daffodil
8 Siberian squill *(Scilla siberica)*
9 Dwarf tulip
10 *Lilium* 'Enchantment'

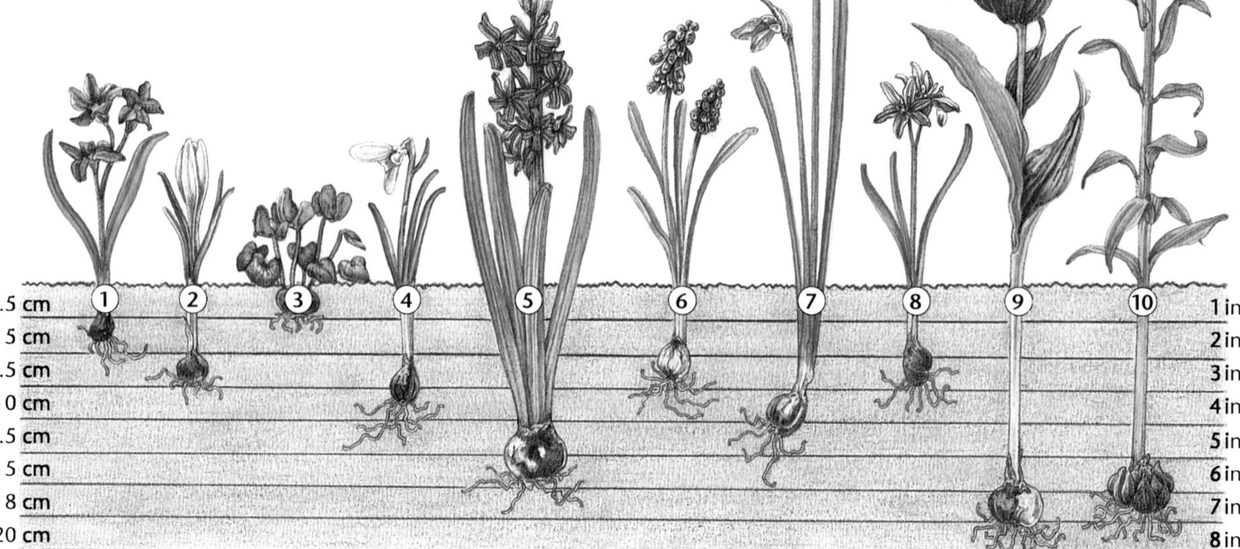

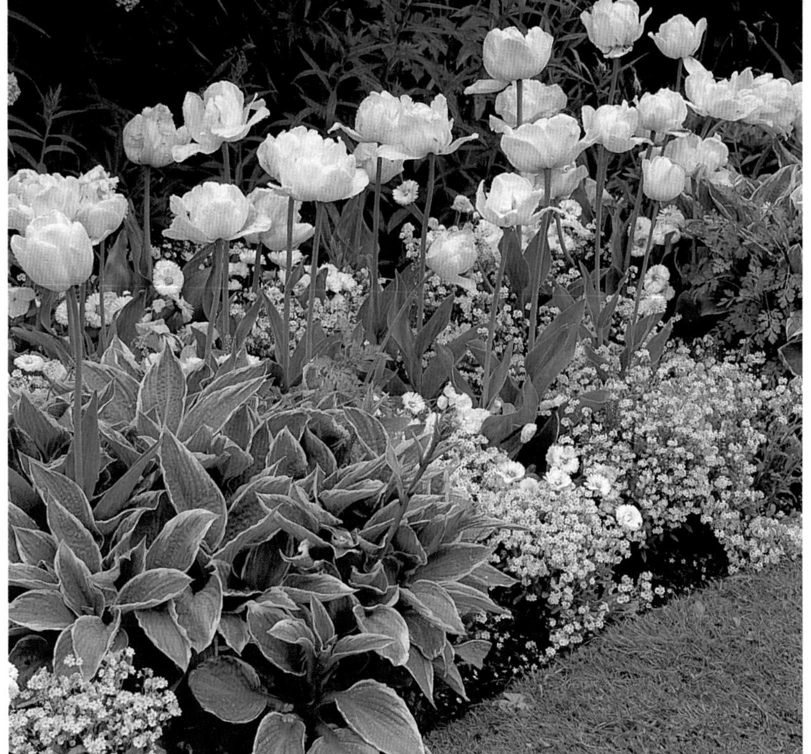

A cool planting scheme of white tulips grows through a ground cover of forget-me-nots and double daisies (*Bellis perennis*), with white-edged hostas providing foliage contrast.

buy from a garden centre, select large, firm bulbs and avoid any that show signs of mould or deterioration. If you miss out on buying dry bulbs in autumn, you can buy pot-grown bulbs in spring from garden centres. They are usually already in bud, so it is easy to imagine what they will look like in your garden. Before planting them, stand them in various places around the garden until you find the right spot.

Planting Hardy bulbs left in the ground undisturbed are planted only once, so they need to be planted properly; use the chart (opposite) as a guide. In soil which does not drain freely, plant tulips and fritillaries on a shallow bed of sand to improve drainage. Crown imperials (*Fritillaria imperialis*) should be planted on their sides to prevent water filling the core and causing the bulbs to rot.

Bulbs planted in a lawn or an area of rough grass give an attractive early spring display year after year. Scatter the bulbs and plant them where they fall using a bulb planter or trowel. Alternatively, lift sections of turf and put the bulbs in place, and then replace the turf. Wait until about six weeks after flowering before mowing the grass so that the bulbs' reserves have time to build up ready for the next year, and do not tie up the dying daffodil leaves to make them look tidy.

Divide colonies of snowdrops just after flowering and replant small clusters in other areas. The colonies soon build up again. Snowdrops sold 'in the green' are easier to establish than bulbs sold 'dry'.

EASY-CARE BULBS

Hardy bulbs offer a bright splash of colour when much of the garden is looking dull. The following varieties are easy to grow and can be left undisturbed to spread and form large clumps.

Anemone blanda Starry white, pink, blue or purple flowers are borne February to April. Reaches 10 cm (4 in). Likes a hot, dry site, but will grow in light dry shade under trees and shrubs.

Dwarf narcissi Spring flowers on plants up to 30 cm (12 in) tall. Happy in sun or light shade. Prefers soil that retains moisture. Hybrids include 'Tête-à-tête' and 'Jumblie'.

Snowdrop Blooms on 15 cm (6 in) stems in February. Prefers moist soil and light shade. Leave undisturbed to form clumps. Good hybrids include *Galanthus* 'Atkinsii' and 'S. Arnott'.

Crocus Dutch hybrids fill the flowering gap between snowdrops and tulips, blooming from mid January to mid April depending on the variety. They will grow in most soils in a sunny position.

Kaufmanniana tulips (water-lily tulip) Dwarf varieties on 20-35 cm (8-14 in) stems in March and April. They need sun, and well-drained soil that remains fairly dry in summer.

The right plant for the problem place

Every garden has at least one problem site where most plants will struggle to survive. To create low-maintenance displays in such sites, you will need plants that are specially adapted to that particular condition. Fortunately, many flowers thrive in extreme conditions: there are those that enjoy a hot, dry spot at the base of a sunny wall; others a cool, shady area under a tree; and a few even thrive in deep shade which has no direct sun at all.

It is essential to choose plants with care, so that they are suited to the conditions in your garden. As a general rule, those perennials and biennials that flower before the end of June tolerate shade, while those flowering later need sun and moisture in order to flourish. Drought-tolerant plants – those with silver or grey leaves – and succulent plants with waxy leaves need full sun and good drainage. Most drought-tolerant plants do well in seaside gardens, even in exposed sites. In windswept gardens, avoid plants with large, soft foliage because it will scorch and shred. (See page 117 for lists of care-free perennials for dry, exposed and seaside gardens.)

FLOWERS AND FOLIAGE FOR BOGGY SOIL

Cold, wet soil conditions in boggy areas cause plant losses in winter. The following plants thrive in such conditions.

Aruncus
Astilbe
Caltha
Cimicifuga
Filipendula
Gunnera
Ligularia
Primula
Rodgersia
Trollius

Drought-tolerant *Artemisia ludoviciana* 'Silver Queen' and *Rosa rugosa* 'Alba' combine to provide the perfect partners for the dark purple iris flowers *(above)*.

In this shady border, Spanish bluebells (*Hyacinthoides hispanica*), *Iris foetidissima*, hostas, hellebores and ferns cover the ground, smothering weeds.

Brightening up shady borders

It is not difficult to find plants that will grow in shade. Indeed, many of the most attractive garden plants prefer a slightly shady situation. For flowering plants to thrive, you will need to assess the depth of shade and the type of soil (see page 20). Plants that grow well in shade can be broadly divided into those that need moist soil and those that prefer drier conditions at their roots. Use the plant selector (right) to choose suitable candidates for your garden. It is also worth adding light-reflecting features such as white pebbles, pale-coloured paving or even a fountain to give sparkling light.

Adding colour Use pale yellow and white-flowered plants to lighten up the shade. As gap fillers between shrubs, choose tobacco plants (nicotiana), which throw up dainty stems of evening-scented blooms from May to October. Another option is sweet rocket (*Hesperis matronalis*), which produces long stems up to 1.2 m (4 ft) tall and stock-like blooms in shades of white through to lilac; it is sweetly fragrant, especially in the evening. To brighten up the front of a border, try one of the silver-leaved lamiums such as *Lamium maculatum* 'White Nancy', or the white-flowered viola, *Viola cornuta* 'Alba'.

Creating a new border When planting a shady border from scratch, first develop a backbone of foliage plants. Choose a combination of shrubs and perennials, including a few evergreens for year-round interest. Some foliage plants, such as *Aruncus dioicus* and *Rodgersia pinnata*, have lush foliage that gives a tropical feel to the border and provides a useful backdrop to show off other seasonal plantings. Many shrubs with variegated foliage, such as spotted laurel (*Aucuba japonica*), *Euonymus fortunei* and *Cornus alba* 'Spaethii' are ideal for shade because they add much-needed colour, and the more subdued light is better for showing off their markings. To cover the ground and suppress weeds, choose hosta, pulmonaria, variegated periwinkle (*Vinca major* 'Variegata') or for large areas, the vigorous variegated ground elder (*Aegopodium podagraria* 'Variegatum').

Improve the soil in a shady border before planting. If the soil is dry, dig a barrowload of well-rotted organic matter into every square metre before planting, water well and mulch after planting. If it tends to become waterlogged, incorporate a bucketful of horticultural grit at the same time as the organic matter to improve drainage. Slugs thrive in damp shady conditions, and can prove a problem with herbaceous foliage plants, especially hosta, ligularia, primula and rodgersia. If so, grow slug-proof alternatives, such as *Alchemilla mollis*, Japanese anemone, geranium (cranesbill) and pulmonaria.

FLOWERS FOR SHADE

Some flowers are well adapted to growing in shade, but fussy about the soil conditions. So make sure you know whether your soil is moist, waterlogged or dry before choosing your flowers.

Perennials for light shade, moist soil
Aruncus dioicus, dicentra, *Primula denticulata*, *P. vulgaris*, *Rodgersia pinnata*, *Smilacina racemosa* (pictured), *Thalictrum delavayi*, tiarella.

Perennials for light shade, dry soil
Ajuga, *Euphorbia amygdaloides* var. *robbiae*, *Geranium macrorrhizum*, hellebore, heuchera, hosta, lamium, pulmonaria (pictured).

Perennials for light shade, wet soil
Astilbe x *arendsii*, *Persicaria affinis* 'Superba', *Trollius* x *cultorum*, viola (pictured), *Zantedeschia aethiopica*.

Bulbs for shade
Allium moly, *Arum italicum*, *Corydalis flexuosa*, *Cyclamen coum* (pictured) and *C. hederifolium*, daffodils, *Eranthis hyemalis*, erythronium, galanthus (snowdrop).

Bedding for shade
Begonia semperflorens, digitalis (foxglove), impatiens, lobelia, lunaria (honesty), mimulus, myosotis (forget-me-not), nicotiana, primula (pictured), viola.

Providing colour in hot spots

The silver and grey-leaved flowering and foliage plants, and the blue-leaved ornamental grasses, such as fescues and blue oat grass (*Helictotrichon sempervirens*), relish free-draining soil and full sun. These generally trouble-free, easy-care plants often have finely cut, lacy foliage (artemisias and *Senecio cineraria*, for example) or very narrow leaves (such as dianthus). But do make sure they are sheltered from cold winter winds.

Alpine plants do not have to be confined to a rock garden. For the front of a well-drained, sunny border, choose drought-resistant kinds such as thrift (*Armeria maritima*), the aromatic *Phuopsis stylosa* or *Saxifraga burseriana*. Other drought-tolerant plants for hot, dry areas include aromatic herbs, such as thyme, origanum, camomile and sage, and succulents, including sedum and sempervivum. Plants with a waxy coating, such as bearded iris and sea holly (eryngium), also perform well in dry conditions.

For a Mediterranean feel to an area surrounding a sheltered patio or a gravel drive, combine drought-resistant plants with specimen shrubs that have strong, sculptural shapes, such as the sword-shaped leaves of yucca or phormium, or large perennials such as *Acanthus spinosus* and *Euphorbia characias* ssp. *wulfenii*.

DROUGHT-TOLERANT BEDDING

The following plants recover quickly after running short of water.

Arctotis
Argyranthemum
Begonia semperflorens
Bidens
Dorotheanthus bellidiformis
***Eschscholzia* (California poppy)**
Felicia
Gazania
Nasturtium
Osteospermum
Pelargonium
Portulaca grandiflora
Salvia farinacea

This Mediterranean-style planting scheme includes agave, cacti and phormium, making an easy-care feature out of a hot spot. Grow not-so-hardy subjects in pots so they can be taken in for the winter.

Colours and scents of the Mediterranean

Dan and Kath James are teachers. They are very busy during term-time, so they do most of their gardening during the holidays. They spend a lot of time in their garden in summer, when they like to eat outside. They do not have any children or pets.

Their south-facing garden is a hot spot, and is ideal for growing Mediterranean-type plants; the area has relatively low rainfall and is sheltered from the wind, and the soil is a thin sandy loam with stones and gravel, giving good drainage. Dan and Kath like to entertain in the garden, which is set below the level of the house. Kath wanted to include scented plants near the patio, and to have plenty of colour throughout the summer. They have an uninterrupted view of the garden from their living room so they want attractive displays through the year.

THE OLD GARDEN It was largely laid down to lawn with narrow borders and a small patio by the house.

DECIDING THEIR PRIORITIES

How much time?
Irregular – 2 hours a week during term-time, more in the holidays.

Essential ingredients?
Somewhere pleasant to sit and enjoy the colour and scent in summer. Plus, garden lighting and a water feature.

Likes and dislikes?
Although time-consuming, they like growing plants in containers, especially scented varieties. They dislike cutting the lawn.

THE NEW GARDEN

The lawn was replaced by a range of easy-care paving materials. Summer-flowering plants predominate, many of them scented.

Paving *A combination of slabs, brick pavers, gravel and pebbles make an attractive, all-weather surface that is practically maintenance free.*

Added privacy *Coloured trellis clothed in scented climbers such as common jasmine increases the sense of privacy.*

Mediterranean atmosphere *On the patio, pots of night-scented stocks, lavender and herbs add delicate fragrance to the air, while the spiky leaves of phormium and yucca provide foliage contrast.*

Summer colour *Flowering shrubs such as ceanothus, hebe and* Genista aetensis *are at their peak in summer. Window boxes filled with geraniums add colour and help to frame the view from the living-room window.*

Water feature *A classical urn gently pours water over heaped pebbles, creating a soothing gurgling sound and adds the finishing touch to a Mediterranean garden.*

Making light work of routine care

If the soil in a flower border is well prepared before planting, then the plants will grow strongly and largely look after themselves. They will establish more quickly and need less attention afterwards. The main tasks of watering and weeding can be kept to a minimum by applying a thick mulch after planting and topping it up each spring when the soil is moist. Other routine tasks, such as feeding, staking, deadheading and tidying, can be done little by little when you have the odd half-hour to spare. However, it is important not to let tasks slip, or they will create more work in the long run.

Close planting of flowering perennials (pink penstemon), foliage (yellow pampas grass) and bulbs (blue agapanthus) smothers out weeds.

No more weeds For an easy-care garden, it is vital that the ground is free from weeds (see page 270). Bare soil encourages weeds, so either use a mulch, such as bark chippings or cocoa shells (see page 264), or cover the ground with plants (see page 268), or use a combination of both. Hoe shallowly areas not mulched or covered with plants to stop germinating weed seedlings becoming established: it is more time-efficient to prevent weeds from growing than to pull them out later.

If perennial weeds have become established in and around plants, apply a systemic weedkiller based on glyphosate to individual weeds, but make sure that none drips onto the plants that you wish to keep.

LABOUR-SAVING PERENNIALS

Flowering borders can be colourful and attractive all year without the need for constant preening. Select from the following plants to fill a gap in an existing border or to create a low-maintenance combination for your garden.

1 ***Centranthus ruber***
2 ***Ajuga reptans* 'Atropurpurea'**
3 ***Hemerocallis* 'Bonanza'**
4 ***Geranium* x *oxonianum* 'Thurstonianum'**
5 ***Lamium maculatum* 'White Nancy'**
6 ***Verbena bonariensis***
7 ***Eryngium alpinum***
8 ***Kniphofia* 'Royal Standard'**
9 ***Penstemon* 'Firebird'**
10 ***Platycodon grandiflorus***

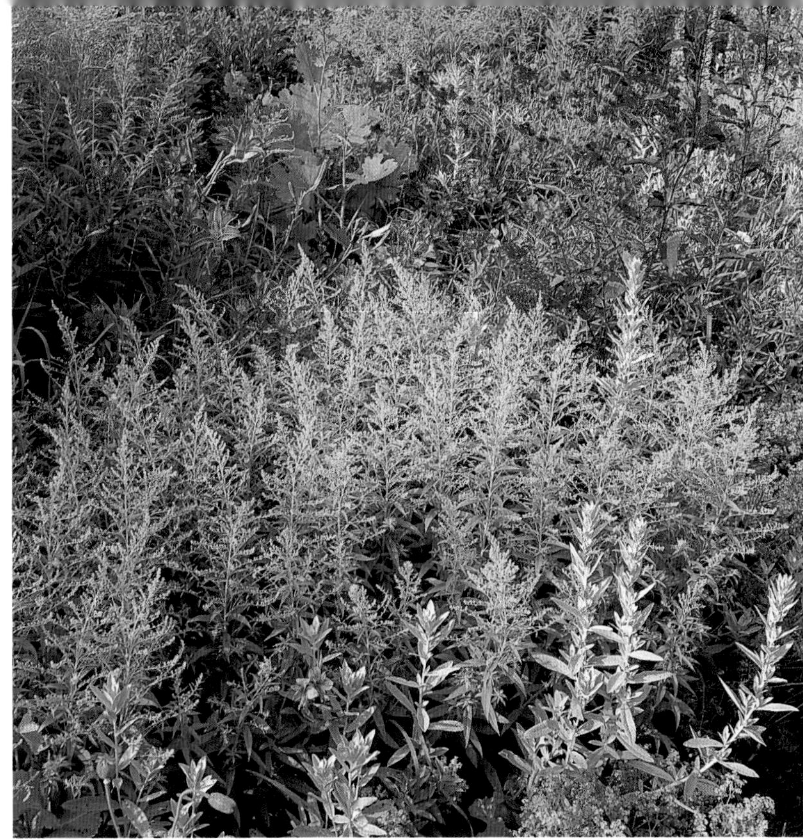

Time saver

Use a garden vacuum to clear up after trimming and deadheading. This is especially useful for plants that can be deadheaded all in one go, such as lavender, using shears or a nylon-line trimmer.

Natural spreaders such as golden rod, alstroemeria and macleaya are easy to look after if left to expand in a vacant site. Here they are teamed with sunflower and *Helenium* 'Moerheim Beauty'.

This is a painstaking job, and for tough weeds it may require several applications, but it is worth doing in the long run. Tackle bindweed by pushing bamboo canes into the ground, allowing the weed to climb up. Lay the canes on a polythene sheet, and spray the foliage with the weedkiller. Alternatively, push the foliage of trailing weeds into a polythene bag and direct the glyphosate spray into the bag. When the spray is dry, remove the polythene and leave the weedkiller for six weeks to give it time to kill the roots. When small plants are surrounded by weeds, cover the plants with an upturned bucket and apply a contact weedkiller or protect plants with a scorch-resistant barrier and use a flame gun to eliminate the weeds (see page 270).

Control self-seeding You don't have to ban plants from the garden because they self-seed, but you do need to act at the right time to stop them getting out of hand. For instance, to control plants such as *Alchemilla mollis*, alliums, bronze fennel, borage or herbaceous campanulas, remove the dead flowerheads before they set seed. If you do want to let the plants provide their own replacements, though, you will need to learn how to distinguish flower seedlings from weeds.

If you want self-sufficient borders that need no weeding or maintenance, fill them with vigorous spreaders, such as *Campanula poscharskyana,* mint, golden lemon balm (*Melissa officinalis* 'Aurea'), gardener's garters (*Phalaris arundinacea* var. 'Picta') and dotted loosestrife (*Lysimachia punctata*). But, avoid using these plants in a mixed border because they spread underground and are difficult to control.

Feed sparingly Too much nitrogen fertiliser causes soft, sappy growth that is vulnerable to pests, diseases and wind damage. It can also reduce the number of flowers produced. How much feed you need to give your plants will depend on the type of soil (see page 20) and on the plant, because some plants thrive on poor soil. On rich clay soils you may not need to feed at all. Free-draining sandy soils in areas of high rainfall tend to be poor in nutrients, so use a balanced feed (such as blood, fish and bone or growmore) once a year in spring and apply an organic mulch in late winter or early spring.

Supporting role To reduce routine care, choose plants that don't need staking. It is tricky to prop up a fully grown plant that has already been damaged, so if you think you may need to stake a plant, make sure that you do this at the planting stage, or in spring before the plant gets too big. Use ready-made interlocking supports that just push into the soil, cutting out the need for individual stakes and twine. The growing plant will soon camouflage unsightly supports.

Longer-lasting displays Most plants will bloom for longer and produce more flowers if faded blooms are removed. The time taken deadheading can be reduced by using a pair of shears when possible. Combine this with the removal of tired-looking foliage on bushy, low-growing plants, including lady's mantle (*Alchemilla mollis*), *Astrantia major* 'Sunningdale Variegated', *Lamium maculatum* 'White Nancy' or 'Pink Pewter', catmint (*Nepeta cataria*), golden feverfew (*Tanacetum parthenium* 'Aureum') and pulmonaria. Clip back these plants close to ground level then water and feed them to stimulate the production of replacement foliage and flowers.

Clipping some bedding and herbaceous plants, including *Erigeron karvinskianus*, petunias, *Senecio cineraria* and *Viola cornuta*, can stimulate another flush of flowers. In the case of plants that produce branched flower spikes, such as foxgloves,

Easy-care flowerbeds

Do avoid disturbing the soil unless necessary. Each disturbance produces a new batch of weed seedlings.

Do keep weeds under control by removing weed seedlings and topping up the mulch before the garden springs to life each year.

Do choose plants which are self-supporting, particularly if your garden is exposed.

Don't choose short-lived plants that need replacing every few years. Avoid using annuals.

Don't overfeed – otherwise plants will become vulnerable to damage.

Don't plant self-seeders near gravel paths or loose-laid paving.

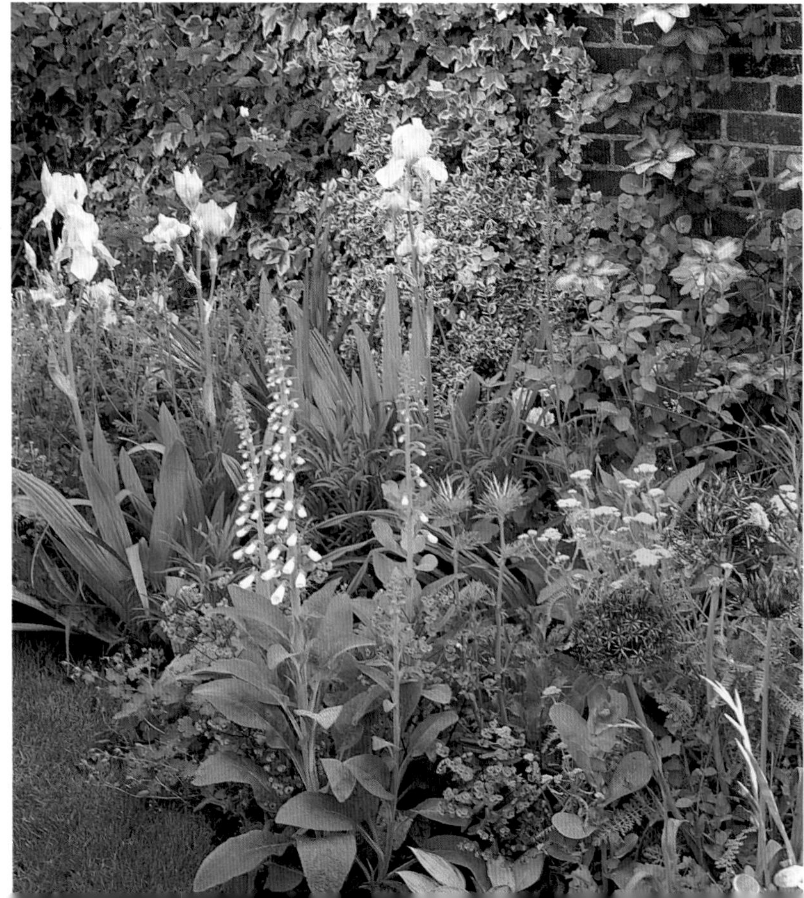

A low-maintenance planting of clematis, self-clinging ivy and self-seeding foxgloves is combined with a weed-suppressing ground cover of crocosmia, euphorbia and yellow iris. Evergreen euonymus at the back gives year-round interest.

PEST AND DISEASE CONTROL FOR FLOWERS AND FOLIAGE

▲ SLUGS

If your garden harbours a large slug and snail population, use slug pellets or surround the plants with sharp grit. You can also use biological controls. Or, plant grey and silver-leaved plants with a woolly or furry coating, such as stachys, because they are rarely attacked.

APHIDS

As well as the common greenfly, aphids occur as pink, grey, black or coated with sticky white 'wool'. The flower stems of lupins, bedding plants and hardy annuals, such as nasturtiums, are particularly vulnerable. Before resorting to spraying with a pesticide, try hand-picking affected shoot tips or rub the aphids off the stem with thumb and forefinger. Severe infestations can be controlled by spraying with pirimicarb. If a plant becomes infested at the end of its flowering season, cut it back hard and remove the debris.

WHITEFLY

Though normally a greenhouse pest, these tiny white triangular insects attack many plants in the garden, especially during hot dry summers or in sheltered sites. They are usually found on the underside of leaves, which become mottled. Spray with a soft soap or with permethrin, following the instructions carefully.

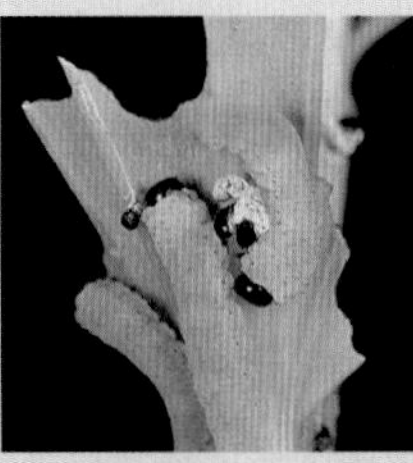

▲ CATERPILLARS

Although not generally a problem on flowering plants, there are a few exceptions, including dahlias, nasturtiums and Solomon's seal. At the first sign of damage, handpick the pest from the plant. Spray with a contact insecticide only if damage is severe or use biological control.

GREY MOULD

This disease has a grey furry appearance and attacks soft plant material, such as blooms and leaves. Remove affected material. Spray with fungicide.

MILDEW

Powdery mildew usually occurs in late summer, especially in dry periods with cold nights. The leaves appear to be covered in a white powder. Remove affected growth. It is difficult to control with a fungicide, but can be prevented by watering plants well and using a mulch to conserve moisture. If the problem recurs, space out plants.

▲ VINE WEEVIL

The adult beetles eat notches in leaf margins. Clear away plant debris so they have fewer daytime hiding places. The C-shaped vine weevil grubs attack the roots of many pot-grown plants. To kill the grubs in the garden, use a nematode biological control.

delphiniums, penstemons and snapdragons, old spikes can be cut off at the base as the flowers fade in order to encourage a second flush of flowers that appear later in the summer.

Do not be too quick to cut down plants in autumn, however, unless you need to control self-seeding. The winter skeletons of many plants, such as astilbe and eryngium, can be very attractive, especially when they are covered in frost. Also, the top growth and leaf litter helps to protect the crowns of more tender plants, such as agapanthus, phygelius and hardy fuchsias. Clear away any remaining top growth in spring before new buds start to break into growth. For tender plants, such as dahlias, cut back the top growth and cover crowns with an insulating layer of compost, leaf-mould or bark chippings. In cold regions and on poorly drained soils, lift tender plants and store them in a dry, frost-free place until replanted in spring.

Clear the ground of overwintered weed seedlings in late winter or early spring and at the same time tidy up any dead plant material left over from the previous year. The task is best left until then because the dead material will pull away much more easily than at the end of the flowering season, even without the use of secateurs.

NO STAKING REQUIRED

Many tall herbaceous plants need staking, or they flop when in bloom. The following are self-supporting.

Anemone* x *hybrida
(Japanese anemone)
***Aruncus dioicus* (goat's beard)**
Cimicifuga (bugbane)
Crambe cordifolia
Digitalis (foxglove)
Echinops (globe thistle)
Kniphofia (red-hot poker)
Rudbeckia (coneflower)
Verbascum
Verbena bonariensis

This cheerful combination, including anemone, phygelius and polygonum, flowers from mid summer into autumn. In a dry hot year, they will start flowering even earlier to give all-summer colour.

Extending colour through the seasons

To create year-round colour in a garden, plant up beds to reach their peak at different times of the year. Separate seasonal beds are most effective when placed at strategic points around the garden in order to catch the eye. As the year unfolds, the centre of interest moves around the garden; bright displays in borders are seen in winter from the house, and fiery planting schemes enjoyed in summer from the patio. Seasonal displays also enable you to do all the work needed in a border in one go – such as putting up supports, feeding and cutting back fading or unwanted growth. Alternatively, for larger borders, where a range of plants can be accommodated, create a seasonal succession of flowers within each bed. For background texture and to extend the period of interest, choose perennials which have attractive foliage.

Most well-designed gardens have beds of seasonal as well as year-round interest, with a mainstay of structural plantings of evergreen and deciduous trees, shrubs, perennials and edging plants.

Effective displays

Plant close Squeeze out weeds by placing plants close to each other. Buy small plants rather than larger ones; they are cheaper and establish faster. Plant out in groups of odd numbers for a balanced effect.

Give support Invest in plant supports that are quick and easy to use and that will last many years. Insert them early in the growing season, avoiding any need to support damaged plants later in the season.

Keep in trim Encourage bigger and longer-lasting flowering displays by regularly removing fading blooms.

Instant spring displays

In March and April, garden centres are full of spring bedding plants, including double daisies, pansies, polyanthus and hybrid primroses, that are already coming into flower. They are ideal for the busy gardener because they can be used to create instant displays, and they avoid having to spend time raising plants from seed. Many spring bedding plants do well in shade and are useful for filling gaps in newly planted borders, beneath deciduous shrubs, under a tree, or on the north-facing side of a hedge or fence.

In addition to bedding plants, a wide range of potted bulbs are available in garden centres from early to mid spring. Buy them when the buds are just starting to show colour. You can then have a good idea of where they might look best in the garden and they will give you a long show. Bulbs will not make a great deal of growth so you need to plant them close together in order to cover the ground straightaway. For the best effect, concentrate them in containers, and group them in beds and borders close to the house.

To cover a large area, it is more economical to buy bedding plants in trays rather than in individual pots. With mixed trays, colours may be tricky to match. If you are buying several trays, empty them out just before planting and group the plants according to their colour.

Anemone blanda is a good ground-cover bulb with early flowers. Place under deciduous shrubs or among herbaceous perennials, which produce growth that emerges later in spring.

SUCCESSFUL COLOUR SCHEMES

It is easier to create an effective display if you stick to one or two colours. Mix and match from the following. S = shade-tolerant.

White scheme
Bulbs: Snowdrops (S), snowflakes (S), tulips (pictured) and hyacinths. Perennials: *Dicentra eximia* 'Snowdrift' (S), *Lamium maculatum* 'White Nancy', *Pulmonaria officinalis* 'Sissinghurst White'(S), *Smilacina racemosa* (S).

Pink scheme
Bulbs: *Chionodoxa forbesii* 'Pink Giant', hyacinth 'Pink Pearl' (S), (pictured), tulip 'Heart's Delight'. Perennials: *Bergenia* 'Baby Doll', double daisies, *Myosotis* 'Victoria Rose' (S), *Pulmonaria rubra* (S).

Yellow scheme
Bulbs: crocuses, daffodils, *Fritillaria imperialis* 'Lutea', hyacinths (S), tulips, winter aconite (S). Perennials: doronicum (S), euphorbia, polyanthus, primrose (S), ranunculus (pictured), trollius.

Blue scheme
Bulbs: *Anemone blanda*, bluebells (S), *Chionodoxa luciliae* (S), grape hyacinth, *Iris histrioides* 'Major', *Scilla siberica* (pictured, S). Perennials: forget-me-not (S), polyanthus, *Primula denticulata* (S).

Early summer colour

There is often a lull in the garden after the main spring flush is over and before summer bedding plants come into full bloom. Several excellent plants bridge this gap. Use them either to enhance an existing mixed border or to create an area devoted entirely to early summer colour.

Peonies offer handsome foliage and extravagant flowers in early summer. They are long-lived and need no lifting or dividing, though most benefit from staking and they can take several years to establish. Double varieties such as 'Sarah Bernhardt' last longer in flower than singles, but are more vulnerable to rain damage. Peonies work well with tall bearded irises, and a foreground of catmint (nepeta) and *Alchemilla mollis*, because they come into flower at the same time.

Other plants for filling the front of the border at this time of year include many cranesbills; for example, *Geranium* 'Johnson's Blue' has pretty cut foliage and a profusion of blooms, and it can be grown in sun or part shade. Heuchera and x *Heucherella alba* 'Bridget Bloom' are also good for edging borders and paths at this time of year.

Knapweeds, such as the deep blue *Centaurea montana*, thrive in a sunny well-drained spot. *C. montana* seeds freely, which is useful because it is not long-lived. The pink-flowered *C. hypoleuca* 'John Coutts' is a choice alternative. Try it with the upright spikes of the indigo *Salvia* x *sylvestris* 'Mainacht'.

For colour in a shady spot, grow one of the carpeting dicentras, which bloom from late spring into early summer. The dainty white snowflake (leucojum) is particularly long-lasting. For early colour in a

Roses are underplanted with the weed-suppressing foliage of *Campanula persicifolia*, *Dianthus* 'Mrs Sinkins', pelargonium and an edging of blue-flowering catmint. The wall makes an attractive backdrop and gives vertical growing space for flowering climbers.

SHADY SIDE OF A WALL

The variegated ivy 'Glacier' provides a backdrop for this May-to-June display of pastel pinks and whites for a shady wall. Lamium and pulmonaria provide all-year ground cover.

1 ***Dryopteris filix-mas***
2 ***Geranium* x *oxonianum* 'Wargrave Pink'** pink flowers to September.
3 ***Hedera helix* 'Glacier'**
4 ***Aconitum* 'Ivorine'**
5 ***Pulmonaria saccharata* 'Argentea Group'** violet flowers in March-April.
6 ***Chaerophyllum hirsutum* 'Roseum'**
7 ***Lamium maculatum* 'Pink Pewter'**

hot scheme, try *Euphorbia griffithii* 'Fireglow' or 'Dixter', which has 90 cm (36 in) tall stems that bear orange-red bracts for weeks. Bush roses and some shrub roses also begin to come into flower at this time of year. They make a wonderful backdrop to early summer perennials. But avoid lupins because their flowers deteriorate rapidly after coming into full bloom; dwarf, modern lupins, though, can be used as a bedding plant, to be cut back after flowering.

Camouflaging gaps To cover up the faded growth and gaps left by early spring bulbs, use biennials for an instant splash of colour. Easy-care biennials include wallflowers, which are available from garden centres for autumn planting, and double daisies (*Bellis perennis*), which are sold in pots and divided trays in spring.

Several easy-care perennials leave ugly holes in the border once flowering is over. For example, oriental poppy (*Papaver orientale*) produces sumptuous tissue-like blooms and large divided foliage, but leaves a gap in the border by July. Remedy this by planting the poppies behind herbaceous plants, such as hardy fuchsia, which start their growth late in the season. The dying growth of the poppies is then camouflaged, or it can be cut back close to the ground shortly after the flowers are over to make way for the fuchsia.

FLOWERS THAT GROW LIKE WEEDS

Some flowers spread naturally by underground runners or by self-seeding. These can form the basis of the ultimate low-upkeep garden (see page 134).

***Alchemilla mollis* (lady's mantle)**
Aquilegia
***Calendula officinalis* (pot marigold)**
Eschscholzia (California poppy)
Geranium endressii
***Hesperis matronalis* (sweet rocket)**
Lunaria (honesty)
Meconopsis cambrica
Myosotis (forget-me-not)
Nigella (love-in-a-mist)
Oenothera (evening primrose)

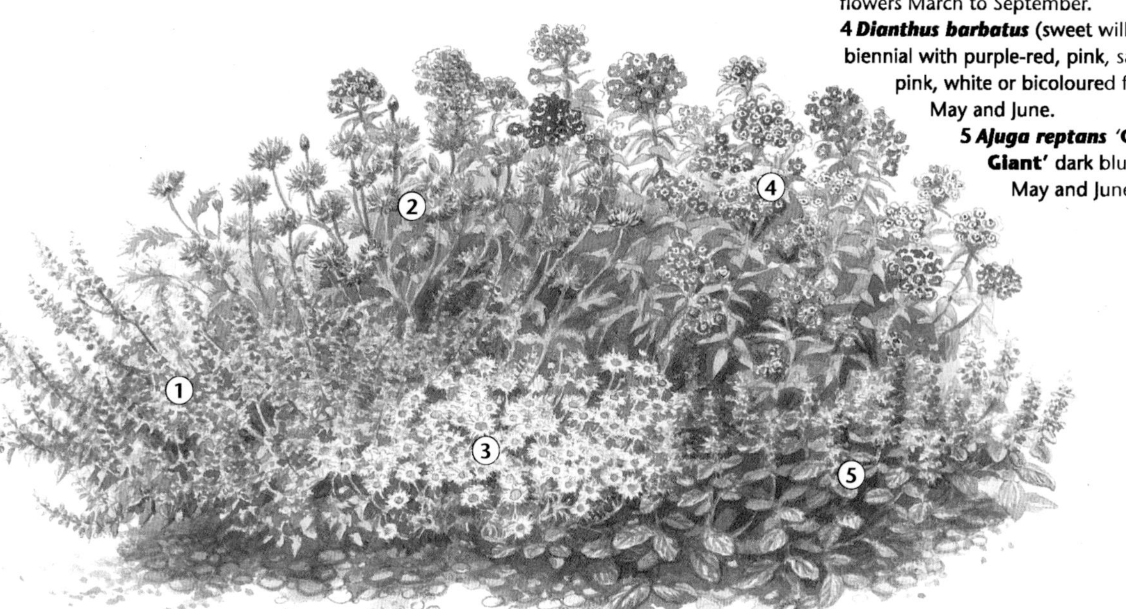

DRY SCHEME FOR SUN

This display of pink, purple and lavender, with silver and white highlights, is best for full sun and well-drained soil. The bronze-purple leaves of the ajuga provide all-year ground cover. The main flowering month of this scheme is June.

1 ***Nepeta x faassenii*** pale lavender-blue flowers June to September.
2 ***Centaurea hypoleuca* 'John Coutts'** bright pink flowers July.
3 ***Rhodanthemum hosmariense*** white flowers March to September.
4 ***Dianthus barbatus*** (sweet william) a biennial with purple-red, pink, salmon-pink, white or bicoloured flowers in May and June.
5 ***Ajuga reptans* 'Catlin's Giant'** dark blue flowers May and June.

ANNUALS AND BIENNIALS FOR EARLY SUMMER

Avoid a lull in early summer by combining bulbs that flower in April and May, such as tulips and ipheion, with any of the following annuals and biennials.

For fragrance In a sheltered spot try sweet william (pictured), wallflower, sweet rocket and brompton stock. Or sow hardy annuals, such as candytuft or poached-egg flower.

In shade In moisture-retentive soil, try biennial viola, foxglove, canterbury bell, pansy, forget-me-not (pictured) or polyanthus. Hardy annual virginia stock will also do well.

As edging Choose viola, pansy or double daisy (pictured) and early flowering hardy annuals such as dwarf cornflower and candytuft. Pots of ranunculus will add a splash of colour.

Middle border Look for hardy annuals such as cornflower (pictured) and pot marigold ('Art Shades' or 'Fiesta Gitana'), and the biennial wallflower and canterbury bell.

Back of border Foxglove 'Excelsior Strain' (pictured) comes in a range of soft pastel shades that blend with most colour schemes. Plant it in clumps or at the back of a border.

Shade-loving bleeding heart (*Dicentra spectabilis*) also leaves a gap after flowering in late spring and early summer. Large hostas and ferns are excellent companions, which produce unfurling leaves that emerge at the right time to fill the space left. Alternatively, plant a foreground of vigorous, bushy or spreading tender perennials, such as helichrysum, marguerite daisies (*Argyranthemum frutescens*) or verbena, which are planted out around the end of May once there is no danger of a late frost.

Extend the flowering After a first flush of flowers, some plants that bloom in early summer can be cut back with shears to near ground level to rejuvenate the plant, encouraging further blooms and preventing mildew. Plants to be cut back at this time of year include *Alchemilla mollis*, *Centaurea montana*, geranium (cranesbill), *Lamium maculatum* 'White Nancy' and 'Pink Pewter', and pulmonaria.

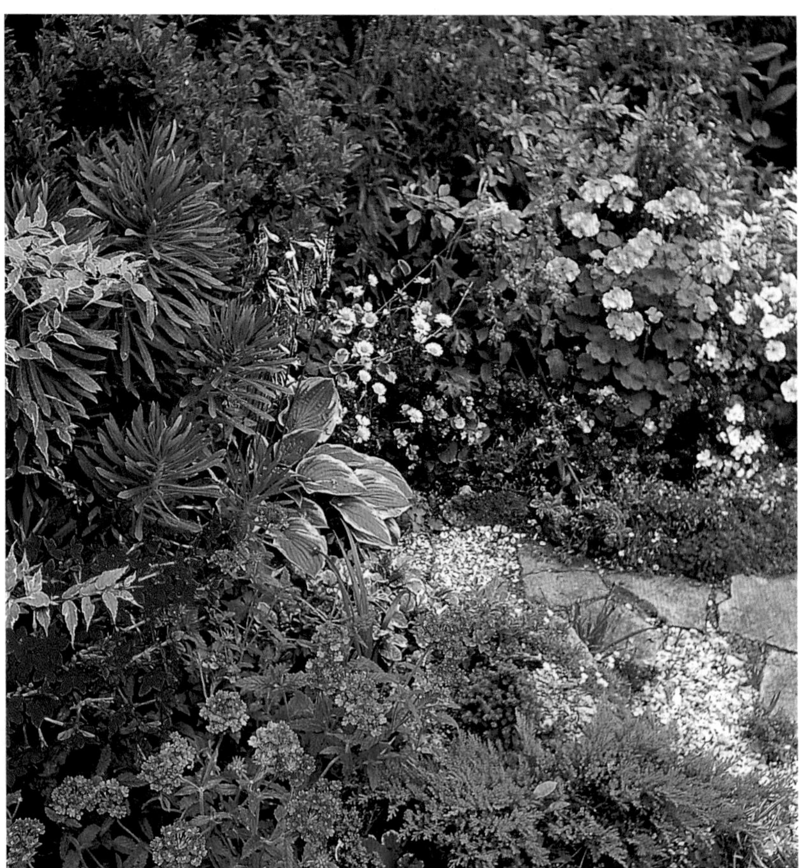

Easy-care, sun-loving bedding plants, such as pink verbena and pelargonium, brighten up a year-round planting scheme. In semi-shaded spots, red-flowered tobacco plants and begonia help to fill the gaps.

HOW TO BUY SUMMER BEDDING

Summer bedding can be bought in a range of sizes, from seed to flowering plants, and is available by mail order or from garden centres. Use the following guide to help you decide what suits your needs, whether it be for mass planting or filling a small container.

SEED
The cheapest way to raise a lot of the same variety. Useful for massed bedding or ground cover. Seed offers the best choice of varieties, including the latest problem-resistant kinds. You also have the pleasure of raising your own plants from seed.

What to buy If you have the space, time and equipment, raise bedding plants that are easy to grow from seed, such as marigold and lobelia, and any needed in large numbers for **displays.**

SEEDLINGS
Easier than growing plants from seed, but still a cheap way to raise a lot of plants of the same variety. There is no need to invest in an expensive propagator.

What to buy
Seedlings are a good way to buy bedding plants that are difficult to germinate, such as pelargoniums, begonias, busy lizzies and petunias. Also worth considering for other bedding plants used in big quantities.

PLUGS
A useful and cheap way to raise several plants of the same variety, possibly for a single-variety container scheme. Plugs are easier than raising plants from seed or seedlings and you get a good selection of most recent varieties.

What to buy They can be bought by mail order or from garden centres. Buy plugs of expensive bedding plants, such as pelargoniums, if you have time to pot them on and a frost-free place to keep them.

TOT PLANTS
A convenient way to buy a few plants for a patio container or hanging basket. You can buy exactly the number of plants that you need. Easy-to-use collections of plants are available, such as by colour scheme.

What to buy A good way to buy young plants of fuchsias, petunias, scaevolas and pelargoniums, especially if you want named varieties. But you must have time to pot them on and somewhere frost-free to keep them.

STRIPS
A cheap and easy way to buy a dozen or so of the same variety, ready to plant out. Useful for bedding displays or large numbers of containers. Most are sold by colour rather than named variety.

What to buy Best for unnamed varieties of bedding plants in flower that are large enough to plant straight into the garden.

Midsummer highlights

Gardens traditionally burst with colour in June and July as many perennial plants reach their peak. Roses are also at their best, and bedding plants in their first flush of bloom. Since so much is out now, it is important to remember to leave space for late summer and autumn plants.

Don't despair if you didn't plant out earlier in the year. Garden centres will still stock many perennials that flower throughout summer, such as geranium (cranesbill), as well as ornamental grasses and other easy-care perennials, such as crocosmia and helenium, in the summer months when they bloom.

For immediate impact, plant closely in groups. Perennials planted in summer, though, will need more watering than those planted earlier in the year. To get them off to a good start, soak the rootball of each plant in a bucket of water before planting. Then dig the planting hole and pour a bucket of water into it so that the soil is really moist. Plant and water again to settle the soil around the roots.

TROUBLE-FREE PERENNIALS FOR LIGHT SHADE

Add colour throughout the growing season to lightly shaded areas with a selection of the following.

Aruncus
Astilbe
Astrantia
Campanula
Geranium (cranesbill)
Hemerocallis (day lily)
Hosta
Persicaria
Rudbeckia (coneflower)
Saxifraga* x *urbium

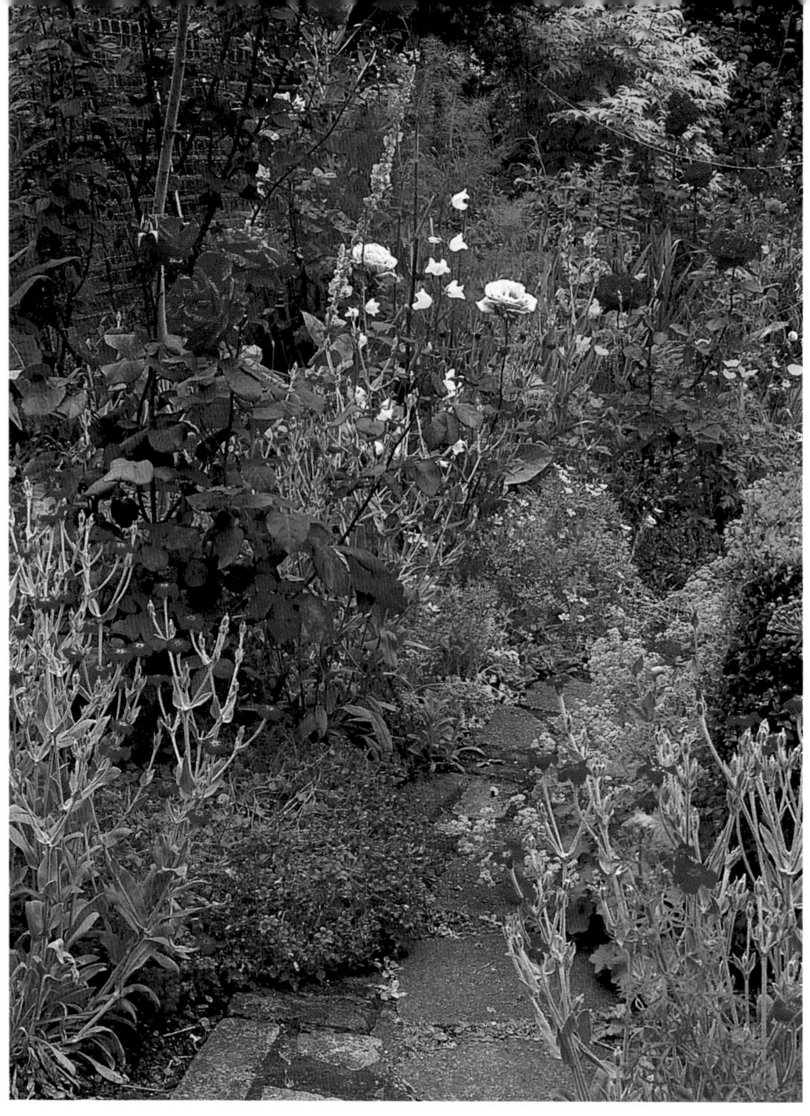

Spreading blue-flowered campanulas combine with self-seeding *Alchemilla mollis* and *Lychnis coronaria* to boost a brilliant, cottage-style summer display.

Exotic touch Hybrid lilies have a relatively short flowering season, but their exotic blooms add a note of luxury and are good for instant planting. Some are also highly fragrant. Once planted, lilies will come up year after year, and if left undisturbed their clumps will steadily expand to give more and more blooms. Although you can buy dry bulbs in autumn and spring, the easiest and most reliable way to purchase lilies is ready grown in pots with several bulbs. A good display is then guaranteed in the first year and planting is simple.

Lilies need well-drained soil rich in humus. Grow them with other plants, such as peonies or shrub roses, that have similar growing requirements and that will help to shade their roots from the hot sun and prop up any leaning, flower-laden stems. Alternatively, modern hybrids are available that are more compact and are self-supporting, such as 'Apollo' and 'Electra', although they tend to lack some of the slender grace of their taller counterparts.

Easy-care cottage borders Many perennials and hardy annuals spread by self-seeding to create the ultimate easy-care garden. These self-sown seedlings establish better than pot-raised plants because their roots are not damaged by transplanting. For colour from spring to early autumn, allow self-seeding of *Alchemilla mollis,* allium, aquilegia, calendula, forget-me-not, foxglove, love-in-a-mist, nasturtium, poppy, wallflower and viola, as well as grasses such as *Stipa tenuissima*.

Some self-seeders will colonise nooks and crannies in walls; such as, *Aurinia saxatile*, *Corydalis lutea*, fairy foxglove (*Erinus alpinus*), wall daisy (*Erigeron karvinskianus*) and wallflower. Others will soon form swathes of colour rooted in paving cracks; including, *Alchemilla mollis*, aquilegia, *Campanula portenschlagiana*, verbascum and *Verbena bonariensis*. To enhance this cottage-garden effect, add gravel areas for the self-seeders to colonise with even greater ease.

FLOWERS UNDER TREES

The following cope well with shade and dry soil. They have attractive foliage and some make excellent weed-suppressing ground cover after flowering. E = evergreen.

Anemone nemorosa
Brunnera macrophylla
***Epimedium* (E)**
Erythronium dens-canis
Geranium nodosum
Galanthus (snowdrop)
Hellebore (E)
Lamium (E)
Pulmonaria (lungwort, E)
***Vinca minor* (lesser periwinkle, E)**

SHADY SCENE FOR WALLS

The gloom of this shady wall is lightened by using variegated and light-coloured foliage and flowers. The scene is at its best in June and July.

1 ***Molinia caerulea* ssp. *arundinacea* 'Variegata'**
2 ***Viola* 'Belmont Blue'**
3 ***Astrantia major* ssp. *involucrata* 'Shaggy'**
4 ***Nicotiana* Nicki Series** flowers also come in mixed colours.
5 ***Hosta* 'Sum and Substance'**
6 ***Dicentra* 'Stuart Boothman'** flowers open in April.
7 ***Ajuga reptans* 'Variegata'**
8 ***Aruncus dioicus* 'Kneiffii'**

PASTEL SHADES FOR SUN

A grouping of cool pinks, blues and white to refresh hot summer days, with *Rosa* 'Iceberg' as the background. These light colours also show up well in twilight. Needs a well-drained site. The main flowering season is June to August.

1 ***Rosa* 'Iceberg'** white flowers to September.
2 ***Eryngium* x *tripartitum*** flowerheads and spiky bracts remain attractive once flowering is over.
3 ***Leucanthemum* x *superbum* 'Snowcap'**
4 ***Penstemon* 'Evelyn'** flowers to October.
5 ***Centranthus ruber*** also white and dark crimson flowers.
6 ***Centaurea cyanus*** the annual cornflower.
7 ***Ajuga reptans* 'Burgundy Glow'** evergreen foliage with flowers opening May to June.

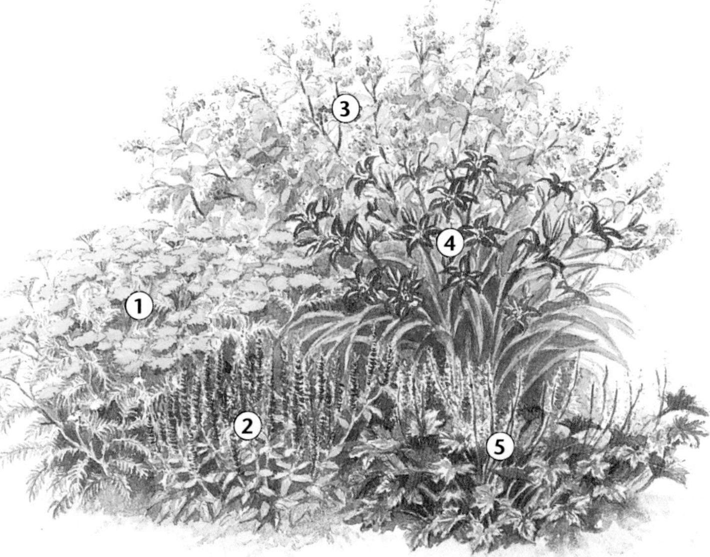

COLOURFUL SCHEME FOR SUN

Bright flowers make the most of a hot spot. Many plants need the strong light to bring out colours, ripen wood or initiate flower buds. The flowering season for this scene is June to September.

1 ***Achillea* 'Moonshine'**
2 ***Salvia nemorosa* 'Lubecca'**
3 ***Ceanothus* x *delileanus* 'Gloire de Versailles'**
4 ***Hemerocallis* 'Stafford'** flowers in June or July.
5 ***Heuchera micrantha* var. *diversifolia* 'Palace Purple'** pink seed heads follow cream flowers.

Time saver

Use the gaps created in late summer by early flowering hardy annuals to plant out winter bedding plants, such as pansies. Alternatively, fill the gaps with late bedding bargains from the garden centre.

Late summer colour

Many tender perennials are at their best in late summer, when they provide a jolly splash of colour. As well as performing well throughout the warmer months, they are more drought tolerant than both annual bedding plants and some classic late summer-flowering perennials, such as border phlox and crocosmia.

Popular tender perennials include: verbena, with varieties such as deep pink 'Sissinghurst' and rich purple 'Homestead Purple'; osteospermums; *Diascia* 'Ruby Field' and *D. vigilis* for a low, pink carpet; bush fuchsias or marguerite daisies for height and substance; and canna or abutilons for a tropical effect.

For tender perennials with particular drought-resistant foliage, helichrysums include silvery *H. petiolare*, lime-green 'Limelight' and cream-variegated 'Variegatum'. The ferny foliage of golden-yellow bidens provides vigorous ground cover. And for edging a sunny border, try the mossy foliage of rock daisy (*Brachyscome multifida*) or the variegated forms of felicia – both flower well.

HOT SPOT

The rich colours of the penstemon and the buddleja give punch to the pastel blues and pinks used in this scheme for free-draining soil. The flowering season is from July to September.

1 ***Buddleja davidii* 'Royal Red'**
2 ***Echinops bannaticus***
3 ***Penstemon* 'Garnet'**
4 ***Calamintha nepeta***
5 ***Osteospermum* 'Stardust'** flowers from May.

COOL AND SHADY

An elegant scheme using white and soft blue to emphasise cool shade. All plants thrive in humus-rich, moisture-retentive soil. Flowering season from July to September.

1 ***Hydrangea macrophylla* 'Mme Emile Mouillière'**
2 ***Aconitum* x *cammarum* 'Bicolor'**
3 ***Phlox paniculata***
4 **Impatiens F1 hybrid (busy lizzie)** flowers start in June.
5 ***Geranium wallichianum* 'Buxton's Variety'** first flowers open in June.

Hardy annuals, such as sweet william (*Dianthus barbutus*) and mignonette (*Reseda odorata*), don't flower for as long as tender perennials or half-hardy annuals, but they are good for filling gaps in late summer. For continuous blooms until the first frosts, sow some extra seeds every few weeks until early June. Alternatively, hardy perennials can be used instead of bedding plants in borders or containers. Choose ones with a long flowering season, such as *Dianthus* 'Doris'.

Longer flowering A garden can start to flag in August when some summer-flowering perennials run out of steam, especially in a dry year. However, many tender perennials and larger-flowered hardy annuals, such as pot marigold (*Calendula officinalis*) and cornflower (*Centaurea cyanus*), will bloom for longer if adequately watered, boosted with a general liquid feed and regularly deadheaded (as a time saver, use shears for those with lots of small blooms).

For additional colour, group together tender perennials that put on a good late-season show, such as the shrubby salvias *S. uliginosa* (clear blue) and *S. fulgens* (red). Or late-flowering bedding plants, such as Chinese aster (callistephus), celosia, coleus (solenostemon), salpiglossis, zinnia, and annual penstemon and rudbeckia. Garden centres also stock compact dahlias and chrysanthemums in bud and flower.

FOLIAGE AND SUN

This August display offers a contrast of leaf size and texture. All plants enjoy moist soil in full sun.

1 ***Cimicifuga* var. *simplex* Atropurpurea Group** white flowers from August to October.
2 ***Miscanthus sinensis* 'Zebrinus'** flowers until November.
3 ***Hosta* 'Royal Standard'** white flowers in August.
4 ***Rudbeckia fulgida* var. *sullivantii* 'Goldsturm'** yellow flowers in August and September.

EASY-CARE PERENNIALS FOR LATE SUMMER

None of these plants need frequent division or staking. All are resistant to disease. As well as late blooms, all have strong foliage interest through the year.

Acanthus spinosus (bear's breeches) Large glossy, dark green leaves appear in early spring. Spires of white blooms with purple bracts. 1.2 m x60 cm (4x2ft). Sun or partial shade.

Anemone* x *hybrida (Japanese anemone) White or pink flowers. Vine leaf-shaped leaves form a clump 1.2 mx60 cm (4x2 ft). Plant in any well-drained soil in sun or light shade.

***Crocosmia* 'Bressingham Blaze'** Orange-red sprays of tubular blooms and grassy foliage in clumps 75x15-20 cm (30x6-8 in). Full sun and good drainage.

Echinops bannaticus (globe thistle) Coarse leaves and stiff-branched, silvery stems 1.2 mx75 cm (4x2½ ft) are topped with soft blue spiny globes. Thrives on poor soils in full sun.

***Aster* x *frikartii* 'Mönch'** Bears long-lasting, lavender-blue flowers on stout stems from July to October. It forms a dense clump 70x35- 40 cm (28x14-16 in).

Grasses and foliage link with the flowers of different seasons in this easy-care combination. In autumn, the yellow daisies of black-eyed Susan (*Rudbeckia fulgida*) provide mid-border highlights.

LONG-LASTING BEDDING PLANTS

The following summer bedding plants will flower into autumn. Those marked with an asterisk don't need deadheading.

Begonia semperflorens*
***Cosmos bipinnatus* 'Sonata'**
Impatiens (busy lizzie)*
***Mimulus* 'Malibu Series'**
Nicotiana (tobacco plant)*
Pelargonium
Petunia
Salvia farinacea* 'Strata'
Tagetes

Added autumn interest

Many reliable, easy-care perennials that perform well in late summer continue their blooms into autumn, when they are joined by the truly autumnal bulbs and perennials, such as autumn crocus (*Colchicum speciosum*) and lilyturf (*Liriope muscari*). Some will even continue to bloom after a few light frosts.

One of the best perennials to flower from late summer and into autumn is the lavender-blue *Aster* x *frikartii* 'Mönch'. It does not need staking and is resistant to mildew. *Sedum spectabile*, such as *S.* 'Autumn Joy', also offer excellent value at the front of a sunny well-drained border. Their rounded, glaucous leaves make attractive ground cover earlier in the year, and are joined by sculptural domed heads of apple-green flower buds that colour to deep pink as autumn arrives.

Other late-flowering perennials that catch the eye include the white or pink-flowered Japanese anemone (*Anemone* x *hybrida*), chrysanthemums, such as 'Anastasia', 'Bronze Elegance' and 'Mei-kyo', and some red-hot pokers (kniphofia).

Problem solver

Frost survivors Many bedding plants collapse with the first hard frost. To ensure an autumn display, include frost survivors, such as lilyturf (liriope), chrysanthemum, moor grass (*Molinia caerulea* 'Variegata'), red-hot poker (kniphofia), schizostylis and sedum.

PLANTS FOR DAPPLED SHADE

A low-maintenance scheme for humus-rich soil in the shade *(right)*. The iris, fern and ivy provide an evergreen foil for the autumn flowers. White stands out well in shade, but it is good to mix it in with a hot colour, such as the scarlet of the berries. Best in September and October.

1 ***Iris foetidissima***
2 ***Hedera helix* 'Little Diamond'**
3 ***Polystichum aculeatum***
4 ***Tricyrtis hirta alba***
5 ***Colchicum speciosum* 'Album'**

AUTUMN FLOWERS IN SUN

This scheme *(left)* peaks in autumn when the schizostylis comes into bloom, but it looks good from July, when the aster daisies appear with the apple-green buds of the sedum. Bright silver artemisia adds sparkle to this soft, pastel grouping.

1 ***Artemisia ludoviciana* var. *latiloba***
2 ***Aster x frikartii* 'Mönch'**
3 ***Sedum* 'Autumn Joy'**
4 ***Schizostylis coccinea***

Hardy bulbs, such as cyclamen, and *Colchicum speciosum* and *C. autumnale*, are useful for planting in lightly shaded areas, such as between shrubs and under trees. If left undisturbed from year to year, they will increase steadily in number with no assistance. For a sunny well-drained spot, such as the base of a south-facing wall, choose *Amaryllis belladonna,* or *Nerine bowdenii* with its rounded clusters of pink starry blooms above clumps of strap-shaped leaves.

Annuals that reach their peak in late summer and early autumn include Chinese asters (callistephus), with their pastel colouring and single or fully double blooms; they are ideal at the front of the border. *Rudbeckia* 'Marmalade' has clear orange daisy-like flowers highlighted by black central cones. This variety works well towards the back of a border mixed with perennials. For edging, select dwarf rudbeckias, such as 'Toto', 'Becky' and 'Sonora'. In hot dry summers, the annual zinnias put on a magnificent show late in the year, but they don't do well in cold or wet summers. Zinnias come in a range of colours and heights, from 25-75 cm (10-30 in).

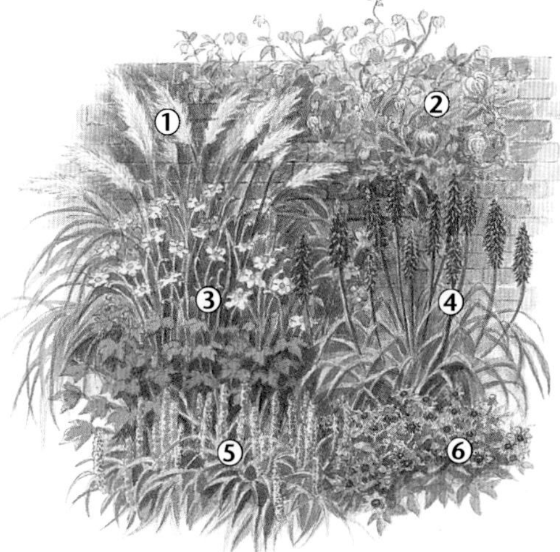

BORDER COLLECTION

The flowers in this scheme would look particularly good against a backdrop of autumn leaf colour. Ideal for full sun and a well-drained soil. At its best from August to October.

1 ***Cortaderia selloana* 'Pumila'** all-year foliage and silvery plumes in late summer.
2 ***Clematis tangutica*** the yellow flowers from July to November are followed by fluffy seed heads.
3 ***Anemone x hybrida* 'Honorine Jobert'**
4 ***Kniphofia* 'Prince Igor'**
5 ***Liriope muscari*** flowers from September to November.
6 ***Rudbeckia* 'Becky'**

Winter flowers

Although it is not possible to achieve the same intensity of colour in winter as in other seasons, there is a surprising variety of winter-flowering bedding plants, bulbs and perennials to choose from. Concentrate colour in pockets, especially in containers by the house, rather than spreading it thinly around the garden. Space bedding plants close together because gaps between them won't close up until well into spring, giving a threadbare appearance.

Winter-flowering pansies, such as the Universal and Ultima Series, are weather-resistant and will flower on and off in mild spells from autumn through to late spring if deadheaded.

WINTER-FLOWERING GROUND COVER

Throughout the year ground-cover plants suppress weeds beneath trees and shrubs. A few will then put on a colour display when the garden needs it most.

***Arum italicum* 'Marmoratum'**
Bergenia* x *schmidtii
Cyclamen coum
***Erica carnea* (winter heath)**
***Pulmonaria rubra* 'Redstart'**

Do not be in a hurry to clear perennial beds. Their frost-encrusted foliage and seed heads *(left)* will provide decorative interest in winter and food for birds.

Change the focus of a mixed border in winter *(below)* by underplanting deciduous shrubs with winter-flowering ground-cover plants such as hellebores, winter aconites and snowdrops.

Winter heaths, such as *Erica carnea* 'Springwood Pink', add colour during the coldest months while providing evergreen ground cover for the rest of the year. They are also good in containers.

They are perfect, teamed with ornamental cabbage, for replacing summer and autumn-flowering bedding plants in patio borders or for adding foreground colour to a planting of evergreen shrubs. For sheltered spots with some sunshine, try hardy primulas, such as the single or mixed-coloured Crescendo Series and 'Wanda' hybrids. New strains of double daisy (*Bellis perennis*) will also produce late winter blooms.

Hardy perennials The handsome evergreen foliage and large, cup-shaped blooms of hellebores provide a perfect foil for early-flowering bulbs, such as snowdrop and *Cyclamen coum,* and later for the silver-spotted pulmonaria and the early-flowering *P. rubra* 'Redstart'. The pure white flowers of Christmas rose (*Helleborus niger*) get weather-beaten, so choose white forms of *H. orientalis* instead. *H. argutifolius* has bold leaves and clusters of apple-green blooms. And don't let the common name of stinking hellebore (*H. foetidus*) put you off; it releases its scent only when bruised. Its glossy, dark green leaves and clusters of acid-green flowers go well with the red winter stems of the dogwood, *Cornus alba* 'Sibirica'.

Bergenia foliage adds a dramatic touch to a winter garden. Some forms turn rich purple-red or beetroot in cold weather. Interplant *Bergenia cordifolia* 'Purpurea' or *B.* 'Bressingham Ruby' with clumps of taller, large-flowered snowdrop, such as *Galanthus* 'S. Arnott', or early flowering dwarf daffodils, such as *Narcissus* 'Tête-à-tête' or 'Peeping Tom'.

Winter-flowering bulbs Most early bulbs are dwarf and prefer a sunny well-drained site, with the exception of woodlanders, such as the winter aconite (*Eranthis hyemalis*), snowdrops, *Cyclamen coum* and daffodils.

Crocus chrysanthus, which comes in a range of colours, forms dense clumps of low-level blooms in February. It is perfect for a rock garden or for the front of a Mediterranean-style gravel border. Another sun-lover for sheltered pockets is *Iris reticulata,* which has dark blue flowers that stand out best against a pale foil. Try it with a ground-covering winter heath, such as *Erica carnea* 'Springwood White'. *Iris histriodes* 'Major' is similar but with more substantial flowers, and there is a range of early-flowering hybrids, mainly in shades of blue and purple.

Bulbs good for using in a lawn around a shrub or tree are the tough, large-flowered *Crocus* x *luteus* 'Golden Yellow', the pale mauve *C. tommasinianus* and the bright blue *Scilla bifolia.*

Buying wild flowers

From seed Specialist seed firms supply the biggest range and provide useful information. A limited range is available in most garden centres and from some seed catalogues. Organically produced seed is also sometimes available.

As plants A few species are available in garden centres. Choose healthy looking plants that are not badly pot bound. Specialist seed firms supply some varieties by mail order and there are several nurseries that specialise in wild-flower plants.

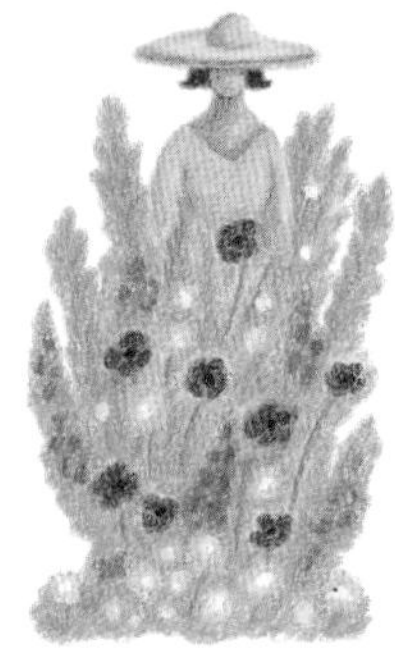

Creating an easy-care garden with wild flowers

Wild-flower gardening requires little time and effort, but it does not mean simply leaving your plot to run wild. If you did so, your garden would quickly become an untidy wasteland filled with brambles and invasive weeds. By cultivating wild flowers, you can achieve a natural-style garden that not only provides a habitat for insects and other wildlife, but also needs much less work than conventional flowerbeds. Wild flowers need low soil fertility and are naturally resilient, so little soil preparation is needed. Nor do they require feeding, staking or pest and disease control, which makes them ideal for gardeners short on time and those not wanting to use chemicals.

You can include wild flowers in a garden in various ways. Use them to turn a rough patch of ground away from the house into a wild garden, teamed with native species of trees and shrubs, such as wild cherry (*Prunus avium*) and guelder rose (*Viburnum opulus*). If you want to attract butterflies and other insects, be sure to grow species that provide food for caterpillars as well as nectar for adults; for example, nettles, verbascum and bird's foot trefoil (*Medicago sativa*). Team wild flowers with early spring bulbs, such as narcissi or bluebells in shade under trees, or blend them with cultivated perennials, such as geranium (cranesbill), which have wild origins.

BLENDING A WILD SCHEME

This combination of wild flowers and 'domesticated' perennials will grow together happily to create a flowering meadow or wild-flower cultivated border.

1 *Achillea filipendulina* 'Gold Plate' 1.2 m (4 ft) tall. Flowers June/July.
2 *Geranium phaeum* (dusky cranesbill) 75 cm (30 in) tall. May/June.
3 *Malva moschata* (musk mallow) 90 cm (36 in) tall. June to September.
4 *Verbascum thapsus* (great mullein) 1.8 m (6 ft) tall. June to August.
5 *Geranium pratense* (meadow cranesbill) 60-90 cm (24-36 in) tall. Flowers June to September.
6 *Phalaris arundinacea* var. *picta* (gardener's garters) 90 cm (36 in) tall. Cream/green-striped grass.
7 *Leucanthemum vulgare* (oxeye daisy) 30-90 cm (12-36 in) tall. May/June.

WILD FLOWERS FOR WOODLAND GARDENS

Combine some of the plants below to create a natural carpet of colour under deciduous trees and shrubs.

Anemone nemorosa
(wood anemone)
Digitalis (foxglove)
Fragaria vesca **(wild strawberry)**
Geum rivale **(water avens)**
Lamium galeobdolon
(yellow archangel)
Primula vulgaris **(primrose)**
Silene dioica **(red campion)**
Vicia sativa **(bush vetch)**
Viola odorata **(sweet violet)**

Cultivated plants, such as this blue-flowering *Camassia quamash*, can be combined effectively with native species in a wild-flower meadow.

A swathe of primrose (*Primula vulgaris*) lights up this area of rough grass in dappled shade during spring. Cut the grass short at Christmas to show the flowers off to best effect then do not cut again until after the primroses bloom.

When choosing wild flowers for your garden, the same rule applies for when selecting cultivated plants – the plant must suit the growing conditions. Some wild flowers prefer damp or boggy conditions, some like shade and others need sun. Check the backs of seed packets for details, or the care labels if buying pot-grown plants. Specialist seed catalogues often indicate which plants are attractive to butterflies. You can also buy seed mixtures for creating 'instant beds' in various habitats, for example, mixtures of seeds which thrive on chalkland or in coastal gardens. Others are specially created to attract bumblebees or the night-flying moths on which bats feed.

Wild-flower gardens need weeding in the same way as normal flowerbeds. By mulching around the plants with bark chippings you can reduce the time spent on this chore to a minimum. Wait until early spring to cut down old wild-flower stems in order to tidy the garden, because during winter the plant remains provide overwintering sites for beneficial insects, such as money spiders.

Once plants are established, deadhead the most successful species to control self-seeding, but leave a few of each type of wild flower to set seed so that natural replacements appear and colonies increase. Leave self-sown seedlings where they appear naturally.

Boundaries and Walls

IF YOU CHOOSE THE RIGHT MATERIALS AND PLANTS, YOU CAN CREATE AN ATTRACTIVE BOUNDARY THAT IS ALSO EASY TO LOOK AFTER

The vertical dividers of a garden – whether they follow the boundary line or form an internal screen – are one of the most crucial elements in its design. They not only provide the framework within which other features are placed, but can also have important secondary roles to play, depending on the situation. They may have to offer privacy, visual interest, security, intrigue, a vertical planting structure and, for an external boundary, a good face to the world.

No other element of your garden has to work so hard, so it is important to make the right choice. Providing a suitable boundary can be expensive, however, which leads many to make the cost the primary consideration rather than ease of maintenance. Unfortunately, what is cheap at the outset can result in greater costs in the long run, especially in terms of time spent maintaining and replacing structures.

The choice of materials is wide, but this is quickly whittled down when it has to satisfy a range of visual and functional demands, as well as being easy to maintain. Make the right choice, and your boundary or screen will require little attention and greatly enhance your garden.

EASY-CARE CALENDAR

SPRING
Tie down the shoots of climbing roses to encourage flowering. Tie in any wayward shoots of all climbers and wall shrubs and cut out any dead or damaged shoots.

SUMMER
Deadhead roses within easy reach by removing old flowerheads with 15 cm (6 in) of stem, cutting just above a leaf joint. Prune philadelphus and other summer-flowering shrubs by cutting back flowered stems to just above the next non-flowering shoot. This treatment effectively deadheads and keeps the plants compact in one go.

MID SUMMER
Continue to deadhead roses. Cut back overlong shoots to keep plants tidy, especially near to an entrance. Sprinkle a high-potash feed to promote flowering the following year.

AUTUMN
Clear leaves from around the base of roses and clematis if they have suffered from a fungal disease.

WINTER
Tidy up any debris before winter. Tie in any wayward stems to their supports.

STARTING FROM SCRATCH

Hire a contractor to erect walls and gate. It will take two days to dig out the footing and lay the foundations. Bricklaying will take a professional about two days for each 1.8x1.8 m (6x6 ft) of wall. Adding supports and planting climbers will take about a day.

Vertical gardening In this garden, easy-care flowering climbers and wall shrubs, including clematis, roses and philadelphus, add seasonal scent and colour to the year-round interest of the evergreen ivy and greater periwinkle.

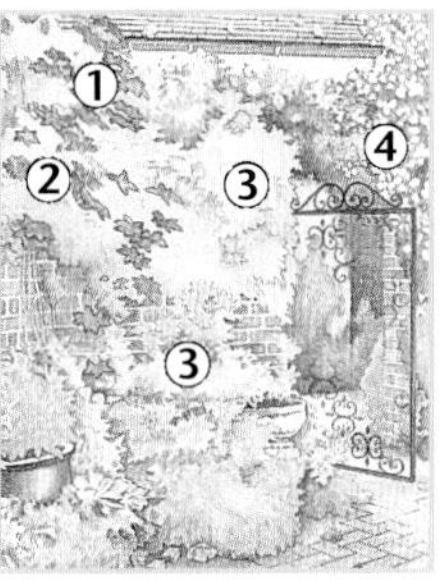

1 CLEMATIS – *'The President' (purple) and 'Nelly Moser' (pink) both flower from June.*

2 CLIMBING ROSE – *they tend to produce their main flush in June with another in late summer.*

3 EVERGREENS – *variegated ivy and greater periwinkle provide year-round interest.*

4 MOCK ORANGE *(philadelphus) – adds orange-blossom fragrance to the air on warm evenings.*

Making the most of garden boundaries

A boundary must not only form an attractive frame for the garden, but also be in keeping with the house and the surrounding buildings and landscape. There is a wide range of options to choose from, and each comes with its own style, character, texture and colour. Boundaries can be soft and natural, such as hedging, or hard, such as fencing or walling. There are low maintenance materials to suit all types of requirements: whether to produce a formal or cottage-garden look, to enhance privacy or hide eye-sores, to create a feeling of depth or mystery, to influence growing conditions, or to keep out intruders or strong winds.

If you prefer a formal look, do not feel restricted to traditional hedging plants that need clipping at least once a year, such as box, beech or yew. Opt instead for evergreens that stay neat with only minimal trimming, such as elaeagnus and aucuba. Alternatively, walls, trellis-work or railings provide an instant formal screen throughout the year with minimal care, and can be enhanced with climbers.

HOW MUCH WORK?

Different types of boundary take varying amounts of time to build and maintain. Use this as a guide.

Boundary	Start-up time	Care	Cost
Walls	•••	•	£££
Fences	••	••	££
Trellis	•	••	££
Railings	••	••	£££
Hedging	••	•••	£

Key to ratings
• (quick and easy) to
••• (time-consuming and hard work)
£ (cheap) to £££ (expensive)

Pyracantha *(above)* makes a prickly, evergreen boundary, providing summer flowers and autumn berries. Here it is left unclipped to form a natural shape.

White argyranthemums shows up well against the autumn hues of *Vitis coignetiae*. The vine will scramble happily over a wall using just a simple support.

Use panels of trelliswork to raise the height of an existing boundary for extra privacy and shelter and to provide an instant support for climbers.

An informal, rustic boundary can be created using wattle hurdles rather than traditional country hedge, such as hawthorn, or expensive dry-stone walls. The hurdles, made of woven hazel or willow stems, can be bought as ready-made panels, so are quick to put up. They last about ten years, or longer if treated with a preservative (see page 152). Just as quick to erect, but cheaper, are picket fences, made from lightweight panels of vertical wooden pales. They are ideal for small rural gardens, and twining climbers will weave through the pales without the need to attach wires.

If you need to enhance privacy because you are overlooked by neighbours, for example, trellis fixed to the top of existing fencing using metal post collars instantly adds height and provides a support for climbers (see below). Trellis can also be used to cover up down pipes or dilapidated structures, and is easily attached to walls (see page 154). Or it can create an illusion of depth in a small garden when used with mirrors or bought as a ready-made trompe l'oeil.

Internal boundaries are another way to add depth and mystery to a small garden – and trelliswork is ideal. Low hedges are a more formal way, as with traditional knot gardens and parterres, but instead of using work-intensive box hedging, it's possible to substitute easier

Trellis makes an attractive garden divider that needs no clipping and little upkeep. Here, a simple trellis arch frames the focal point beyond.

Problem solver

Improving privacy Use metal post collars to extend existing fence posts so that decorative trellis or other fencing material can be added which can then be used to support climbers.

alternatives, such as the lavender varieties 'Hidcote', 'Munstead' or 'Nana Alba', a rounded low-growing hebe, such as *Hebe rakaiensis*, or the upright rosemary, *Rosmarinus officinalis* 'Miss Jessopp's Upright'.

The height and size of the boundary will have an impact on the growing conditions in your garden. For example, if you put up a high wall with a south-facing aspect it will become a sun trap – a possible site for a pergola or seating area, and an ideal place for the busy gardener to relax. It will also increase the range of plants you can grow, particularly slightly tender climbers benefiting from the warmth and the shelter from cold winds. Conversely, building a high wall will increase the amount of shade on the north-facing side, adversely affecting sun-loving plants, including grass. To avoid patches of the lawn dying, it would be better to opt for a picket fence or a screen wall which would let some light through. If you are worried about intruders, and you want a low boundary, the spiky appearance of a picket fence or metal rail is more of a deterrent than a flat wall. Near bus stops or schools, low walls can also become used as make-shift seating areas, so go for hedging, fencing panels or railings instead.

Enhancing boundaries with climbers

Karen and Phill Lloyd, both in their late thirties, work from home as independent financial advisers. Their office is in the converted loft of their Edwardian house. The couple's main aim was to introduce a greater feeling of width to their garden, and to do something about the stark, overpowering nature of the closeboard fencing.

The Lloyd's wanted a low-upkeep garden so that Karen could concentrate on her hobby – raising vegetables and flowering plants from seed in the greenhouse at the bottom of the garden. She gets up at five o'clock each morning to walk their Yorkshire terrier and to spend an hour in the greenhouse before starting work, even in winter. Working at home meant that the couple wanted a garden that was visually pleasing all-year round, especially the areas close to the house. It also meant that they could pop out to do the occasional tying in of climbers and training of wall shrubs. They have no children, but plants need to be sufficiently robust to cope with their dog. Karen grows her vegetables beyond the greenhouse as she wanted to keep this area separate from the rest of the garden.

THE OLD GARDEN This odd-shaped garden is a bit like a wedge of cheese – wide at one end and narrow at the other. The closeboard fencing makes for a harsh boundary, with little effort having been made to soften it. The line of stepping stones sit proud of the lawn surface so are awkward to mow around.

DECIDING THEIR PRIORITIES

How much time?
Karen would like to concentrate her time spent in the garden working in the greenhouse. On the rest of the garden, she and Phill do not want to spend more than 4 hours a week.

Essential ingredients?
Climbers to soften the hard, vertical lines of the fencing. Easy-care flower borders that do not encroach too much on the lawn.

Likes and dislikes?
They both like flowers, and the more colourful the better. They also like plantings that have a lush, natural look. They dislike formal gardens with a lot of hard surfaces.

Solid boundaries placed in a windy position can cause eddying and turbulence and panel fencing, especially the less robust waney-edged type, is easily damaged. Use semi-solid boundaries instead because they filter and slow down the wind. Options include hedging or hit-and-miss fencing, which comprises a double layer of alternate slats that allows the wind to pass through but is a barrier to prying eyes. Protection from the wind also means that border plants will need less staking and watering. On the other hand, hedges grow less quickly in exposed areas, so they will need less trimming.

For a boundary adjacent to a busy road, opt for tough evergreens, such as elaeagnus or cherry laurel (*Prunus laurocerasus*). If litter is a problem, avoid prickly plants, such as holly or pyracantha because it will make clearing out the hedge difficult. An occasional hose down with water will clean off dust and dirt from the leaves. Elaeagnus and cherry laurel will tolerate most conditions – including heavy shade.

The spikes and strong verticals of these railings are softened by the relatively disease-resistant *Pyracantha rogersiana*.

THE NEW GARDEN Various design devices have been used to create a sense of width and depth, while keeping beds narrow.

Arbour *The greenhouse is hidden behind the back of an arbour to create a false end to the garden.*

Climbers *These are chosen for their narrow growing habit, and include* Actinidia kolomikta *and clematis.*

Obelisk *Used to create an instant, year-round vertical. For fragrance, sweet peas will be planted near the pathway.*

Lush planting *Borders are densely planted to screen the boundary and to suppress weeds.*

Angled step *The step is built at an angle to make the garden look bigger than it really is. The angle is softened by curving it.*

Stepping stones *They are recessed to lie flush with the lawn, so the lawnmower can pass straight over them.*

Choosing a boundary wall

Walls are the easiest type of boundary to maintain, but the most costly to build. They should last more than a lifetime and only need repointing every 10 to 15 years, if that. A brick wall is the most expensive type, because it requires skill to lay and the units are small, but bricks are attractive and you can choose from a wide choice of bonds, colours and styles. Concrete blocks are quicker to lay, and they make for a cheaper, long-lasting wall which can be made attractive by rendering or painting (see below). However, rendered or painted walls need regular maintenance.

Screen blocks, available in diamond and leaf patterns, are dated in appearance because of their popularity in the Fifties and Sixties, but they are quick to lay and make a good semi-transparent wall. Only use them for walls less than 1.8 m (6 ft) high, because they are not strong and must be reinforced with piers strengthened by iron rods.

Reconstituted stone is made from crushed natural stone mixed with cement and compressed into blocks. A range of designs is available, including 'instant' dry-stone walling, which come as blocks joined together to form larger units. These are particularly useful for the gardener with little construction experience because they can be 'glued'

Blue salvia brings out the beauty of this dry-stone wall. Leave a 30 cm (12 in) gap at the back of the border for easy upkeep.

Use plants to soften walls and frame gateways. This rose is trained over an arch to give depth and kept within reach to make pruning easier.

Revamp an old wall

You can extend the life of an old brick wall, provided it is still safe. Cap with coping using engineering bricks, which are water-resistant, or tiles laid on the slant, so water easily runs off.

Preparing Cover nearby plants with plastic sheeting, then rake out loose areas of mortar using a wire brush.

Repairing Repoint the wall where necessary using a ready-made mortar mix to save time mixing your own.

Finishing off Paint on silicone sealer to extend the wall's life and stop algal growth on shady walls. Apply two coats of masonry paint.

Making a planting wall

Low walls, especially in the front garden, can be greatly enhanced by planting. The quickest option for a modern setting is to use interlocking planters that are easy to slot together. Use a single course for a low wall or several courses to make a retaining wall.

Dig a trench For a permanent feature dig a trench 20 cm (8 in) deep and 60 cm (24 in) wide.

Fill with hardcore Add rubble, hardcore or gravel, then level and compact by treading firmly.

Lay the first course Slot together the interlocking D-shaped planters to form a low wall. No mortar is required.

Fill with soil Fill the bottom 5 cm (2 in) of each planter with gravel to provide drainage and top up with good garden soil.

Planting Water the soil thoroughly to help it settle. Allow to drain, then plant up with suitable easy-care varieties (see above). The wall illustrated is for a sunny position.

Easy-care plants

The following are all drought-tolerant plants ideal for wall planting.

Sunny wall Try alyssum, aubrieta, cerastium, alpine phlox, moss campion, sea campion, thymes and valerian.

In shade Arabis, *Campanula portenschlagiana*, *Corydalis lutea*, *Cymbalaria muralis*, saxifage, soft shield fern (*Polystichum setiferum*) or perennial violas.

together using an epoxy adhesive. Walls under 60 cm (24 in) can be laid dry, without glue or mortar, so are even easier. Although quick to construct, reconstituted stone walls are expensive and can look out of place in gardens that already have natural stone features.

Another quick option, especially for retaining walls, are gambions – steel mesh or wooden cages that can be filled with stone or rubble. They are available from builders' merchants. However, they need dressing up with soil and wall plants to look good.

Planting for walls It is better to 'build' the plants into a gambion or dry-stone wall than to push them into existing crevices (see above for a list of suitable, easy-care plants). Lay the rootballs as you would a stone in a wall, surround with compost and then lay a stone on top.

To enhance the appearance of rendered or painted walls, plant climbers on a trellis frame that is 'hooked' on and can be lifted off and laid flat on the ground (see page 194). This will save you from having to cut down the plants each time you redecorate.

Ivy is a vigorous grower and can easily run rampant on a wall. To remove it, cut through the stem at the base, wait until the branches are dry and brown, and then peel off the wall, cleaning the trace-marks with a wire brush. Finally, kill the ivy stump with a brushwood killer in spring so that the plant doesn't regrow.

Problem solver

Loose arris rails Panel fences shrink with age, causing loose-jointed arris rails to fall out. These can be easily repaired using a special bracket that holds the rail securely in place.

Fencing options

Fencing is the easiest hard boundary to erect and requires less maintenance than hedging. For DIY assembly, ready-made panels are the simplest (see below). Alternatively, a contractor can erect a longer-lasting type of fencing, such as closeboard fencing with vertical boards nailed onto horizontal rails. This is useful when posts are not at standard distances, and it means you can renew individual sections rather than a whole panel. Use pressure-treated softwood to avoid having to apply preservative every three to five years.

Putting up a panel fence the quick way In summer, use a glyphosate-based weedkiller to clear the weeds when they are actively growing. If there are neighbouring herbaceous plants, then wait until winter, when they will have died down, to make access easier.

For fences up to 1.2 m (4 ft), use fence spikes hammered into the ground to hold up the posts, checking every few strikes with a spirit level that the posts are going in straight. If you are unable to use fence spikes, either because you are erecting a boundary fence, which needs to be stronger or higher, or because the soil is stony or there are other obstructions, buy ready-mixed bags of concrete for the fence-post foundations. Save time digging holes by hiring a petrol-powered, post-hole borer, which acts like a corkscrew in the soil (see page 300), but first make sure that there are no cables or pipes on the boundary line.

THE CHOICE OF PANEL FENCES

Waney edge Widely available in standard-sized panels. It's easy to erect and the cheapest material for fencing. However, it can look flimsy and stark, and is prone to damage by strong winds, vandalism and children playing. It should last between 10 and 15 years.

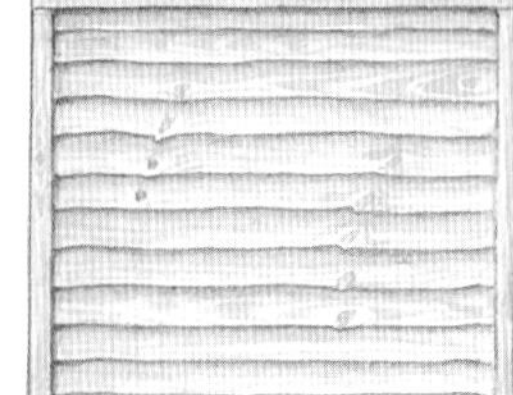

Picket fence Low fencing good for small or front gardens. It lets in light and is quicker to put up than larger panels. But it is more difficult to stain than other types. Panels are usually made of pressure-treated softwood, but are also available in plastic and ornate wire.

Diagonal board More expensive than waney edge panels but longer-lasting. Generally available only from fence specialists. Fewer repairs will be needed because it is sturdy. The wood is planed, so is easier to treat and requires less stain or paint than rough surfaces.

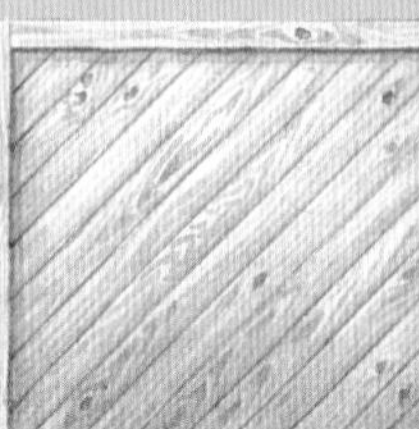

Wattle hurdle Hand woven, usually hazel or willow stems, for a rustic look. Some are clad with heather. They last about ten years, but their life can be almost doubled by treating with a 50/50 mix of turpentine and boiled linseed oil. More expensive than softwood panels.

Interwoven Made from thin strips of pressure-treated softwood woven between vertical strips, held in position by support timber at the edges. Similar in price and life expectancy to waney edge panels, but they are less stark, especially early on, before plants mature.

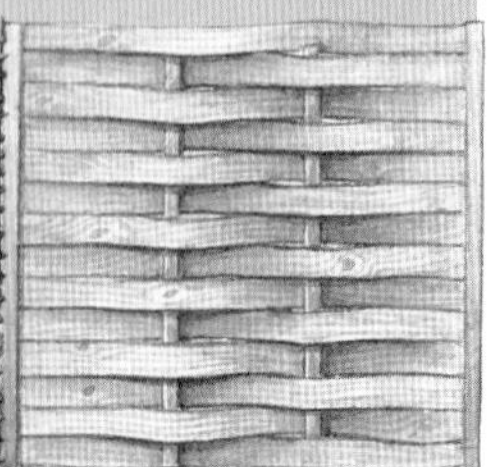

Time saver

If you have more than 30 m^2 (323 sq ft) of fence to stain, hire a paint sprayer, but warn neighbours first and use it only on a still, dry day. Make sure the stain is suitable for the sprayer. Otherwise, use a 10 cm (4 in) brush.

Rustic-style diamond fencing provides a natural support for these dahlias and solidago, as well as letting in light to the base of the plants so they don't go leggy.

Start by erecting the first and last posts of the fence. At every stage, use a spirit level to ensure that all posts are upright. Then, peg in a taut line between the posts, 30 cm (12 in) above ground level, to ensure that the fence runs straight. Nail in another taut line to the top of the two posts to ensure that the intermediate posts are at the same height. These two lines are also a quick way of checking that the posts are vertical along the line of the fence. Use a tape measure, or a bamboo cane cut to the width of the panel (usually 1.8 m/6 ft), to measure the distance between posts.

Attach panels to posts using 5x5 cm (2x2 in) U-shaped brackets rather than less durable, L-shaped brackets. You will need help, though, to slide the panels between the brackets. To give extra strength, use galvanised screws rather than nails, and a powered screwdriver to make the job easier and quicker.

Finishing off To avoid panels rotting at the base, put gravel boards at the bottom of each panel, or make sure the panels are not in contact with the ground. Fit water-shedding caps or finials on the fence posts to increase their life. To prevent weeds from growing through from the neighbours', tack a polythene membrane to the bottom of the fence to form a vertical wall extending 45 cm (18 in) underground.

For a coloured finish, apply a water-based rather than oil-based stain to the timber, avoiding the need to cover plants when painting. Work out the area you need to cover before buying the stain, and allow an extra ten per cent for rough wood. Remember that the fence will deteriorate faster if you grow climbers because the stems, especially of vigorous plants, will prise open any gaps in the fence.

The simplicity of low-level picket fencing is ideal for a cottage-style front garden *(below)*. It is quicker to erect than panel fencing, but staining takes longer.

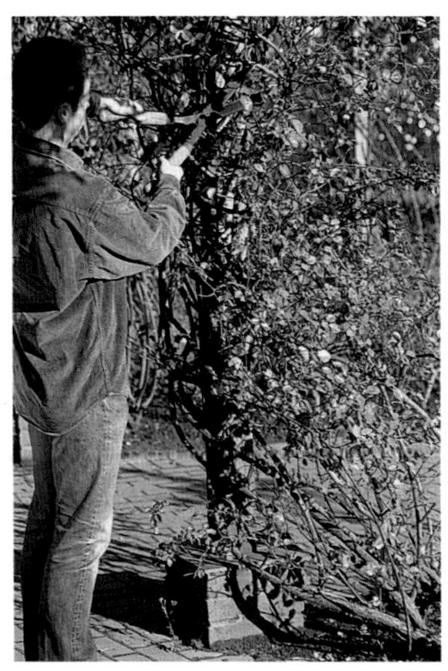

Wind new shoots of climbing roses around the support and tie in as horizontally as possible to encourage flowers. After flowering, tidy up new growth with shears.

Trellis, screens and plant supports

Apart from providing a support for climbing plants, trellis is a quick way of extending walls and fences and is an ideal screen for less attractive parts of the garden, such as sheds, dustbin areas and compost heaps. Available in a wide range of sizes and shapes, trellis can be square or diagonal, with a wavy or straight top edge, or designed as a trompe l'oeil, adding illusory depth.

Trellis is available in several materials, but timber is by far the most common. Choose a pressure-treated softwood, or a hardwood, which needs no treating but is about four times the price. You can buy trelliswork stained with a particular colour from specialist suppliers. If you do it yourself, use stain rather than paint because with age it fades rather than flakes (see page 153).

Plastic trellis is maintenance-free because it doesn't rot or need treating with a preservative. It is widely available in white, blue, green or wood-coloured. It costs about the same as pressure-treated softwood, but it does not have the same resilience, especially at the joints, so avoid it if you want a support for heavy climbers.

Woven hazel or willow trellis is a rustic option, but best used to complement similar materials in the garden. It is more expensive than softwood trellis and is more variable in quality. However, it looks good as a wall decoration without plants or as a support for

CREATIVE PLANT SUPPORTS

Freestanding plant supports can make a feature out of a climbing plant in any part of the garden. They will need to be strong and well-anchored.

Lattice trellis *Sturdy panels available in various widths; some have a concave and others a convex top edge. Used for adding interest to a wall or for dividing a garden.*

Single post *Slot a post into a fencing spike for a quick and easy way to add colour and variety to an existing border, as well as immediate height.*

Post and rope *Fence posts with finial tops linked by rope. Ideal for dividing a garden without creating a lot of shadow and for adding height at the back of a border.*

lightweight climbers. If left untreated it should last up to ten years; if you want it to last longer either apply a wood preservative or treat with a special mix of boiled linseed oil and turpentine (see page 152).

Metal trellis is available from specialist suppliers, such as gate manufacturers or ironmongers. It's the strongest and longest-lasting option, provided that the metal is galvanised or plastic coated.

Adding height Attaching trellis to the top of a wall has several advantages: it enhances security, cuts down on wind eddies and allows you to grow bigger plants. For windy sites or to support heavy climbers, bolt timber posts to the side of the wall with an upstand for attaching the trellis. Otherwise, a quick method is to fix the support posts to the top of the wall using galvanised 5x5 cm (2x2 in) L-shaped brackets. Screw two brackets to the bottom of each post, then screw the brackets to the top of the wall so that the posts are spaced correctly. Finally, attach the trellis to the posts using U-brackets.

Trellis as a fence Trellis makes a good fence where privacy is not required. Use 7.5x7.5 cm (3x3 in) posts because they look neater and are easier to handle than the larger-sized ones used for fencing. Then attach battens each side of the post and nail (or screw) trellis to that, or simply secure trellis to the front of the post.

This trompe l'oeil (or perspective) trellis clad with clematis provides a frame for the box topiary. It is an effective feature needing little work.

Obelisk *Ready-made designs are available in wood and metal, or you could make your own out of trellis. Useful for creating a focal point or adding height to a border.*

Arbour *Available in various sizes and styles. Creates a secluded seating area that doubles as a plant support and point of interest in the garden.*

Attaching trellis

Good air circulation To allow air to circulate behind the trelliswork, fix a frame of 5x5cm (2x2 in) battens to the wall. Start by marking on the wall the four corners where the battens are to be attached. For speed, apply a waterproof universal adhesive to the back of the battens. Press the battens onto the wall, maintaining pressure for the recommended time. Allow to dry for a day. Or, use a drill to fix the battens with galvanised screws.

Detachable trellis For easy access to the wall for repairs or painting, attach the trellis to the battens using hooks at the top and bottom. This allows the trellis, together with climbers, to be removed from the wall and replaced later.

In summer, the green leaves of the climbing *Vitis coignetiae (above)* provide a perfect foil for purple berberis and silver *Brachyglottis greyi*. By autumn *(right)*, the foliage of the vine turns bright red and becomes the centre of attention.

Easy-care planting for boundaries

Growing climbers and shrubs against boundaries or internal screens adds interest to a hard or unattractive surface, and is the best use of space in a small garden. Choosing the right plant for the right site is the key to minimising work; in particular, you will need to consider the plant's eventual size, and its preferred aspect.

To work out the aspect of a wall or fence, use a compass or observe where the sun rises (east) and sets (west). Sites that face north and east receive less warmth from the sun, and unless they are sheltered are exposed to cold winter winds. Frosts lift more slowly here, so plants need to be hardy. On east-facing walls, grow later-flowering plants, such as pyracantha, since early flowerers, such as camellia, will have their blooms damaged by the rapid thaw that occurs when morning sun follows a frosty night.

Choosing the right plants It is important to choose plants to match the size of their supports if you want to avoid constant rounds of cutting back and tying in. If the climber or wall shrub does need drastic pruning, cut it back by a third, or remove a few larger branches at the

Planting climbers

Do put up the support before planting. Make sure it is the correct size and strength for the climber.

Do kill weeds before planting.

Do add compost when planting and use a mulch to reduce the need to water and weed.

Do invest in long-handled pruners or loppers to cut back tall climbers.

Don't plant large plants where they will need constant cutting back to keep within bounds.

Don't remove canes from new climbers. They will use them to clamber easily onto the support.

EASY-CARE CLIMBERS WITH ATTRACTIVE FOLIAGE

The following climbers need no pruning other than to keep within bounds.
E = evergreen

Akebia quinata
Hedera canariensis
'Gloire de Marengo' (E)
***Hedera colchica* 'Dentata',**
'Dentata Variegata' and
'Sulphur Heart' (E)
***Hedera helix* 'Buttercup' (E) and**
'Goldheart' (E)
***Humulus lupulus* 'Aureus'**
***Hydrangea serratifolia* (E)**
***Jasminum officinale* 'Fiona Sunrise'**
Parthenocissus
Vitis coignetiae

Euonymus fortunei 'Silver Queen', with an edging of crested male fern, provides a low-upkeep 'cladding' for this shady wall.

base (see page 89). Self-clinging climbers, such as ivy and climbing hydrangea, should be cut back hard when planted because only new growth, rather than existing growth, will cling to the wall. After that, they will need no extra support. Other climbers, such as those that climb by twining (such as honeysuckle and common jasmine) or by using tendrils (such as clematis and passion flower), will need to be positioned so that their growing canes are angled into the wall in order to enable them to scramble up the trellis or wires.

Avoid covering old, crumbling walls with self-clinging climbers because they will speed up the decaying process. Also avoid plants with woody stems and any which grow to more than 4.5 m (15 ft), including wisteria, because they will need a very solid, well-anchored support otherwise they can collapse under their own weight.

Wall shrubs are freestanding shrubs suited to growing against a wall. There are three types. Some, such as pyracantha and chaenomeles, respond well to clipping, and to training flat against a wall. Others, such as *Forsythia suspensa* and *Jasminum nudiflorum,* are naturally lax shrubs that need to be tied into a support or to flop over a low wall for them to be seen at their best. The third type are slightly tender shrubs, such as fremontodendron, that take well to training on a wall, and need the extra warmth from a south or west-facing aspect.

Even climbers and wall shrubs that don't need annual pruning will need cutting back if they outgrow their situation, so it is essential to choose the right-sized plant for the spot, otherwise you will be forever

A green cascade of climbing golden hop, *Clematis armandii* and *C. montana*. Trim with shears if they become too unruly.

EASY-CARE WALL SHRUBS

The following wall shrubs need no pruning other than to keep within bounds. S = shade-tolerant, F = fragrant.

Carpenteria californica **(F)**
Ceanothus
Chaenomeles (S)
Cotoneaster dammeri **(S),**
C. horizontalis **(S),** ***C. x suecicus*** **(S)**
C. microphyllus **(S),**
Cytisus battandieri **(F)**
Euonymus fortunei **(S)**
Fremontodendron
Garrya elliptica **'James Roof'**
Pittosporum tenuifolium
Pyracantha (S)

cutting it back – especially when planting round doorways and windows. Check the eventual width of wall shrubs and avoid planting them in narrow borders near pathways.

Sunny walls and fences Warm, sunny sites on south and west-facing walls provide an opportunity to grow a wide range of more tender climbers and wall shrubs. Soil dries out quickly in these situations, so to save time on watering add plenty of well-rotted organic matter to the planting hole. Or choose one of the many easy-care plants, such as fremontodendron or *Carpenteria californica*, that flower best in the poor soil commonly found near house walls. Aftercare is also straightforward, because these plants either require no pruning or can simply be chopped back with shears when they get too large. Fragrant plants in particular, such as *Carpenteria californica* and the pineapple-smelling *Cytisus battandieri*, need a sunny spot for maximum scent.

Shady walls and fences Many climbers that cope with shade need good soil, so always dig in plenty of organic matter when planting and mulch afterwards. Climbers tend naturally to scramble upwards, so make it easier for them by ensuring that branches are angled towards a suitable prop, whether it is trellis, wires or a host plant.

A sunny wall gives you the opportunity to grow more tender plants, such as this Moroccan broom *(Cytisus battandieri)*.

This red-flowered chaenomeles *(below)* is perfect for a north-facing wall. Secure the main stems with wall nails and ties.

Soften structures with climbers. Here, the living roof of *Clematis montana* needs only an occasional trim if it has sufficient room.

Drought-tolerant wall shrubs, like this *Fremontodendron californicum (below)*, rarely need watering.

Before choosing your climber, assess whether the shade is dry, such as that found under the canopy of a large tree, because this will limit your choice of plants. Ivy is the obvious climber for this situation, but in moister spots, the range increases. Shade-loving climbers tend to produce their flowers and foliage higher up, unless encouraged to bloom lower down by pruning and tying in, so combine them with easy, shade-tolerant shrubs, such as vinca or *Cotoneaster horizontalis*, that will cover the bare stem bases.

Covering up eyesores Ugly chain-link or wire-mesh fencing can be transformed into a living green barrier by planting it with ivy. One large-leaved ivy or two small-leaved varieties planted every 1.8 m (6 ft) will be sufficient to form a barrier 1-1.2 m (3-4 ft) high within four years. The leaves of *Hedera helix* 'Buttercup' turn a butter-yellow in the sun, while for bigger, variegated leaves try *Hedera colchica* varieties 'Sulphur Heart' or 'Dentata Variegata'. Leave the ivy to grow without clipping or, for a formal look, clip it once it reaches the top of the fence. For a more elaborate display, mix ivy with euonymus and *Jasminum nudiflorum*. Other suitable climbers include the evergreen *Lonicera japonica* or the vigorous, yellow-flowered *Clematis* 'Bill MacKenzie', which has attractive fluffy seed heads in autumn.

Time saver

A quick-fix alternative to tying in climbers to their support with garden twine or wire is to use proprietary plant ties and clips, especially for fiddly, delicate stems. They come ready cut to length and galvanised against rust.

The branches of the climbing rose 'Parkdirektor Riggers' have been spread as horizontally as possible along the bottom lattice to encourage a good display of flowers at eye level.

Trouble-free climbing roses

Roses are rewarding plants, offering a wide range of colour, flower shape, scent and habit. For easy care, keep pruning methods simple (see calendar, opposite) and choose varieties with resistance to black spot and mildew. When planting, add plenty of organic matter, such as well-rotted compost, to the soil in order to keep the plant healthy and trouble free. Most roses need to be in the sun for almost all day, but avoid scorching-hot, dry spots unless you are prepared to water and use a fungicide regularly. Plant the rose at least 45 cm (18 in) away from the wall, or other kind of support, to encourage good air circulation and reduce disease problems.

There are two main types of climbing roses: ramblers and climbers. Ramblers are closer to the original wild rose; they grow vigorously and bear huge trusses of small flowers in one flush in summer. Climbing roses, on the other hand, tend to produce fewer, but larger flowers, and bloom throughout the summer. While ramblers flower on the previous year's wood, climbers flower on young wood made in the same year, so less old wood needs cutting out when pruning.

Improved results

More flowers When tying in branches, bend them down horizontally. This will produce more flowers, as well as reducing the vigour so that the plant is more likely to keep within its allotted space and need less cutting back.

Fewer disease problems If your soil is light and sandy, installing an automatic watering system (see page 266) will reduce the incidence of fungal diseases. Also, mulch twice yearly, in spring and autumn.

Roses for pillars or posts If you have no time to train a rose against a wall, compact varieties of climbing roses can be tied in to vertical structures in the border. Choose roses with an upright habit and that grow no taller than their support. For posts and pillars lower than 2.4 m (8 ft), try yellow-flowered 'Good as Gold' or the orange-red 'Warm Welcome'. For structures up to 3.5 m (12 ft), good choices include red-flowered 'Parkdirektor Riggers', pink-and-gold 'Phyllis Bide' or yellow 'Golden Showers'. Alternatively, wrap the stems of larger climbers in a spiral around the pillar or post to encourage horizontal stems from which flower-carrying sideshoots can grow.

Thornless roses Some varieties of climbing rose have almost no thorns, making them safe for children, easier to prune, and an ideal choice for use near pathways. Easy-care varieties include the climber 'Zéphirine Drouhin' and the ramblers 'Lykkefund' and, for a sunny wall, *Rosa banksiae* 'Lutea'.

Less pruning Choose a rambler that needs only light pruning – the removal of dead, diseased or spent wood, as well as damaged shoot tips (see below). Give it plenty of space to spread, such as over a shed, large wall or garage, because some ramblers can grow to 12 m (40 ft). Indeed, the variety 'Kiftsgate' will produce up to 3.5 m (12 ft) of new growth a year, so needs a large tree or a big wire fence to scramble over. If a rambler growing through a tree or over a large structure becomes too big, or growth too congested resulting in failing health, cut the whole plant back to 1.2 m (4 ft) in winter. It will rejuvenate, although it will take vigorous climbers a year or two to flower again.

TRAINING AND PRUNING CLIMBING ROSES

Buy well-branched plants and train immediately after planting to create a framework that is easy to prune and that will flower where you want it.

SPRING
Just before growth begins, prune repeat-flowering climbers by removing dead and exhausted shoots. To get flowers all along stems, tie in large shoots horizontally in a rough fan shape, once growth starts. Over the growing season, spread out and tie new shoots.

SUMMER
Deadhead ramblers, where possible, and once-flowering climbers by removing old flower heads with 15 cm (6 in) of stem – or 30-45 cm (12-18 in) if vigorous. To get new growth on old ramblers, cut a few old, spent flowering shoots to ground level.

AUTUMN/WINTER
Leave pruning of repeat-flowering climbers to spring. If roses have suffered mildew or black spot, clear leaves to prevent spores overwintering. To rejuvenate rampant ramblers on large structures, cut them back to 1.2 m (4 ft) from ground level.

EASY-CARE CLIMBERS AND RAMBLERS

Roses offer a colourful display, whether in one strong burst or by flowering throughout summer. All the following offer resistance against black spot or mildew.

Attractive flowers and hips 'Bobbie James', 'Dortmund', 'Hamburger Phönix', 'Madame Grégoire Staechelin', 'Maigold' (pictured), 'Parkdirektor Riggers', 'Rambling Rector'.

Repeat-flowering 'Aloha', 'Compassion', 'Dublin Bay', 'Golden Showers', 'Hamburger Phönix', 'Harcomp', 'Macba', 'Madame Alfred Carrière', 'Sympathie', 'Phyllis Bide' (pictured).

Double flowers that resist rain 'Aloha', 'Arthur Bell', 'Delmur', 'Golden Showers', 'Hardwell', 'Highfield, 'Macha', 'New Dawn' (pictured), 'White Cockade'.

Easy-to-prune ramblers May flowers: *Rosa banksiae* 'Lutea'. June flowers: 'Lykkefund, 'Rambling Rector', 'Sanders' White Rambler (pictured). 'Seagull', 'Veilchenblau'.

Good for scent 'Aloha', 'Compassion', 'Madame Grégoire Staechelin', 'Maigold', 'Rambling Rector', 'Sanders' White Rambler', 'Seagull', 'Veilchenblau' (pictured).

Time saver

Multi-stemmed clematis provide the quickest cover, so when buying look for a plant with three or four healthy stems. If there is only one stem, cut it back to the lowest pair of buds after planting to produce more stems.

Clematis for all seasons

There is a variety of clematis that flowers for every month of the year in myriad colours and shapes, including bells, saucers and lanterns. In the wild, clematis use their leaf stalks to grip onto branches of small trees and shrubs. The fluffy, white autumn seed heads give them the common name, old man's beard. In the garden, they need to climb over trellis, wires or a shrubby plant.

The natural habit of clematis is to grow a twisted 'rope' of stems with 'bird's nest'-like growth spreading out higher up. Hard pruning after planting (see below) encourages plenty of stems to give a better plant shape when the clematis is grown over trelliswork or a wall. If you are growing the plant through a shrub or tree, this need not be done because the 'rope' of stems will help the clematis reach the shrubby plant's canopy, where it will flower.

Choose vigorous, no-prune clematis (see right) for places that are hard to reach, such as sheds or walls, or where stems will be difficult to pull out, such as through trees or shrubs. Smaller, no-prune clematis are better for fences or trelliswork, because they can still be cut

Successful planting

The top of the clematis rootball needs to be up to 15 cm (6 in) below soil level to safeguard against the fungal disease clematis wilt. Deep planting also produces a reserve of buds that will grow into new stems if the plant is damaged above ground. For drought-resistance, add plenty of well-rotted organic matter.

Dig a hole 45 cm (18 in) wide and deep. Add garden compost or leaf-mould to the base.

Position the plant The lowest pair of buds needs to be positioned below soil level, with the plant angled towards the support. Don't remove canes until new growth starts.

For effective watering Next to the roots sink a short pipe or plastic bottle with the base cut off and fill with gravel to make watering easy.

Mulch the surface Once the planting hole is filled, mulch with stones or bark chippings to keep roots cool and moist, and to reduce the need to water.

Encourage more shoots After planting, prune the plant to the lowest pair of visible buds. When new stems appear, tie them in the direction that you want them to grow.

Keep roots moist Water the clematis regularly until established by running the hose into the gravel-filled pipe or cut-off plastic bottle.

Quick training

To avoid having to tie in, choose a vigorous clematis species, such as *Clematis montana*. When planting, cut back to the lowest pair of buds to ensure lots of flowering stems. If you want the plant to grow over a structure, such as a pergola or arch, plant on the north side so that the shoots grow over the structure and flower towards the sun, still keeping the roots cool in the shade.

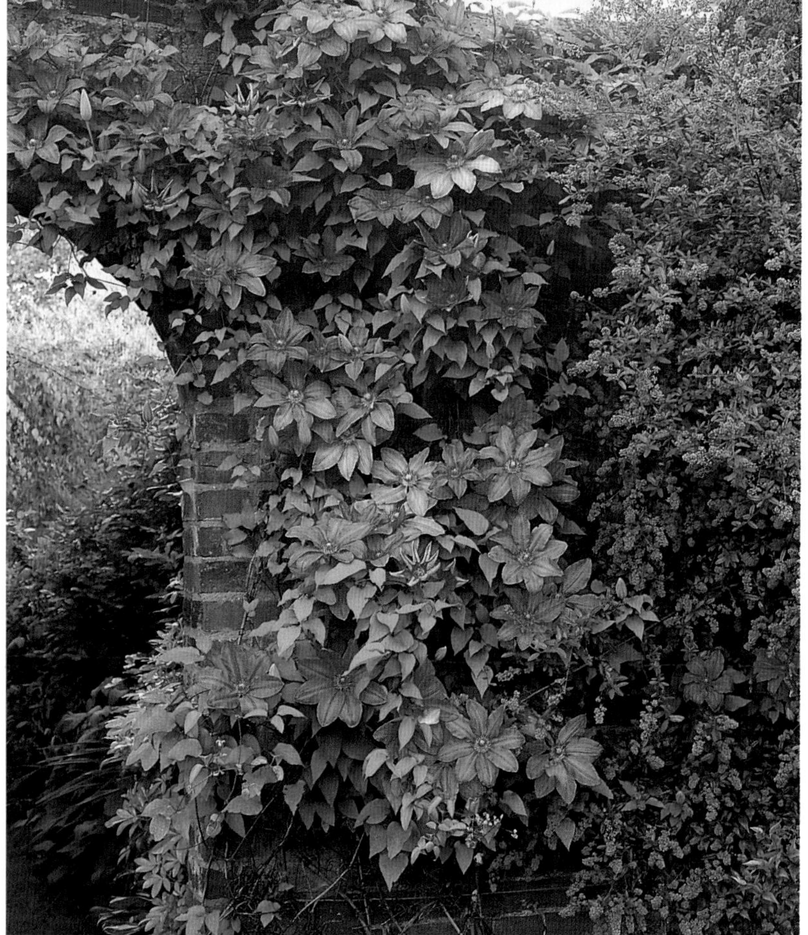

Clematis 'Lawsoniana', which needs only a light prune in early spring, is a perfect early-summer companion for *Ceanothus* 'Cascade'.

back hard if the support needs treating. Choose hard-prune clematis for obelisks and containers: hard pruning will keep growth compact, with dense growth right from the base.

Pruning made simple If you have inherited a garden with clematis and are unsure whether to prune, use this as your guide.

Small flowers in spring (early-flowering species). No pruning needed, but the plant can be cut down to 60 cm (24 in) immediately after flowering if they outgrow their allotted space – this may mean a missed season of flowering, though. These include: *Clematis montana*, *C. alpina* and *C. macropetala* both with dainty, bell-shaped flowers.

Large, saucer-sized flowers (large-flowered hybrids). For those that flower in June or earlier, remove dead or damaged top growth in February. Those that flower after June can be hard pruned in February. Cut back all stems to 15 - 30 cm (6 - 12 in) above ground level. For both groups, cut back to a pair of healthy buds.

Late-flowering species that flower in late summer and early autumn, such as *C. orientalis* and *C. tangutica*, and *C. viticella*, have the same pruning instructions as for early-flowering species (see above).

TROUBLE-FREE CLEMATIS FOR EVERY SITUATION

From a big wall to a small obelisk, there are types of clematis for all situations. Species clematis are particularly self-sufficient, with the viticella group the most resistant to clematis wilt. Flowering months are shown in brackets.

Against sheds and walls *C. armandii* (Mar), *C. montana* (May), viticella group (July-Sep), 'Jackmanii Superba' (July-Sep), orientalis group, such as 'Bill MacKenzie' (pictured, Aug/Sep), *C. flammula* (Sep), *C. tibetana* (Oct).

Over trellis and fences *C. alpina* (Apr), *C. macropetala* (May), early large-flowered hybrids, like 'Vyvyan Pennell' (pictured, May-July), texensis group (July-Sep), viticella group (July-Sep), orientalis group (Aug/Sep).

In containers and on obelisks *C. alpina* (Apr), *C. macropetala* (May), texensis group (July-Sep), late large-flowered hybrids, such as 'Perle d'Azur' (pictured, June-Sep), viticella group (July-Sep).

In shade *C. alpina* (Apr), *C. macropetala* (May), *C. montana* (pictured, May) and large-flowered hybrids 'Comtesse de Bouchard', 'Henryi', 'Marie Boisselot', 'Nelly Moser', 'Victoria' and 'William Kennett'.

Double-value climbers

Planting two climbers together on the same support makes good use of space, particularly in a small garden. If you combine climbers which have the same cultural requirements and flower at different times, they can be as easy to look after as a single climber and yet provide a longer season of interest.

Alternatively, if you want to grow climbers, but don't have a suitable wall or fence, you can use a tree or a large shrub as a climbing frame. Some climbers, roses in particular, have a tendency to have bare stems at the base, so planting another climber up them is a simple way of filling the gap. It also saves you the bother of having to put up wires or trellis.

For climbers and shrubs to combine with ease, it is essential to match the vigour of the plants so that one doesn't swamp the other. Provided that the plants have similar requirements for soil type and aspect, as well as maintenance, such as pruning and watering, you can double the impact without doubling the work. For example, any two large-flowered hybrid clematis flowering at the same time can be grown together – it is only a matter of harmonising colour schemes. Alternatively, many clematis that need little or no regular pruning can be grown over large, established no-prune climbers without fear of competition. For example, *Clematis macropetala* grown through a rambling rose.

Choosing a support plant Deciduous shrubs with a short flowering season and plain evergreens, especially those with foliage dark enough to make a good backdrop for flowers, can be put to extra work in the garden by growing climbers through them. The same applies to trees, but large trees need more vigorous climbers in order to make an impact (see right).

Either grow climbers through plants that need no pruning, such as the deciduous shrub *Clerodendrum trichotomum* or the evergreen *Viburnum rhytidophyllum*, which both grow to 5 m (16 ft). Or through plants which have the same pruning requirements, such as the viticella group clematis, *Clematis* 'Ville de Lyons' through *Buddleja davidii*, or an ornamental elder such as the purple-leaved *Sambucus nigra* 'Guincho Purple' or *S. racemosa* 'Sutherland Gold', which has golden, finely cut foliage. All these can be hard pruned in early spring.

Many types of clematis are particularly suitable for clambering through trees and shrubs because this is what they do in

Perfect props

Choose any plant in Group A and team it up with any in Group B or Group C. Companions from Group B require no pruning, companions from Group C should be hard pruned in February.

Group A *Garrya elliptica* 'James Roof', *Hedera canariensis* 'Gloire de Marengo', *H. colchica* 'Sulphur Heart' or 'Dentata Variegata', *Hydrangea anomala* ssp. *petiolaris*, *Pittosporum tenuifolium* 'Silver Queen', climbing roses and ramblers (see page 161 for recommended varieties), *Schizophragma hydrangeoides* and *Trachelospermum asiaticum*.

Group B All varieties of *Clematis alpina*, such as 'Frances Rivis', and *Clematis macropetala*, such as 'Blue Bird' and 'Markham's Pink'.

Group C Large-flowered clematis that flower after June. All varieties of viticella, including 'Etoile Violette', 'Madame Julia Correvon' and 'Purpurea Plena Elegans'.

Clematis 'Gravetye Beauty' (tulip-shaped) and 'Purpurea Plena Elegans' are easy to look after because they can be hard-pruned together in February.

GOOD COMPANIONS

Climbers are ideal for teaming up with existing plants in the garden and this is an easy way for the busy gardener to add a new climber without having to go to the trouble of providing a support. Choose climbers that live harmoniously with their support, thrive in similar conditions, and flower in a different season to give longer interest.

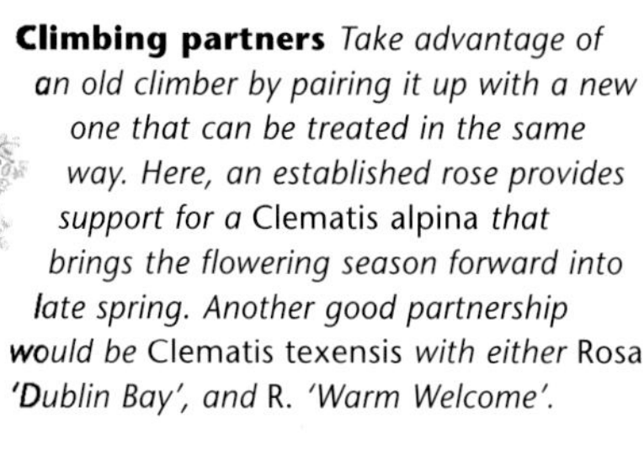

Climbing partners *Take advantage of an old climber by pairing it up with a new one that can be treated in the same way. Here, an established rose provides support for a* Clematis alpina *that brings the flowering season forward into late spring. Another good partnership would be* Clematis texensis *with either* Rosa *'Dublin Bay', and* R. *'Warm Welcome'.*

Brighten up a dull shrub Humulus lupulus *'Aureus' adds summer interest to a mature* Viburnum rhytidophyllum. *Other good climbers to use with shrubs include:* Clematis texensis, C. viticella *and large-flowered hybrid clematis; Chilean glory vine* (Eccremocarpus scaber); *and the perennial pea* (Lathyrus latifolius).

Add interest to an old tree *Choose a climber that will reach up into the canopy and not require pruning. If it's a fruiting tree, avoid climbers with vicious thorns. Here,* Clematis x jouiniana *'Praecox' adds summer colour to the canopy.*

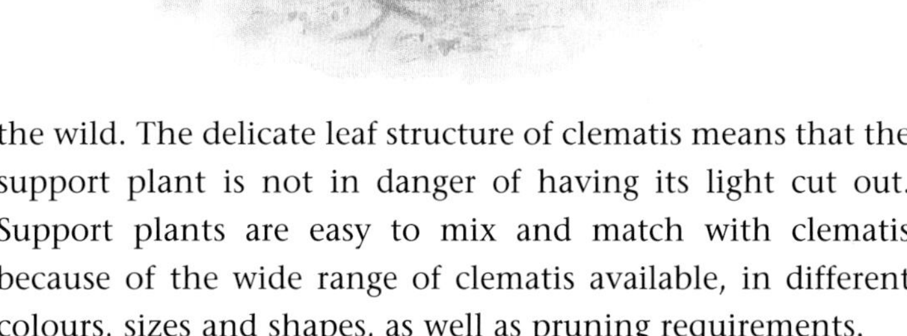

the wild. The delicate leaf structure of clematis means that the support plant is not in danger of having its light cut out. Support plants are easy to mix and match with clematis because of the wide range of clematis available, in different colours, sizes and shapes, as well as pruning requirements.

Other lightweight, herbaceous climbers that don't mind being chopped back with the support shrub during the dormant season include the vigorous golden hop (*Humulus lupulus* 'Aureus'), the purple-flowered perennial pea (*Lathyrus latifolius*) and Chilean glory vine (*Eccremocarpus scaber*), which will need to be grown as an annual in less mild areas.

Dead trees make good supports for more vigorous climbers, such as *Clematis montana* and parthenocissus. To make the tree safe – as it may fall down – trim off the branches to leave a tall trunk and stubs to act as the climbing support. Climbers can also be used to add interest to mature live trees (see above).

To make an informal hedge, *Kerria japonica* needs only a thinning out of the oldest shoots from the base in June.

An easy way to hedge your boundaries

Hedges make long-lasting barriers and a wide range of attractive plants are available to do the job – some with evergreen leaves for all-year privacy, and others with flowers and berries. The main tasks associated with hedges are planting and trimming, but you can limit the work by choosing resilient plants that have a slow rate of growth.

The style of hedge that you choose – formal or informal – dictates the amount of work needed. Formal hedges of yew, holly or beech need trimming once a year, in mid August, and privet or box-leaved honeysuckle (*Lonicera nitida*) every six to eight weeks, from late spring to autumn, if they are to be kept neat. In any case, avoid formal hedges more than 1.5 m (5 ft) high because they are difficult to reach when cutting, or consider hiring a contractor (see page 302).

An informal hedge is an easy-care alternative. Shrubs such as *Elaeagnus* x *ebbingei* or *Aucuba japonica* (see below), which grow no higher than 3 m (10 ft), need only an occasional trim to stop them becoming straggly. They are better used for short boundaries, though, because they need to be pruned with secateurs, otherwise their broad, shiny leaves turn brown and messy looking if sliced in two. Alternatively, use shears or a hedge trimmer just before the main flush of growth in spring so that the new shoots hide the damaged leaves.

If the boundary is adjacent to a busy road, avoid prickly evergreens, such as berberis and pyracantha, which have thorns that will make picking out the inevitable litter difficult. And, if you live in an area

WHICH HEDGE?

Many hedges can be grown either as formal clipped specimens or informal natural screens. More informal hedges **often have flowers and berries too.**

Elaeagnus* x *ebbingei *Good evergreen shelter hedge. Glossy, dark green leaves, silver underneath. Small, fragrant flowers mid autumn to spring. Size: clipped 1.5 m (5 ft); unclipped 2.4 m (8 ft).*

Osmanthus delavayi *Compact evergreen. Dark green leaves. Fragrant flowers are produced in April and May. Blue, black fruits in autumn. Size: clipped 90 cm (36 in); unclipped 1.2 m (4 ft).*

Griselinia littoralis *Bright, glossy green leaves. Only moderately frost hardy. Good hedging plant in mild, coastal areas because it is salt-tolerant. Size: clipped 90 cm (36 in); unclipped 1.8-2.1 m (6-7 ft).*

with a high snowfall, choose a deciduous hedging so that you won't have to knock off the snow.

For an instant screen, the temptation is to select Leyland cypress, which grows about 90 cm (36 in) each year. However, it needs trimming at least twice a year, so it is better to select Lawson cypress, which grows at a lesser, yet still vigorous, 30 cm (12 in) a year.

A wildlife hedge, such as this one with native elder and dog rose, not only provides you with ingredients for elderflower wine and rose-hip syrup, but can also be left to care for itself for years.

Wildlife hedge If you live in a rural area and have plenty of space, consider a wildlife hedge – it will grow to about 2.4x1.8 m (8x6 ft) and can be left to its own devices for years. Use plants that make up field hedgerows in your area, choosing one species – for example, hawthorn, sloe or hazel – to make up three-quarters of the hedge. Add a mixture of other shrubs such as guelder rose (*Viburnum opulus*), elder (sambucus) and dogwood (*Cornus sanguinea*) for extra seasonal interest. If the hedge gets too big, take out some larger branches in winter, when time is less precious. Bramble, rose and ivy will self-sow in the base of the hedge, making an impenetrable barrier and a home for nesting birds, along with hedgerow plants and wild flowers, such as lady's smock, primroses and bulbs, depending on the soil conditions of the area where you live.

Aucuba japonica (spotted laurel)
Evergreen with glossy green leaves. Tolerates most conditions, including deep shade where little else with grow. Size: clipped 90 cm (36 in); unclipped to 3 m (9 ft).

Escallonia rubra* var. *macrantha
Evergreen with toothed, dark green leaves. Best in mild areas. Crimson flowers from summer to early autumn. Size: clipped 1.5-1.8 m (5-6 ft); unclipped to 3 m (9 ft).

Hedges near borders

If you're planting a hedge near a plant border, avoid hedges that are very hungry and thirsty, such as x *Cupressocyparis leylandii* and privet, because they will take away nutrients and water from the border plants. Also avoid plants that drop prickly leaf litter, such as holly, pyracantha, berberis and hawthorn; they will make working in the border unpleasant. Leave a 45 cm (18 in) path behind the border for easy access for hedge trimming and so that clippings do not fall on plants.

Time saver

Make trimming hedges at the back of a border quick and safe by sinking well-firmed stepping stones in front of the hedge, and using them as a solid base for the ladder. Use a ladder support when clipping a tall hedge.

Planting and aftercare of hedges

The most economical way to set a deciduous hedge is to buy bare-root plants for planting in the dormant season. Evergreens, on the other hand, need to be bought as pot-grown specimens and planted in spring so that they have time to establish themselves in their new position before the arrival of drying winter winds.

Before planting a deciduous or evergreen hedge, clear the boundary line of perennial weeds using a glysophate-based weedkiller for speed. Then dig a trench and fill it with organic matter to help to retain moisture, keeping watering to a minimum. Run a seep hose along the boundary line so that the hedge can be easily watered in the first few years until it is established. After planting, cut back the plants by a third to encourage dense growth. Always plant borders at least 60 cm (24 in) from the front of the hedge to minimise competition for nutrients and moisture, and to make hedge cutting easier.

Easy hedge trimming Reduce the amount of hedge trimming needed by spraying the hedge once a year, after trimming, with a growth regulator. This will prevent extension growth and make the hedge thicker so that even a vigorous hedge will need trimming just once a year, at the end of the summer. The spray is suitable for privet and

CALENDAR OF HEDGE CARE

SPRING

Planting Plant evergreen hedging, giving it time to establish before winter arrives. Space plants 45 cm (18 in) apart and cut them back by a half immediately after planting for faster, bushier growth. Consider installing a seep hose for easy watering. Mulch after planting.

Rejuvenating old hedges Hard prune a deciduous hedge in early spring, and an evergreen hedge in mid or late spring (see opposite).

Feeding Sprinkle a handful of growmore per metre of hedge in late February.

Trimming Spring-flowering hedging plants that do not produce berries, such as *Forsythia* x *intermedia*, need clipping once they have finished flowering.

SUMMER

Trimming Many formal hedges, including yew, beech and holly, are clipped once a year in mid August. For young hedges, top lightly with shears to encourage bushy growth. Tall hedges are best trimmed with taut lines of string stretched between an A-frame so that the hedge can be cut easily at an oblique angle, with the base wider than the top. This lets light in to the bottom of the hedge, stopping it from forming a top-heavy shape – and it means you won't have to knock off the snow in winter. Place plastic sheeting underneath to catch clippings. For a big hedge, hire or buy a shredder to produce mulch for borders to reduce the need for weeding and watering.

AUTUMN

Planting Plant deciduous hedging as bare-root plants 45 cm (18 in) apart, incorporating plenty of organic matter so the plants establish themselves quickly. Cut back by at least a third to encourage bushy, faster growth.

Collecting leaves Don't bother removing hedge leaves from borders. Turn them into a mulch by placing compost over the top to prevent them blowing around. Use a rotary mower to collect and shred leaves on the lawn. Use a leaf sweeper with an in-built shredder for a quick clear-up of leaves elsewhere.

WINTER

Trimming Cut out old branches from wildlife hedges with a pruning saw or use long-handled loppers for easy reach.

Weedkilling Use a residual weedkiller based on dichlobenil under the hedge to prevent weeds from forming and spreading to neighbouring beds, in particular perennial weeds such as bindweed. However, if you want hedgehogs to hibernate in your garden, avoid using chemical weedkillers and allow fallen leaves to remain around the base of the hedge. Encourage them further by buying a special hedgehog house and positioning it in a secluded spot at the bottom of the hedge.

COPING WITH OVERGROWN LEYLANDII

It is not uncommon for a Leyland cypress hedge to reach 9 m (30 ft) or more. This makes Leyland hedges time-consuming and awkward to trim. For a drastic remedy, you can cut them down to a metre high, and hope that they recover. They can also be rescued if they go brown at the base. Get professional help if the hedge is 3 m (10 ft) or more above the height of your stepladder (see page 302).

Grown too tall *In late spring, cut down the main trunk to a height of 1 m (3 ft). For safety, do this in several stages if the hedge is tall. It's possible that the hedge will not recover, but then it will be at a manageable height to uproot.*

Brown at the base *For a quick way to cover up any dead, lower branches that have turned brown, plant periwinkle (vinca) or ivy at the base of the hedge – both these plants are able to cope with the dry, shady conditions cast by dense evergreen hedges.*

many other popular, fast-growing hedging plants. Buying or hiring powered equipment will make the job of trimming hedges faster and easier, although large-leaved plants are best clipped with secateurs (see right). The model that you choose will depend on whether you have access to a power source and the size of the hedge. Provided the space isn't confined, use longer blades for quicker cutting. Gloves and goggles are recommended for safety regardless of the method used, and long trousers and tough boots or shoes for powered trimmers.

Hard pruning If a hedge has grown out of hand, it is usually possible to cut it back hard in mid or late spring and start again. You will need to feed and mulch plants in the season before cutting back and in the season that follows. For deciduous hedges, cut back all twiggy growth on one side of the hedge to the main stems in winter or early spring. Wait a year and, if growth is good, do the same on the other side. Topdress the surrounding soil with a general fertiliser, such as growmore, and apply a mulch to help the plant to make a good recovery. For evergreen hedges, carry out the work in mid or late spring.

Hedging plants that respond well to this treatment include deciduous beech, berberis, hawthorn and hornbeam, and evergreen holly, box-leaved honeysuckle (*Lonicera nitida*), privet, yew and cherry laurel (*Prunus laurocerasus*). Such drastic cutting is not suitable, though, for many conifers. For pruning of the fast-growing Leyland cypress and Lawson cypress, see alternative methods outlined above.

Trimmer choice

Choosing the right tools for the job will make hedge trimming less hard work.

Secateurs Hedge plants with large leaves, such as spotted laurel and holly, need pruning with secateurs otherwise their leaves look messy. Trim new growth to the desired height or width, cutting each stem just above a leaf joint. You can use shears or a hedge trimmer, though, just before new growth appears.

Shears Slow and time-consuming on anything but small hedges. Small one-handed shears are available for easier access. Cheap and safe.

Hedge trimmers There are three types of powered hedge trimmer:

Petrol Heavier, noisier and more expensive than electric. Larger and more powerful. No cable to worry about. Higher on maintenance, but quicker to refuel than to recharge a battery. Good for areas more than 30 m (100 ft) away from the house.

Battery Good for small gardens with hedges of an area less than 45 m^2 (50 sq yd) or which are far away from a power source. Batteries need recharging about every half hour, but there is no cable to worry about. Generally lightweight and quiet, so more convenient to use. More expensive and slower than electric.

Electric Lightweight and quiet, medium-priced, but needs an extension cable if power source is far away. Always use a residual current device (RCD) for safety. Cable can be inconvenient, but no stopping to refuel or recharge. Cannot be used in the wet.

Patios and Containers

FOR THE GARDEN TO BECOME A TRUE OUTDOOR LIVING SPACE, IT MUST PROVIDE ADEQUATE ROOM FOR ENTERTAINING AND SITTING OUT. THE EASIEST ANSWER IS TO BUILD A PATIO

Creating a patio is one of the most labour-saving additions that can be made to a garden. A hard surface requires minimal maintenance when compared with a lawn or flowerbeds, and can safely be left to look after itself for long periods. However, a patio can be an expensive investment, so it is important to get it right first time.

First, make sure that you design the patio to match your needs, whether for regular barbecues, a quiet place to sit or for evening entertaining. Although paving materials are relatively low maintenance if the patio is properly constructed, some require more care than others.

Like any indoor room, the patio will need furnishing. Fill decorative containers and raised beds with colourful flowers and foliage; use high-performance plants that can cope with drought, provide fragrance and year-round colour, and soften the edges of hard landscaping materials.

Easy-care furniture and accessories, such as a barbecue, help to complete the outdoor living area, while lighting adds atmosphere and extends the hours of use.

1 CONTAINERS – *mulch pots with bark chippings or pebbles, and group together for easy watering.*
2 POT PLANTS – *grow drought-tolerant plants; tender varieties can be moved indoors in winter.*
3 BEDDING – *bedding plants grown in the border will need watering less than those in pots.*
4 PATIO – *combine two different paving materials for an attractive finish to cover the ground.*

EASY-CARE CALENDAR

EARLY SPRING
Plant up spring bedding. Tidy up permanent plant displays in containers. Sweep the patio and remove any algae, moss or other accumulated dirt using a pressure washer or patio cleaner. Apply path weedkiller if needed.

LATE SPRING
Buy sufficient container compost and slow-release fertiliser ready for summer displays, but do not plant up containers with summer bedding until the risk of frost is over (unless you have a frost-free place to keep them). Set up and test automatic watering systems.

SUMMER
Replace spring bedding with summer bedding. Check and adjust automatic watering so that each container is getting sufficient water. Check plants for signs of pests and diseases and take any remedial action immediately. Deadhead fading blooms.

AUTUMN
Remove faded summer bedding. Move tender perennials under cover and keep frost free; replace them with hardy plants that will give winter colour. Clear fallen leaves from the patio.

STARTING FROM SCRATCH
If you are an able DIY enthusiast, you could build a small patio like this in two weekends once the materials have been delivered. This should be left to settle for a week or two after construction. It would then take an additional weekend to plant up the containers and surrounding borders.

Plant lover's retreat Given an effective watering system, a patio can be a low-maintenance option. This sunny terrace makes an attractive place to relax, and is home to a range of tender exotics all grown in terracotta pots, such as citrus, cordyline, crassula and trachycarpus.

Patio design options that create a new dimension

The most suitable place for a patio is adjoining the main living-room of the house, with access through patio doors or french windows. If it is easy to reach, the patio is more likely to be used to the full, and tidying up and caring for plants in containers will be less work than if the patio is at the other end of the garden. However, at times there may be a case to place a patio at some distance from the house; on a site where it is sunnier, more sheltered, has a better view, or is less overlooked by neighbouring properties. This may also provide the opportunity for an adjoining gazebo or summer house to store chairs.

There are three main types of material: hard surfaces, including bricks, slabs, pavers and setts; a wooden surface, in the form of decking; and a gravel surface, either loose or self-binding (with a clay content high enough for the stones to bind together). Hard surfaces need the most ground preparation and take longer to lay, but once built are the easiest to look after and the most durable (see pages 50 and 174).

Raised beds bring planting nearer to eye level and cut down on back-breaking maintenance work. Timber tones add a natural, warm finish to this sunken patio.

The best place for a patio is usually next to the house, giving ease of access and making routine gardening less of a chore.

If a patio is to blend into the garden's overall design, consider the style and size of the plot as well as the purpose of the patio. Patios in small gardens are the most difficult to integrate because they occupy a high proportion of the available space, but you can still achieve attractive results by using the right materials in the right way.

The overall shape of a patio doesn't have to be square; circular and semi-circular patios are now as easy to build as square ones with the use of a special kit of interlocking blocks. You can also play around with paving materials. For example, laying slabs at a 45 degree angle to the house makes them look more inviting than if laid square. And the patio can be jazzed up by combining paving material types. Look for contrasts of colour, size and texture, such as gravel with timber, or use lines of pavers or setts to break up an area of slabs. Extra care will need to be taken, though, to achieve a level surface, but your task can be made easier by combining paving of the same thickness.

To make a paved area appear smaller, remove or add the occasional slab at the edge of the patio to break up straight lines and blur the patio's edges. Alternatively, you can replace individual slabs with boulders, stone chippings or gravel. Use plants to soften a hard surface by making planting pockets in the patio (see right), building a raised bed (see page 192) or allowing the plants in the surrounding borders to cascade over and hide the edges.

Problem solver

Plants in paving Before starting the foundations, decide on the position of plants around the patio and in planting pockets within the patio. Once the works are over, replace the topsoil of the planting areas with John Innes No. 3 compost. This will ensure a weed-free growing medium with the right nutrients so plants establish rapidly.

A shady patio Choose a light-coloured paving material; paint walls a light colour; and use a mirror for extra reflection. Grow luxuriant, shade-tolerant plants, such as ferns, ivies and hostas (though variegated varieties may lose their leaf markings in dim conditions) and evergreens with glossy leaves, such as photinia. Use textured slabs and lay them with a slight slope for drainage, because many surfaces turn slippery in damp, shady conditions.

Topiary shapes, such as the box balls on this renaissance-inspired patio, may look a lot of work, but they are easier than caring for pots full of bedding plants.

PAVING MATERIALS

Use the following guide to help you choose the right paving materials for your patio design.

Type	Start-up	Care	Cost
Slabs	••	•	£
Bricks/blocks	••	•	££
Crazy paving	•••	•	£
Gravel	•	••	£
Tiles	•••	•	£££
Decking	••	••	£££

Key to ratings
• (quick and easy) to
••• (time-consuming and hard work)
£ (cheap) to £££ (expensive)

Designing and building your patio

A patio can transform the appearance and enjoyment of a garden, but building one is a lot of work. The quickest and simplest option is to employ a contractor to build it for you. However, if you are keen to do it yourself, it is possible to do the job in a couple of weekends provided that not too much preparation work is needed.

A patio must be laid on a firm, level base so choose a site which is fairly level to start with. Clear the site of any vegetation by spraying with a path weedkiller. Hire a cable-and-pipe locator to check the position of utility supply pipes and cables below the patio area. If you find an obstacle underground, lay a marker tape on the surface, and make a rough sketch of the positions for future reference. If necessary, choose a patio surface which allows access to the pipes, such as pavers laid on sand. Manholes can be disguised using recessed drain covers.

Design the pattern of the paving to scale using graph paper. Keep the design simple. Straightforward patterns, such as basketweave or running bond, are the quickest to design and lay (see below). A random effect, in particular one that uses two types of paving material, is more complicated, so you will need to take more time planning to ensure that it looks right when finished.

For an easy-care, long-lasting patio lay paving materials on a foundation of 10 cm (4 in) hardcore. If next to the house, the final surface must be at least 15 cm (6 in) below the damp-proof course and have a slope of 1 in 100 away from the building to drain off rainwater.

Hard paving materials The larger the unit of material used, the quicker the patio will be to lay. However, large units are often heavy. Slabs, for example, may produce the quickest results, but they weigh about 15 kg (33 lb) each. Lay them on a 5 cm (2 in) bed of sharp sand or – for a lasting finish – on blobs of mortar over the hardcore base. Smaller units of paving materials, such as bricks, pavers or setts, give more design flexibility and are easier to move around – pavers and

COMBINING PAVING MATERIALS EFFECTIVELY

If only one paving material is used, the patio in a small garden can dominate the overall design, while in a larger garden the patio can look stark and unintegrated with the rest of the garden. By combining two or more paving materials, you can break up the outline of the patio and help to prevent it from dominating its surroundings. Lay small paving blocks in attractive patterns, like those shown below. Do not overdo it, though, because a paved area using a multitude of shapes and styles looks overly fussy.

Slabs with brick edging

Bricks in running bond pattern

Bricks and tiles

setts, for example, weigh only about 3 kg (7 lb) each – but small units are more complicated to lay. The simplest method is to create a solid border using brick or concrete edging. Then lay the pavers or setts on a level 5 cm (2 in) bed of sharp sand and firm into position using a hired vibrating plate compactor. Also hire a powered barrow or sack trolley to move materials around, and a block splitter to cut pavers or an angle grinder for slabs. To control weeds, lay a permeable membrane beneath the sand.

Gravel Like pavers, loose gravel needs a firm edge to hold it in place. Spread a 2.5 cm (1 in) layer of gravel with a rubber-tined rake over weed-suppressing permeable membrane on a prepared base. Gravel is usually sold by the yard (cubic yard): one yard of gravel covers at least 20 m^2 (24 sq yd) at a depth of 2.5 cm (1 in). For a fine finish use pea gravel.

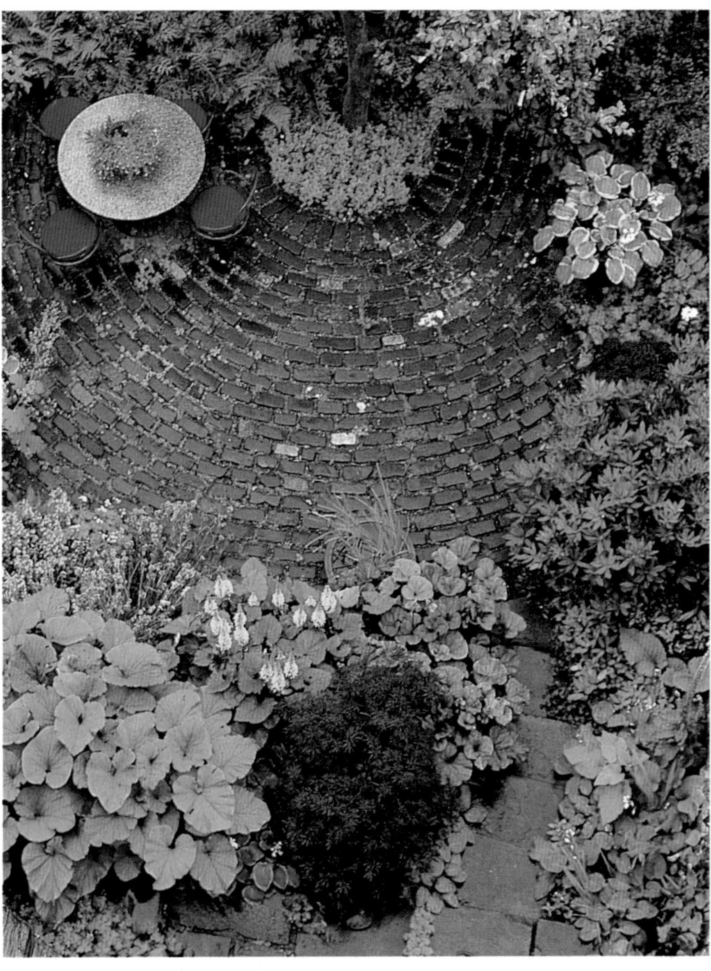

Self-seeding perennials have been allowed to colonise this patio area, helping to soften the appearance of the paving so that it blends into the garden landscape.

Timber decking Build a deck on brick or concrete pillars, or directly onto a solid concrete bed covered with a damp-proof membrane. Construct the timber deck and secure with non-corroding screws. Timber squares are also available which can be laid directly onto a sand bed in the same way as paving slabs or bricks. Use angled nails to fix the squares together. Decking is particularly useful for covering difficult areas because it can be raised off the ground, but this takes more skill.

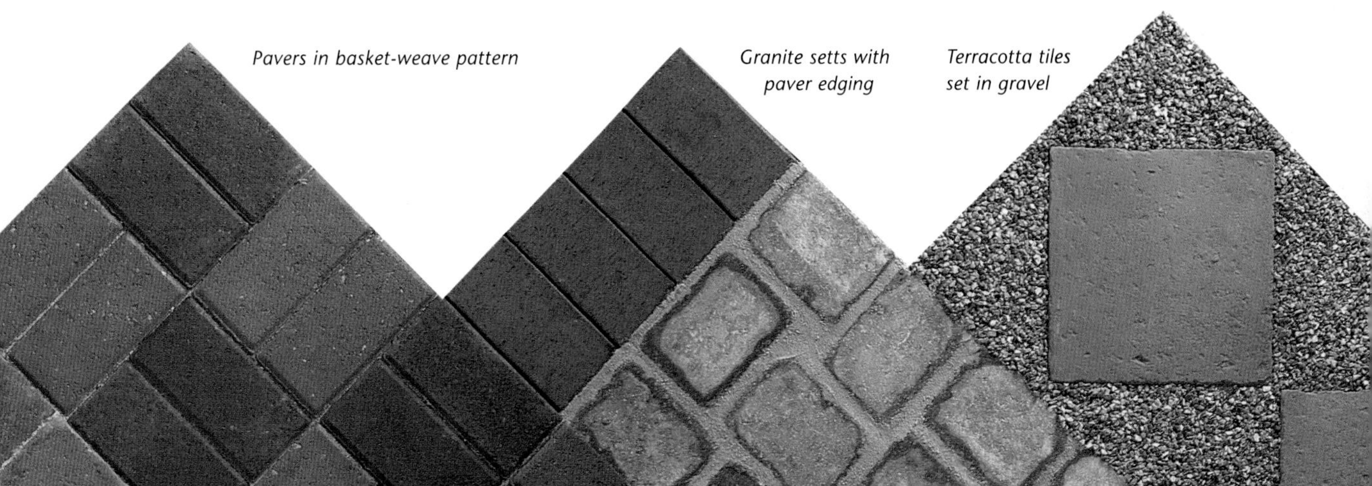

Pavers in basket-weave pattern

Granite setts with paver edging

Terracotta tiles set in gravel

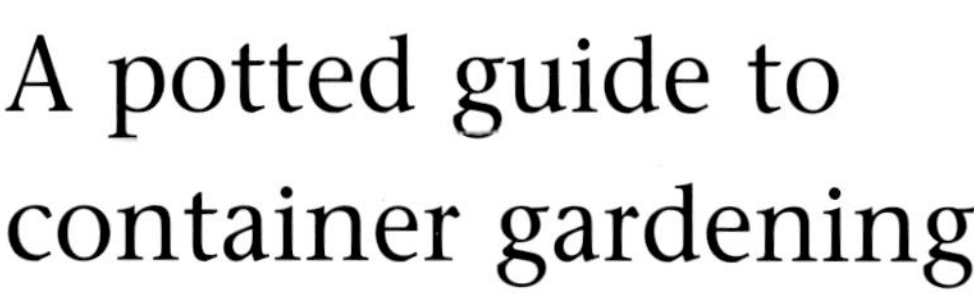

A potted guide to container gardening

Plants in containers provide colour and interest on the patio over a long season, and the containers themselves can also be decorative. The drawback is that containers are labour intensive. This is because the plants in them have only a small amount of compost in which to grow, limiting the availability of water and nutrients. If container plants are to grow well over a period of time, they will need almost constant attention. Fortunately, several products and techniques can be employed to make the task a lot easier. For example, simplify watering by installing an automatic watering system (see page 188), or add a water-retaining gel to the compost before planting to lengthen the period between waterings.

Choosing containers The size, shape and material in which a container is made affects how much time it will take to look after. For example, a 40 cm (16 in) hanging basket holds about three times as much compost as the standard 30 cm (12 in) basket, while a 45 cm (18 in) pot holds four times as much compost as a 30 cm (12 in) pot of a similar design. This makes the larger containers far less prone to drying out and so easier to look after. However, don't forget that large containers full of compost and plants are heavy to move, though a sack trolley or a special wheeled platform can make the job easier. When choosing a shape, opt for a good, stable design that makes

Which compost?

There are two main types of compost: soil-based (John Innes) and soil-less, which may be based on peat or a peat substitute, such as coir.

Soil-based composts These are heavy, retain water well and provide a long-lasting supply of nutrients. They are the best choice for permanent plants in containers and for plants that grow tall and are top heavy. For permanent displays, use John Innes No. 3 because of its high level of nutrients.

Soil-less composts These are lightweight, clean and easy to handle, but dry out quickly and contain few nutrients. Soil-less composts are best for temporary displays, such as bedding plants and hanging baskets. Peat-based composts are the most consistent in quality, though alternatives, such as those based on coir and bark, are improving all the time.

WHAT TYPE OF CONTAINER?

Terracotta Porous and well drained, which suits Mediterranean-type plants. For the busy gardener, the main drawbacks are that terracotta pots need more frequent watering, are heavy to move, need more cleaning and some need protecting from frost (look for pots that are guaranteed frost-proof).

Plastic Lightweight and easy to move, plastic pots need less watering than clay ones. They tend to become brittle after exposure to sunlight, but are less fragile than clay pots. They are also more frost-proof so can be used for year-round displays. Convincing clay lookalikes are now available and are a useful option for the busy gardener.

Wood Well-made wooden containers have an attractive, natural appearance. Choose hardwood or pressure-treated softwood to avoid the need for regular treatment with a timber preservative. Usually heavy, but some can be fitted with wheels to make moving easy. Good for growing top-heavy plants.

Glazed Earthenware and ceramic pots are now widely available in attractive colours. Glazed pots are heavy and fragile, and some are not frost-proof. Those without drainage holes are the busy gardener's choice for a simple water feature or for creating an instant focal point.

An empty container, such as this earthenware pot, provides an instant, rich contrast to the green and silver foliage.

Using permanent plantings, such as the box and *Alchemilla mollis* in this display, eliminates the need to replant yearly.

Concrete Available in a wide range of designs and mouldings. Robust and heavy, so good for permanent plantings. Can be cemented permanently into position for security. Not suitable for acid-loving plants unless treated with sealant. Frost-resistant.

Reconstituted stone Ground stone chippings moulded into shape like concrete. The material looks like real stone and is much cheaper but it is slow to weather. Robust and heavy, so good for permanent plantings. Frost-resistant.

Fibreglass Containers come in bright, primary colours as well as more subdued, earthy tones. Many have a high-gloss finish, including metallic. They are lightweight, frost-resistant and well insulated. Self-watering versions are particularly useful for the busy gardener and can be used indoors or out.

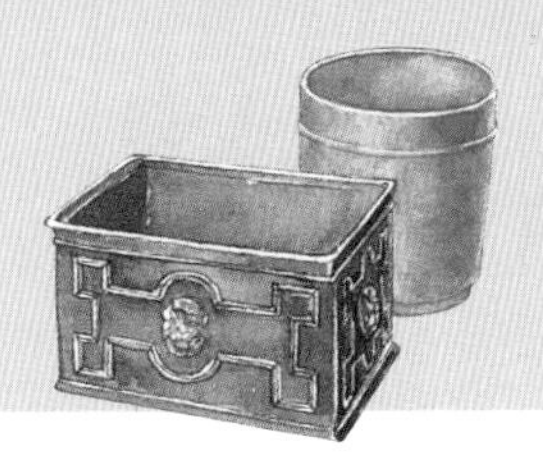

Metal Those made from galvanised steel lend a clean, modern look. If they don't have drainage holes, put the plant in a pot that does and stand it in the metal pot – this will also counteract metal's poor insulation. Lead containers are very expensive and come in traditional, decorative styles.

Drainage matters

Good drainage The compost must be able to drain freely. Permanently sodden compost deprives the roots of air, which will kill the plant. Check that the container has efficient drainage holes. Enlarge them or add extra if necessary (use a hot skewer or a drill on plastic pots).

Unobstructed drainage holes Place broken pots or rubble over the drainage hole before filling the pot with compost. Stand the container on bricks or special pot feet to raise the base from the ground in winter.

repotting easy – a standard pot shape is ideal. Beware of decorative containers that look elegant, but are impractical for growing plants; very shallow or narrow containers that do not hold enough compost to keep the plants growing well, or waisted or narrow-necked jars that make it virtually impossible to remove or repot the plants that they contain.

Some pots have a built-in reservoir that helps reduce the frequency of watering. These are a good option for the busy gardener, especially for isolated containers that cannot be easily integrated into an automatic watering regime.

Specialised containers A wide range of containers are made for specific situations, such as to hang from walls or beams, or to be placed on a windowsill. Hanging baskets and wall-mangers made from an open-weave design are usually lined with moss or special liners. However, this type of basket needs to be watered frequently – twice a day in hot weather – because the porous liner is exposed to the air, which quickly

Planting an easy-care hanging basket

You can make a hanging basket a lot easier to look after by using the right plants and materials to start with. Reduce the need for watering by choosing a large basket and using container compost.

Basket Choose a large basket, at least 36 cm (14 in) wide. It will contain a lot more compost, so will require less frequent watering.

Liner For a permeable liner, such as moss, create a water reservoir by placing a saucer in the base before filling. Or line the bottom of an open-mesh basket with polythene to reduce water loss.

Compost Use a hanging-basket compost that has been formulated to retain moisture for longer. Alternatively, add water-retaining gel to ordinary potting compost.

Fertiliser Use slow-release fertiliser pellets when planting to feed the plants all season.

Plants Select drought-tolerant plants that can cope with drying out between waterings (see panel, right).

Planting Wrap the plants' top growth before pushing them through from the inside of the hanging basket. This will prevent damaging the roots.

Combine plants with similar maintenance needs in a hanging basket. To cut down on watering, hang the basket in a sheltered site, away from the midday sun in summer.

dries out the soil. Solid-sided baskets require less-frequent watering and some models incorporate self-watering devices and saucers to further reduce the workload.

Feeding If you choose a soil-based compost, plants will need feeding after three months, while those in soil-less compost will need feeding after about six weeks, once the soil's nutrients are used up. The easiest way to feed container plants is to add a slow-release fertiliser at the time of planting to provide sufficient nutrients through the growing season. Otherwise, you will need to feed weekly during the growing season, which is easiest done by applying a liquid feed while watering.

Positioning containers If you want to reduce the frequency of watering, place pots in a sheltered, well-lit spot that doesn't get too hot and is in shade during the hottest part of the day. Most easy-care plants will thrive in this situation (see panel, right). Containers on a sunny patio should be grouped together to make watering easier and mulched with bark chippings or pebbles to conserve moisture. In shady areas, in summer, plant containers full of shade-tolerant, trouble-free plants such as *Begonia semperflorens*, fuchsia, impatiens, pansies, primulas, polyanthus and hostas, although you will need to apply slug pellets to protect the hostas' growth.

PLANTS FOR AN EASY-CARE BASKET

A selection of colours and plant shapes, including upright and trailing, are needed to give visual interest to a hanging basket. Choose a balance of plants for both foliage and flowers from the following drought-tolerant groups.

Trailers There are trailing varieties of many popular plants, such as fuchsias and pelargoniums, as well as more unusual subjects, such as *Anagallis monellii* (pictured), *Lotus berthelotii*, sanvitalia and sutera.

Colourful flowers Ever-reliable impatiens, pelargonium, petunia, verbena and viola – such as *Viola* 'Jackanapes' (pictured) – are available in a wide range of colours and forms. Others include portulaca and *Scaevola* 'Saphira'.

Foliage plants Many cascading plants have attractive foliage, including *Glechoma hederacea* 'Variegata' (pictured), *Hedera helix* 'Glacier', *Helichrysum petiolare*, *Lysimachia nummularia* 'Aurea' and *Plectranthus forsteri* 'Marginatus'.

Upright plants These give height to the basket, helping to balance it visually. Bushy lobelia, or upright varieties of osteospermum, fuchsia, pelargonium (such as *Pelargonium* 'Friesdorf', pictured), petunia or verbena.

Choosing the right plants for containers

Gardening with containers will give you the chance to produce instant effects; whether a splash of colour or a key focal point. Dull walls can be enlivened, doorways given a seasonal lift, existing planting highlighted, manholes disguised, or a touch of exoticism added by using pots to introduce frost-tender plants that either last a season or can be easily moved indoors over winter.

No digging and little weeding is required for gardening with pots. But plants will need regular watering, feeding and deadheading, and permanent plants need occasional repotting. Bedding plants will also need replacing twice a year – in early summer and autumn.

Containers can be planted up with any type of plant, but because they are often used to give an instant lift to a dull corner, it is the short-lived displays that tend to be most effective – bulbs and bedding plants, whether annuals, tender perennials or biennials. With permanent displays, which use trees, shrubs or hardy perennials to provide a framework of interest year after year, it is particularly important to choose the right plants to keep down the workload: you will need to use plants that survive all weathers, from drought, to autumn winds and winter frost, because the roots of plants in containers are more exposed to the elements than those grown in the ground.

Spring displays A flash of spring colour works brilliantly to revive flagging spirits following a gloomy winter. In autumn, once the summer bedding displays have finished, fill pots with violas, polyanthus, primroses and double daisies (*Bellis perennis*) to provide the first blooms of spring, add bulbs such as muscari, hyacinths, crocus and short-stemmed daffodils to boost the colour displays. Position them so that they can be viewed from the house. These early bulbs

Time saver

Buy bedding plants in single, named colours rather than mixed-colour boxes. This will make it quicker and easier to decide what to put where. A unity of colour will also lead to more cohesion in the garden's design.

Spring-flowering plants are clustered together for maximum effect. For an instant display, buy potted plants already in flower.

Use easy-care plants for containers, such as these summer favourites: argyranthemum, pelargonium, fuchsia, blue lobelia and silver helichrysum.

can be followed by tulips; the more compact greigii tulips, such as 'Red Riding Hood', are particularly good for containers, and many have mottled leaves for extra interest. For a long-lasting seasonal display, plant bulbs that flower at different times in layers in the same pot or for an instant display buy potted bulbs already in bud.

Spring bedding can also be used as an underplanting for a shrub or tree in a container. Try purple crocuses under Japanese maple (*Acer palmatum*) to extend its season of interest or dark-coloured violas to complement the white, star-shaped flowers in early or mid spring of *Magnolia stellata* – one of the few magnolias compact enough to grow in a pot. Both shrubs, however, need a sheltered site.

Summer displays Once all risk of frost is over, remove any remaining spring bedding plants, and replace them with tender perennials. Traditional bedding, such as trailing lobelia, are a lot of work because they need to be kept constantly moist, which can mean watering twice a day in hot weather. However, by choosing easy-care plants that can survive temporary periods of drought (see list, right), you can get a continuous flowering display until the first frosts without much effort. For an instant border display, or to bring colour to a doorway or a corner of the patio, plunge pots of exotic tender perennials, such as cannas or abutilons, directly into the soil without taking them out of their containers.

PLANTS THAT NEED LESS WATERING

Use drought-tolerant plants to cut down on watering containers. They can often be identified by the following characteristics. (All the examples are suitable for pots.)

Spiky leaves Plants such as agave, cordyline, phormium and yuccas, or those that have tough narrow leaves such as thrift and *Dianthus gratianopolitanus* (pictured).

Grey, hairy leaves Including, *Brachyglottis* (Dunedin Group) 'Sunshine' (pictured), *Convolvulus cneorum*, *Helichrysum petiolare*. For neat foliage, cut back brachyglottis and helichrysum in spring.

Thick, waxy leaves Succulent plants such as echeveria, lampranthus, mesembryanthemum, *Sedum spurium and S. spathulifolium*, and *Sempervivum tectorum* (pictured).

Aromatic leaves These include lavender, *Helichrysum italicum* and *Salvia microphylla*, as well as evergreen herbs, such as thyme (pictured), rosemary, sage and sweet bay.

Sun-loving flowers These include summer bedding (such as gazania and pelargonium, pictured); perennials (osteospermum and *Convolvulus sabatius*); and shrubs (hibiscus).

Use containers as an easy way to extend border displays onto the patio. Here, this has created a colourful flower garden, mixing bedding plants with perennials.

Buying bedding plants You can buy your summer bedding in various ways (see below, and page 133). Plants in pots, strips or large plugs (plants raised in individual cells in trays) are available from nurseries and garden centres from mid to late spring. They can be planted directly into containers.

If you have a frost-free area to grow on plants, mail-order suppliers sell small plugs or tot plants (small plants in individual pots) of more unusual varieties, but you will have to place your order in early winter. If you need large quantities of one particular variety, it may be worth growing plants from seed.

Whichever way you buy your plants, choose healthy specimens. The compost must be moist, with no matted roots growing through the base. Potted plants should have plenty of buds, but not many open flowers: prematurely flowering plants may be suffering from overcrowding or drought.

Close planting in containers, and the subsequent competition for nutrients, water and root space, helps to ensure early flowering. But this must be balanced with the need to give plants sufficient room to develop into bushy specimens to last throughout the season. Regular watering and feeding of densely planted containers is essential.

WHAT SIZE PLANT?

Pelargoniums can be bought as seed, seedlings, plugs, tots and plants from most garden centres in spring. They are expensive to buy as seed and can be difficult to germinate, so buying young plants is a convenient option – especially if you do not have the time or facilities for raising plants from seed yourself.

1 Plugs *Small plants sold in trays of 12 or more. Many new varieties are available, but they need to be potted up and kept frost free.*

2 Seed *Time consuming but rewarding to raise own plants from seed. Requires heat to germinate and a greenhouse or plenty of windowsill space to grow on.*

3 Tots *Mini-plants sold in individual pots. Good range of named varieties, but need growing on before they can be planted out.*

4 Seedlings *Easier than seed, but limited range of varieties available. You will need a windowsill or greenhouse.*

5 Plants *Much more expensive, but can be bought in flower ready to plant to create instant displays.*

Creating a courtyard retreat

Alison and Denis Kennedy have full-time jobs based in the city. They have no children, two cats, and would like to use their small garden as a place to relax on spring and summer evenings, and at weekends.

The garden needed to look as interesting as possible all-year round, without requiring a lot of maintenance because the Kennedys' long working hours and regular trips overseas meant they could only devote irregular bursts of attention to their garden. They wanted a paved, sheltered area where they could relax on fine days, with plants growing in-between the cracks, or small beds around the edges. The paved area was to be surrounded by evergreens, as well as a few deciduous shrubs and perennials for shelter and seasonal interest. They wanted to create attractive garden boundaries that would provide privacy from neighbouring gardens and from the alleyway running along the end of the garden. They also needed space for storage, but they did not want a shed that looked too functional.

THE OLD GARDEN This small, patchy lawn, edged with a few uninspiring shrubs, is neither attractive nor easy to maintain.

DECIDING THEIR PRIORITIES

How much time?
Variable, but 1 hour a week on average.

Essential ingredients?
A paved area with sufficient privacy and shelter for relaxation. Containers filled with interesting, easy-care plants. Shade for hot days.

Likes and dislikes?
They want scent and colour for as much of the year as possible, and are anxious to avoid regular chores such as weeding.

Optical effects *A tool-shed at the foot of the garden provides a frame from which to hang a large mirror. Reflections add to the attractiveness of the plants, as well as creating an illusion of greater light and space.*

Containers *Different shapes contrast with the strong, straight lines of the paving. Large pots have been chosen because they need less watering.*

THE NEW GARDEN Decorative paving, mirrored reflections and lightly coloured trelliswork create a feeling of light and space, while the subtle planting scheme evokes a mood of peace and relaxation. The ornamental containers and planting pockets, filled with drought-tolerant plants, help to ensure all-year colour and an attractive view from the house whatever the weather.

Planning the paving
Different-sized paving stones with a light base colour have been laid in different directions to help to extend visually the length of an otherwise short garden. The actual length of the garden is 6 m (20 ft) and the width 3 m (10 ft).

Plant selection *A dominant colour scheme is carried through from the plants in the containers to those in the planting pockets in-between the paving stones.*

Permanent perennials for containers

While spring and summer bedding may provide instant colour and interest, it will need buying and planting afresh each season, which takes time. Hardy perennials can provide a low-maintenance alternative since they go on year after year. Many popular perennials, such as hostas, die down in autumn, but some others are evergreen, including several euphorbias.

Perennials in containers can be used either as a specimen plant, grown on their own to provide a focal point – acanthus and hostas are good for this – or they can be part of a balanced, mixed planting that also includes a few seasonal bedding plants, shrubs and trees.

Choose a container at least 25 cm (10 in) wide and deep to avoid frequent watering. In spring or autumn, check whether the roots are growing through the base of the pot, in which case the plant could be potbound and need repotting into a larger container, or dividing and repotted in the same container. Use a soil-based John Innes compost, which will supply nutrients over a longer period than soil-less compost.

Time saver

Cut down on the need to water and feed permanent potted plants by encouraging them to root through into the ground below. Don't use crocks in the base and keep the area under the pot moist.

HOT COLOURS FOR SUN

Combine drought-tolerant perennials in a large pot *(below)* to reduce the need for watering. This fiery display lasts from May until October.

1 ***Thymus serpyllum* 'Coccineus'** Flowers June-Aug.
2 ***Schizostylis coccinea* 'Major'** Flowers Aug-Nov.
3 ***Achillea millefolium* 'Paprika'** Flowers May-Sep.
4 ***Phormium* 'Sundowner'** Evergreen sword-shaped leaves.
5 ***Sedum* 'Ruby Glow'** Red-stemmed. Flowers Sep/Oct.

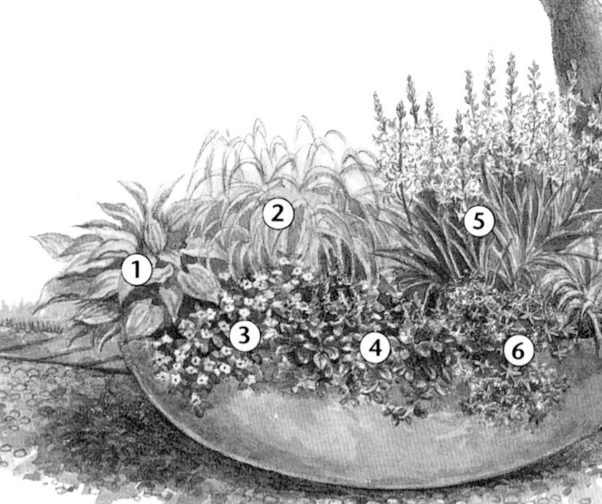

ADDING LIGHT TO SHADE

Some perennials are ideal for uplifting a shady corner in late spring *(above)*. Keep in dappled shade for best foliage colour.

1 ***Hosta fortunei* var. *albopicta*** Mauve flowers in July.
2 ***Milium effusum* 'Aureum'** Semi-evergreen grass.
3 **Impatiens** Bedding plant for colourful summer-long display.
4 ***Ajuga reptans* 'Atropurpurea'** Blue flowers in May and June.
5 ***Camassia leichtlinii* 'Alba'** White flowers in May.
6 ***Galium odoratum*** Starry flowers May to July.
7 ***Luzula sylvatica* 'Aurea'** Yellow-leaved, grass-like perennial.

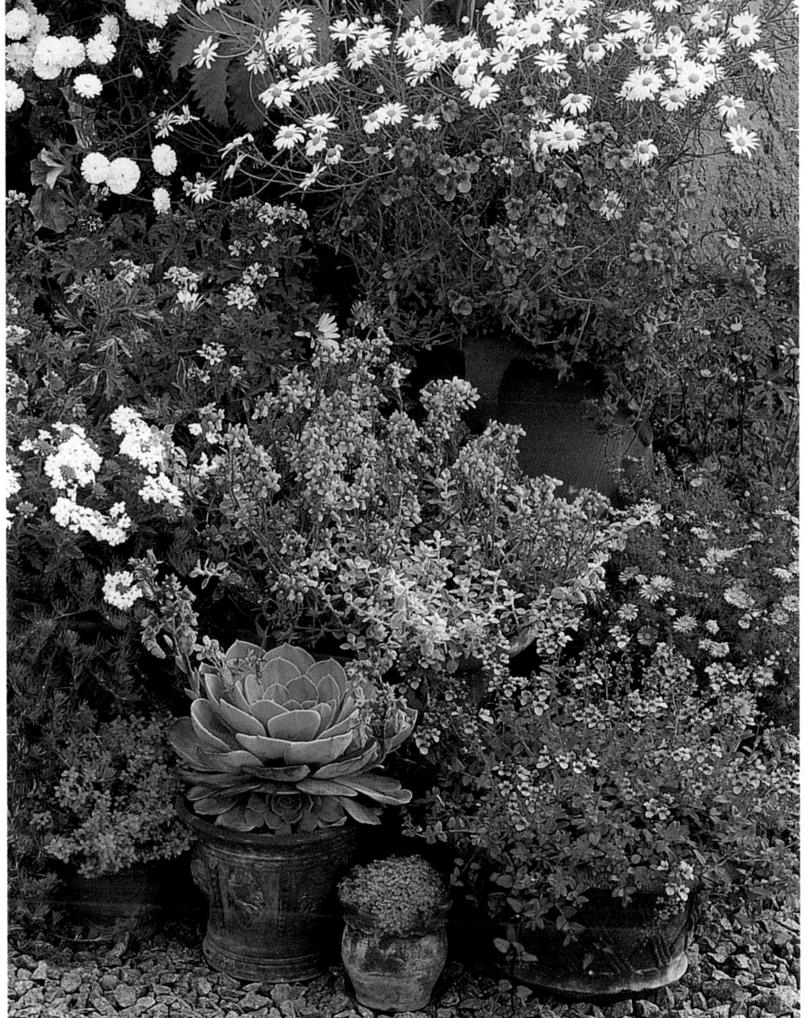

Clustering small pots together lends itself to easy watering and creates a greater visual impact than spreading pots around the patio.

Choosing perennials Select plants that need no staking and that are not easily damaged by rain and wind (see list, right). Choose plants that shed their dead flowers naturally or those which have faded flowers that can be left in place, such as acanthus, euphorbia and sedum. Or choose plants which have flowers that fall to reveal ornamental seed heads, such as agapanthus, or good foliage plants such as the purple-leaved *Heuchera micrantha* var. *diversifolia* 'Palace Purple'.

Grasses Many ornamental grasses can survive on poor, free-draining soil with little water, especially those originating from dry grassland areas. The blue tufts of *Festuca glauca* (see right) look good against a gravel mulch. For taller grasses, the stipa genus includes several striking varieties, including the densely tufted *Stipa tenacissima* and *S. gigantea*. For partial shade and moister conditions, the striped foliage of *Hakonechloa macra* 'Aureola' looks impressive in a terracotta pot, but buy a large specimen because it's slow-growing.

TOP PERENNIALS FOR CONTAINERS

These plants need little upkeep, and they all provide interest, either foliage or flowers, for more than half the year. All but the hosta need well-drained soil.

Artemisia ludoviciana A neat mound of downy, silver-green leaves. Good for cooling a mixed planting with bright colours. Likes full sun. Eventual height 1.2 m (4 ft).

Euphorbia characias* ssp. *wulfenii Whorls of evergreen, blue-green leaves. Large, cone-shaped flowerheads in spring with lime-green bracts. Full sun. Grows to 1.2 m (4 ft).

Festuca glauca This low-growing evergreen grass has spiky, silver-blue foliage that is more intensely coloured in summer. Full sun and good drainage. Grows to 23 cm (9 in).

***Geranium* 'Johnson's Blue'** Forms a mat of deeply divided, soft-textured leaves with light lavender-blue flowers carried in profusion through the summer. Grows to 30 cm (12 in).

***Hosta* 'Wide Brim'** Heavily puckered, heart-shaped leaves. Spikes of pale lavender flowers in summer. Likes partial shade with moist soil. Height 60 cm (24 in), spread 90 cm (36 in).

Shrubs for containers

Like any other plants in the garden, plants grown in pots need a basic framework to provide a year-round structure. Shrubs are ideal candidates because they continue from year to year with little need for upkeep, and many of them are evergreen, with their foliage providing interest in the drab winter season.

Avoid vigorous varieties since they will need more frequent repotting, and more regular watering and feeding. Even so, many mature shrubs will need planting in containers at least 45 cm (18 in) wide to accommodate their root growth. For easy manoeuvring, buy pots with wheels or move existing pots on a wheeled trolley. If you want to avoid the need to repot, remove the top 2.5-4 cm (1-1½ in) of compost each spring, fork over the surface and add fresh compost. Or, take the plant out of its pot, trim away no more than a third of its root system, and then repot in the same pot with fresh compost.

Gardening in containers also means that you can provide the right soil conditions for a particular plant. Camellias and azaleas, for example, need acid soil. If your garden has neutral or alkaline soil, you can still grow these plants in pots filled with ericaceous compost. For an all-evergreen display, underplant with the fern *Blechnum spicant*.

Evergreen shrubs In winter, the patio often provides the main view of the garden from the house, while its hard surface makes it the area most likely to be visited when other parts of the garden are wet and muddy. Several shade-loving, evergreen shrubs that adapt well to pots have flowers or berries in winter, including *Viburnum tinus*,

EVERGREEN SHRUBS

The following shrubs make trouble-free specimens in containers. Mix them with colourful bulbs and perennials for best effect.

***Aucuba japonica* 'Gold Dust'**
Choisya ternata
***Euonymus fortunei* 'Emerald 'n' Gold'**
Fatsia japonica
***Juniperus squamata* 'Blue Star'**
***Picea glauca* var. *albertiana* 'Conica'**
Rosmarinus officinalis
***Skimmia japonica* 'Rubella'**
Viburnum tinus

WINTER INTEREST

Several evergreens suitable for growing in containers are useful for adding much-needed colour to the winter patio. Here, the shrubs skimmia and gaultheria are combined with ivy, bergenia, winter-flowering pansies and the short-stemmed daffodil, 'February Gold'.

1 ***Bergenia* 'Wintermärchen'** A small-leaved bergenia which turns a brilliant scarlet in winter. Deep rose-pink flowers are produced in March and April.
2 ***Skimmia japonica* 'Rubella'** A compact, evergreen male form. Flowers red in bud over winter opening to white in March.
3 ***Gaultheria procumbens*** Dark red fruit all winter and urn-shaped white flowers in summer. Evergreen mat-forming foliage.

with pink buds that open to white flowers followed by blue-black fruit, and the slightly tender *Fatsia japonica,* with creamy white flowers in autumn followed by black fruit.

Large glossy evergreen leaves, such as those of fatsia and aucuba, or variegated foliage, such as that of certain aucuba varieties and euonymus, are good for brightening up shady patios throughout the year. Conifers offer a wide range of colours, including blue and golden, as well as all types of sizes and forms. They do particularly well in containers because of their shallow roots, but they need sun.

Small shrubs can spend a year or two in a pot before planting in the garden. Here, *Spiraea* 'Fire Light', heather and skimmia, with hakonechloa, give an autumn show.

Specimen plants Shrubs trained as standards (such as holly, sweet bay or *Viburnum tinus),* clipped evergreens (such as box), flowering deciduous shrubs (such as hydrangea), or those with a strong sculptural form (like the columnar *Juniperus scopulorum* 'Skyrocket') look good planted on their own as a specimen plant to draw the eye. For best effect, use specimen plants to mark a spot – a doorway, a corner, or at the end of a path.

Winter bedding Winter-flowering pansies are ideal for sprucing up containers of shrubs in full sun or partial shade between autumn and spring. They come in lots of colours – from violet to bright yellow and coppery red – but they can stop flowering in cold spells (see Problem solver). For permanent reliable winter colour, use low-growing shrubs such as winter-flowering heathers or a compact skimmia, such as the male *Skimmia japonica* 'Rubella' for deep red winter buds or the hermaphrodite *S. japonica* ssp. *reevesiana,* with bright red berries.

Problem solver

Reliable colour Winter-flowering pansies are good for planting under shrubs, but they peter out in very cold spells. For reliable winter colour in a sunny site, try ornamental kale instead, especially if being viewed from above.

Easy ways to water containers

Use containers made from non-porous materials, such as plastic, or line porous containers, such as wood or terracotta, with polythene to make them impermeable (see box opposite). Go for a few big containers rather than lots of small ones. Add water-retaining gel so that the compost can hold more water, and a slow-release fertiliser to feed the plants right through the growing season. After planting, cover the container surface with a mulch, such as bark chippings or pebbles, to reduce the amount of water lost through evaporation. Leave 2.5 cm (1 in) between the top of the mulch and the top of the pot to allow space for easy watering.

Watering equipment A wide range of equipment is available to keep to a minimum the amount of time spent watering by hand. If you only have a small number of containers, self-watering pots are viable. You can even convert existing pots using strips of capillary matting. If you have a lot of hanging baskets, buy a hose lance; some models have a built-in fertiliser dispenser so that you can apply feed at the same time. Otherwise, buy a self-assembly kit that allows you to plumb in all your containers for automatic watering.

Time saver

Water-retaining gel helps cut down on watering time. If you didn't add it when planting, push a cane into the compost and trickle in dry crystals of the gel. Plug holes with compost and stand the pot in water overnight to soak.

Group containers together to make watering easier and keep roots shaded and cool.

AUTOMATIC WATERING

A micro-irrigation system that operates automatically saves hours of watering time. Choose one consisting of a supply pipe that carries the water around the garden and micro-tubing that can be fitted with individual nozzles that drip water at an even rate (some types are adjustable). Starter kits are available for self-assembly and you can buy extra pipes, connectors and nozzles to extend the system. Connect the system to an outside tap and turn on and off by hand or automate it by adding a timing device or water computer.

Water timer *These are invariably electronic, run by a computer chip. Set it to come on in the evening so that less water is lost through evaporation.*

Positioning *Lay out the supply pipe and micro-tubing in position before trying to join it together to make sure that the various joints are in the right place.*

Flush out the system *Before adding the nozzles, flush out the assembled pipework with clean water to remove any accumulated dirt.*

Hard-water areas *Prevent blockages caused by limescale by washing the system out with a chemical limescale remover at the end of the season.*

Large containers *Space drip nozzles around the pot or use a T-connector to fit a ring of porous pipe to the micro-tubing.*

HOW TO CONSERVE WATER

▲ LINE POROUS CONTAINERS
Wooden containers are porous so require more frequent watering, especially during the summer. However, you can avoid the problem by lining the container with polythene before planting but don't cover the drainage holes. Terracotta is also porous and can be lined with polythene. Again pierce small holes in the bottom for drainage. Another option is to use a plastic pot slightly smaller than the terracotta one as a non-porous liner.

▲ SELF-WATERING CONTAINERS
The range of self-watering containers now includes standard pots, tubs, troughs and hanging baskets. These are useful for places that are awkward to water, such as window boxes, especially those in sites exposed to full sun. Made from plastic or glass fibre, they have a reservoir built into the base and a wick connecting the reservoir to the compost. Many also have a sight glass or float so you know when the reservoir needs topping up.

▲ ADD A WATER-RETAINING GEL
Polymer crystals hold up to 400 times their own weight in water. Mix with compost before planting.

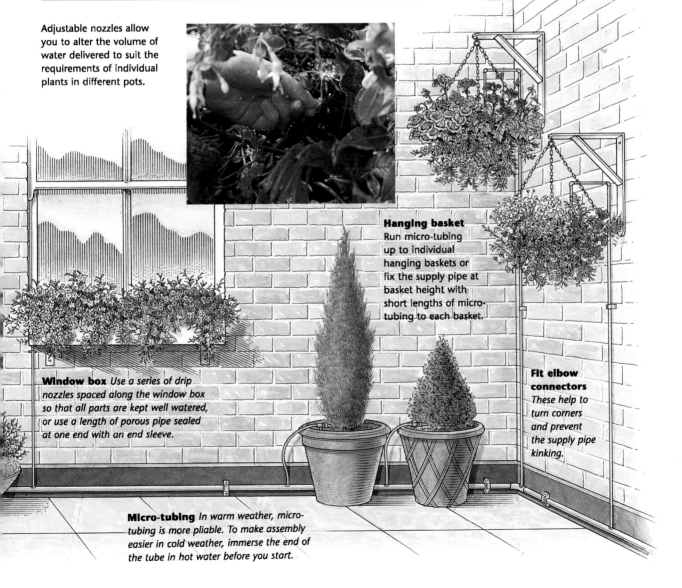

Adjustable nozzles allow you to alter the volume of water delivered to suit the requirements of individual plants in different pots.

Hanging basket Run micro-tubing up to individual hanging baskets or fix the supply pipe at basket height with short lengths of micro-tubing to each basket.

Window box *Use a series of drip nozzles spaced along the window box so that all parts are kept well watered, or use a length of porous pipe sealed at one end with an end sleeve.*

Fit elbow connectors *These help to turn corners and prevent the supply pipe kinking.*

Micro-tubing *In warm weather, micro-tubing is more pliable. To make assembly easier in cold weather, immerse the end of the tube in hot water before you start.*

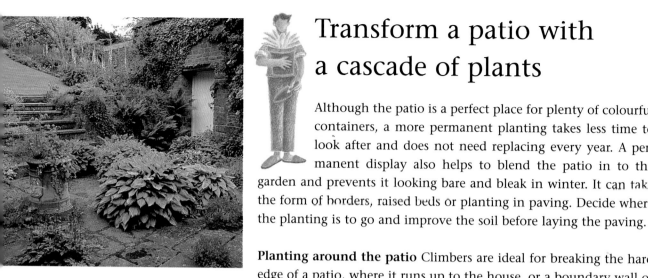

This sunken garden contains low-maintenance perennial plants, such as hostas and campanulas, that provide flowering interest in spring and summer.

Some plants, including thyme, dianthus and campanula, like reflected heat from the paving. Here, the paving joints have been mortared to prevent self-seeding.

Transform a patio with a cascade of plants

Although the patio is a perfect place for plenty of colourful containers, a more permanent planting takes less time to look after and does not need replacing every year. A permanent display also helps to blend the patio in to the garden and prevents it looking bare and bleak in winter. It can take the form of borders, raised beds or planting in paving. Decide where the planting is to go and improve the soil before laying the paving.

Planting around the patio Climbers are ideal for breaking the hard edge of a patio, where it runs up to the house, or a boundary wall or fence (see page 198). Around the outer patio edges, raised beds are easy to maintain (see page 192), and afford a certain amount of privacy and shelter. Planting can be graded from trailing plants cascading over the front walls to taller plants towards the back, where the rest of the garden begins. These plants should not obscure the view of the garden, but lead the eye towards the horizon. Raised beds are free-draining, so they are best planted with drought-resistant plants.

PLANTS FOR PAVING

These low, creeping plants tolerate a dry site and being trodden on occasionally.

Acaena microphylla
Armeria juniperifolia
Campanula carpatica
Dianthus deltoides
Erica carnea
Iberis sempervirens
Lychnis alpina
Mossy saxifrage
Parahebe catarractae
Sagina subulata* var. *glabrata
Thymus serpyllum

Statues provide an instant year-round focal point. Having stood proud of the border all winter, this statue is engulfed by the foliage during the growing season.

A ground-level bed bordering a patio should have flowing lines on the garden side to reduce formality and to soften the transition from one area to another. Edging, such as clay rope-top edging, on the bed's patio side will help to stop plants and soil overspilling. Keep the use of containers to guiding the way up steps, marking gateways, softening sharp angles or hiding eyesores, such as manhole covers.

Linking the patio and garden The patio area can be linked to the rest of the garden by careful planting or by the use of hard structures. Plants in the main garden can be repeated on the patio – in their dwarf form if necessary. Colour and form can also be echoed, such as a flowering forsythia at one end of the garden with a planting of dwarf yellow tulips on the patio. An archway or piece of decorative trelliswork on the patio may frame a statue or imposing plant at the other end of the garden, or create a view that tempts people off the patio to explore the garden itself. Pergolas, steps and paths can form direct links from the patio to the rest of the garden.

Planting in the paving Soften and break up large areas of paving by using low-growing plants in cracks or in planting pockets created by lifting paving slabs or bricks. Most paving plants cope with an occasional tread of feet but not with constant traffic. Moderately resistant plants include acaena, the creeping thymes (*Thymus serpyllum*) and the non-flowering camomile (*Chamaemelum nobile* 'Treneague'). Plant them away from thoroughfares so they pose no hazard and only the foliage extremities get damaged.

Break up the stark appearance of a patio by planting creeping herbs and perennials in gravel and in paving pockets. Here, alpine plants are used for seasonal flowers as well as all-year evergreen foliage.

This raised bed helps to link two areas of the garden. On the lower level, part of the paving has been removed and planted to soften the overall effect.

Low-maintenance raised beds

A raised bed is the biggest type of 'container' for growing plants on a patio. It holds a much larger volume of soil or compost than other types of containers so plants need less watering and feeding, and less replanting since there is room to include a greater number of permanent plantings of perennials and shrubs.

A raised bed has several advantages over a ground-level bed. It minimises the need to stoop; raises low-growing, scented varieties and small-flowered plants closer to nose and eye level; allows plants to be grown under particular soil conditions (see box opposite); and adds a three-dimensional element to your garden. They are also a good way to deal with a slope because they are a form of terracing.

Design and construction Choose a style of raised bed that complements the patio and house. For easy construction, raised beds are available as a split-log roll or as a kit of interlocking wooden mini-sleepers or concrete blocks that don't need mortaring (see below). Alternatively, build a raised bed yourself from individual concrete blocks or bricks. Steer clear of natural stone, because it requires skill and expertise to achieve good results. You will need to build the bed high enough to tend it without too much bending, and narrow

RAISED BEDS MADE EASY

Raised beds can be made from a range of materials, including brick, concrete blocks, railway sleepers and natural stone. Easier options include vertical logs, mini-sleepers or multi-blocks that are glued together with epoxy adhesive.

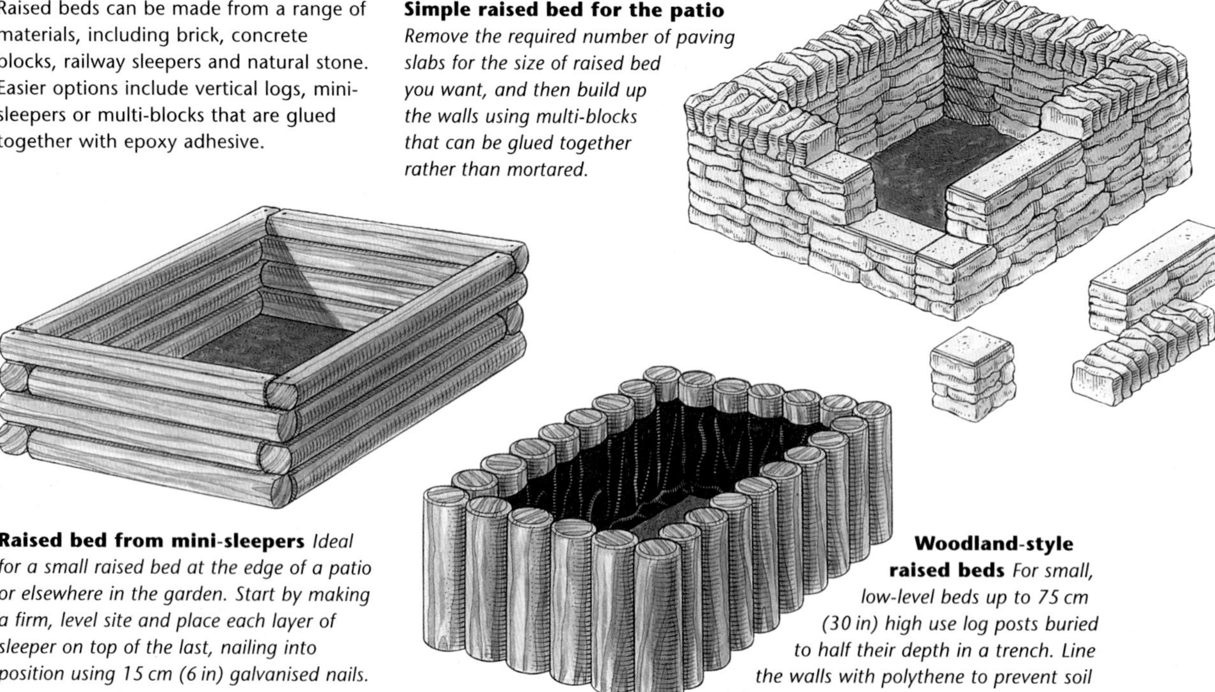

Simple raised bed for the patio *Remove the required number of paving slabs for the size of raised bed you want, and then build up the walls using multi-blocks that can be glued together rather than mortared.*

Raised bed from mini-sleepers *Ideal for a small raised bed at the edge of a patio or elsewhere in the garden. Start by making a firm, level site and place each layer of sleeper on top of the last, nailing into position using 15 cm (6 in) galvanised nails.*

Woodland-style raised beds *For small, low-level beds up to 75 cm (30 in) high use log posts buried to half their depth in a trench. Line the walls with polythene to prevent soil falling through the cracks.*

enough to reach to the middle from either side, but not less than 45 cm (18 in) wide, or the soil will dry out too quickly.

On an existing patio surface that is in good condition, foundations are not necessary. Once the walls are built, put 15 cm (6 in) of rubble, such as hardcore or gravel, at the bottom of the bed to improve drainage. If using mortar-bonded bricks or concrete blocks, you must allow for additional drainage by creating weep holes near the base of the raised bed – one every 90 cm (36 in) of length – by leaving small holes of 1.5 cm (½ in) diameter in the mortar.

Building a raised bed directly on soil allows for better drainage and a deeper root run for plants. First, clear the ground of all plant growth, using a glyphosate-based weedkiller or flame gun if necessary. For stone or brick walls more than 30 cm (12 in) high, you will need to lay a concrete footing which is twice the width of the wall. Otherwise, firm the soil by tramping on it with your feet.

Finishing off Fill the bed with good-quality topsoil or bagged compost (see box). Allow to settle for a couple of weeks before topping up and planting, and mulching the surface (see page 264) to cut down on watering. Part of the raised bed can be turned into a rudimentary garden seat by placing coping stones on top of one of the walls.

Special conditions

Raised beds enable you to grow plants not naturally suited to your soil.

Acid lovers For plants that cannot tolerate lime, such as camellia, line the base of the bed with a sheet of polythene punctured for drainage. Then fill the bed with ericaceous compost. Mortared walls containing lime will need coating on the inside with bitumen paint.

Bog garden To create a bog garden, line the inside of the raised bed with polythene, punctured for drainage. Fill the bed with moisture-retentive soil and water well.

Alpine plants Most alpine plants need free-draining conditions, which are provided naturally by raised beds. Fill with a three-to-one mix of good topsoil and horticultural grit.

This bold modern design using railway sleepers and gravel is planted with easy-care sculptural plants such as agave, hostas and grasses.

A rose arch adds vertical interest as well as providing shade in summer. Choose climbers that need little pruning, and try to position the arch to frame a view.

Using climbers to soften a patio

Climbing plants grow upwards and outwards to quickly cover vertical surfaces. Unlike wall shrubs, true climbers have some means of support, whether it is twining stems or leafstalks (such as honeysuckle or clematis), aerial roots (such as ivy) or coiling tendrils (such as sweet pea), so are less time-consuming to maintain.

Uses and benefits Climbers will clothe house walls adjoining the patio, reinforcing the link between garden and house. They can also be grown on pillars, pergolas, arches and other patio structures.

Where space for plants is limited, climbers make maximum use of all available growing areas. They are usually used to add a vertical dimension to the garden, but less vigorous varieties of climber, such as small-leaved ivies, can also be allowed to trail from raised beds to help to soften the edges of hard landscaping.

As long as there is a reasonable depth of soil beneath the patio surface, a climber can be planted in a small bed adjoining a wall or other support. Because most of the root area will be covered by paving, moisture loss is kept to a minimum, and weed growth is not likely to be a problem.

Problem solver

Easy maintenance Attach trellis to the supporting fence using large hooks rather than screws. This will allow you to remove the trellis quickly and easily if you need to carry out maintenance work on the fence.

LOW-LABOUR PATIO CLIMBERS

Choose climbers that need little regular tying in or pruning.

Actinidia kolomikta
Clematis alpina
Clematis macropetala
***Hedera colchica* 'Dentata Variegata'**
***Humulus lupulus* 'Aureus'**
***Lonicera japonica* 'Halliana'**
Parthenocissus henryana

Tips for easy care Before planting, prepare a large, deep bed of good-quality topsoil or compost because existing soil near house walls is often full of rubble and very shallow, and will not support healthy growth. When you plant the climber, dig the planting hole 30-45 cm (12-18 in) from the wall and angle the cane on which the climber is growing towards the wall's surface. To make watering easier and to ensure that the water reaches the roots, sink in a length of plastic drainpipe or a cut-off plastic bottle (see page 162).

In its early stages, a climber may need tying in to a support. Use plastic-covered wire to tie in plants – it is quicker to fix than twine. Avoid prickly stemmed climbers near thoroughfares because they will need continual pruning back to prevent them becoming a nuisance.

When growing climbers in containers, use a support that can be moved around with the container – a tripod of poles, for example. Special tubs are available with cane holders in the base for stability.

LOOKING AFTER AN EASY-CARE PATIO

SPRING

Clean sweep Hire or buy a power washer in order to clean the patio quickly and easily. Spot treat any particularly stubborn stains with patio cleaner. Apply weedkiller if necessary.

Patio repair Replace or repair cracked or uneven slabs.

▲Clean pots Prepare containers for replanting by cleaning inside and out. For a quick job, use a power washer or a strong jet from a hose. Discard damaged containers, or use as ornaments.

Pot up Buy plants and compost. Plant up pots and raised beds once the risk of frost is over. Incorporate a slow-release fertiliser that will feed plants all season.

SUMMER

▲Water containers Water plants regularly as weather conditions and plant growth dictate (see page 188 for quick-and-easy watering). This may mean watering up to twice a day.

Feed If a slow-release fertiliser is not used, apply a liquid feed once a week while watering.

▲Deadhead This is time-consuming, but worth while since it can extend and improve the flowering display. Otherwise use plants that don't need deadheading, such as allium and impatiens.

Problems patrol Check plants for pests and diseases, and deal with outbreaks immediately.

Remove weeds Weeds in containers and raised beds are easy to pull out by hand when the compost is moist. Apply a glyphosate-based weedkiller if there are problem weeds, such as couch grass or bindweed, in beds around the patio. By late summer weeding should be unnecessary because the rapidly growing bedding fills out and smothers weeds.

AUTUMN

Fallen leaves Clear up fallen leaves while they are dry; after rain they become much more difficult. For small areas, use a broom or garden vacuum, for large patios a leaf sweeper (see page 61) will be more efficient.

Tidy up Remove summer-flowering bedding plants as they pass their best. Leave herbaceous growth of perennials which have sculptural interest, such as agapanthus.

Winter colour Replant containers and beds for winter interest; plant spring-flowering bulbs.

Store furniture Clean and store away garden furniture.

▲Wrap up Give temporary protection to permanent plants during the worst winter weather by wrapping in fleece. Move containers of tender plants to a frost-free place.

WINTER

Check drainage Make sure compost is not too wet. Raise pots on 'feet' or bricks if necessary to improve drainage.

Make plans Plan planting schemes for the following year.

Directors' chairs are ideal for sitting back and viewing the garden at the end of the day. They are comfortable, and easy to fold and store.

Swinging seats are peaceful and relaxing. Enhance them with scatterings of pots planted with scented flowers, such as lilies and nicotiana, on each side.

Furnishing the patio with indoor style

A patio is somewhere to relax, so having a comfortable place to sit is important. Special garden furniture will mean no more lugging indoor furniture outside and then having to remember to bring it indoors again. Some types of garden furniture can be left out all year, only needing a light brushing in spring to get rid of accumulated winter debris, while other types, such as those using fabric, need bringing in if rain is forecast.

When choosing garden furniture, select a style that complements the house, adjacent planting and the rest of the garden. Try to stick to this style for all the furniture, so avoiding a mishmash of forms and colours. Go for furniture that needs little or no upkeep, and that can be left outside all year or is easy to store (see chart, left). You will also need to consider what you will be using the furniture for; a lightweight folding chair that it is easy to carry; a more sophisticated lounger model with adjustable footrest for a relaxing read; a rigid, upright non-folding chair for working or eating at the table – possibly a bench for two people or more; or a hammock strung between metal frames that can be moved around easily.

Tables need to be large enough to seat the whole family. Parasols are a useful additions for supplying adjustable shade, whether freestanding or part of the table (see page 200).

CHOOSING FURNITURE

Use this guide to select outdoor furniture to suit your patio and what you do in your spare time.

Material	Care	Cost	Ease of storage
Softwood	••	£	••
Hardwood	•	£££	n/a
Cast iron	••	££	•••
Aluminium	•	££	n/a
Plastic	•	£	•
Resin	•	££	•
Stone	•	£££	n/a
Reconstituted stone	•	££	n/a

Key to ratings
Care and storage:
• (quick and easy) to
••• (time-consuming and hard work)
Cost: £ (cheap) £££ (expensive)

Permanent features Chairs or benches that can be left out all year can also act as low-care focal points – under a spreading tree or at the end of a path, for example. Timber kinds are good for this. Hardwoods, such as teak or iroko, are the most durable and require no maintenance, although a teak oil can be used to keep the wood's original reddish brown colour from fading to silver-grey. Softwood furniture must be pressure-treated, but it can suffer from woodworm.

On the patio, stone benches and seats can make an effective permanent focal point. Metal furniture made from cast-aluminium or aluminium alloy can all be left outside provided the fittings are non-rust. Although durable, all these materials are unforgiving and uncomfortable unless you take a cushion to sit on.

Today, the most popular option is patio furniture made out of resin. It is more durable than its cheaper plastic predecessor, so can be left outside all year. Like plastic, it is easy to wipe clean and is lightweight; most designs have either folding or stackable chairs and loungers to make storage easier. It is available in a range of colours and styles.

Protective covers Even durable furniture will get dirty and covered in algae if left outside for very long. To save time having to clean furniture each time you want to use it, use an all-weather cover to protect it when not in use. There are special designs for everything from a single chair to a whole patio set. They are not durable enough to be used for protecting furniture overwinter, however. Fabric cushions should be kept indoors when not in use.

Keep the style of furniture in line with the garden's overall character and size. This roughly hewn wooden bench fits in with the tropical-style vegetation and requires no maintenance or winter storage.

Maintenance tips

Wood Clean with a pressure washer or stiff brush and water; sand down rough areas; apply wood preserver to non-treated softwoods, and apply, if desired, teak oil to hardwoods once a year to keep their colour.

Cast iron Clean with a damp cloth. It rusts slowly when exposed to air. You will need to sand down damaged areas and apply a rust converter, followed by an undercoat and topcoat of paint.

Aluminium Wipe down with a damp cloth, and oil all fittings and moving parts.

Plastic and resin Clean with a damp cloth and detergent, or with a proprietary spray cleaner.

Stone Clean with a pressure washer or stiff brush and soapy water.

Upholstery Use a proprietary liquid or spray for cleaning.

Time saver

To avoid marking the paving and time-consuming cleaning later on, keep some sand near the barbecue and sprinkle it on any fat spillages as soon as they happen.

Entertaining outdoors

The patio area should be seen as an extension of the house. Not only is it for relaxing, reading a book or taking in the rest of the garden, but also for eating and entertaining. A well-sited barbecue is the most convenient way of eating outside, avoiding lots of unnecessary walking to and fro from the kitchen because the food is cooked near to the table. But to make the most of your patio, you will want to use it in the evening, once the sun has set, so you should consider installing some kind of lighting system as well.

Barbecues They must be quick and easy to set up and use in order to take advantage of fine evenings on the spur of the moment. The cost of equipment varies widely, and the most expensive barbecues are not necessarily the easiest to use.

Barbecues are either built-in or portable. A built-in barbecue is a permanent, integral part of the patio. In most climates, it is used for only a few months of the year, so it should not occupy a prominent position but must be convenient to use. Typically, the surround is a brick structure, into which a barbecue grate and grill is slotted. The grate and grill are easy to clean, and take up little storage space.

Portable barbecues, on the other hand, can be used anywhere, but take up more storage space. Disposable barbecues are the most basic type of portable barbecue. They are the ultimate in convenience – ideal for picnics or very small gardens, even balconies. They usually consist of a foil tray, integral grill and charcoal, and they cook only small amounts.

The most popular portable barbecues are freestanding models set on legs. Open, brazier barbecues must have a windshield to ensure an even heat. They offer flexible cooking – potatoes can be baked on the coals – and the grill height is adjustable. Kettle barbecues are similar but have a domed lid that retains heat and smoke, so it cooks food more quickly. Food can be baked, roasted, braised as well as grilled. And you can use them throughout the year.

Gas and electric barbecues are switch-controlled, clean and come in different sizes. They heat a layer of reusable lava

A well-designed barbecue will make cooking outdoors enjoyable for all the family. This built-in barbecue is in a convenient position, with good access. It is also away from plants so that flowers and foliage are not affected by the smoke.

This candle-lit den makes a tranquil hideaway on a summer's evening and is brought alive by a scattering of colourful cushions. The picture is enhanced by the large, glossy leaves of the variegated ivy and the luxuriant growth of the ferns.

Lighting allows busy gardeners to appreciate and to make the most of their garden after dark. Here, it is also used to enhance the garden's design.

rock, taking 10 minutes to reach cooking temperatures against 30-45 minutes for charcoal. Gas barbecues use refillable cylinders.

For fuel, briquettes burn for twice as long as lumpwood charcoal and produce a more even heat. Their relative slowness to light can be quickened by using special firelighter blocks or fluid. The grill is ready to use when the surface of the charcoal is covered in fine white ash.

Bringing light To carry on entertaining throughout the evening, you may need lighting. Candles or flares can be effective and create atmosphere, but they need constant replacement. For subtle lighting at the touch of a switch, use spotlights placed around the patio. To install low-voltage lighting, plug a transformer into an indoor socket and run low-voltage cable outside, either underground or clipped to features such as fencing. Adjustable spotlights are useful for achieving dramatic effects, from uplighting, downlighting, or backlighting to pick out particular plants or features.

Individual lamps on soil spikes are available as a kit. They attach to a low-voltage cable by a simple snap fitting. For areas far away from the house, consider solar-powered lighting. But the number of hours of lighting will depend on the amount of sunlight during the day.

A mains security light attached to the house wall will illuminate a large area, but the light is too strong for comfortable outdoor living. An ordinary porch lamp would be a better option. Lights powered by mains electricity should be installed by an electrician.

Siting barbecues

Do line the charcoal tray with aluminium foil for easy disposal of the charcoal. Alternatively, buy an ash-dump grate.

Do shelter the barbecue from the wind or use a windshield.

Do build a barbecue that you can easily dismantle and put elsewhere by laying bricks or blocks, without using mortar, to form a honeycomb pattern for stability.

Don't site a barbecue too close to plants because it can damage them.

Don't place the barbecue a long distance away from the kitchen.

Providing shade Most people prefer a patio to be situated in full sun, but when eating or reading in summer a little shade is welcome. Many plants also need protection from direct sunshine, and providing them with some shade will reduce the amount of watering required. To give a better idea of the type of shade required and the best position for it, observe the site for a few weeks in summer. Draw a rough sketch and keep a note of the sunny and shady areas through the day. A permanent structure will provide some shelter from the sun each day – the amount, position and duration of the shade varying according to the sun's position – it may also give much-needed protection from the wind as well as making the patio more private.

Solid shade is cast by walls and fences, while lighter, dappled shade can be provided by a strategically placed deciduous tree or by screens made out of trellis or concrete screen blocks with a diagonal or leaf pattern. A light-roofed structure, such as a pergola with the option of training climbers over the crossbeams, provides more hours of shade, while a wide, plant-clad arch creates a pleasant arbour. Often it is best to experiment with temporary shade first before investing in a more

Quick results

Use trelliswork covered with an annual climber such as morning glory, or a deciduous climber such as a clematis that is hard pruned each February (see page 162), to vary the density of shade throughout the seasons. This will give most shade in summer, when the climber is in full leaf, and less in winter, when the extra light during the short days is welcome.

CREATING SHADE ON THE PATIO

Various features exist for creating as much or as little shade as is needed even on the most sun-drenched of south-facing patios. Some items offer deep shade, others light. Many can be moved around the patio.

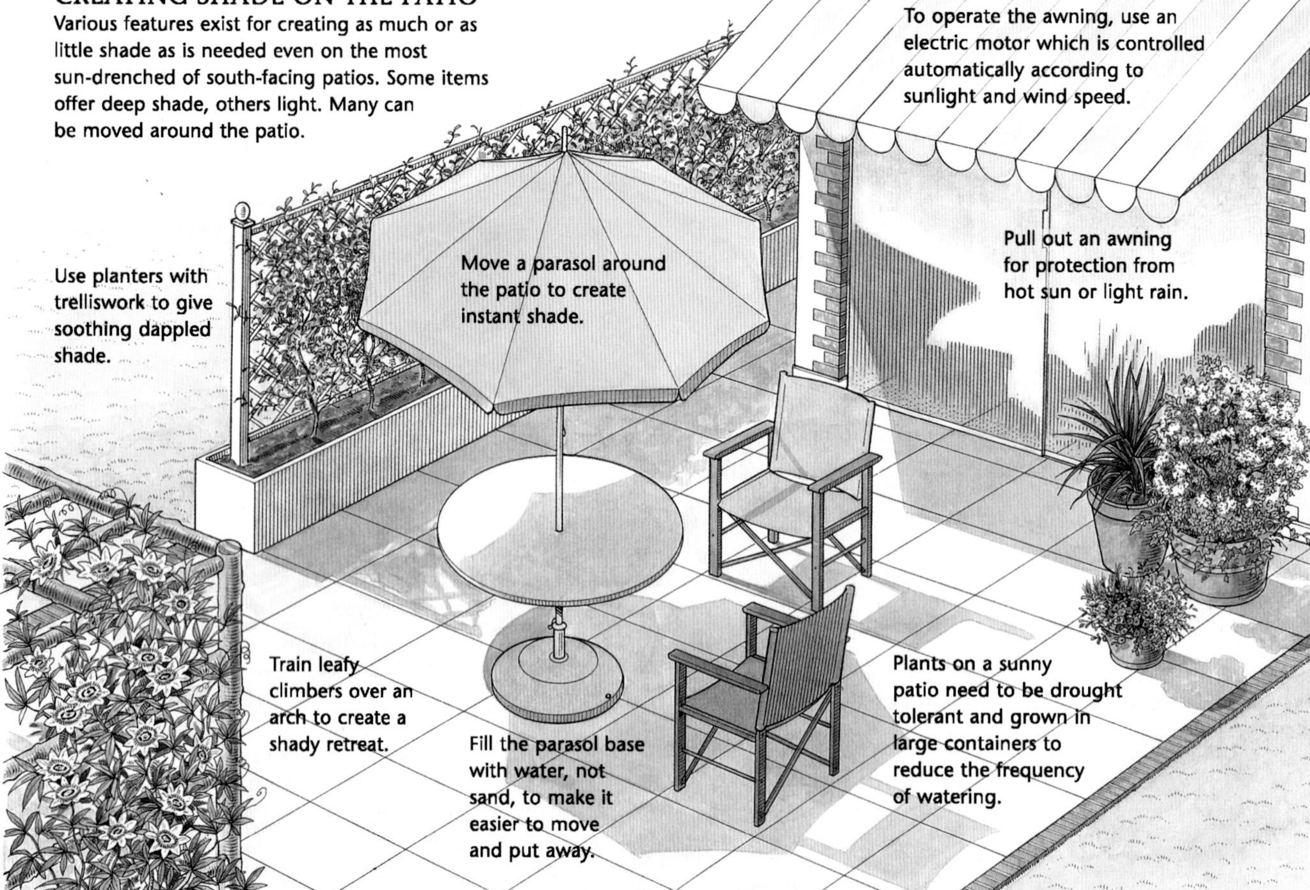

To operate the awning, use an electric motor which is controlled automatically according to sunlight and wind speed.
Use planters with trelliswork to give soothing dappled shade.
Move a parasol around the patio to create instant shade.
Pull out an awning for protection from hot sun or light rain.
Train leafy climbers over an arch to create a shady retreat.
Fill the parasol base with water, not sand, to make it easier to move and put away.
Plants on a sunny patio need to be drought tolerant and grown in large containers to reduce the frequency of watering.

Enliven a simple bird table *(above)* with ornaments in summer. In winter, when you feed the birds, use non-germinating seed – or you'll have more weeding to do.

Stone dogs are easier to look after than the real thing. These two, though, would be better placed on gravel, otherwise you'll need a trimmer to cut the grass.

permanent screen. For example, a parasol can be moved about the patio and put away when not needed: a tilting top allows you to vary the area of shade. An awning is generally attached to the house, often over patio doors. It can be pulled out as required and also provides protection from light rain.

Canvas gazebos are also available – like a marquee but without sides. The roof is supported by lightweight metal poles fixed to the patio surface with coach bolts. A canvas gazebo provides overhead protection from sun and light rain, but is time-consuming to erect, and must be dismantled in windy weather and put away in winter.

Statues and ornaments For permanent year-round interest that won't die from neglect, statues and ornaments are an obvious choice. The selection available extends to more than just a sundial or naked nymphet; animals can stalk around your garden, grass-like plants can grow out of the top of a sculpted head, or a wind chime can tinkle or ding – depending on your taste – in the wind.

Ornaments may be made of anything. For those set on the functional as well, bird tables now come in ornamental forms along with birdbaths. Bear in mind how the material will weather; for example, rough stone will become encrusted with lichens. In some cases, this weathering may add to the attraction of the feature.

Ornamental touches

Flash of interest Pinpoint the area in your garden that cries out for more interest – the end of a path, a corner or next to a water feature – and use an ornament to bring it to life.

Keep in scale Make sure that the ornament is in scale with its surroundings. One large piece may be all you need to form a striking focal point on the patio.

Small is not always beautiful Try not to clutter up the garden with too many small ornaments. However, a few small sculptures can be effective set unobtrusively among plants.

Simple is easy If in any doubt about what goes with what, choose an ornament with a very simple form, in particular if you are mixing styles and ages of ornaments.

The conservatory

Originally, conservatories were designed for the cultivation of tender plants. Now they are more often used as a light and airy extra room – a protected extension of the garden, a place to sit and enjoy the view on a chilly spring or autumn day. The position of a conservatory is often chosen for maximum sun – fine for colder months, but not for summer. To reduce the need for shading and watering in hot weather, be prepared to compromise on brightness, and consider a conservatory with a tiled roof and stone or brick half walls.

Hanging basket For easy watering and effortless hoisting up and down, hanging baskets are available on pulleys.

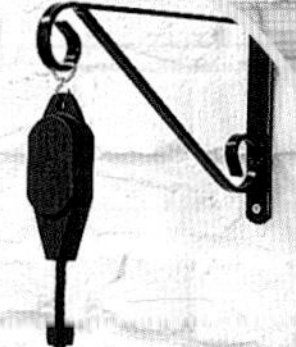

If you want to grow a lot of plants consider installing a raised bed, which is easier to maintain than individual pots.

Water supply
Fit a tap inside the conservatory for quick and easy watering. Even better, install an automatic system.

Use the conservatory to grow plants which would not survive the winter outdoors, such as brugmansia and citrus trees.

Furniture should be tough. Soft furnishings look good, but sunlight can cause colours to fade.

On which wall?

Which way a conservatory is facing can dramatically change its usefulness:

South-facing A conservatory that faces south may be a pleasant place to sit in winter, but will be too hot to use in summer without shading.

North-facing A conservatory that faces north is cooler in summer and useful for most houseplants, which dislike strong direct sun.

East or west-facing These are the best aspects for a conservatory, but will need shading in summer.

Create an extension of the garden by using the same floor materials as the patio, or be sure flooring resists water.

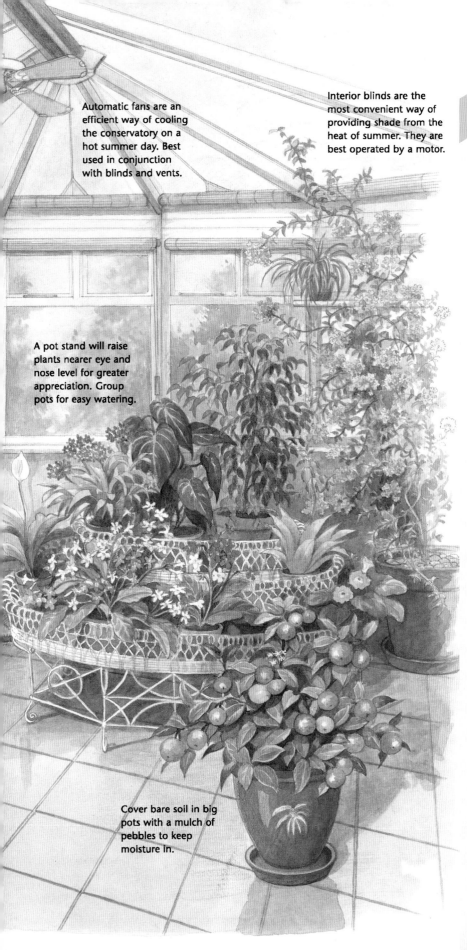

Automatic fans are an efficient way of cooling the conservatory on a hot summer day. Best used in conjunction with blinds and vents.

Interior blinds are the most convenient way of providing shade from the heat of summer. They are best operated by a motor.

A pot stand will raise plants nearer eye and nose level for greater appreciation. Group pots for easy watering.

Cover bare soil in big pots with a mulch of pebbles to keep moisture in.

PLANTS FOR A FROST-FREE CONSERVATORY

A conservatory gives you the chance to grow more exotic plants. All these are evergreen. They will need to be kept at not less than 4°C (40°F) in winter.

***Brugmansia* x *candida* 'Grand Marnier'** Strongly scented, trumpet-shaped flowers in summer and autumn. All parts of the plant are toxic if swallowed. Can reach 1.8 m (6 ft).

Clivia miniata From the same family as the amaryllis. Strap-shaped, dark green foliage. Large heads of flowers in spring or summer. Height 40 cm (16 in), spread 60 cm (24 in).

Nerium oleander (oleander) This upright shrub is often seen at home in the Mediterranean area. It flowers in spring and summer. All parts are poisonous. It grows to 3 m (10 ft).

Prostanthera rotundifolia (mint bush) Its small, round leaves smell of mint when crushed. Purple, bell-shaped flowers in profusion in spring. Reaches 1.8 m (6 ft).

Strelitzia reginae (bird of paradise) A clump-forming perennial with coloured spathes and flowers from winter to spring. Height at least 90 cm (36 in), spread 75 cm (30 in).

Water Gardening

EVEN THE SMALLEST GARDEN CAN FIND THE SPACE FOR A BEAUTIFUL POND. IF YOU GET THE DESIGN RIGHT AND CHOOSE TROUBLE-FREE PLANTS, A WATER FEATURE CAN PRACTICALLY LOOK AFTER ITSELF

A water feature adds a completely new dimension to a garden. Whether it be formal or informal, ornamental or natural, a well-designed pool will produce a relaxing atmosphere and provide relief to the stresses of a busy gardener's life. Even a simple water feature can add light, colour and movement that could be used to improve areas of the garden which lack interest. In a small garden, the reflective nature of water can create the illusion of space, while a natural pond can be constructed to provide the perfect habitat for frogs, toads, insects, birds and a wealth of other wildlife.

It is essential to get the siting of a water feature right from the outset if it is to be low maintenance. Ideally, it should be sited in the open, in full sun away from tall buildings and trees. A pond in a sunny location looks better, providing reflections and changes of mood, especially if the water is moving. But don't forget, if you want a moving water feature, such as a fountain or cascade, or pond lighting for added interest at night, you will need an electricity supply too.

EASY-CARE CALENDAR

SPRING
Plant new additions to the pool, and lift and divide any marginal plants that are getting too big.

SUMMER
Top up the pond during hot weather to compensate for water lost through evaporation. Feed fish. Scoop out blanket weed by twisting it round a bamboo cane.

AUTUMN
Net the pool to keep out fallen leaves from nearby deciduous trees and shrubs. Feed fish with a high-protein diet to build them up for winter. Float a ball on the surface of the pool before it freezes to help to protect the pond liner from damage caused by expanding ice.

WINTER
If the pond freezes over, melt a hole in the ice by standing a saucepan filled with hot water on the surface. This will allow any noxious gases to escape that would otherwise build up under the ice and kill the fish.

STARTING FROM SCRATCH

To make a small pond, like the one pictured, will take you the weekend to excavate the hole by hand or half a day if you hire a mechanical digger, motorised barrow and skip to remove the spoil. It will take about a day to position, fill the pool and trim the liner, plus half a day to conceal the edges with paving and plants. Stocking the pool will take up another half day, but should be left for a week or two after construction, when the water is clear.

1 EASY-CARE PLANTS – *elegant hostas, day lilies, polygonum and grasses conceal the edges.*
2 SHELVING EDGE – *easy access for wildlife.*
3 FLOATING PLANTS – *water-lily leaves cover more than half of the surface to help prevent algae.*
4 MARGINALS – *rushes offer year-round interest.*
5 VIEWING POINT – *a paved edge provides a secure vantage point to see and feed the fish.*

Sited in a sunny glade This small informal pond contains a balance of aquatic plants and fish. An easy-care planting of large-leaved hostas, pampas grass, polygonum and day lilies helps to create a seamless transition into the surrounding garden.

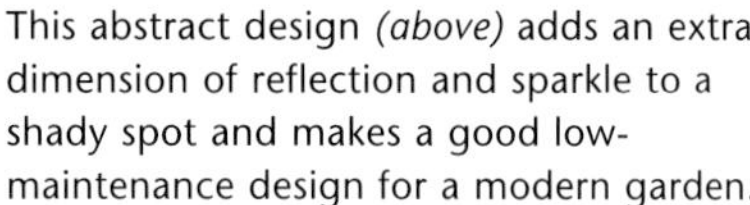

This abstract design *(above)* adds an extra dimension of reflection and sparkle to a shady spot and makes a good low-maintenance design for a modern garden.

A small 'wildlife' pond *(above, right)* is surrounded with cranesbill, annual poppies and bergenia to give a natural look. True bog garden plants would soon outgrow the space available.

WHAT TYPE OF POND?

Use the following guide to help you to decide which style of pond to choose for your garden.

Type	**Start-up time**	**Care**	**Cost**
Formal	••	•••	£££
Informal	••	••	££
Ornamental	••	••	££
Raised	•	•	£££
Bog garden	••	•••	££
Wildlife	•••	•	£££

Key to ratings
• (quick and easy) to
••• (time-consuming and hard work)
£ (cheap) to £££ (expensive)

Dipping into the pool of simple design options

The design of a water feature and the arrangement of the plants is a matter of combining personal taste with the plants' requirements. However, by choosing a style of water feature that suits the garden you can ensure that it sits comfortably within the surrounding landscape. Formal ponds are created from geometric symmetrical shapes, such as squares, rectangles and circles, with their straight lines and definite curves. Whatever shape you choose, try to follow existing lines in the garden. Straight lines should be parallel with nearby features, while curves should broadly echo those of a nearby border or path.

The aim with an informal pool is to create an abstract shape, without straight lines or sharp angles, where irregular curves blend in with the natural landscape. Use a mower to mark the outline of an informal pool in a lawn; the edges will then be easy to build and to maintain. Or, use a hosepipe as a guide. Keep the shape simple; avoid fussy niches and contortions, which will require a lot of upkeep. A natural pond may appear to be easier to look after, but the tangled informality of the wild look can be more difficult and time-consuming to create convincingly than the disciplined order of a formal pond.

Although a pond sunk into the earth creates a more natural appearance, many people prefer a pool that is raised above the ground. Indeed, a raised pond offers many advantages over other styles for the busy gardener (see table, left). It is easier to construct because you don't have to excavate a large hole or dispose of the spoil and routine care is more straightforward. Any container that holds water is potentially a raised water feature, whether it is a half barrel, a sink or an old water tank. A raised pond is a good practical choice next to a sitting area or on a patio. Small containers also provide a range of creative opportunities where space is limited because it is possible to move them around.

Simple babbling brooks and small cascades that don't contain plants or fish are another easy-care option for the busy gardener. They are particularly suited to modern styles of garden especially when surrounded with a sympathetic planting of lush foliage or bog plants. But with all ponds which have moving water or lighting displays, you will need to make sure that an electricity supply is installed before you start building your feature.

A sparkling pebble pool *(right)* surrounded by a lush planting of hostas, ornamental grasses, ferns and ivy is practically maintenance free.

Raised for easy viewing, this small sink garden *(below)* is filled with a variety of rushes. It nestles in a quiet shady corner surrounded by an attractive planting of white polemonium, viburnum, primula, lamium, ferns and foxgloves.

Choosing the best site

Selecting the site for a pond is critical because it makes the difference between a low-maintenance feature and a constant time-consuming struggle to achieve success. An easy-care pond needs to be sited in a well-lit position, preferably in full sun away from overhanging trees and deep shade cast by buildings. In a sunny position, plants supported by a pond will grow vigorously and remain healthy. It will also be easier to develop a natural balance between plants, fish and wildlife, so that the feature becomes largely self-sustaining. Small water features containing fish should not be sited in a hot spot because the small volume of water will heat up rapidly, which may kill the fish. Water features that do not contain fish can be sited in shady spots, indeed they are particularly useful for adding light, sound and movement to shady corners. In a small garden, the options will be limited, but even here you should choose the best site possible and then design any other garden features around it.

The most natural and often the most attractive position for a sunken pond is at the lowest point in the garden. The site must always be well drained, otherwise rising ground water during the winter will cause the lining of the pond to bulge and become displaced, or lift completely out of position.

It is also important to consider what the reflection in the water is going to be like. It should be attractive when viewed from the house, patio or any other areas of the garden where you might stop and admire the scene. Reflections are particularly useful for adding subtle light, colour and movement to a garden.

Consider the position of buildings and trees around the pond. Avoid areas where tall buildings and trees cast a shadow over the pond for most of the day as the sun moves across the sky. Also make sure that the area you intend to excavate is free from underground drainpipes, gas

Before you start

Do site a pond at the lowest point of the garden for a natural look.

Do make sure that the pond site is clear of underground services such as pipes and cables.

Do choose an open situation in full sun for most of the day.

Do arrange the electricity supply before you start to build a water feature which needs one.

Don't site a pond near buildings or trees because of the shade.

Don't choose a site that has a high water table.

An open, sunny site at the lowest point in the garden means that the easy-care pond *(below)* blends naturally into the garden landscape.

Positioned at the edge of a gravel path where it catches the afternoon sun, this mini-pond *(left)* is almost hidden from view by a planting of alchemilla, ornamental grasses and pots of hostas.

Problem solver

Wind-blown leaves Most leaves blow into a pond rather than fall straight into it. Before leaf fall, erect a temporary fence of fine mesh netting 60 cm (24 in) high around the pond. Collect and compost or throw away leaves as they accumulate.

mains or electricity and telephone cables because any damage caused will be costly to repair. Carefully consider how the pond is to integrate into the rest of the garden. If you want to include a bog garden or to surround the pond with other planting schemes, make sure there is sufficient room. To check how well the pond will blend in with the rest of the garden design, mark out the proposed position of the pond using a piece of hosepipe and canes to indicate the spread of the surrounding plants and borders.

If you want moving water, such as a fountain or a waterfall, you can either run a low-voltage line to the pond from a transformer plugged into the mains or get an electrician to lay an underground mains cable to the pond ensuring it meets the required safety standards. A pump powered by a solar panel may be worth considering, particularly in isolated locations.

It is also prudent to ensure a source of fresh water nearby, because even the most well-positioned pond will require topping up at some point to compensate for evaporation. If the pond is a long way from the nearest tap, do ensure that the garden hose is long enough.

A simple spout pouring water into a half barrel adds relaxing sound to the cool foliage of ferns and hostas. A moving water feature like this is an ideal way of adding interest to a shady corner.

Avoid siting a pond downhill from a lawn or next to a path or road where it could be polluted by water containing fertiliser, weedkiller or oil. This could promote rapid algal growth or even poison the pond water and kill the inhabitants.

The trouble with trees Site the pond far enough from trees to prevent problems with shading and the pond being clogged by autumn leaves. Horse chestnut leaves are particularly toxic, and the leaves of willow contain a chemical similar to aspirin, which can kill fish. Other trees to avoid include laburnum, holly, laurel and rhododendron. Trees with vigorous root systems, such as poplar and willow, can soon cause problems underground because their roots can lift, crack and disrupt the pond liner. Other trees play host to overwintering populations of troublesome aquatic pests. Decorative and edible cherries and plums, for example, give sanctuary to the water-lily aphid. If you wish to grow trees near to water, choose fibrous-rooted evergreens, such as conifers and Japanese maples.

Adding a pond for gentle relaxation and enjoyment

Joanna and Richard Robinson work full-time; she is a senior local government officer and he is a lawyer. They decided to commission a garden designer to create a practical, yet attractive design in keeping with their newly built terraced house. They particularly liked the idea of a pool and fountain combined with a shady pergola, and Mediterranean-style planting on the terrace.

The Robinsons have no children and wanted a garden that they could use as additional living space – with a formal patio area for sitting out in the evening, and for weekend entertaining and meals in the summer. Richard wanted to introduce fish to the pond and to encourage wildlife, such as frogs and birds, to the garden. With little time available, the Robinsons have to condense their gardening activities into occasional bursts. They needed to create an easy-care environment that did not limit the enjoyment they were seeking from their garden, and from the water feature in particular. Because time was scarce, they felt it was worth having the hard work carried out by a contractor, leaving them time to enjoy the result.

THE OLD GARDEN When Joanna and Richard bought their Georgian-style house, the only feature in their long, narrow garden was the lawn, which led the eye to an ugly brick wall at the end. Being set at an angle, the wall seemed to emphasise the lack of space in the garden. The waney-edge fencing gave them privacy from neighbours, but the strong vertical lines made them feel hemmed in.

DECIDING THEIR PRIORITIES

How much time?
2 hours per week on average, a little more at the start and end of the growing season.

Essential ingredients?
A formal patio area for entertaining at weekends and some evenings. A garden pond with moving water and fish. Plus planting schemes that provide scent, summer colour and an attractive sitting area.

Likes and dislikes?
They would like a garden that attracts wildlife, is colourful and easy to relax in. They wanted some storage space to keep garden tools.

A pond in shade Shady ponds are not suitable for fish and the choice of plants that will grow in shade is limited. In fact, you will get far better results by keeping the number of aquatic plants to a minimum and use shade-loving plants, such as ferns, to wreath the edge of the pool in foliage from the outside. If you want to include aquatic plants instead of using water lilies, which will not thrive in shady conditions, choose pond lily (*Nuphar lutea*) which is more shade tolerant. It has smaller flowers than the typical water lily, but its leaves look much the same. Most plants which grow under water cannot tolerate shady conditions, but the hornwort (*Ceratophyllum demersum*), which does not root to the pond floor but is suspended just beneath the water surface, will grow quite happily in gloomy places. Other plants that are ideal for stocking a shady pond include: water plantain (alisma), kingcup (*Caltha palustris*), rush (juncus), golden club (orontium) and water fringe (*Nymphoides peltata*). To make a real feature of a shady pool add moving water such as a waterspout or fountain.

Quick results

Instantly improve the stark appearance of a patio pool by arranging groups of plants in containers in front. Choose both upright and trailing plants, so they appear as a seamless extension of the pond planting. Containers without drainage holes are an ideal way to grow striking bog garden plants, such as *Cyperus longus* or the vigorous *Gunnera manicata*, that could otherwise grow too big for the garden pond.

THE NEW GARDEN A formal pool and covered walkway clothed with climbers, such as scented roses, are combined to form a single feature.

Secluded shed *The garden shed hides the brick wall and provides storage space. It has been camouflaged with foliage to make the garden seem larger.*

Style of pool *The formal design fits in visually with the house, and being 2.5x5.8 m (8x19 ft) is of sufficient size to maintain a natural balance.*

Garden lighting *Hidden lights add drama to the pool and garden during twilight and darkness.*

Design and construction

The larger the pool, the easier it will be to look after. If you have the space, a pool with a surface area of more than 5 m² (54 sq ft) sustains a natural balance between its inhabitants. Aim for a depth of around 60 cm (24 in) with a marginal planting shelf at around 15 cm (6 in). A large volume of water also means that the temperature of the pool does not change quickly and it is less likely to turn green and get choked with algae. Below this size, much time and effort will be necessary to maintain the natural balance and keep the water clear. A small pool is easiest to manage if it has only a fountain and does not contain any plants or fish.

Pond liners are the quickest and easiest way to install a pond. There are two main types – flexible liners and preformed (rigid) shells. Soil conditions influence which material is most appropriate. In sandy or very stony soil it is much easier to install a rigid shell than to fit a flexible liner. On the other hand, in heavy clay you can easily create an accurate shape and the contours needed to fit a flexible liner.

Flexible liners A pond constructed with a flexible pond liner can be any size or shape. There are several materials available: polythene is the cheapest but least durable; PVC, LDPE and butyl rubber are more expensive but last longer (see the table, opposite, to choose the right material and use the calculation below it to work out the size). To install a flexible liner, excavate a hole of the required size and shape,

Hide the edge of the liner in a formal pool by laying paving stones so that they project 5 cm (2 in) over the water.

EDGING THE POOL

Providing a neat and practical edge can greatly improve the appearance of a pond. Use the following ideas to create an edge to suit the style of pond you want to create.

Formal edge (below) *A neat formal edge can be made with paving laid on a bed of mortar. The liner is securely trapped between the soil and the paving, above the pool's water level.*

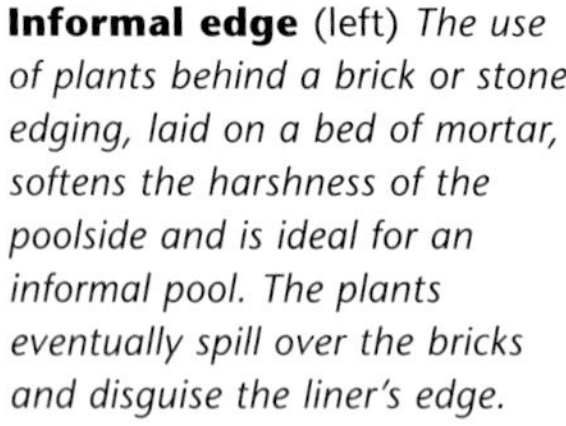

Informal edge (left) *The use of plants behind a brick or stone edging, laid on a bed of mortar, softens the harshness of the poolside and is ideal for an informal pool. The plants eventually spill over the bricks and disguise the liner's edge.*

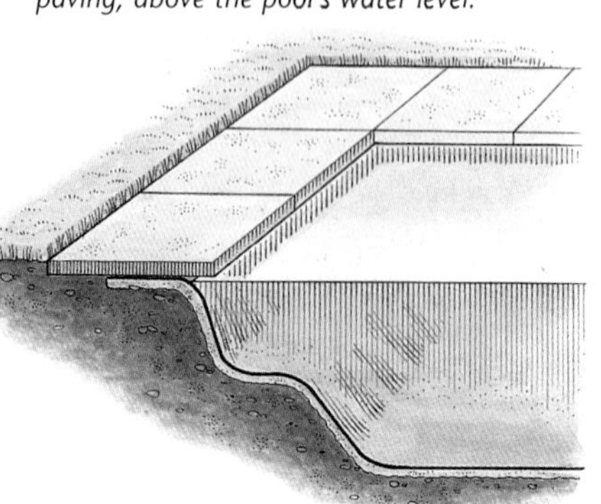

Natural edge (right) *A shallow beach of pebbles allows easy access for wildlife and is better than soil, which tends to muddy the pool. Behind, long grass provides hiding places for wildlife and a natural transition to a lawn.*

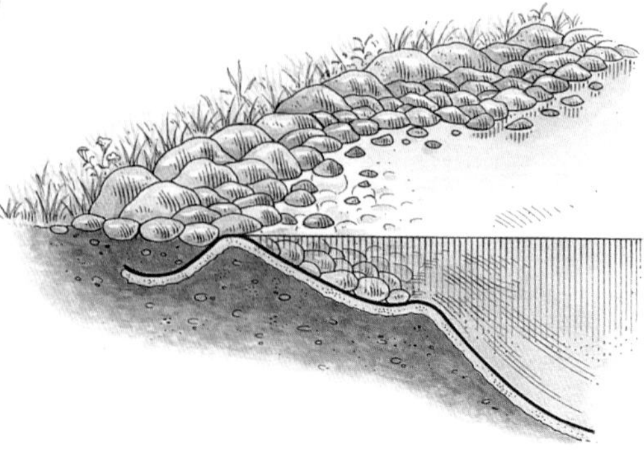

CHOOSING A POOL LINER

The following flexible and rigid liners are all widely available

Liners	Strength	Expected life	Cost	Ease of installation
PVC	●●	10-15 years	££	●
Butyl rubber	●●	15-20 years	£££	●●
LDPE	●●	15 years	££	●●
Polythene	●	5 years	£	●
Glass fibre (rigid)	●●●	15 years	££	●●●
Plastic (rigid)	●●●	10 years	££	●●●

Key to ratings Strength = ● (not very durable) to ●●● (very durable); Cost = £ (cheap) to £££ (expensive); Installation = ● (easy) to ●●● (hard).

What size flexible liner?

Pond size Mark out the area with a hosepipe. Then measure the longest and widest points, and decide on the depth. In this example, the length is 3 m, the width is 2 m and the depth is 50 cm.

Quick calculation Add the length to twice the depth (total: 4 m). Then add the width to twice the depth (total: 3 m). So the liner needs to be 4x3 m.

remove any large stones or roots, then line it with sand or special fleece (available from garden centres). Lay the pond liner in the hole, weighing the edges down with stones. Leave for a couple of hours to warm up and stretch, then slowly fill it with water. Help the liner to fit the contours of the hole by easing it gently at the edges. Once filled, trim the liner to leave a 15 cm (6 in) overlap on all sides.

Preformed (rigid) shells Available in plastic and glass fibre, in a limited range of shapes and often with poor accommodation for plants. Installing a preformed shell is more time-consuming. Excavate a hole about a third the size again of the shell and roughly the correct shape. Place the shell on a bed of sand in the hole and adjust it until it is level both from side to side and end to end using a spirit level and a straight piece of timber. Use battens to hold the shell in position and weigh down the shell with 5 cm (2 in) of water. Carefully backfill with soil around the shell, checking that the pond is still level as you work. The shell must be well supported so make sure that there are no gaps under the marginal shelves or around the sides.

Quick results

Use a flexible liner because it is the quickest and easiest to fit. Stick to simple shapes with gentle curves. Make sure the edge of the pond is level and keep sides sloping at about 20 degrees to the vertical and corners rounded. Line the hole with a 5 cm (2 in) layer of sand to help to prevent puncturing and lay out the pond liner on a warm day when it is more flexible and easy to mould into shape.

These water lilies help to maintain a natural balance, with their shade-creating leaves checking the growth of algae.

Problem solver

Planting narrow shelves It is often difficult to use a planting basket in a preformed pool with narrow marginal shelves. Instead take a pair of old tights, fill them with aquatic planting compost and mould to the shape of the ledge. Make small holes in the tights to plant through.

Selecting the right plants

It is important to choose the right combination of plants for your pond. This not only affects its visual impact, but also the natural balance and subsequent maintenance requirements. There are four main groups of pond plants (see lists opposite). Avoid invasive plants, such as water mint (*Mentha aquatica*) and pond sedge (*Carex riparia*), which swamp their neighbours even when they are confined in a planting basket. Some tall plants, such as the great reed mace (*Typha latifolia*), should also be avoided because they get top heavy in their planting baskets and tend to tumble into the water even in quite light breezes.

Submerged aquatic plants are vital for the well-being of the pool because they mop up excess nutrients, which algae would otherwise feed upon, and produce life-giving oxygen to plants and fish, as well as providing cover for spawning fish. There are two submerged plants which produce beautiful flowers. The easiest to grow is the water crowfoot (*Ranunculus aquatilis*), a ferny leafed underwater plant which produces occasional clover-like floating leaves and masses of cup-shaped white blossoms with golden centres during late spring and early summer. The water violet (*Hottonia palustris*) flaunts upright spikes of off-white or pale lilac flowers during early summer.

Many floating plants provide colour and interest on the water surface over only a short period of time, but a few are good value. The frogbit (*Hydrocharis morsus-ranae*) and water chestnut (*Trapa natans*) form winter buds and fall to the bottom of the pool at the first hint of autumn, reappearing in late spring when awakened by the slowly warming water. The prickly leafed water soldier (*Stratiotes aloides*), which looks like an elegant olive-green pineapple top, remains suspended under the water all winter and bobs to the surface when the sun begins to shine. Fairy moss (*Azolla caroliniana*) disappears only if the weather is particularly harsh, otherwise its delicate filigree foliage carpets the water surface for most of the year.

Deep-water aquatics, such as the water hawthorn (*Aponogeton distachyos*) and water fringe (*Nymphoides peltata*) are easy to grow, and there are many water lilies (nymphaea) to choose from (see list, right). Select a variety which suits the depth of your pool.

Grow plants suited to the shallows (marginals) around the edge of the pond. The variegated irises give the best value. Both *Iris laevigata* 'Variegata' and *I. pseudacorus* 'Variegata' have striped leaves for much of the growing season, and blue or yellow flowers respectively in early summer. The zebra rush (*Scirpus* 'Zebrinus') and variegated sweet flag (*Acorus calamus* 'Variegatus') also produce attractive foliage.

Planting made easy

To reduce maintenance, grow all plants in purpose-made plastic baskets with lattice-work sides. The baskets are much more stable in the water than ordinary pots. The plants can be moved about and if one becomes overgrown more quickly than the others, it can be removed from the pool to be divided with minimum disruption.

Line the basket Use hessian to line standard baskets to prevent soil escaping. Micromesh baskets come ready lined.

Add aquatic compost This is formulated for use in ponds. Ordinary compost will release soluble plant foods rapidly into the water, encouraging algae.

Top up with gravel Add a 2 cm (¾ in) layer of pea gravel to prevent fish and other aquatic life stirring up the compost.

Soak the basket This will drive out all the air, so the compost will not bubble up when the basket is lowered into the pool.

EASY-CARE POND PLANTS

A low-maintenance pond should contain a mixture of floating and submerged plants. Cover a third of the surface with floating plants and add ten submerged plants per square metre. Choose from the following lists of easy-care plants.

Deep-water plants
Aponogeton distachyos, *Nymphaea* (water lily, such as 'Arc-en-ciel', 'Aurora', 'Ellisiana', 'Froebeli', 'Hermine', and 'Pygmaea Helvola' for shallow pools), *Nymphoides peltata* and *Orontium aquaticum* (pictured).

Marginal plants
Acorus calamus 'Variegatus', *Butomus umbellatus, Caltha palustris* 'Flore Pleno', *Iris laevigata* 'Variegata', *Myosotis scorpioides, Pontederia cordata* (pictured), *Scirpus* 'Zebrinus', *Typha minima*.

Floating plants
The following are the only reliably hardy floating plants that are easy care: *Azolla caroliniana, Hydrocharis morsus-ranae, Stratiotes aloides* (pictured), *Trapa natans, Utricularia vulgaris*.

Submerged plants
Ceratophyllum demersum, Eleocharis acicularis, Elodea canadensis, Fontinalis antipyretica, Hottonia palustris, Lagarosiphon major, Myriophyllum spicatum, Potamogeton crispus, Ranunculus aquatilis (pictured).

Raised pools for the patio

A raised pool can be an absolute delight on a patio. As you sit and relax, you can see the fish and plants at close quarters. It is also an ideal choice for the busy gardener because there is no need to excavate a large hole, and routine maintenance such as planting and cleaning out is much easier. Raised pools are now available in kit form from garden centres, or you can make your own using a freestanding container or by constructing a retaining wall and lining it with a pond liner.

A freestanding half-barrel is the easiest way of creating a patio pool (see opposite). If you want something a little larger, you can construct a pool from a glass-fibre container. Place it on the patio, add enough water to ensure that it remains in position, and add a decorative surround. A log roll – such as those sold by garden centres for use as border edging – can be secured tightly around the container using strong adhesive. Or fix the log roll to stout posts about a foot from the container, and fill the gap between the roll and the pond edge with soil and plant it to make a combined pond and raised garden.

Another option is to build a brick structure and fit a pond liner inside. The walls will need to be at least two bricks thick and lined with a 5 cm (2 in) thick layer of expanded polystyrene for insulation before adding the pond liner.

Topping up

Water loss All water features require topping up, especially in summer to compensate for water loss through evaporation. Reduce the impact of water as it is added to the pond by putting the end of the hose into a watering can, old sock or large perforated polythene bag and secure it with a jubilee clip. The water then flows out of the hose gently without disturbing any gravel or compost. If the pool needs regular topping up all year round, the liner may have been punctured so the pool will need to be drained and repaired.

Pebble-filled terracotta pots *(above)* make a novel and attractive gurgle fountain in a low-maintenance raised pond on a patio.

A raised pond featuring an old pump overgrown with ferns and ivy *(left)* is surrounded by foxgloves and Japanese maples that together transforms a shady corner into an oasis of texture and sound.

A quick and simple pool

Use a half-barrel or a sturdy plastic tub to make a miniature pond on a firm, level site. If you choose a barrel, paint it with preservative and allow it to dry thoroughly.

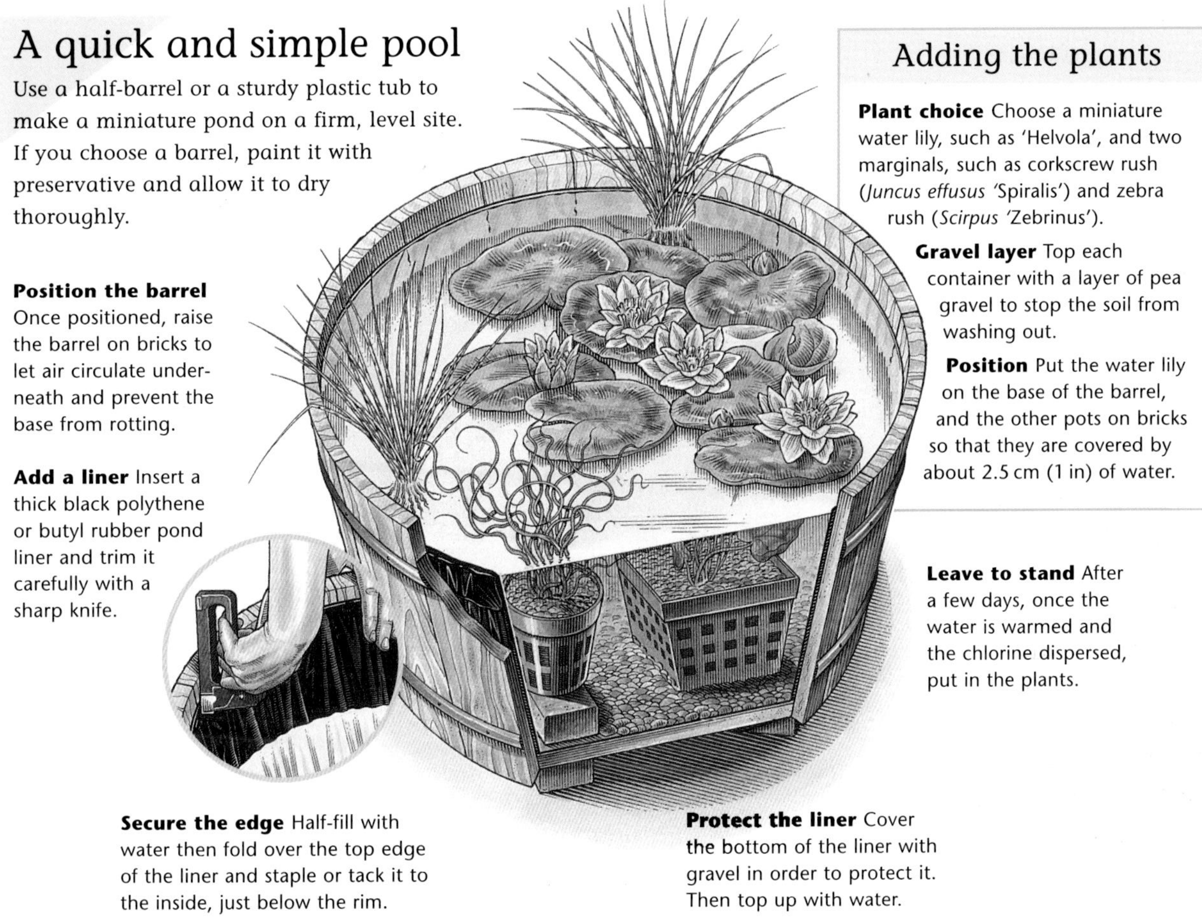

Position the barrel Once positioned, raise the barrel on bricks to let air circulate underneath and prevent the base from rotting.

Add a liner Insert a thick black polythene or butyl rubber pond liner and trim it carefully with a sharp knife.

Secure the edge Half-fill with water then fold over the top edge of the liner and staple or tack it to the inside, just below the rim.

Protect the liner Cover the bottom of the liner with gravel in order to protect it. Then top up with water.

Leave to stand After a few days, once the water is warmed and the chlorine dispersed, put in the plants.

Adding the plants

Plant choice Choose a miniature water lily, such as 'Helvola', and two marginals, such as corkscrew rush (*Juncus effusus* 'Spiralis') and zebra rush (*Scirpus* 'Zebrinus').

Gravel layer Top each container with a layer of pea gravel to stop the soil from washing out.

Position Put the water lily on the base of the barrel, and the other pots on bricks so that they are covered by about 2.5 cm (1 in) of water.

Scented plants A raised pool can be planted conventionally (see list right), but you may prefer to choose plants which not only look good but are aromatic too. For example, water mint (*Mentha aquatica*) and the closely related *Mentha cervina*, have sweetly fragrant foliage, but both need pinching back to keep within bounds. The variegated foliage of *Acorus calamus* 'Variegatus' has a strong aroma of tangerines if it is rubbed gently. If you plant the free-flowering water hawthorn (*Aponogeton distachyos*), the air will be filled with the fragrance of vanilla and the water lily variety 'Rose Arey' emits an aniseed scent.

Winter care for small water features In small containers, plants may need winter protection especially in colder areas. The easiest option is to empty the barrel and move it to a frost-free place such as a garage or sheltered part of the garden, and then refill it. Or you can store the water lilies in the mud at the bottom of a container, provided that the mud does not dry out. Most marginal aquatic plants can be stored in the same way, but discard any floating plants which grow beneath the water's surface and replace them in the spring.

PLANTS FOR SMALL PONDS

It is essential to choose the right pond plants if space is limited. Combine several of the following easy-care plants for an attractive feature.

Corkscrew rush
Fairy moss
Miniature water lily
Umbrella grass
Water chestnut
Water hyacinth
Water lettuce
Zebra rush

BOG GARDEN PLANT SELECTOR

The following plants are worth incorporating into your bog garden scheme because they are generally trouble free and offer a long season of interest.

***Astilbe* x *crispa* 'Perkeo'** Compact plant with dark green, deeply cut leaves up to 15 cm (6 in) high. Bears attractive plumes of pink flowers in July/August. Prefers partial shade.

***Cardamine pratensis* 'Flore Pleno'** (lady's smock) Mounds of ferny foliage reaching 30x60 cm (12x24 in). It bears fully double pale lilac blooms in April. Likes sun or partial shade.

***Ligularia dentata* 'Desdemona'** Large, heart-shaped leaves that are purple underneath. Orange flowers are borne on 90 cm (36 in) stems from July to September. Needs some shade.

***Lobelia* 'Queen Victoria'** Stems 1.5 m (5 ft) tall that bear scarlet blooms from July to October. The leaves are a magnet to slugs. Tender in cold regions. Likes sun or partial shade.

Schizostylis coccinea Produces grassy foliage with distinctive freesia-like blooms on 60 cm (24 in) spikes from late summer to early winter. Good for adding colour late in the year. Prefers sun.

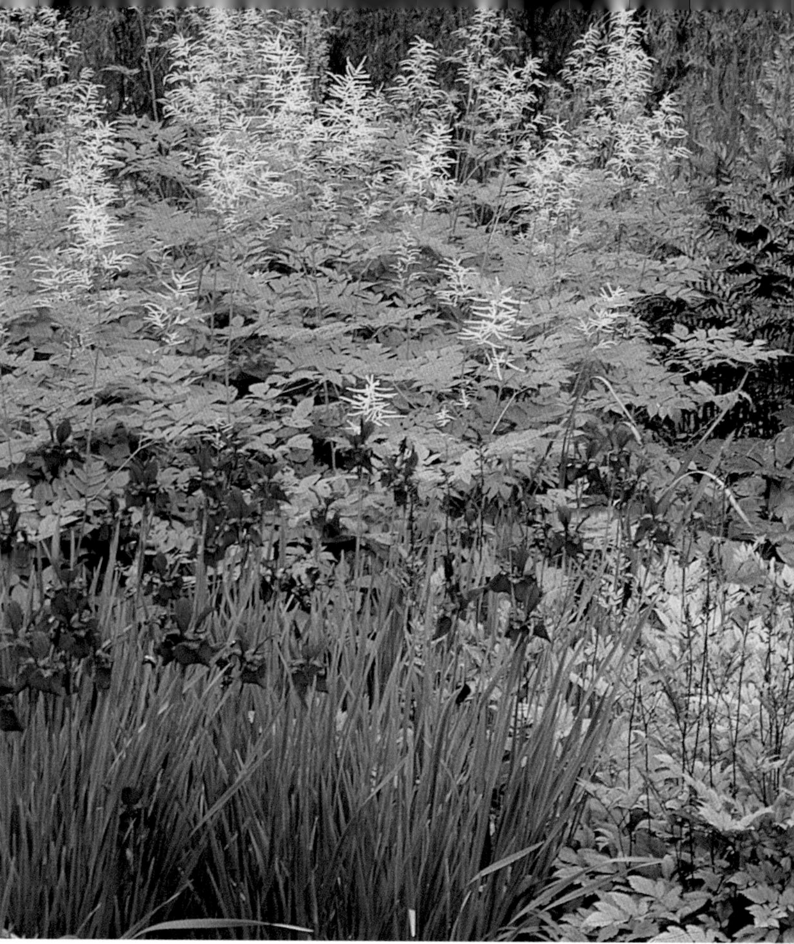

Creating a bog garden

A bog garden is an area where the soil remains permanently wet and is used to grow plants that originate from marshes and wet pastureland. Many bog garden plants associate very well with a pond and help to create a natural setting that allows a water feature to harmonise with the rest of a garden design. If you have heavy soil that remains constantly moist, you should be able to grow bog garden plants without making a special area.

A bog garden can be constructed as an integral part of the pool, or as a stand-alone feature. If it is to be part of the main pool, excavate it at the same time as building the pool. Adding a bog garden as a separate project afterwards is a lot more work, and a satisfactory result is more difficult to achieve. The bog garden should form a spreading shallow area 30-45 cm (12-18 in) deep. If you are using a flexible liner for the main pool, purchase one which is larger than required and use the extra to incorporate the bog garden (see illustration, right).

Separate the pond and bog garden with a row of stones and fine-mesh netting. This barrier retains the soil, but allows the water to percolate through to keep the soil mix constantly wet. Add a mixture of the excavated soil and well-rotted

garden compost, leaf-mould or other richly organic matter to at least 5 cm (2 in) above the water level. If it is difficult to integrate a bog garden into the pool surroundings, the right conditions can also be achieved by excavating part of the garden and lining the hole with a perforated PVC or butyl rubber pond liner. Mix the excavated soil with organic material then fill the hole. Install automatic irrigation (see page 188) because you will need to water frequently to keep the bog area wet.

Choosing plants Most bog plants are best planted in early spring, although some are readily available in containers and can be planted at any time. Avoid invasive plants, such as houttuynia and the creeping lysimachia. More restrained plants include: astilbe, filipendula and primulas, as well as ferns such as the ostrich feather fern (*Matteuccia struthiopteris*) and the royal fern (*Osmunda regalis*).

A lush waterside planting of moisture-loving plants *(left)* includes irises, rodgersia, *Astilbe* x *arendsii* 'Granat', *Salix alba* 'Tristis'.

Making a bog garden next to a pond

A bog garden is the best way of making a low-lying pond look natural with a range of moisture-loving plants growing in the moist soil around the water's edge. Don't make the bog garden more than 1.8 m (6 ft) across otherwise it will be difficult to maintain. It is easiest to build it at the same time as installing the pond.

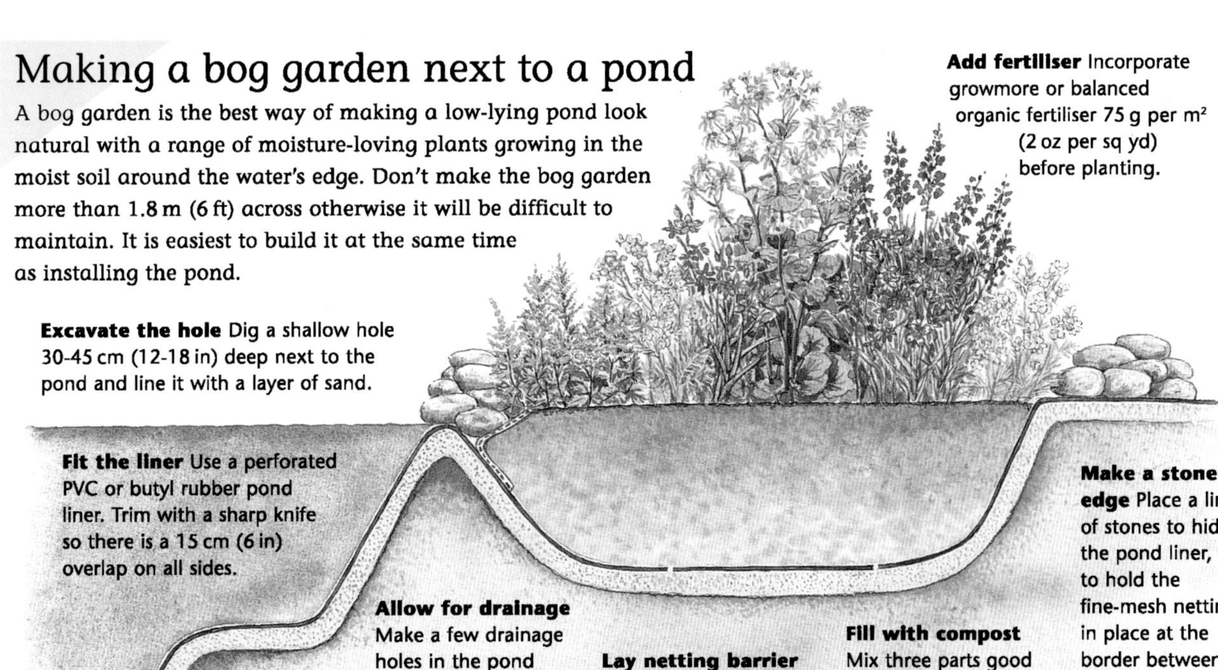

Add fertiliser Incorporate growmore or balanced organic fertiliser 75 g per m² (2 oz per sq yd) before planting.
Excavate the hole Dig a shallow hole 30-45 cm (12-18 in) deep next to the pond and line it with a layer of sand.
Fit the liner Use a perforated PVC or butyl rubber pond liner. Trim with a sharp knife so there is a 15 cm (6 in) overlap on all sides.
Allow for drainage Make a few drainage holes in the pond liner. Or place a 5 cm (2 in) layer of gravel over the bottom of the liner.
Lay netting barrier Position fine-mesh netting along the border between pond and bog garden to prevent soil from washing out.
Fill with compost Mix three parts good garden soil with one part well-rotted organic matter and use this to fill the bog garden.
Make a stone edge Place a line of stones to hide the pond liner, and to hold the fine-mesh netting in place at the border between pond and bog garden.

Creating a wildlife pond

By including the right plants and features, you can convert an existing pond or build a new one from scratch that will be a magnet for wildlife. Not only will you help to preserve our native species, but you can enjoy watching them up close. When designing a wildlife pond make sure that animals will be able to use the pond safely. Build a sloping beach down to the water's edge so they can drink and to act as an escape route for any that fall in. Also choose your plants carefully to avoid the need for constant pruning.

Attracting birds

Birds are attracted to wildlife ponds for food and water, and in order to bathe. They provide an enormous amount of pleasure, but they can bring problems, especially for gardeners in rural areas. Birds often pick up pesticides on their feathers so if they bathe in the shallow edge of the pond it can lead to pollution problems, which may kill the fish. You can reduce the likelihood of this happening by installing a separate birdbath nearby.

Plan some deep areas with water at least 90 cm (36 in) deep. These will remain cooler than the rest of the pool and provide pond life with a reservoir of oxygen in hot weather.

Marginal plants are essential to provide breeding areas for insects and safe havens where they can shelter from predators.

Surface walkers Pond skaters (pictured), water measurers and whirligig beetles skim or swim on the surface of the water.

A gently sloping shoreline allows amphibians and birds access to the water's edge.

Snails There are many kinds, including ramshorn snail (pictured), great pond snail and horny orb snail. All help to keep the pond clean.

Bottom dwellers such as water stick insects, water scorpion, flatworms and rat-tailed maggots live in the sediment at the bottom of the pond.

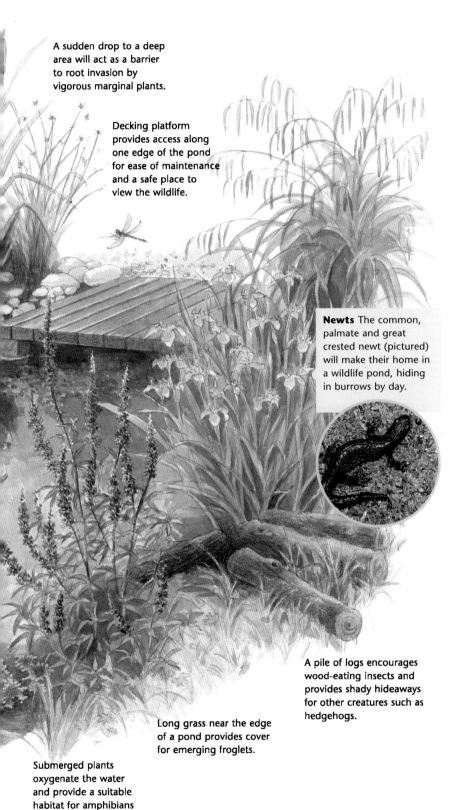

A sudden drop to a deep area will act as a barrier to root invasion by vigorous marginal plants.

Decking platform provides access along one edge of the pond for ease of maintenance and a safe place to view the wildlife.

Newts The common, palmate and great crested newt (pictured) will make their home in a wildlife pond, hiding in burrows by day.

A pile of logs encourages wood-eating insects and provides shady hideaways for other creatures such as hedgehogs.

Long grass near the edge of a pond provides cover for emerging froglets.

Submerged plants oxygenate the water and provide a suitable habitat for amphibians and insects.

TROUBLE-FREE PLANTS FOR NATURAL PONDS

Create the richest environment for wildlife by growing native plants, which are easy to find at garden centres. The following make an easy-care combination.

Carex pendula Almost evergreen marginal plant with pendant catkin-like flowers followed by hard seeds. Provides cover and is a good food plant. Height 1-1.2 m (3-4 ft).

Nymphaea alba The white flowered water lily has spreading rounded, dark green leaves which provide excellent cover for fish and amphibians. Naturally pollinated by beetles.

Myriophyllum spicatum This totally submerged, very fine-leafed plant attracts aquatic insects and makes an ideal place for the deposition of fish spawn. Fish also like to eat it.

Lythrum salicaria Spires of purple flowers during the summer attract many insects. The attractive lance-shaped dark green foliage is carried on tall stems. Height 1-1.2 m (3-4 ft).

Azolla caroliniana Beneficial surface shade is provided by this floating fern. The trailing roots become home to aquatic insects. The foliage turns bright red when grown in full sun.

Time saver

Reduce the number of times a water feature needs topping up by installing a large reservoir and by not siting the feature in a hot or windy position where the water evaporates more quickly.

A simple bell fountain in a sunken half-barrel *(right)* makes an attractive feature, adding gentle movement and sound to the atmosphere of the garden.

Use your imagination to create eye-catching and humorous water features. Below, a pile of log slices have been 'skewered' on a piece of copper pipe in an irregular way to give an informal but balanced effect.

The sight and sound of flowing water

The sparkle of a sunlit waterfall, the reflections of lights from a pond in twilight and the sound of a babbling brook make the garden a perfect place for evening relaxation or for entertaining friends. You do not need a large space to enjoy water in the garden; there are many smaller water features – from a water garden in a tub to bubbling pebble fountains and wall masks. They are quick to create, take little time to maintain and are quite safe if there are children about. Most can be made and planted within a day. Whether the water feature includes moving water will influence the types of plants used, because few plants flourish in turbulent water (see list on page 224).

Fountains Small fountains are among the most popular and effective small features and a modern submersible pump provides changeable fountain jets. The simplest display can be created by placing the pump so the jet is just below the surface or hidden from view in a pile of pebbles. Alternatively, the outlet pipe on the pump can be connected to a statue to produce either a gentle trickle or a forceful spray,

Making a safe pebble fountain

This attractive small water feature is safe and fun for children to play with because the water reservoir is securely covered. You can buy special preformed liners for a standard pebble fountain or create your own design using a plastic central-heating expansion tank.

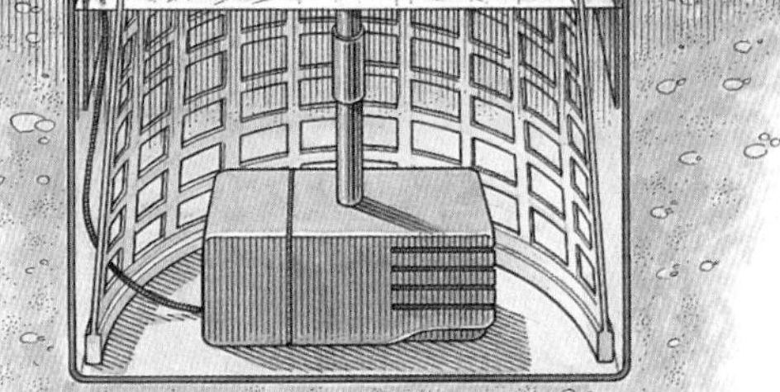

Add pebbles Wedge large pebbles to fill in the gap between the laundry basket and the rim of the tank. Top up with pebbles to disguise the fountain jet and cover the catchment area.

Position the reservolr Dig a hole large enough so the top of the tank is about 2.5 cm (1 in) below the soil surface. Then fill around the edges to support the sides.

Cover the reservoir Use an upturned plastic laundry basket to cover the pump and provide a platform to support the pebbles.

Create a catchment area Slope the area around the tank so that water will drain back into the reservoir. Line this area with a flexible pond liner (see page 213).

Add the pump Place a small submersible pump (see page 225) on the bottom of the reservoir so that the fountain head is above the water and hidden among the pebbles.

depending on the atmosphere you wish to create. The shape of the fountain spray is controlled by attaching different nozzles or jets to the pump, or perhaps linking the outflow to an ornament. Spray patterns vary widely from single waterspouts to multiple outlets that produce multi-tiered sprays, elaborate hemispheres or even whirling sprays. A specialist water garden centre will usually have the widest range to choose from (see page 306).

Pebble fountains (or gurgle ponds) are the easiest type of small water feature to build and require practically no maintenance. Water bubbles up through large pebbles producing an attractive gurgling sound. The quickest way to create a pebble fountain is in a waterproof half-barrel placed in an open, sunny site close to an electricity supply.

Millstone fountains are similar in construction except the jet of water spouts through the central hole in the millstone and flows gently over the edge. You need not worry about finding a suitable stone – garden centres now offer quite convincing replica millstones in either reconstituted stone or glass fibre. Millstone fountains can be constructed in barrels, although they are visually more appealing when sunk into the ground. The millstone sits on a bed of pebbles that forms a catchment area which drains the water back into a sump reservoir beneath. The water can then be recirculated by the submersible pump placed in the sump.

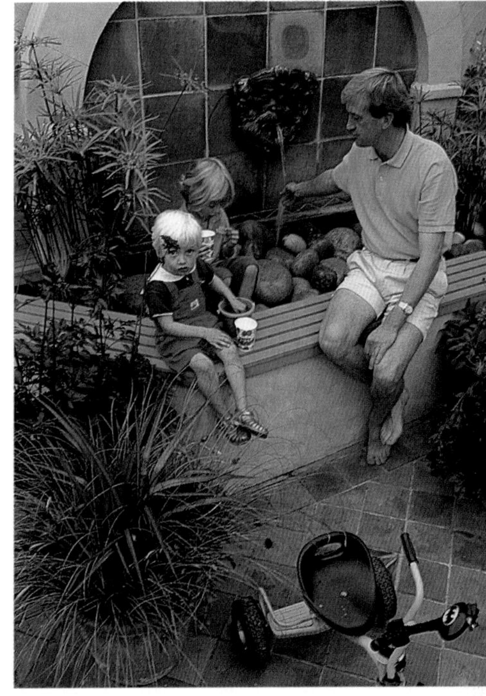

With the reservoir securely covered, this raised pebble pool and wall fountain is a safe option for a family garden.

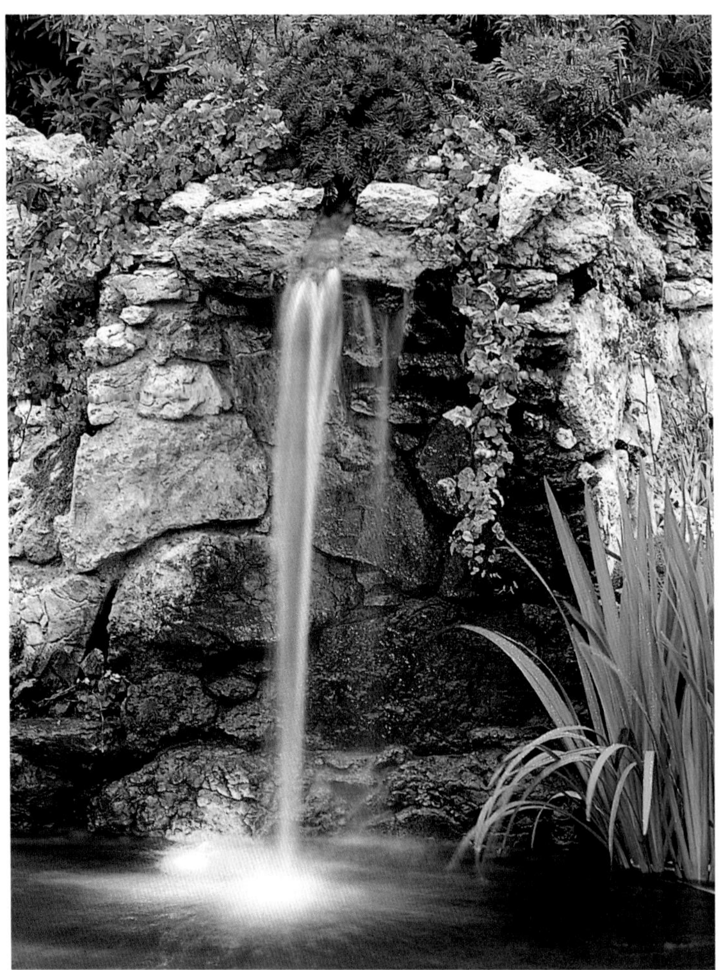

An underwater spotlight illuminates the cascading column of water, adding drama to the pond as dusk falls.

There are many preformed wall fountains which have a built-in pump that can be added to the garden and be functional within an hour. The fountain merely needs to be hung on a wall, then connected to a water reservoir and electricity. If you already have a pond, a wall mask fountain which spouts water can look beautiful. The mask needs to be fixed to a fence or wall so that it produces a satisfactory water flow, and the water and electricity supplies are completely hidden from view.

Streams and waterfalls If you want a moving water feature to run down a slope, use one of the ready-made waterfall or cascade units rather than trying to create your own with a flexible pond liner. Waterfalls built using a pond liner or concrete take a long time to construct and rarely look convincing. Plastic or glass-fibre units are guaranteed to be water tight and are moulded so that the water flows attractively over them. For a cascade to appear natural it is important to surround it with an attractive planting scheme. Unfortunately, the soil around ponds and cascades lined with butyl rubber is often dry so choose plants such as *Aurinia saxatilis* and *Persicaria affinis* 'Superba' that are not invasive and can cope with dry soil conditions. Avoid clump-forming perennials, such as bamboos and ornamental grasses, because they throw up shoots that can puncture the liner.

PLANTS FOR MOVING WATER

Water lilies will not prosper in a pond with a fountain unless they are kept out of the line of the spray. The following plants are quite at home in moving water.

Bog bean
***Caltha palustris* 'Flore Pleno'**
Myriophyllum spicatum
Water crowfoot
Water forget-me-not
Water irises

Choosing a pump Water and electricity make a dangerous combination. When installing a pump always use a waterproof armoured cable and a waterproof connector (available from aquatic specialists). If you already have electricity in your garden – perhaps in a greenhouse or shed near to the pond – you can plug the pump into the socket fitted with a residual current device (RCD). If you want a permanent outdoor electricity supply hire an electrician to do the job for you. Low-voltage pumps, a safer option, are now widely available. Submersible pumps are very reliable and sit on the floor of the pond. See 'What size pump?', right, to select the best model for your feature.

For isolated water features where laying on a power supply is impractical use a solar-powered pump. These produce sufficient power for a small fountain or water feature even when the weather is overcast.

Lighting One of the best times to enjoy water in the garden is in the evening as the stillness of dusk descends. At this time garden lighting can be used to create an added dimension to your appreciation of the water features. A simple underwater spotlight can be added to any fountain or waterfall feature. For example, tulip fountains – where the water rises in a central jet and then tumbles evenly around to give the appearance of a tulip – look particularly stunning when lit from below by a simple underwater spotlight. Uplighting is also an ideal choice for the hemispherical spray pattern – an elaborate two-tiered jet system with contrasting spray arrangements.

Spotlights are available with a choice of coloured lenses. For the more adventurous, multiple colours can be achieved with a colour changer – a revolving disc which is attached to the fountain unit. A sequence of colours can accompany changes in spray pattern and can even be linked to mood music.

What size pump?

Use the information below so that you can buy an appropriate pump for your water feature. (The flow rate tells you how much water needs to be pumped.)

Small feature For a small fountain or pebble fountain buy a pump with a flow rate that is more than 450 litres per hour.

Large feature For a wall or display fountain you will need to buy a pump that produces more than 650 litres per hour.

Waterfalls Most cascade units require an output of at least 950 litres per hour to provide a thin sheet of water and 1150 litres per hour to provide a deep, continuous flow.

Building a cascade with lighting

A simple waterfall assembled from preformed glass-fibre cascade units is very easy to make. Dig the hole as for an ordinary pond and use the soil to landscape a raised area for the cascade units. Keep the top 15 cm (6 in) of soil to one side, and add it to the raised area last.

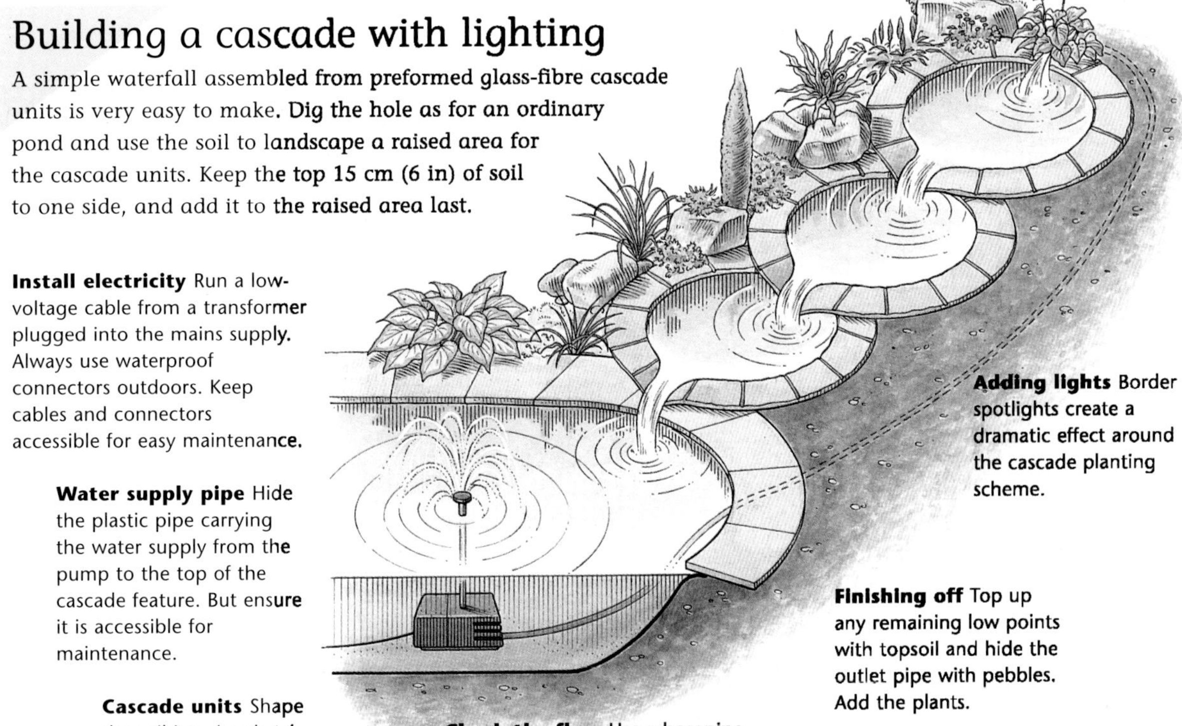

Install electricity Run a low-voltage cable from a transformer plugged into the mains supply. Always use waterproof connectors outdoors. Keep cables and connectors accessible for easy maintenance.

Water supply pipe Hide the plastic pipe carrying the water supply from the pump to the top of the cascade feature. But ensure it is accessible for maintenance.

Cascade units Shape the soil into 'pockets', one for each cascade unit. Bed each unit on sand and check that it is level.

Check the flow Use a hosepipe to check the flow of water down the cascade before fixing the units in place using a wet mortar mix.

Adding lights Border spotlights create a dramatic effect around the cascade planting scheme.

Finishing off Top up any remaining low points with topsoil and hide the outlet pipe with pebbles. Add the plants.

How to find your pond's natural balance

A pool which is established with the correct balance of plants and fish requires minimal maintenance. If it is protected from falling autumn leaves, it rarely needs cleaning out completely – usually every five or six years. Only if something exceptional happens, such as a dead fish decomposing and fouling the water, or a spillage of fertiliser or pesticide, is it necessary to take urgent remedial action by cleaning out the pond.

By creating a healthy balance you will prevent algal problems in the water. The pond should be at least 1.8x2.5 m (6x8 ft) if it is to maintain its own natural balance without human intervention. Ponds smaller than this will require more time for maintenance. The water temperature in small ponds changes so rapidly that algal growths will develop irrespective of the type and number of plants used. Small ponds can also become rapidly depleted of oxygen, killing the fish.

Plants The submerged plants use up enough nutrients from the water to starve the algae and control its growth. However, this control will work only if the compost used in the planting containers is properly

Keeping it healthy

Calculate the surface area of the pool excluding the marginal shelves, then use the following simple formula to ensure health and clarity in the pool.

Submerged plants For every square metre allow ten bunches of submerged aquatic plant. (These can be grouped together in containers or distributed evenly over the pool floor)

Floating plants Plant to ensure that at least a third of the surface area is covered by floating foliage.

Fish There should be no more than 45 cm (18 in) length of fish per square metre of water surface area.

Fish help to keep a pond healthy by eating insects and adding nutrients to the water through their droppings.

Problem solver

Algae control New ponds often turn green to start with because the water is laden with minerals and nutrients. Once a balance is reached it should clear. Established pools that turn green can be cleared using a biological or chemical pond treatment or chemical-free barley straw pads (pictured), all are available from garden centres.

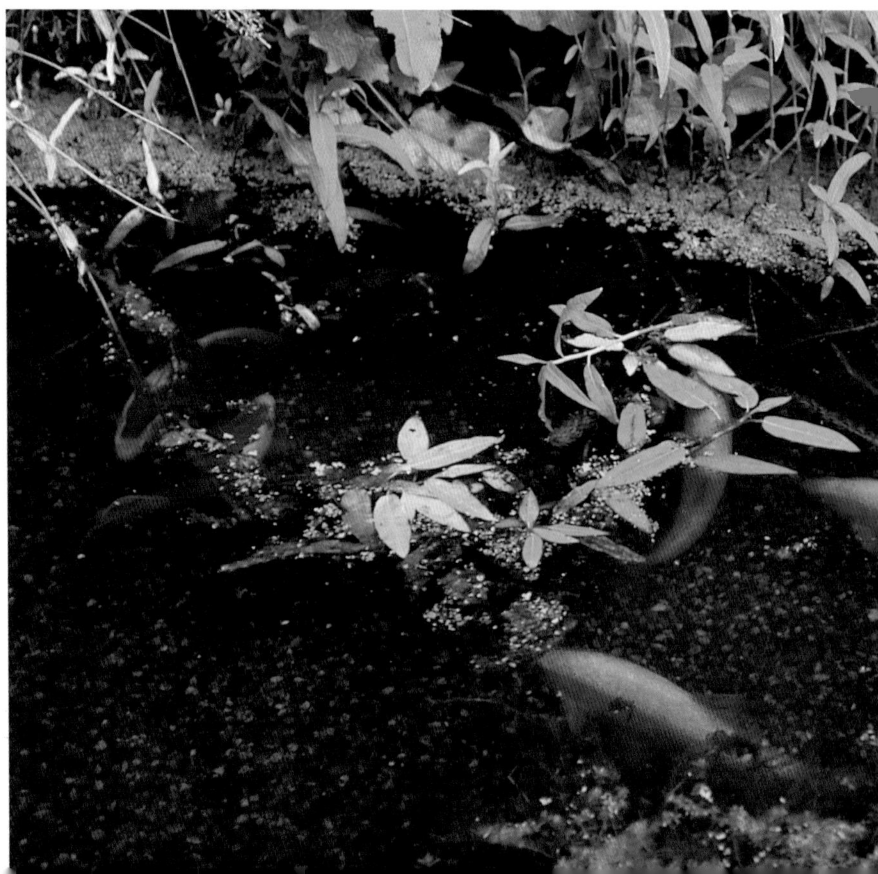

CALENDAR OF CARE

How much time you need to spend maintaining your pond will largely depend on the style of water feature you have. Anything with plants and animals will need some care throughout the year.

SPRING

New plants Planting time for a new pool. Also add replacement submerged aquatics.

▲ Overcrowded plants Lift and divide established plants which are becoming overcrowded.

Position pump Remove the pool heater and replace with the submersible pond pump.

EARLY SUMMER

Tidy plants Dead head and cut back plants as necessary.

Pests and diseases Watch out for pests and diseases and treat immediately.

Top up water During hot weather keep an eye on the water levels. Top up as necessary.

▲ Feed fish Regularly feed fish using a proprietary fish food.

LATE SUMMER

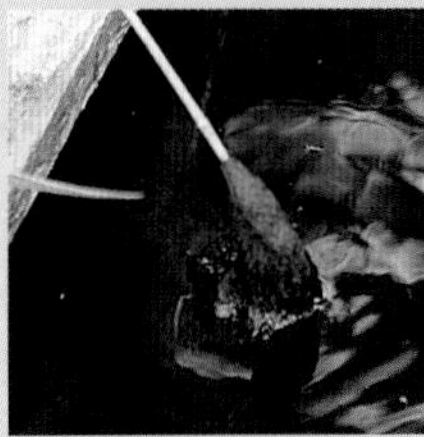

▲ Blanket weed Remove filamentous algae by twisting it round the tip of a garden cane. Leave the algae next to the pond for a day or two to give pond creatures in it the opportunity to return to the water. Put water weed onto the compost heap.

Top up water Add water as necessary.

AUTUMN

Tidy plants Tidy up plants for the winter.

Remove pump Replace with a pool heater.

Feed fish Before the weather turns cold, feed fish with a high-protein food to build them up. Don't feed them in winter.

▲ Net pool Cover or surround the pool with a fine-mesh net to keep out fallen leaves.

WINTER

Water-lily aphids Spray plum and cherry trees with winter wash to kill off overwintering water-lily aphids.

▲ Protect the liner If you don't use a pond heater, float a ball on the surface to help to prevent damage. Stand a pan of hot water on the ice to melt a hole to release noxious gases from beneath.

formulated for use in ponds and contains only slow-release fertilisers. Do not use ordinary potting compost because it releases large amounts of highly soluble nutrients into the water. Algae thrive in bright light, so the surface foliage of water lilies and floating aquatics contributes to its control by cutting down the amount of light falling directly into the water.

Fish They contribute to keeping the plants healthy by eating insects and by providing nutrients through their droppings. When buying fish choose those that are swimming evenly and have bright eyes and erect fins. The bodies should show no signs of damage, and all their scales should be intact. There should be no sign of white spots or black patches on the body, nor any hint of a fine cotton wool-like growth which can indicate the onset of a fungal attack. Healthy fish are never bloated and should not show any signs of trailing faeces.

Fish sometimes succumb to fungal diseases and occasionally fin and tail rot. As soon as a fish looks unwell, carefully remove it from the pool and place it in a bucket of water. Inspect the fish closely, noting down obvious symptoms. There are treatments available from aquatics' specialists which cure all of the common diseases.

The Kitchen Garden

GROWING YOUR OWN FOOD CAN BE A HIGHLY SATISFYING PART OF GARDENING. YOU CAN KEEP WORK TO A MINIMUM BY PLANTING TROUBLE-FREE VARIETIES AND USING MODERN TECHNIQUES

Eating your own home-grown fruit, vegetables and herbs is such a pleasure that even a very busy gardener might be tempted to try growing a few food plants. All crops, especially salad leaves, potatoes and strawberries, are so much tastier when eaten freshly picked from the garden that you may decide that it is time well spent. New and improved varieties, and labour-saving techniques and products, such as growing under crop covers and using automatic watering systems, help to make home-grown produce a realistic option even if time is at a premium.

Herbs, tomatoes and salad crops are the best plants for the novice vegetable gardener to start with because they are highly productive and can be grown in small spaces. Success on a limited scale may inspire you to extend your range of crops, or even to tackle a whole vegetable plot or a fruit garden. Fruit trees and bushes are a particularly good investment because, once established, they will produce crops year after year. Annual applications of well-rotted organic matter to the soil reduce the need to water.

1 PERMANENT DEEP BEDS – *no digging, limited weeding and easy watering.*
2 PERENNIAL CROPS – *a bay tree and rhubarb will crop for many years with little maintenance.*
3 TROUBLE-FREE PLANTS – *easy-to-grow herbs, such as chives and thyme, are always useful.*
4 EASY ACCESS – *all-weather paths make it easy to tend and harvest crops.*

EASY-CARE CALENDAR

MID SPRING
Prepare soil and apply a balanced general feed. Sow hardy varieties or put out bought plants after hardening off. Close planting and mulching will help to prevent weeds.

LATE SPRING
Plant out frost-tender vegetables. For an organic solution for combating pests and diseases, cover crops at risk with insect-proof mesh. Set codling-moth traps in apple trees. Hoe once a week to keep down weeds.

SUMMER
Harvest fruit and vegetables as necessary. Water selectively. Stay vigilant for pests and diseases; treat outbreaks promptly. Feed strawberry plants after harvesting.

AUTUMN
Harvest and store apples and pears. Clear debris from plots and attach sticky grease bands to apple trees to prevent pests climbing up the trees.

WINTER
Plant garlic. Prune apple trees and cut down autumn-fruiting raspberries. Apply winter wash to dormant fruit bushes and trees to kill overwintering pests. Order vegetable seed or plantlets.

STARTING FROM SCRATCH
You can create an easy-care no-dig bed for growing vegetables in half a day. A new fruit garden is best planned as a whole and planted in one go. Allow at least an hour per tree for correct planting, staking and mulching. Plant herbs straight into the soil or pots.

Pots of pleasure Just a few hours each week should be enough to maintain a selection of vegetables, fruit and herbs. Most of the work is concentrated in spring and summer.

Time saver

Buy courgettes and tomatoes as young plants – you will need only a few. Vegetables sown little and often, such as salad crops, are best raised from seed sown directly outside in rows.

Planning for success

Good planning is the key to growing fruit and vegetables successfully when time is short. Work out how many hours you can spend each week tending your plot, then concentrate your efforts on crops that will give maximum rewards for the time you have. Try to spread the workload throughout the year by completing non-seasonal tasks during the winter months.

You don't need a large garden or even a dedicated area of the garden to grow your own produce. Some crops, especially herbs, salad vegetables and strawberries, can be raised in containers. If you want to grow just a few plants, then start with a pot or two on a patio. It is not only easy to do, but you get quick results because no ground preparation or weeding is required. However, once you have more than half-a-dozen containers, the time spent planting, watering and feeding mounts up and would be more productively spent on looking after crops planted in the ground.

Some food crops make attractive additions to the flower border. Chives or strawberries, for instance, make an easy-care edible edging,

A garden to provide a family's fruit and vegetables

Sarah Deal and her two children, aged 3 and 7, live in an end-of-terrace town house with a long, narrow garden. Sarah wanted to grow her own fruit and vegetables. Previously, she had cultivated only a few herbs in containers on her sunny patio.

Sarah is a vegetarian and was keen to grow the widest possible range of fruit and vegetables, although she had time to spend only 4 hours a week tending her town-house garden – half of which would be dedicated to the fruit and vegetable plot. She was keen to grow her crops organically, but was prepared to use chemicals as a last resort.

For at least part of the day, most of Sarah's garden is in shade from nearby trees; the sunniest area is near the house. Since most fruit and vegetables require a sunny site to thrive, the productive plot had to be positioned near the house. The soil along boundary walls and fences was poor and needed improving. Tree roots were also taking a lot of moisture from the soil, making it dry for much of the year.

THE OLD GARDEN This sunny spot near the house was the best place to grow fruit and vegetables, so the plot needed to be attractive as well as productive.

DECIDING THEIR PRIORITIES

How much time?
Sarah can spend 4 hours per week on average on her garden. More time is available during Easter and summer holidays.

Essential ingredients?
A decorative vegetable plot that is easy to look after and productive. The garden also needs to have areas where the family can relax together and the children can play.

Likes and dislikes?
All the family like apples and bush fruit as well as a wide range of vegetables. No one likes beetroot or redcurrants.

while fruit trees can be trained to grow against a wall or fence alongside a flowering clematis or rose, or used as a productive garden divider. Cropping will be reduced, however, if plants have to compete with others for light, moisture and nutrients.

A plot dedicated to fruit and vegetables avoids problems of competition and is easier to protect from pests and diseases. You can take a lot of hard work out of growing vegetables by using a raised, no-dig bed with paths in between (see page 239).

A vegetable bed can be a decorative feature as well as a practical one. For example, geometric beds containing vegetables can be combined with archways covered by runner beans or perhaps a trained courgette plant. Many vegetables are surprisingly attractive plants. For colourful leaves, try beetroot, red cabbage and red 'leaf lettuce'; ruby chard has brilliant red stems. You can make the productive plot blend in with the rest of the garden by growing flowers for cutting, such as chrysanthemums and dahlias. Sweet rocket, nasturtium, pot marigold, viola and pansy, all have edible flowers that are ideal for adding to salads or cold summer drinks.

Make the most of your crops

Do grow only the crops you know that you and your family want to eat.

Do plan ahead and work out how much time you can spend each week before deciding what to grow.

Do draw up a cropping plan of what you will grow during which season and where in the plot.

Do choose pest and disease-resistant varieties where they are available.

Do invest in fruit cages and crop covers to protect your produce.

Do concentrate on growing fewer crops well.

Don't grow too much of one thing or it will go to waste.

Don't bother with crops that are difficult to grow or that are unreliable performers.

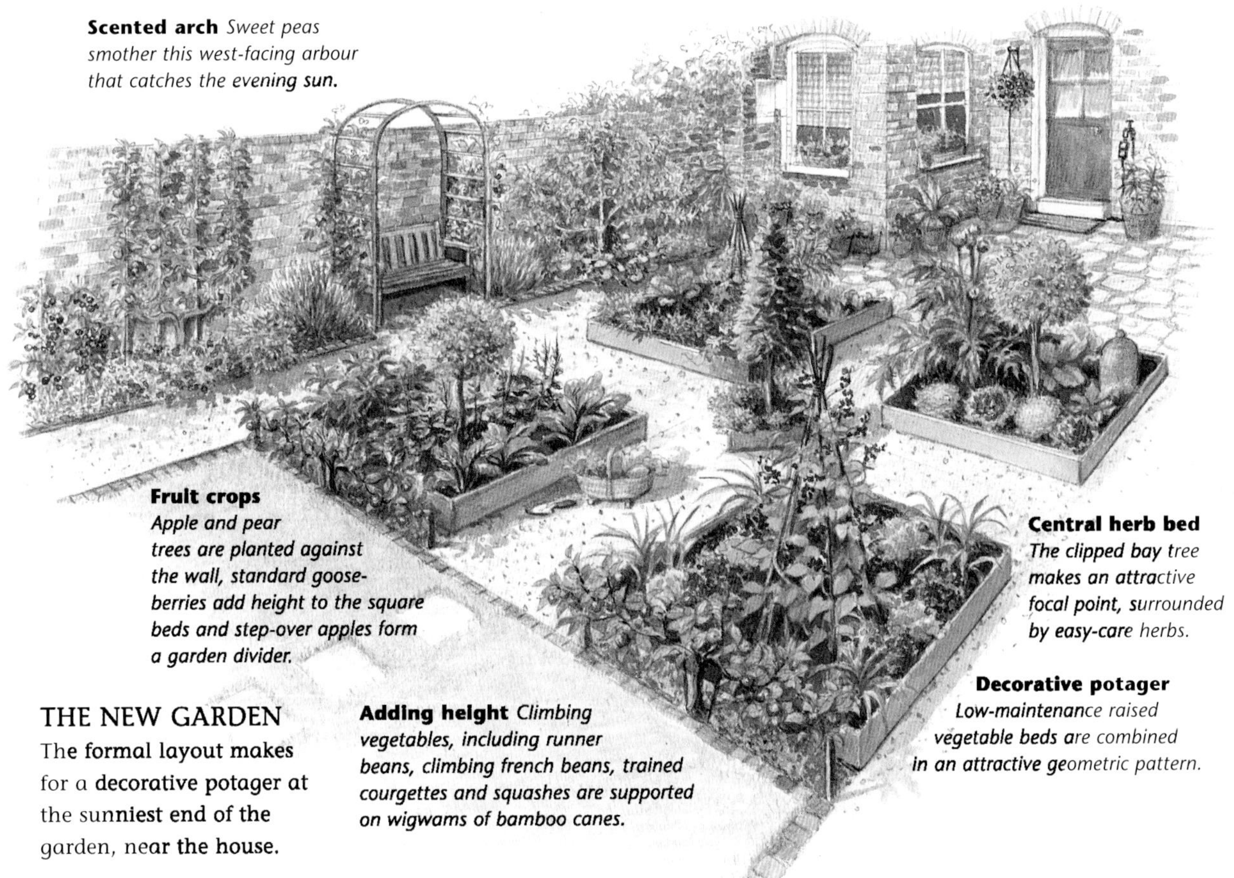

Scented arch *Sweet peas smother this west-facing arbour that catches the evening sun.*

Fruit crops *Apple and pear trees are planted against the wall, standard gooseberries add height to the square beds and step-over apples form a garden divider.*

Central herb bed *The clipped bay tree makes an attractive focal point, surrounded by easy-care herbs.*

Decorative potager *Low-maintenance raised vegetable beds are combined in an attractive geometric pattern.*

Adding height *Climbing vegetables, including runner beans, climbing french beans, trained courgettes and squashes are supported on wigwams of bamboo canes.*

THE NEW GARDEN
The formal layout makes for a decorative potager at the sunniest end of the garden, near the house.

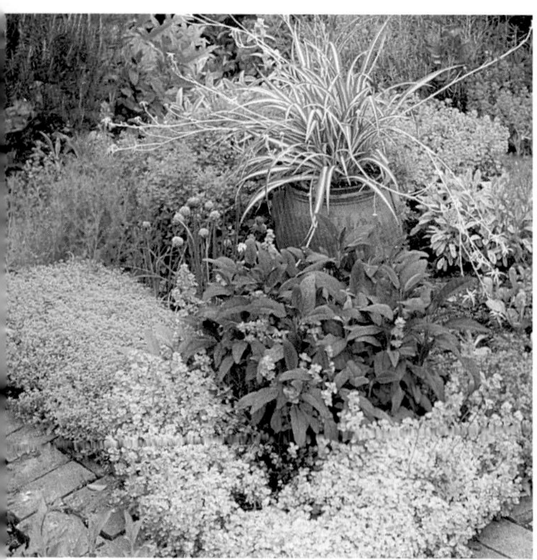

A formal herb garden with permanent paths contains easy-care herbs including sage, oregano, thyme and rosemary.

Sweet-smelling recipes for a herb garden

Few people realise how easy most herbs are to grow. Many herbs should be planted in well-drained soil in a sheltered, sunny site, but some prefer moist, cool conditions. Concentrate on growing those that you will actually use. Few cooks venture far into the garden in the middle of cooking, so place your herb garden as close as possible to the kitchen door, or at least next to a paved area for easy access. Choose a site with sun for at least half of the day. If your garden is small, save space by blending your herbs in ornamental borders or as edging.

Containers Herbs can be grown successfully in containers provided they have adequate drainage. Containers make it easy to group plants according to how quickly and vigorously they grow and by the type of care that they need. Because they are portable, herbs in containers can be moved to a convenient position outside the kitchen door when they are ready

Fennel, purple sage and many other herbs are ideal for growing among other plants. Evergreen mat-forming thyme makes an excellent edging plant.

GROUPING HERBS

Permanent herb beds soon look straggly and untidy because short-lived herbs die and vigorous perennial types outgrow their allotted space. Keep your collection productive and attractive by growing herbs as single subjects in containers. The containers can then be grouped together.

Individual pots of herbs *will be easier to water if plunged rim-deep in gravel in a window box.*

This segmented hexagonal planter *allows you to replace short-lived herbs without replanting the whole bed.*

to use. Most herbs will thrive in containers that are at least 15 cm (6 in) deep. However, fennel, which has a long root that needs deep soil, and bay trees, which are big when mature, are best in larger containers such as a half barrel.

Window boxes can be used for growing both upright and prostrate herbs. For ease of maintenance, grow the herbs in separate pots; if one has been cut particularly hard, you will then be able to replace the pot without disturbing the rest of the container. Fill the window box with gravel, burying the pots up to their rims. This will make watering easier. Terracotta pots are an attractive, popular choice because they are porous, which reduces the risk of waterlogging. However, herbs in this type of pot will require frequent watering during summer.

Avoid urn-like containers with planting pockets set in the sides, such as strawberry planters, because they are fiddly to plant up and difficult to water thoroughly, especially if you are in a hurry. A similar decorative effect can be achieved by grouping together several simple terracotta pots with a different herb in each. Hanging baskets are suitable for herbs that creep and spread, such as thyme, oregano and prostrate rosemary, and can be hung near the back door.

EASY-CARE HERBS

The following are easy to grow and take little time and effort to maintain. To minimise the work, combine herbs of similar habit and vigour. All are moderately vigorous unless otherwise stated.

Basil Annual, 30 cm (12 in). Grow in pots on a sunny windowsill. Sow in spring to avoid slugs. Although the least attractive, sweet basil is the most useful in the kitchen.

Chervil Annual, 60 cm (24 in). Short-lived, but self-seeds freely. Copes well with light shade in summer, but in winter needs sun, or can be grown under cover.

Chives Perennial, 30 cm (12 in). Likes sun or partial shade. Cut back several times a season to get new leaves. Divide every few years, preferably in autumn, or replace.

Dill Annual, short-lived, 60 cm (24 in). Likes sun and shelter. Best raised from seed because it does not transplant well. Leave to self-seed. Ready to eat six to eight weeks after sowing.

Mint Perennial, 60 cm (24 in). Likes moist, rich soil. Applemint is a tasty variety. Mint can be invasive. To restrain, see page 237.

Continued on p. 234

EASY-CARE HERBS

Continued from p. 233

Parsley Grown as an annual, 30 cm (12 in). Likes partial shade, but protect it from slugs. Buy pot-grown plants in spring or summer. Broad-leaved types are flavoursome and easiest to grow.

Rosemary Evergreen shrub, 15 cm to 1.2 m (6 in to 4 ft) depending on variety. Needs sun and well-drained soil, otherwise not reliably hardy. The upright form is good for smaller spaces.

Sage Perennial, 60 cm (24 in). Likes sun and well-drained soil. Replace plants every four or five years. The green-leaved form is hardier than the coloured types and has more flowers. Vigorous.

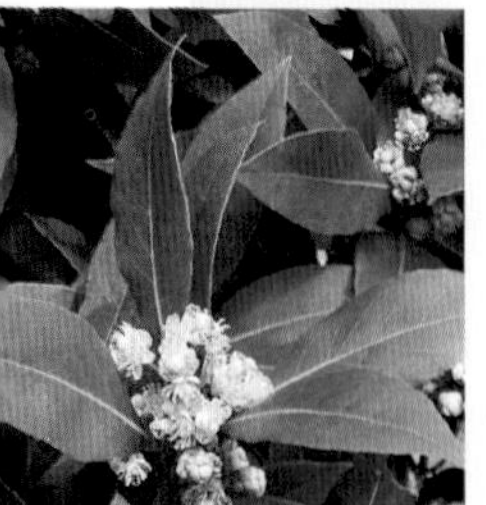

Sweet bay Vigorous evergreen shrub, 1.5 m (5 ft) if in a container and kept trimmed. Likes sun and shelter from cold winds. In cold areas, move indoors in winter when small. Harvest all year.

Thyme Perennial, 30 cm (12 in). Hardy evergreen for dry, sunny spots. Replace after three or four years. Prostrate thymes have ornamental appeal. For cooking, choose *Thymus vulgaris.*

Knot gardens The traditional formal knot garden, edged with box, rosemary, lavender or thyme, has romantic appeal. But a knot garden is time-consuming to plant and is more difficult than other planting schemes to maintain. The edging needs trimming at least once a year and competes with the herbs for nutrients, light and moisture. For a formal scheme, edge the bed with Victorian-style tiles or old bricks set on end instead of plants. It will also make weeding easier.

Raised beds Herbs are easy to look after and to gather if they are grown in a raised bed. If you want to grow herbs and your garden has heavy clay soil, a raised bed is a good solution. However, they do take time and effort to construct. The rewards will come in summer when the raised bed, with its larger volume of soil or compost, will need less frequent watering than smaller containers. A raised bed is a good way for growing herbs that like a Mediterranean climate, such as thyme, oregano, sage and rosemary. For a low-maintenance feature, mulch with gravel or pea shingle to help retain soil moisture and to suppress weeds. (See page 192 for other ideas.)

A brick raised bed can look good in a modern garden. Choose the building materials to blend in with the rest of the garden and build up the sides of the raised bed to a comfortable height, approximately 45 cm (18 in). If you construct the bed so that its north-facing side is two or three courses of bricks higher than the south-facing side, the

A raised herb bed which contains a mixed planting including the taller borage and sage, and low-growing camomile and thyme. Run your hand through the small plants to release their delicate scents.

Making a raised herb bed for a patio

Create the perfect environment for growing herbs by building a wooden raised bed on a sunny patio. The bed will require less watering than small pots and makes an attractive feature. Use timber that has been pressure-treated with preservative to make the posts and the sides of the bed.

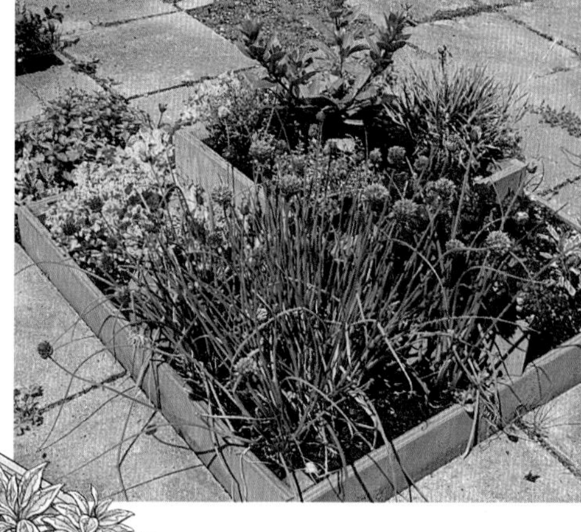

Select the site Lift a group of paving slabs from the sunniest area of the patio. Measure the size of the square then cut the boards to length.

Stain the wood Use a water-based wood stain to change the colour of the wood without harming plants.

Build the sides Cut a 5x5 cm (2x2 in) post 30 cm (12 in) long for each corner and nail the box frames together.

Position the first tier Check the frame is square then hammer in the posts. Fill with free-draining soil or a grit-and-compost mix.

Add the other tiers Repeat the procedure for the second and third tiers, so that their corners rest on the sides of the tier below. Firm the soil down to remove air pockets.

Mulch with gravel After planting the herbs, mulch between them with a layer of gravel to show off the plants and to reduce water loss.

Planting

A 90x90 cm (36x36 in) bed will accommodate chives, variegated sage and marjoram in the lowest planting pockets. Various thymes in middle pockets, as well as mint (plant in a sunken pot to prevent it spreading). In the top tier, plunge a potted bay tree – it can be moved into the house in winter.

surface of the herb bed will slope towards the sun and absorb more warmth during the day. Wooden raised beds are easier to construct than brick beds and can make an attractive feature (see illustration, above). Although railway sleepers are often recommended for this purpose, they are expensive, very difficult to manoeuvre and cut to size, and they ooze creosote. Instead, use pressure-treated timber that is widely available from garden centres and DIY stores.

Sunny borders If you have a border in full sun and which has well-drained soil, you can cut down on watering and weeding during summer by planting herbs in any gaps between the ornamental plants. Shrubby herbs that are needed in small amounts, such as rosemary, can be grown as single specimens. Those herbs that are needed in greater quantities, such as chives and parsley, are best grown in groups. Low-growing coloured sages and mat-spreading thymes also make good plants for edging.

Time saver

Pick up pot-grown herbs, such as basil, chervil, chives, marjoram, rosemary and mint at the supermarket. Although forced, they are ideal for growing on the kitchen windowsill.

Buying herbs

Herbs to buy big Buy sweet bay as a specimen plant and grow in a border if you have a sheltered, sunny site. Mature plants are less likely to need protecting in winter and leaves can be used fresh all year round.

Herbs to buy small Most herbs, including basil, chives, dill and parsley, can be raised from seed, but it is easier to buy small plants in 9 cm (3½ in) pots from a garden centre.

Check plants carefully When buying mint or marjoram, check the underside of leaves for small orange spots, which are a sign of a disease called rust – and avoid such plants.

Colourful herbs Variegated versions of common herbs, such as rosemary, sage or thyme, are attractive, but they are less hardy and grow less prolifically than the all-green versions.

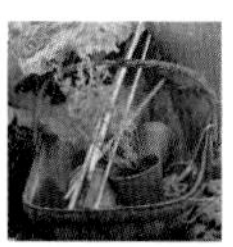

Keeping herbs productive

Herbs need very little aftercare once they are planted, although most need replacing every few years. Remove any all-green shoots from variegated varieties. Deadheading encourages new foliage and prevents unwanted self-seeding, but chives or marjoram can be left to bloom since their flowers are edible and can also be used as a garnish. Trim thyme with shears after it flowers to keep it neat and tidy. Prune shrubby herbs, such as sage and rosemary, after they flower to keep plants compact and bushy. Do not cut back into woody stems because this can kill the plant. Use the prunings for cooking or as cuttings to grow new plants. Harvest herbs regularly even if you don't use them in order to encourage new growth.

In spring, apply an organic mulch, such as bark chippings, around herbs that prefer a moist soil, including chives, parsely, sorrel and tarragon. This will cut down on the amount of watering necessary in the summer. Apply a grit mulch to low-growing Mediterranean herbs, such as thyme, marjoram and sage, in order to keep the leaves clean. As well as retaining soil moisture mulches will also help to prevent weeds growing between the plants. Make watering herbs in pots

PROPAGATING HERBS

If you are short of time it is not worth propagating most herbs as they are easily bought as small plants. If you are keen to raise your own, many herbs can be raised from cuttings, division, layering or seed.

Cuttings *Take cuttings of bushy perennial herbs such as rosemary, sage and thyme from late spring to early autumn. Cut off a 5-7.5 cm (2-3 in) long shoot. Strip off leaves from the lower half of each cutting and push three cuttings around the edge of a pot of compost. Water in. Cover with a polythene bag and put on a windowsill.*

Sowing *Many herbs, such as parsley and basil, are easy to raise from seed. Sow three seeds in a 7.5 cm (3 in) pot of compost in spring and place on a sunny windowsill.*

Division *Clump-forming herbs, including chives, lemon balm and thyme, can be lifted and divided in spring. If you want more mint, simply pot up rooted runners.*

Layering *A few shrubby herbs, such as thyme, rosemary and sage, can be propagated without any equipment. In summer, lay a shoot down onto soil that has been improved with compost, holding it down with a stone. It will root naturally by the autumn, when it can be separated from the parent.*

Rosemary, basil, thyme, parsley and mint *(above)* can be kept growing throughout the winter in pots on a windowsill.

Sun-loving herbs, such as this purple sage *(left)*, like a well-drained root run so are ideal for growing in containers. They are then easy to move around and can be conveniently placed close to the back door or on a nearby sunny patio.

easier by leaving a 2.5 cm (1 in) space when planting between the surface of the compost and the rim. In autumn, throw away annuals, and old, woody herbs. Buy fresh stocks the next spring.

Herbs suffer from few pests and diseases. Pick off caterpillars and slugs that you find while harvesting and remove any damaged leaves. Check over mints for the tell-tale signs of mint rust – orange spots on the lower stem and under leaves. Destroy all affected plants.

Fresh herbs in winter Many herbs can be 'forced' in order to produce fresh leaves throughout the year. Place a cloche over hardy herbs, such as parsley, chervil and chives, growing in beds and borders to extend their growing season. For winter crops of annual herbs, such as basil, parsley, leaf coriander and chervil, sow seeds in small pots in late summer and grow them indoors on a warm, sunny windowsill. They can then be planted out in the garden the following spring.

Keep perennial herbs, such as mint, marjoram and oregano, producing fresh leaves by lifting and dividing clumps in early autumn. Discard older, woody sections and pot young, healthy divisions in small pots on a sunny windowsill. Dig up clumps of chives in early autumn. Put them in a pot and bring indoors. They will then produce a crop over winter, and you can plant them outdoors again in the spring.

Problem solver

Taming invasive herbs Plant mint in an old bucket with drainage holes punched into the base, or in a large old flower pot. This will confine the plant. Sink the container in the ground, so that the rim protrudes at least 2.5 cm (1 in) above the soil to prevent the runners spreading.

Drumhead cabbage, curly kale, peas and courgettes, a variety of herbs, plus Californian poppy and *Allium hollandicum* 'Purple Sensation', make this vegetable garden both attractive and productive.

Reaping the rewards of growing vegetables

As well as the benefit of fresh, tasty and interesting produce without the need to visit the supermarket, many busy people also find vegetable gardening an enjoyable way to exercise and relax. A productive plot can be easily maintained as long as you follow a few time-saving golden rules. The first is to grow only what you and your family like to eat and in appropriate quantities. Consider when it will need to be harvested and make sure that this will fit in with the other parts of your life. For instance, if you go away every August, grow vegetables that crop before and after then. Above all, make good use of your time by growing a few vegetables well rather than many badly.

Digging This chore can be almost eliminated by separating the walking areas from the growing areas using a no-dig bed system (see right). Create a series of beds with paths in between for easy access. Add a raised edge, such as gravel boards made of pressure-treated softwood, to help to prevent the beds spilling onto the paths. Once the no-dig bed is built, apply a thick mulch of well-rotted organic matter each autumn, letting earthworms incorporate it into the ground for you over the winter. Although deep beds take longer to construct and prepare, they will repay the effort with time saved over the long run.

Crops grown in no-dig beds are easier to look after because they root more deeply and can be spaced closer together, reducing weeding and watering.

When to water

Do water all newly planted and sown vegetables. If the soil is dry, water for a couple of weeks until established.

Do water vegetables grown in containers daily if necessary.

Do water leafy salads daily to keep the soil constantly moist.

Do water regularly fruiting crops such as beans and courgettes, and tomatoes when in flower and when the fruit is swelling.

Don't water, once established, root crops, such as beetroot and carrots (except in a drought), perennial crops such as asparagus and globe artichoke, or winter crops such as spring cabbage and winter kale. Their roots will penetrate deep into the soil, where moisture is available.

Making a no-dig bed for vegetables

The easiest way to grow vegetables is in a raised bed with paths in between. The soil doesn't become compacted because it is never walked on – so eliminating the need to dig. The deep bed allows for closer spacing and, combined with regular mulching, reduces the need for weeding and watering. Make each bed 1-1.5 m (3-5 ft) wide so you can reach with ease into the centre of the bed from the path.

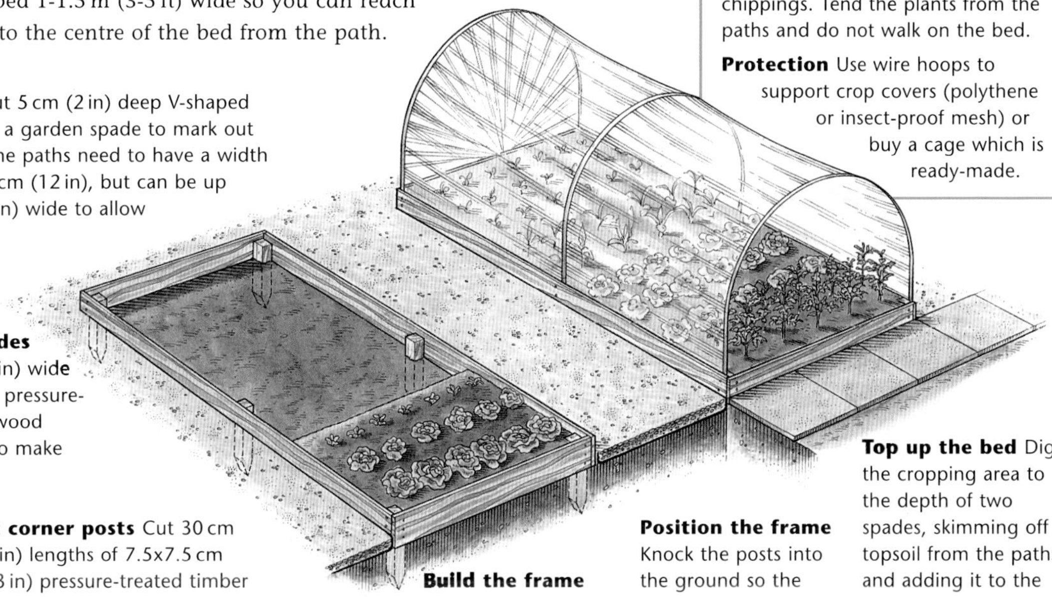

Mark out Cut 5 cm (2 in) deep V-shaped trenches with a garden spade to mark out the design. The paths need to have a width of at least 30 cm (12 in), but can be up to 60 cm (24 in) wide to allow access with a wheelbarrow.

Make the sides Use 15 cm (6 in) wide gravel boards pressure-treated with wood preservative to make the sides.

Cut corner posts Cut 30 cm (12 in) lengths of 7.5x7.5 cm (3x3 in) pressure-treated timber to make the posts at each corner and at the centre of the longest sides.

Build the frame Use 7.5 cm (3 in) galvanised nails to fix the boards to the corner posts. Ensure corners are square.

Position the frame Knock the posts into the ground so the sides sit in the trench. Ensure that the sides are level.

Top up the bed Dig the cropping area to the depth of two spades, skimming off topsoil from the paths and adding it to the beds. Top up with mushroom compost.

Finishing off

Make the path Lay down a sheet of water-permeable membrane to prevent weeds. You can disguise the sheeting with gravel or bark chippings. Tend the plants from the paths and do not walk on the bed.

Protection Use wire hoops to support crop covers (polythene or insect-proof mesh) or buy a cage which is ready-made.

Watering Reduce the need for watering by applying a mulch in early spring to keep moisture in the ground. Water only those crops that will benefit most (see 'When to water', left). Apply the water to the rooting area, doing the job thoroughly every week – or consider investing in an automatic watering system.

Weeding For quick results, destroy perennial weeds when preparing a plot with a glyphosate-based weedkiller. For a seedbed, after preparing the ground, cover it with clear polythene to warm the soil and to encourage weed seeds to germinate. Hoe off the weed seedlings before sowing the vegetables: hoe shallowly so that you don't bring a fresh crop of weed seeds to the surface. Concentrate on hoeing around young vegetables before their leaves start to touch between the rows. The crops will then create so much shade that no further weeds will germinate. Hoe on a regular basis so that weeds do not develop beyond tiny seedlings; they can then be left to shrivel up and die on the soil surface and you won't have to clear them up. Hoe on dry, sunny days only because many weeds will reroot in damp soil.

Time saver

You can practically eliminate having to hand water your vegetable plot by laying a leaky or seep hose. Fit the hose to a water timer which is set to deliver 20 litres per sq m each day.

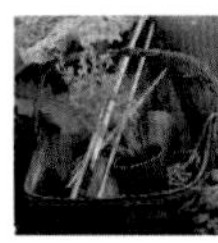

Easy-to-grow vegetables

Most vegetables are annuals so they need sowing or planting afresh each year. Hardy vegetables are easier to start off than tender types, which need frost protection. But tender plants, such as courgettes and runner beans, are easy once frosts have passed provided you grow only a few plants. Vegetables vary as to how fussy they are about soil conditions and the amount of attention they need. You will get better yields from those that can more or less fend for themselves (see 'Vegetable selector', opposite).

To spread your workload during the garden's busiest time – in spring and summer – create two beds, one for hardy crops and the other for frost-tender ones. Prepare and plant the one for hardy vegetables in March or April and the other at the end of May. You will

VEGETABLES TO AVOID

These crops are either difficult to grow or have a short harvest period.

Cauliflower
Celery
Outdoor cucumbers
Fennel
Peas
Spinach
Sweetcorn

VEGETABLES IN CONTAINERS

If you do not have space for a vegetable bed you can grow a few crops successfully in containers. Pots will need regular watering and liquid feeding (use a balanced feed for leaf crops, a tomato feed for fruiting crops). They need to be at least 20 cm (8 in) deep and to have drainage holes. Start with easy crops, such as runner beans, early potatoes, carrots, tomatoes, spring onions and salad crops.

Tomatoes *Choose a trailing variety such as 'Tumbler' for a hanging basket. Plant after the last frosts have passed. Spray plants against blight in mid summer.*

Runner beans *Use a large pot and keep well watered. Choose the variety 'Pickwick'.*

Spring onions *Pull 12 to 14 weeks after sowing as required. Choose the variety 'White Lisbon'.*

Potatoes *Use an early variety, such as 'Rocket', in a container at least 30 cm (12 in) deep and wide. Plant sprouted tubers in late spring.*

Carrots *Use a short variety, such as 'Suko', for growing bags. Pull when 5-7.5 cm (2-3 in) long.*

Salad crops *Loose-leaf lettuce can be grown in containers 15 cm (6 in) deep. A window box or trough is an ideal size.*

then be able to stagger the work of soil preparation and planting. Only the bed for hardy crops needs to be weeded and watered between March and the end of May, while the other is kept covered with black polythene in order to stop weed growth. This method will also give you a good spread of vegetable types.

Overwintered onions are an easy winter crop to grow. Plant them as sets in mid autumn; by late spring you can start pulling the biggest, then harvest the rest by early summer. With some crops, such as runner beans and courgettes, you will need just a couple of plants to get lots of produce, but you will need to pick them over regularly in summer. When following a recipe, easy-to-grow vegetables can substitute difficult ones; leaf beet, for example, is easier to grow than spinach, and leeks and spring onions can replace onions because they are less fussy about soil and less likely to run to seed, or 'bolt'.

Since the choice of vegetable varieties changes rapidly, the table below indicates what features to look for in order to help you choose the best from the seed catalogues.

VEGETABLE SELECTOR

Many vegetables are easy to grow and are an ideal choice for the busy gardener. Some vegetables need a little attention to get established but are worth the effort.

Vegetable	Easy to grow	Worth the effort	Keeps well in the soil	Features to look for when choosing a variety
Beetroot	✓		✓	Bolt resistant (e.g. 'Boltardy')
Bean, broad	✓		✓	Short ones need less support
Bean, french	✓			Dwarf ones need less support
Bean, runner	✓			Reliable (e.g.'Desiree', 'Polestar')
Calabrese		✓		Easier than cauliflower or broccoli and more productive.
Carrot	✓		✓	Early varieties grow faster than main crop (e.g. 'Early Nantes')
Courgette		✓		Compact varieties take up less room, but give the same crop.
Garlic	✓			Any variety
Leaf beet		✓		Easier to grow than spinach
Leek		✓	✓	Reliable (e.g. 'Musselburgh')
Lettuce		✓		Bolt resistant
Onion, spring	✓			Reliable (e.g.'White Lisbon')
Pea	✓			Mangetout easy to prepare
Potato		✓		Early ones (e.g. 'Maris Bard')
Radish	✓			Any variety
Ruby/Swiss chard		✓	✓	Easier to grow than spinach
Tomato, outdoor		✓		Bush or trailing types

REPEAT PERFORMERS

A few vegetables are perennials so once planted they will produce crops year after year. The following are worth trying.

Asparagus Once established, a bed will last 10 to 20 years. Asparagus needs a well-drained site. Plant 30-45 cm (12-18 in) apart. Plants are easier than crowns or seed. Choose an all-male hybrid, such as 'Franklin', that can be cut in its second year.

Rhubarb Can crop for 5 to 10 years or so. Needs rich, well-drained soil. Plant a virus-free division in winter in soil enriched with organic matter. Mulch each spring. Remove flowering stems. Try 'Timperley Early', good for forcing, or 'Victoria'.

Jerusalem artichokes Tolerant of rough ground and heavy soil. Plant tubers in spring. Plants will need supports because they grow to 3 m (10 ft) high. Cut off flowerheads. Cut back stalks in autumn. Try 'Fuseau' for ease of cleaning.

Sorrel Ideal for partial shade. The leaves have a sharp lemon flavour and can be picked through winter in mild areas if cloched. Pick outer leaves first, leaving middle leaves to grow. Remove seed heads. Plants are very hardy and last for three or four years.

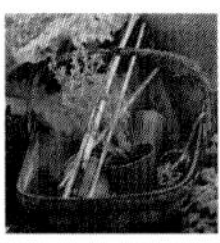

Growing healthy crops

Take early steps to prevent pests and diseases in order to save time in the long run. Keep your vegetable-growing area clear of rubbish and remove dead plant material immediately – put it on the compost heap or, if it is diseased, put it in the dustbin.

Always buy healthy plants – potatoes, in particular, should be certified virus-free, so check before you buy. Vigorous plants are less likely to succumb to pests and diseases than weak ones, so aim to build up a fertile soil that is rich in organic matter.

Crop covers in modern materials were developed for commercial growers and can be a boon to the busy gardener. There are two types of crop cover: garden fleece and insect-proof mesh. Garden fleece is laid loosely over newly planted tender plants to protect them from unseasonal frosts and flying pests, while allowing water through. Leave the fleece on for about four weeks after planting, then remove once the weather gets warmer. Clean it at the end of the season by putting it in a washing machine. Insect-proof mesh is a more durable netting that is better ventilated than fleece so it can be left on all

PEST OR DISEASE-RESISTANT VEGETABLES

The following varieties are claimed to have resistance or tolerance to specific problems (check seed catalogues).

Calabrese 'Trixie'
Carrot 'Fly Away', 'Sytan'
Courgette 'Defender'
Leek 'Conora'
Lettuce 'Dynamite', 'Musette'
Parsnip 'Avonresister
Swede 'Marian'
Tomato 'Shirley'

Preventing pests and diseases

If the same crop is grown on the same soil year after year, pest and disease problems will build up. If you grow a wide range of vegetables, it pays to plan a crop rotation. Make feeding and soil improvement easier by grouping vegetables of the same family. In the three-year rotation (year one shown below), cabbage family crops are grown on soil previously used by the pea family to take advantage of the legumes' ability to 'fix' nitrogen in the soil. Grow salad crops in between slower-growing crops anywhere on the plot.

Vegetable families

Cabbage family (brassicas) Includes broccoli, brussels sprouts, cabbage, calabrese, cauliflower, kale, kohl rabi, swede, turnip and radish.

Pea family (legumes) Includes mangetout peas, french beans, broad beans and runner beans.

Onion family Includes onions, garlic, leeks and shallots.

Root crops Include parsnip, beetroot, carrots, turnips and swedes.

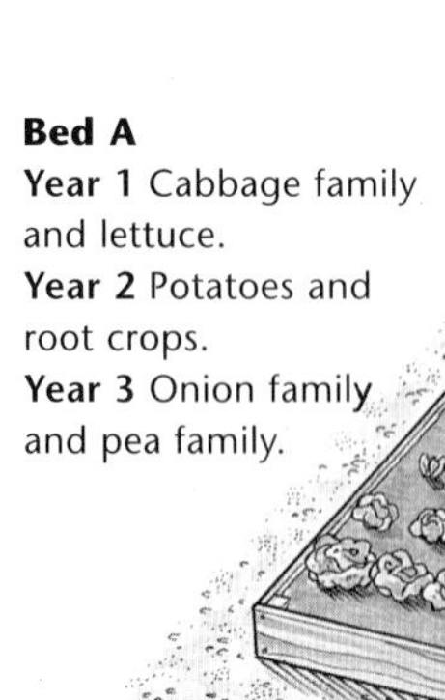

Bed A
Year 1 Cabbage family and lettuce.
Year 2 Potatoes and root crops.
Year 3 Onion family and pea family.

Bed B
Year 1 Onion family and pea family.
Year 2 Cabbage family and lettuce.
Year 3 Potatoes and root crops.

Bed C
Year 1 Potatoes and root crops.
Year 2 Onion family and pea family.
Year 3 Cabbage family and lettuce.

WHAT TO DO ABOUT PESTS AND DISEASES

▲ **CLUBROOT**
A fungal disease of brassicas which deforms and rots the roots. Spores can remain in the soil for many years. Remove and burn affected roots. In future, lime the soil to pH 7.5 and start brassicas in pots before planting out. Try resistant varieties.

SLUGS/SNAILS
Large holes in leaves and other plant tissues. Use slug pellets after planting young plants.

APHIDS (GREENFLY)
Weaken plant and can spread viruses. Spray plant (including undersides of leaves) with pirimicarb or dimethoate. Pull up and dispose of plants with root aphids. Black-bean aphid can be controlled by pinching out growing tips of broad beans after four flower trusses have set.

▲ **EELWORMS**
Serious soil pests with few control methods. Move your vegetable plot to a different part of the garden or grow in containers.

BIRDS
Pigeons can attack brassicas and take pea and bean seeds. Net crops in early spring.

BEETLES/WEEVILS
Telltale signs are small holes in young leaves or nibbled leaf edges. Dust brassica seedlings with derris. Next year use a crop cover for protection.

MICE
They can eat pea and bean seeds. Raise plants in pots and plant out once established.

ROOT PESTS
Cabbage root fly eat roots of brassicas, lettuce and root crops. Work soil insecticide into the top 5 cm (2 in) of soil before planting. Use brassica collars.

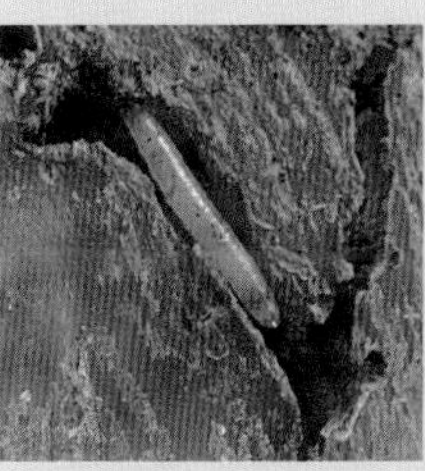

▲ **ROOT FLIES**
Affect carrots, cabbages and onions. Flies lay eggs at soil level; these hatch into small grubs which attack the roots. Use a crop cover to stop flies laying eggs next year.

▲ **RUST**
Causes orange spots on leek foliage. Remove diseased leaves. There is no cure.

ROOT ROTS
Widespread leaf discoloration or wilting is often the first symptom. Remove and destroy affected plants. Improve soil conditions (see page 238).

CATERPILLARS
Butterflies and moths lay eggs on the underside of leaves. Pick off by hand; spray or use a biological control (*Bacillus thuringiensis*). Use a crop cover to prevent the problem reoccurring.

BLIGHT
Attacks potatoes and tomatoes. Cut off top growth from affected plants to limit the spread. Spray in early summer with copper-based fungicide in wet periods.

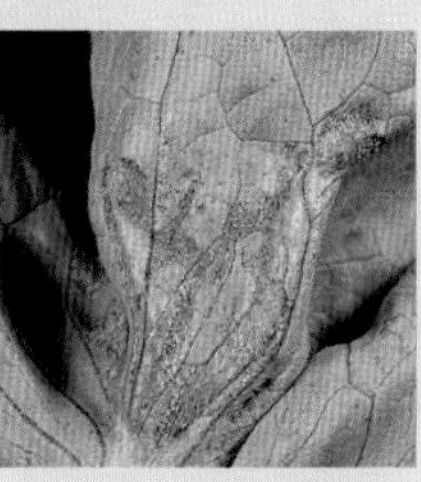

▲ **DOWNY MILDEW**
Causes the yellowing of brassica and lettuce leaves, and makes the tips of onion foliage die back. Remove affected specimens, thin the remaining plants and spray them with mancozeb.

summer, but it does not provide any frost protection. Plants can be watered through the covers so remove them only when the plot needs weeding or the plants pollinating.

You can also help to prevent pest problems by taking a leaf out of the organic gardener's book and enlisting the natural enemies of plant pests. Aphids, for example, are eaten by birds and ladybirds, while slugs are eaten by frogs. Encourage these beneficial creatures to forage in your garden by providing a suitable habitat (see page 270).

As soon as you see any pests, eggs or any diseased leaves, remove them by hand. If a serious pest or disease outbreak occurs, apply a ready-to-use spray to save time diluting and mixing concentrated chemicals. Remove plants suffering from viruses – shown by their yellow-streaked, mottled or spotty leaves – since there is no cure and the virus can easily spread to other plants.

DISEASE-RESISTANT POTATOES

Many varieties are resistant to particular pests and diseases but are often prone to others. The following are good all-round varieties that have resistance to at least two diseases.

'Accent'
'Cara'
'Romano'
'Wilja'

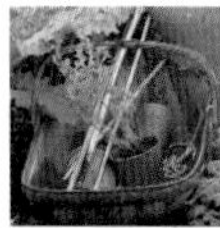

Buying and growing vegetables

Garden centres have begun to sell a range of vegetable plants in spring. By starting off with small plants rather than seed you will save yourself the chores of sowing and pricking out, however, your choice of varieties will be restricted.

Mail-order seed catalogues offer a wider range of bolt-resistant and disease-resistant varieties than you will find in garden centres. You can also get any seed ordering and planning completed in winter. Any unsown seed from previous years can be used – apart from parsnip seed – if it has been kept cool and dry in an airtight tin.

Sow seed in modular trays (illustrated below) so that each seedling has plenty of space to grow. This will also make transferring seedlings from trays into pots unnecessary. Young plants started off indoors will need 'hardening off' – to get used to colder conditions – before they can cope with being outside. The easiest way to do this is in a coldframe. Place plants in the coldframe with the lid just slightly open for a few hours during the day. Close the lid and cover with a double layer of garden fleece at night. Over a ten-day period, open the lid wider for longer periods during the day. If you do not have a

To get a continuous supply of lettuce through the summer you will need to sow in batches little and often. A cloche helps to warm the soil before sowing.

SUCCESSFUL SOWING

Raising plants from seed is so rewarding that even the busy gardener often wants to find the time. Keep the work to a minimum by sowing only those crops you find difficult to buy as plants. Use the following tips to keep the workload down.

Quick and easy *Save time sowing, planting out and weeding by sowing several seeds per module for lettuce, onions, leeks, cabbage, calabrese and beetroot. Plant out as a clump two to three times normal spacing.*

Instant rows *For an early start, sow peas and beans in guttering under cover. When plants are large enough, slip out the row into a prepared wide drill. Sow later crops outside in a staggered row rather than sowing in several single rows because the resulting wide row is easier to care for.*

Sowing outdoors *The easy way to make a seed drill outdoors is to press in a bamboo cane. If the soil has lots of weed seeds or is stony, cover seeds with potting compost to retain moisture and facilitate hoeing as rows are easier to see.*

Cloches

A cloche will buy a busy gardener valuable time. Choose one that is easy to ventilate and move around. A cloche offers protection from wind if well secured to the ground, and raises the soil and air temperature around the plants. Soils dry out more readily under cloches so use a length of seep hose for easy watering.

Early start You can sow or plant 10 to 14 days earlier under a cloche than in open ground. Try lettuce and carrots this way.

Added warmth Use cloches in summer to speed up ripening of strawberries or to dry off onions.

Late finish A cloche helps to extend the growing season of lettuce and other leaf crops.

Storage methods

Many vegetables can be kept for use in winter by simple storage. Damaged vegetables should be used fresh.

Storing dry After drying, store onions, shallots and garlic in a frost-free shed or garage. Store only those that are firm and keep them in net bags hung up so the air can circulate around them. Potatoes, provided they are kept in the dark, and winter squashes can also be stored like this.

Freezing Only top-quality, fresh produce is worth freezing, so aim to pick and freeze the same day. Freeze leaf beet, baby carrots, french beans, calabrese and broccoli.

Leaving in the ground Beetroot, carrots, celery, leeks, parsnips and winter cabbages can be left on the plot in winter, but cover them with cloches or fleece to protect them from severe frost damage.

coldframe, stand your plants outside on fine days, but bring them in at night, for two or three weeks before planting. Plants from garden centres may also need hardening off, so check when you buy them.

Planting Apply a balanced general feed, such as blood, fish and bone, or growmore to the soil a few weeks before planting. Vegetables that are not fully hardy should be planted out after the last frost (usually between mid May and early June). Water the plants thoroughly in their pots (add a dilute liquid feed if they have been in the pots for several weeks). When planting, lay a marked stick on the soil to make spacing plants easier. Water again after planting and apply a mulch.

Aftercare Once the key time-consuming tasks of digging, watering and weeding have been streamlined (see page 238), aftercare of all crops takes much less time. Fast-growing crops may need a second application of balanced fertiliser during the growing season; sprinkle the fertiliser between the rows and hoe or water in.

Harvesting Harvest courgettes and mangetout peas early. Pick over runner beans regularly to keep them producing. Root crops and cabbages can be left on the plot for weeks, even months (see table, page 241) before they are picked. Onions, garlic, shallots and winter squashes must be dried off in the sun before storing.

Time saver

At the end of the season, pick all remaining, full-size tomatoes that are still green. Place them in a bowl with a ripe apple or banana to speed the ripening process. Keep out of direct sunlight.

Fruitful pickings that require little effort

Fruit crops require less work in spring than vegetables and, once established, they require little attention and will bear rich rewards for many years. You can reduce maintenance time by choosing easy-care fruit and by growing them in the correct situation (see illustration, opposite). The best site to grow most fruit is one that gets sun for at least half the day, but is sheltered, with well-drained soil that retains moisture in summer. To save time, position fruit crops where they will be easy to water and prune. Some of the more decorative fruit trees can be incorporated into the ornamental part of the garden.

An apple tree makes a good focal point in a lawn. Choose a half-standard with a 1.2 m (4 ft) trunk; a bush tree with a trunk about half this length; or a 'Ballerina' tree, which forms a natural column without pruning and casts little shade. After planting and staking, lay a sheet mulch (available ready-cut in 45 cm (18 in) or 90 cm (36 in) squares). Disguise black plastic with bark chippings, but wool-mix sheets look acceptable as they are. A sheet mulch will prevent weeds from competing with the young fruit tree for moisture and nutrients, so less time needs to be spent on improving the soil (see page 264).

Most fruit is easy to grow if given the right conditions – these strawberries, raspberries, redcurrants and white currants will grow in a sunny position.

A gooseberry bush grown as a lollipop-shaped standard *(below)* will make a neat and attractive bush that fits comfortably into a decorative planting scheme.

Sunny fences or walls are an ideal site for trained fruit, such as plums or pears and hybrid berries. Although training involves a little extra work and skill, the benefits include an attractive cover to the fence with two seasons of interest. By training the tree you will make picking the fruit easier. Cordon apple or pear trees can be a productive alternative to a conventional screen or barrier in a garden. You will need full access on at least one side for pruning and tying in new growth to supporting wires.

A walk-in fruit cage is an excellent time-saving investment. It keeps birds off the crop all year round and removes the need to net each individual bush. Another bonus is that fruit quality often improves under a cage because it provides some shelter. You can buy ready-built fruit cages made of tubular metal (invest in a good-quality solid frame) or you could build your own using timber. Maintenance is minimal, but check for damage to the netting frequently. If you live in a snowy area, use a larger mesh that will let the snow through.

FUSSY FRUIT

Decent crops of the following fruit are unlikely unless you have a south-facing wall and are prepared to provide extra care.

Apricots
Figs
Grapes
Nectarines
Peaches
Pears
Plums

WHERE TO GROW FRUIT

Choose the right type of fruit for the situation. Use the illustration below to help you decide where to plant fruit in your garden.

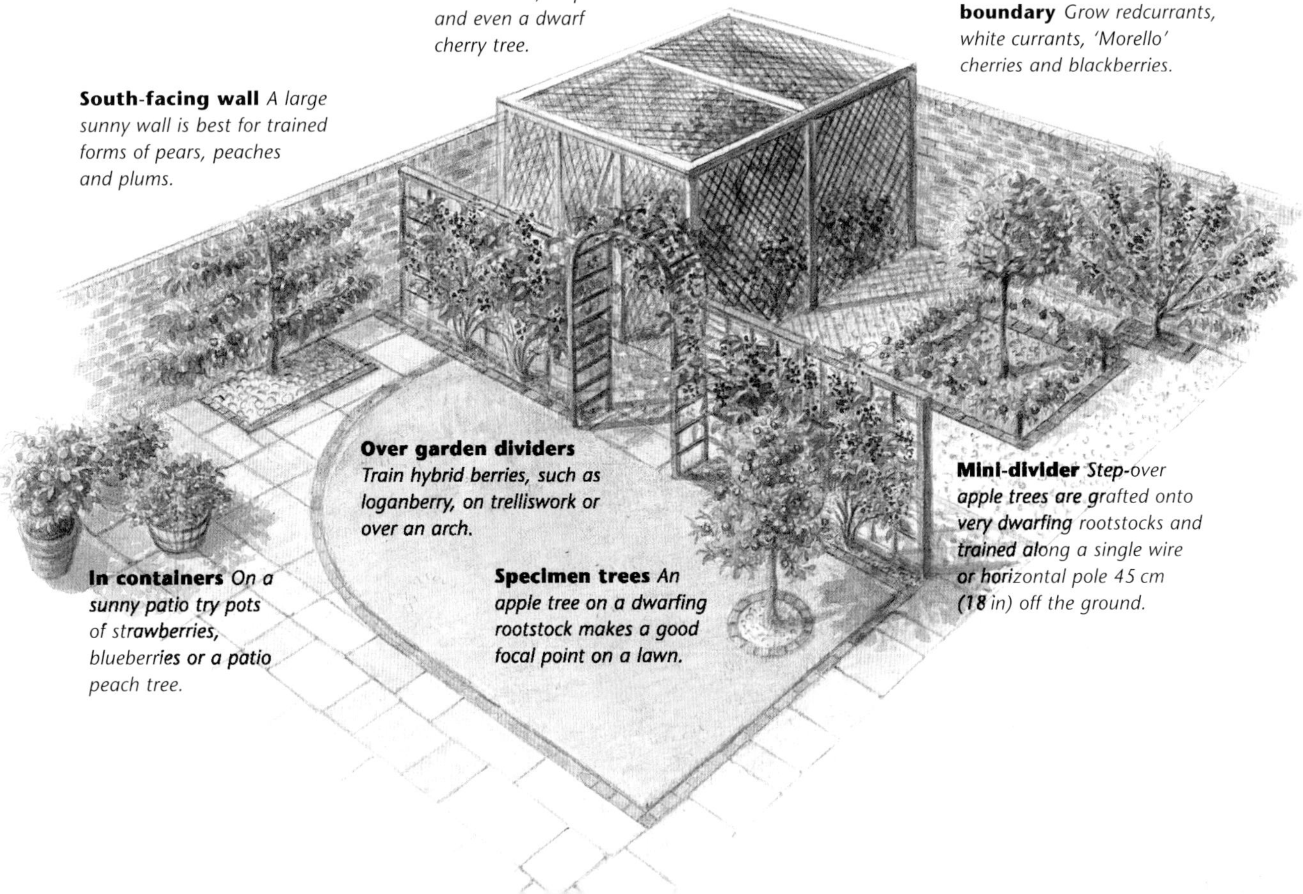

In a fruit cage *This is the best place to grow soft fruit because it provides protection from birds and shelter from the wind. In a small cage, grow fruit that will benefit most from the protection – redcurrants, strawberries, raspberries and even a dwarf cherry tree.*

West or north-facing boundary *Grow redcurrants, white currants, 'Morello' cherries and blackberries.*

South-facing wall *A large sunny wall is best for trained forms of pears, peaches and plums.*

Over garden dividers *Train hybrid berries, such as loganberry, on trelliswork or over an arch.*

Mini-divider *Step-over apple trees are grafted onto very dwarfing rootstocks and trained along a single wire or horizontal pole 45 cm (18 in) off the ground.*

In containers *On a sunny patio try pots of strawberries, blueberries or a patio peach tree.*

Specimen trees *An apple tree on a dwarfing rootstock makes a good focal point on a lawn.*

A redcurrant trained as a double cordon makes good use of wall space. It is easy to prune and pick. Prune each arm as for single cordons shown on page 253.

Step-over apple trees (*below right*) can look effective as a productive edging for a fruit or vegetable plot. Prune horizontal stems in the same way as a cordon (see page 252).

The easiest fruit to grow

Apples, raspberries, redcurrants and strawberries are easy to cultivate, as well as being useful in the kitchen. Apples are the easiest tree fruits to grow because they are hardy and suitable for most soils – even neglected trees produce some crops. The size of the mature tree is determined by the particular rootstock (see below). You need two or three different varieties to cross-pollinate each other. To save having to grow more than one tree, check that there are other suitable apple or ornamental crab apple trees in neighbouring gardens. Alternatively, choose a 'family tree' which has different varieties grafted onto the same rootstock. Late-flowering varieties are less likely to suffer from frost, which damages flowers and prevents pollination. Some varieties, such as 'Charles Ross' and 'James Grieve', can be used both as cooking and dessert apples.

Pears are less hardy and less tolerant of wind than apple trees and need more shelter and warmth. However, they can be trained as single-stemmed cordons against a warm wall. Pears also need another compatible variety nearby to pollinate the flowers.

Plums blossom early so they are prone to frost damage. Varieties of plums that are fan-trained are easier to protect from frost because you will be able to use netting. Choose self-fertile varieties, such as 'Victoria' and 'Czar', so that only one tree needs to be grown.

The fruit of large-growing cherries is often devoured by birds before harvesting. Trees on dwarfing rootstocks are easier to grow and to protect with netting. 'Morello' cherries are the only tree fruit that will

KEEPING TREES SMALL

Fruit trees are available on a range of different rootstocks. The rootstock determines the vigour of the tree and how big it will grow. If the rootstock is not stated on the label, don't buy the tree.

Fruit	Rootstock	Size of tree
Apple	M27	1.2-1.8 m (4-6 ft)
	M9	2.5-3 m (8-10 ft)
	M26	3-4.5 m (10-14 ft)
Pear	'Quince C'	3-3.5 m (10-11 ft)
Cherry	'Colt'	3.5-4 m (11-13 ft)
Plum	'Pixy'	1.8-2.5 m (6-8 ft)
	'St Julien A'	3.5-4 m (11-13 ft)

grow in the shade, including on a north-facing wall. However, they are suitable only for cooking. A few varieties of cherry are self-fertile, including 'Stella', so they do not need another variety to act as a pollinator.

This fan-trained 'Victoria' plum is self-fertile so does not need a second plum variety to act as a pollinator. It is a very heavy cropping dual-purpose variety that can be used for eating and cooking.

Bush and soft fruit Check out specialist fruit catalogues for varieties of soft fruit offering disease resistance. New varieties are being introduced each year.

Blackberries are too vigorous for most gardens, although unlike most other fruit they tolerate wind and shade. Hybrid berries, such as the thornless loganberry, are tasty and pretty in flower. They can be trained against a sunny fence.

Blackcurrants are easy to grow, though fiddly to pick. The fruit is of limited use fresh, but makes excellent jam and desserts. Redcurrants are sweeter than blackcurrants. They are easy to grow, but protection from birds is essential. Cordon-trained plants produce the heaviest crops, and are the easiest to pick, prune and protect from raiding birds.

Gooseberries are spiny, so picking and pruning can be unpleasant. Vertical cordons produce larger fruit which is easier to pick. Like currants, they need to be shaded from hot summer sun. Thin fruit in early summer and use the small, unripe fruit for cooking, leaving the rest to mature on the plant. The plants are long-lived.

Raspberries are easy to pick and very versatile, whether used fresh or frozen. Summer-fruiting types are usually grown in a line with a wire support. After fruiting, the old canes are cut out and the new canes tied in. The easiest to grow are the autumn-fruiting varieties such as 'Autumn Bliss'. They need no supports and are simply cut down to ground level in February.

Strawberries crop a few months after planting, making them a popular choice of fruit. They grow best planted through a mulch of black polythene in mounds of raised earth. Use cloches or netting to protect them from birds. Plant new stock every two to four years on a new site. Alpine strawberries make pretty, easy plants for shaded areas of the garden. The fruits are small and tasty but not juicy.

Time saver

If you have a well-established fruit tree you can reduce the need for pruning by grassing over the soil underneath. This will provide competition that will reduce the vigour of the tree.

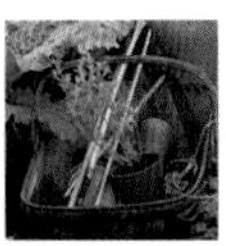

Preventing pests and diseases

A lot of problems can be avoided by keeping the garden tidy and taking action before they start. For instance, by picking up windfalls and diseased leaves in autumn, you can prevent fungal spores from overwintering on them. A garden vacuum will save time. In October or November, attach grease bands, available from garden centres, to the trunks of apple trees to prevent female moths climbing up to lay their eggs. Place the bands 60 cm (24 in) from the ground and check them regularly to make sure they are in good condition and that the barrier is not breeched by leaves or other debris. Leave them in place till April. Also put up pheromone traps (see below) in late spring to catch the male codling moths.

When crops are growing, be vigilant for signs of attack. Use the chart opposite to identify serious problems and take remedial action immediately. When checking crops, remove and destroy foliage with grey mould, eggs or aphids (greenfly) on them, and pick off any caterpillars that you see. Preventive spray programmes are not worth while because they have to be applied at such precise times with so many precautions that it is rarely practical, except perhaps on the smallest trees. For the busy gardener, a low level of pests and diseases should be considered acceptable on fruit, especially tree fruit. Also, by not spraying, you can enjoy pesticide-free produce.

If pests do become a problem, prompt action will save time and effort in the long run. For instance, aphids must be controlled because they spread rapidly, weakening plants by sucking their sap and spreading viruses. Options include winter wash (see 'Quick

APPLES

There are hundreds of apple varieties, but the following are widely available and have good general disease resistance.

'Charles Ross'
'Discovery'
'Greensleeves'
'Jonagold'
'Jupiter'
'Lord Derby'
'Redsleeves'
'Sunset'

In late spring prevent damage by codling moth by putting up pheromone traps. The sticky traps, which are available from garden centres, lure male moths by using the scent of the female moth. One trap should protect five trees.

Easy-care fruit

Do choose varieties that are naturally resistant to diseases.

Do provide the best possible site and growing conditions.

Do keep weeds under control – maintain a 90 cm (36 in) diameter weed-free zone around young fruit trees, and a 45-50 cm (18-20 in) wide strip on either side of cane fruit.

Don't choose complicated, trained forms – they take longer to prune.

Don't allow fruit to go short of water, particularly when swelling.

PESTS AND DISEASES TO LOOK OUT FOR

Few pest and disease outbreaks on fruit are worth worrying about because you will still get a good crop. However, the following can severely damage the crop or weaken the plants and so action is necessary.

BLACKBERRIES AND HYBRID BERRIES
Can be spoilt by raspberry beetle grubs in fruit. Control with contact insecticide after flowering.

CURRANTS

▲**Big bud mite** They cause swollen buds on blackcurrants, eventually weakening bushes. Pick off stems showing symptoms.
Aphids Pucker leaves and weaken the plant. Use contact insecticide.

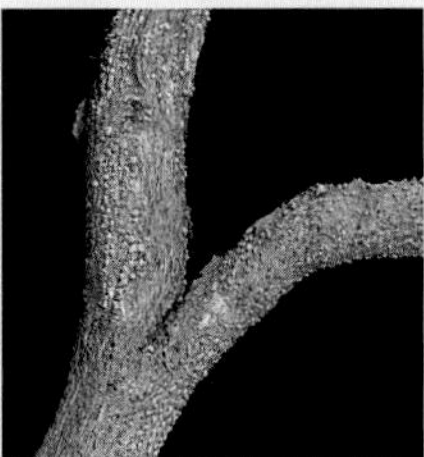

▲**Coral spot** This appears as small red spots on stems. It particularly affects redcurrants, and should be pruned out.

APPLES
Codling moth Tunnelling larvae damage fruit making them unusable. Prevent damage by hanging up pheromone traps in late spring. These trap male codling moths. One trap will protect up to five trees.

Scab It is a waste of time storing apples with scab (brown patches on fruit and leaves). There is no effective control, so prune out affected twigs and prevent future outbreaks by clearing away windfalls and fallen leaves in autumn.

▲**Powdery mildew** This affects young shoots and leaves, which should be removed and destroyed.

Canker Causes sunken patches on branches. Cut out affected wood when seen.

RASPBERRIES
Many pests and diseases attack raspberries, but if plants still produce edible fruit simply cut out affected canes.
Raspberry beetle Maggots found in the fruit – but 'Autumn Bliss' is rarely affected. Control with contact insecticide after flowering.

GOOSEBERRIES
Mildew A common and serious problem. Spray with a systemic fungicide. Replace plants with a resistant variety such as 'Invicta' or 'Greenfinch'.

▲**Sawfly** Caterpillars eat leaves and can defoliate whole stems during late spring. Pick off any caterpillars you see or use a contact insecticide.

STRAWBERRIES
Grey mould Affects fruit in wet summers or when the plants are watered from overhead. Pick off mouldy fruit when you see it and clear away dead leaves.
Slugs Apply pellets to prevent slug damage.

results', right) or summer spraying. In early summer, a soap-based spray or an aphid control based on pirimicarb can be used if aphids are visible. Some raspberry varieties are resistant to raspberry aphid.

Serious diseases, such as honey fungus, fireblight or red core (which affects strawberries in particular) are best dealt with by removing and destroying the plants, and then starting again on a fresh site. To avoid the risk of root disease when replanting fruit trees or bushes, do not plant on a site where previous crops grew.

Other diseases that attack the woody framework of the plant can be fatal, too. Canker on apple or pear trees needs to be pruned out. Red spots on the wood are a sign of coral spot, which can spread onto live wood and should therefore be cut out immediately.

Over the years, soft fruit can be progressively weakened by viruses, so replace plants when their yields become low. Buy fresh, healthy stock rather than propagating your own – not only is this quicker, with less risk of viruses, but you have the opportunity to try out newer disease-resistant varieties.

Quick results

Winter washes deal with many types of overwintering pests including greenfly and winter moth. Winter washes are based on tar oil, and are ideal for cleaning up dormant fruit trees in late winter – eliminating any unresolved summer or autumn pest problems. However, they are unpleasant to use and also kill beneficial insects so should be used only when necessary.

Buying and growing fruit plants

Garden centres and seed catalogues sell a limited range of fruit, but the biggest selection of newer varieties and disease-resistant varieties are available from fruit specialists. Orders are taken in autumn and winter and plants are dispatched during the dormant season – from November to March. Strawberries are the exception: they should be bought container-grown in summer (runners are cheaper, but harder to establish). Buy virus-free plants and avoid any with foliage that has yellow mottling or streaks. Many types of soft fruit are sold 'certified' as being pest and disease free. This guarantee is worth paying extra for.

By tucking a thick layer of straw around the strawberry plants when the small green fruit start to swell, you will stop the fruit touching the soil and prevent them from rotting.

Planting Bare-root specimens should be planted straightaway in order to prevent the roots from drying out. Otherwise, put them in a shallow trench with the roots covered until you get a chance to plant them properly. Container-grown specimens can be planted at any time of the year, but for the least work do it in autumn, when the ground is naturally moist. Avoid planting during dry spells. Before the fruit is planted, the ground should be free of perennial weeds.

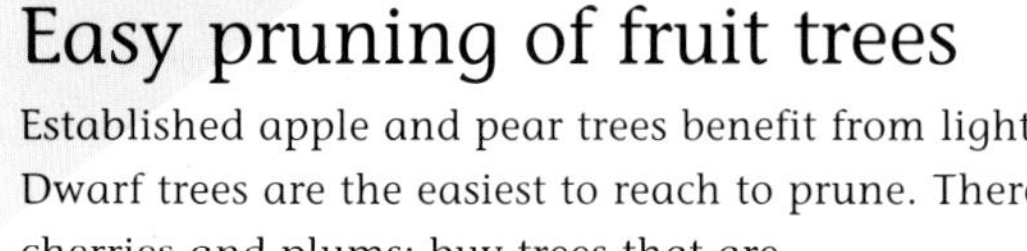

Easy pruning of fruit trees

Established apple and pear trees benefit from light pruning each winter. Dwarf trees are the easiest to reach to prune. There is no need to prune cherries and plums; buy trees that are already trained to a good shape.

New growth Shorten about half the new sideshoots to maintain the tree's overall shape.

Awkward branches Prune out any upright branches that are difficult to pick and that shadow other branches.

Dead wood Remove any diseased or dead wood, cutting back to just above a bud.

Overcrowded branches Remove crossing and overcrowded branches to make the tree less congested.

Pruning cordon trees

Cordons, espaliers and fans of apple or pear trees are trained in the same way. Treat each branch of espaliers and fans as single cordons.

In summer Prune new sideshoots along the main stem back to three buds beyond the rosette of leaves at the base.

In winter Cut back the tip of the main stem to a convenient height (around 1.8 m/6 ft) to keep the tree easy to reach for picking.

PRUNING FRUIT BUSHES AND CANES

Cane fruit are simple to prune. Easiest of all are autumn-fruiting raspberries, which can be cut back to ground level in February. New shoots will then grow in spring and fruit in autumn. For summer-fruiting raspberries, see right. Blackcurrants are the easiest bush fruit to prune (see 'Time saver', below). Other established bush fruit, such as gooseberries and redcurrants, need pruning in both summer and winter (see below).

Gooseberry and redcurrant bushes *In winter* (right)*, cut back the leaders by half their length and remove any dead, diseased or damaged wood.*

Summer-fruiting raspberries *Cut old canes that have fruited right back to the ground either after harvesting or by autumn. Select strong new canes and tie them in 10 cm (4 in) apart. Remove all others.*

In mid summer (above)*, prune back the new sideshoots to about 10 cm (4 in), but leave the leading shoots.*

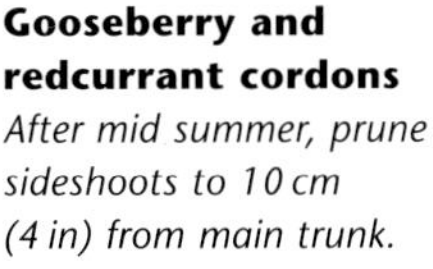

Gooseberry and redcurrant cordons *After mid summer, prune sideshoots to 10 cm (4 in) from main trunk. In winter, shorten the leader by a third.*

Time saver

When the fruit is ripe, cut back fruiting stems of blackcurrant bushes to within 2.5 cm (1 in) of the base of the shoot. You can then remove the fruit from the pruned stems at your convenience.

Aftercare A thick organic mulch of well-rotted manure, garden compost or bark chippings is essential. Top up the mulch once a year in spring. At the same time, apply a general-purpose, balanced fertiliser, such as blood, fish and bone, growmore or a rose fertiliser. For fruit trees, apply fertiliser over an area just beyond the spread of the branches. Do not apply fertiliser to strawberries unless grown in a container. Give plants extra water when the fruit is swelling.

Harvesting Most fruit needs harvesting in the summer, and dry evenings are a good time. Pick the fruit carefully, especially if you want to store it. Use shallow containers, such as seed trays, to prevent crushing soft fruit that is needed whole. Leave apples and pears on the trees as late as possible. Pick early apple varieties from August onwards and use straight away because they don't store well. Leave late varieties until early to mid October and harvest before bad weather damages them or blows them to the ground.

Storing fruit

Storing dry Good-quality apples are worth storing. Don't store bruised or holed fruit or windfalls. There is no need to wrap apples singly, simply put them in polythene bags with a few holes in and tie the bag loosely. These can then be kept in the garage or other cool, dry place for 6 to 8 weeks. Check them regularly and remove any deteriorating fruits.

Freezing Raspberries and prepared apples freeze well, as do currants and gooseberries.

Preserving Blackcurrant jam and redcurrant jelly are a delicious way of storing fruit. Freeze the currants until you have time to make preserves.

The easy-care greenhouse

A greenhouse allows you to raise plants when it suits you. Controlling the environment requires attention, but modern materials and equipment can help to automate some tasks. Larger greenhouses take less work than smaller ones, because smaller ones are prone to extremes of temperature and ventilation is difficult. Glass is the best cover. Plastic materials are available, but they do not age well. ***Aluminium frames need little care but wooden frames are attractive. Choose a durable wood such as western red cedar.***

Efficient greenhouse ventilation relies on the 'chimney effect' by which hot air rises and escapes through ridge vents and is replaced by cooler air drawn in through side vents.

Automatic vents As the temperature rises, the resin-filled piston expands, forcing open the roof vents and letting out hot air.

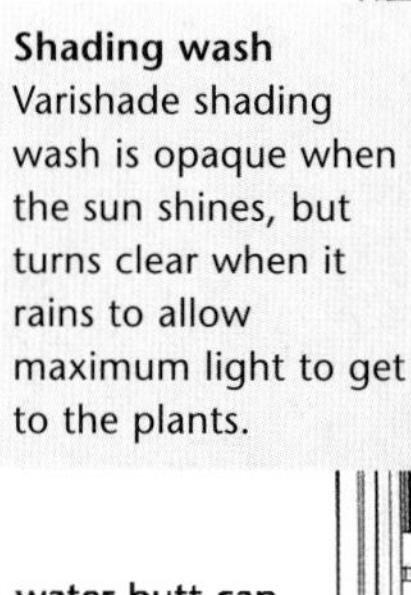

Shading wash Varishade shading wash is opaque when the sun shines, but turns clear when it rains to allow maximum light to get to the plants.

Use sheets of bubble polythene to insulate the sides and roof during cold spells.

Shading External roller blinds are an efficient way of keeping a greenhouse cool, but they need to be securely fitted.

A water butt can be used to collect rainwater for lime-hating plants. Raise on blocks to make filling a watering can easier. Cover to prevent algae.

A well-designed greenhouse has an all-weather path and a door with a low threshold that is wide enough for a barrow.

ELECTRICAL EQUIPMENT

A mains electricity supply helps the busy gardener to make the most of the greenhouse. Hire a professional electrician to connect up the supply. Remember that electricity in the moist environment of a greenhouse is potentially hazardous, so install a residual current device (RCD). Use weatherproof switches and armoured cable or PVC cable inside a plastic conduit.

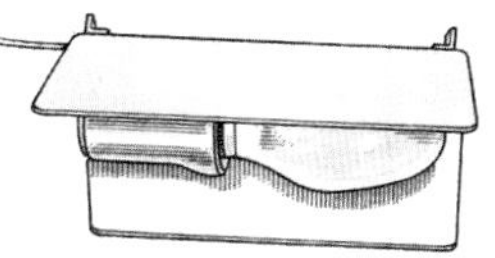

Lighting *Enables you to extend the growing season – especially useful if you want to raise seedlings early in the year.*

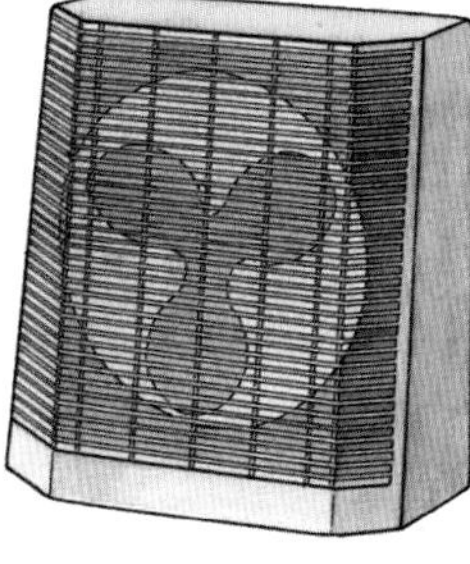

Electric mat *Lay on staging. Place pots and trays of seedlings on top to keep root area warm. The mat can be rolled up after use.*

Propagator *Choose one with a thermostat. Worthwhile accessories include a water mat (to raise humidity) and tray covers (to reduce moisture loss).*

Reliable heating *A specially designed electric fan heater with a thermostat is the easiest way to heat a greenhouse. It also circulates air, reducing the risk of disease. For tender plants in winter, aim for at least 4°C (40°F).*

TENDING THE EASY-CARE GREENHOUSE

EARLY SPRING

Young plants Order them from seed catalogues. Pots of seedlings and young plants will be available from garden centres too, but do not rush to buy unless you have time to care for them.

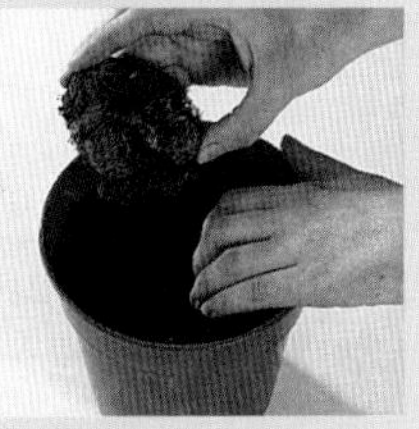

▲**Flowers** Pot up gloxinia tubers; sow coleus seed.

Tender plants Pelargoniums and fuchsias overwintered as plants or cuttings can be moved into the light and watered sparingly.

Automatic watering Set up a capillary or drip watering system. Make sure the system is working properly before it is needed.

MID SPRING

Feed Apply a dilute liquid feed to any plants you do not have time to pot on.

Shade Use a curtain of shading fabric to protect young plants until you apply shading paint.

Sow Seeds of various vegetables and ornamentals can be sown from March, but most will wait until April. Sow unusual favourites unlikely to be sold as seedlings or young plants.

▲**Pot up** Young plants ordered by mail could arrive now. Water, pot up and put in a frost-free greenhouse as soon as possible.

Seedlings Water with a copper-based fungicide to prevent damping-off disease.

Plant tomatoes Set out plants in pots or a growing bag.

Harden off Move half-hardy plants to the coldframe to get them acclimatised to conditions outdoors.

Pest control Put up a yellow sticky trap to monitor flying pests. Check plants for signs of attack. Control outbreaks immediately.

LATE SPRING

Tomatoes Train up string supports and remove sideshoots. Feed every week as the fruits begin to swell.

Tender plants Outdoor containers can be planted up and kept in the greenhouse until all danger of frost has passed.

Harden off Continue to move plants to the coldframe to harden them off.

SUMMER

Keeping cool Apply a shading wash. Increase the humidity in very hot weather by leaving a seep hose running over the path. Ventilation might now be needed at night as well as during the day.

Feed Apply liquid feed weekly to plants.

Tomatoes Harvest fruit and remove the growing tip from plants when seven trusses have set.

Sow Try schizanthus and calceolaria for spring flowers.

AUTUMN

▲**Tidy greenhouse** If overwintering tender plants, wash glass and insulate greenhouse with bubble polythene. Clear tomato plants.

Tender plants Take under cover before the first frost. Pot up if necessary. Don't overwater.

Heat Use a fan heater to keep greenhouse frost free if it contains tender plants.

WINTER

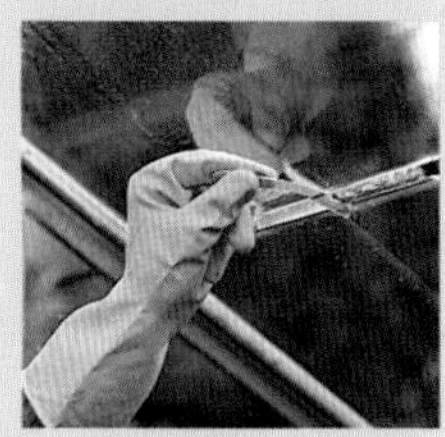

▲**Clean greenhouse** If the greenhouse is not heated in winter, clean it out on a mild, sunny day. Pay particular attention to clearing dirt from around glass panes to discourage the growth of moss, which can crack the glass. Clean pots with a hose and a stiff brush.

Growing plants in your greenhouse

Once you have mastered the environment, plants in your care will grow quickly, producing earlier and better crops. Install semi-automatic watering systems such as capillary matting and drip irrigation to make this task easier. Pests, too, will relish the cosy conditions and the ready supply of food offered by the growing crops and flowers, so be on the lookout for early signs of attack by checking over plants at every opportunity. Many common pests can be controlled using biological controls (see right), but this means you cannot use chemical sprays for other problems otherwise you may kill the biological control organism as well.

Biological controls

Save time spraying plants against pests such as whitefly and spider mite by using their natural enemies. Use a yellow sticky trap to monitor pest levels, removing it before adding the control (see page 306 for suppliers). Timing is crucial and using biological controls will limit the pesticides that can be used.

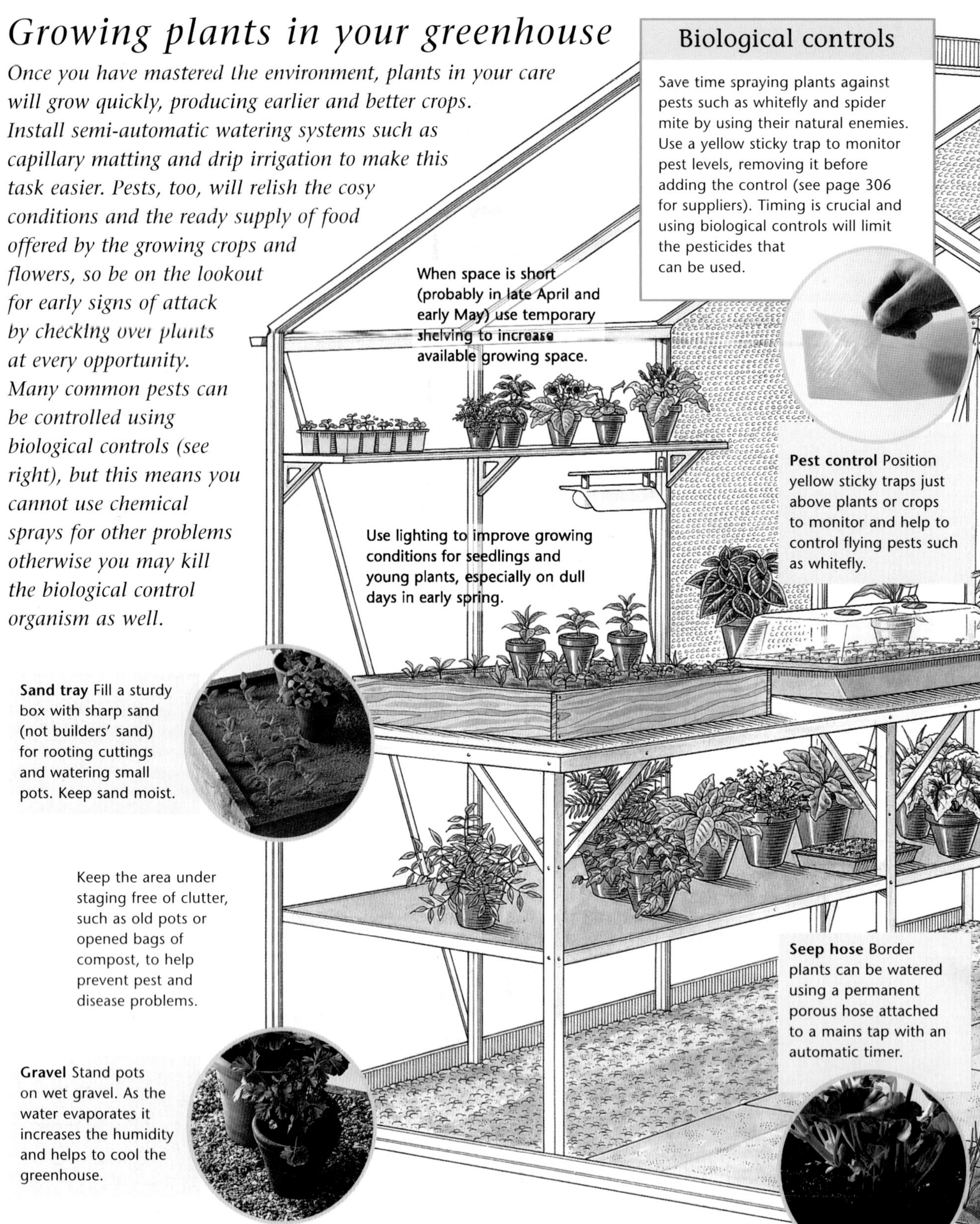

When space is short (probably in late April and early May) use temporary shelving to increase available growing space.

Use lighting to improve growing conditions for seedlings and young plants, especially on dull days in early spring.

Pest control Position yellow sticky traps just above plants or crops to monitor and help to control flying pests such as whitefly.

Sand tray Fill a sturdy box with sharp sand (not builders' sand) for rooting cuttings and watering small pots. Keep sand moist.

Keep the area under staging free of clutter, such as old pots or opened bags of compost, to help prevent pest and disease problems.

Seep hose Border plants can be watered using a permanent porous hose attached to a mains tap with an automatic timer.

Gravel Stand pots on wet gravel. As the water evaporates it increases the humidity and helps to cool the greenhouse.

Watering made easy

You can set up a capillary matting system to do time-consuming watering automatically. Water containers from the top to start them off. Don't use pots with rims on the base because the capillary system will not work.

Check the base Make sure that the staging is firm and level, then lay capillary matting on top of a sheet of heavy-duty polythene.

Quick set-up For a simple temporary system, drape one end of the capillary matting into a plastic trough filled with water. Top up as necessary.

Long-term displays Attach guttering along the edge of the staging to replace the trough, and cover the capillary matting with a sheet of black polythene to reduce evaporation. Cut holes in the polythene for individual pots.

Gravity-fed drip systems and growing bag reservoirs make watering easier.

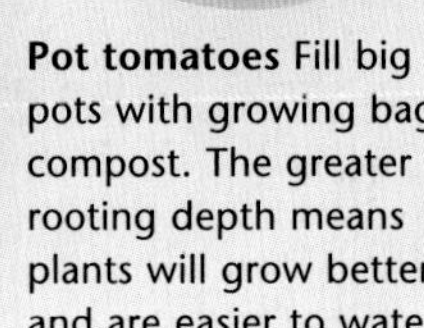

Pot tomatoes Fill big pots with growing bag compost. The greater rooting depth means plants will grow better and are easier to water.

Squash the sides of growing bags with boards to increase rooting depth and reduce need for water.

Automatic watering Install a drip irrigation system with a timing device or water computer to keep growing bags constantly moist (see page 188).

TROUBLE-FREE ORNAMENTALS

Add colour to your greenhouse by potting up a few spare bedding plants in large pots. The following easy-care ornamentals will also add interest to your greenhouse.

Pelargoniums Scented-leaf types can be appreciated in the warmth of the greenhouse. Regal types are best grown under glass, where their blooms are protected.

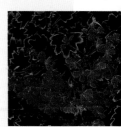

Gloxinias Colourful trumpet flowers for shady, humid corners are easy to grow from tubers. Half bury the tubers in pots of compost in early spring for flowers in summer.

Coleus A single packet of mixed seed will produce a range of brightly coloured leaves with different markings. Sow the seed each spring in a propagator, or buy plants.

Schizanthus (poor man's orchid) Grow in a minimum temperature of 5° C (41° F). Sow in late spring for blooms in late summer, or in late summer for early spring flowers.

Amaryllis (hippeastrum) Buy a large bulb in early autumn. Pot up so half the bulb is above the compost. Water sparingly until growth starts, and then keep compost moist.

Time-saving Techniques

USE MODERN TECHNIQUES AND MATERIALS TO CUT THE TIME SPENT WORKING IN THE GARDEN AND INCREASE THE TIME YOU SPEND ENJOYING IT

Gardening is constantly changing as new plants, ideas, methods and products are developed. Increasingly, gardeners try to work with nature rather than battling against it using an armoury of sprays, feeds and pruning tools. Gardening with nature does not mean letting the garden go wild, but choosing plants that will thrive with minimum intervention. By gardening 'green' you can save time too. Keep chemical spraying to a minimum and encourage natural predators, such as ladybirds and hoverflies, to control the pests for you.

It is always more time efficient to take preventative action. Reduce the time you spend on the chores of weeding and watering by using mulches to conserve moisture and prevent weed growth. Using ground-cover plants and spacing other plants so that they form a natural leaf canopy will help suppress weeds too. If weeds do appear, act promptly and remove them as seedlings; they will be prevented from setting seed and causing problems later. Also stay vigilant for major pest and disease outbreaks – taking remedial action quickly.

The busy gardener needs to avoid unnecessary work. Water only when you need to and restrict applications of fertiliser to annual crops and plants in containers. There is no need to feed most ornamental plants growing permanently in borders.

New innovations and products can be the busy gardener's best friend. For example, you can cut down on the workload by installing an automatic irrigation system for plants that need regular watering – focus on groups of plants that have high water needs, to keep the system simple.

Buying healthy plants

Busy gardeners are more likely than most shoppers to be tempted to buy on impulse. However, if you spend a little time making a list in advance and choosing good plants in the first place, you will save a lot of time in the garden in the long run

Plants that have not experienced stress can put all their efforts into growth and establishing roots. Poor and neglected plants need more aftercare and can bring problems, such as weeds, pests and diseases. A good-quality plant will have been raised under ideal conditions and delivered recently to the shop. It should be established in its pot, but not potbound – the roots should hold the compost but not be a solid mass, tightly coiled around the bottom of the pot. Don't be shy about carefully turning plants out of their pots to inspect the roots.

Selecting plants

Plants left on display benches for too long start to suffer from stress. They can run short of water and nutrients in their small pots and this can lead to wilting, premature flowering and discoloured foliage. Overwatering on the display benches can also be a problem – waterlogged roots cannot survive for long and are vulnerable to fungal disease. Liverwort or moss on the surface of the compost is a sign that it has been kept too wet. Avoid plants left sitting in water (except aquatic species).

Health check

Avoid importing problems into your garden by inspecting shoot tips, young leaves (including the undersides) and roots for signs of pests and diseases. Check fuchsias, alcea (hollyhocks) and roses for rust spots beneath the leaves, alpines and herbaceous plants for grey mould, and the tell-tale 'webs' of the spider mite under the leaves of fruit trees and plants sold under cover. Also look for limpet-like scale insects on woody plants and powdery mildew on fruit trees, roses and perennials. Vine weevil is a serious problem on many types of garden plant and

What to look for

Climbers Check stems near the base of the plant because they are easily damaged.

Herbaceous perennials Buy small, 9 cm (3½ in) pots in spring, but larger pots in summer, which have more space for the roots to develop. Hardy perennials can be bought in autumn even if top growth has started to die back, but check roots first for signs of damage.

Conifers It is vital to find out whether the speed of growth and size of plant is suitable for the site. Draw up a list before buying and buy only named varieties. True dwarf varieties cost more because they are slower-growing, but are essential in a restricted space.

▲ **Trees and shrubs** Look for a good shape that is not lop sided or leggy to save having to prune it into shape. Check the rootball to make sure the plant is not badly pot bound.

Patio and bedding plants Don't buy too early; let the retailers have the bother of protecting plants from frost. Bedding plants are sold at various stages of maturity (see page 133). The more mature the plant the less nurturing it will need, but you'll get less choice of varieties and they will cost more.

Bulbs Those bought as plants about to flower give instant results and are often more successful than dry bulbs. This applies both to spring flowers, such as dwarf narcissi, and to summer-flowering plants such as lilies.

is difficult to treat. The adult makes notches on leaf edges, and if this is on young foliage then they have probably laid eggs in the compost too and the resulting grubs will eat the roots. Also avoid plants with unnatural mottling or streaking of foliage because these are symptoms of virus disease for which there is no cure.

Pull off any weeds and remove the top few centimetres of compost before planting the new plant in your garden.

Where to buy plants

Buy from tidy, well-organised outlets with weed-free plants that have a high stock turnover. Avoid visiting garden centres at peak times – bank holidays and weekends, particularly in fine weather. Shop during late-night opening, on rainy days, on Friday afternoon or early Saturday morning when shops are fully stocked for the weekend.

If you have a plant list to shop from, group your list by types of plant – herbaceous, alpines, shrubs, trees, climbers and patio plants – because this is how most garden centres are laid out. Ensure you have the Latin names of hardy plants because most are displayed alphabetically in this way.

Plant labels are designed to sell the plants, not to tell you how much effort they will be. For example, the label will not mention whether the plant is invasive, self-seeding, needs annual pruning or is not reliably hardy, so check in a reference book before you buy to see how much work a plant needs.

Shopping from home

Buying by mail order can spread the workload over the year because, for hardy plants, most ordering and delivery takes place in the dormant season (autumn to winter). Plants to buy this way include large quantities of bulbs, hedging plants, ground cover, unusual varieties of perennials and roses.

Beware of cash with order adverts in newspapers and magazines. Seek out specialist suppliers via personal recommendation and visits to garden shows. *The RHS Plant Finder* is a good starting point for tracking down suppliers of more unusual plants.

Unpack deliveries straightaway. Left unopened, the plants will start to grow and will be drawn and leggy due to the lack of light. If you cannot plant out immediately, pot up bare-root plants or plant them temporarily to protect exposed roots. Contact the supplier as soon as possible if you have problems, such as inadequate or dried roots, rotting crowns or if plants have been damaged or delayed in transit.

Ready-planted containers

You can ask a garden centre or nursery to plant your choice of summer bedding in a container, then collect it after the last frosts in your area. Alternatively, visit a garden centre at the end of May and buy a ready-planted container.

Tailor-made Choose your planting scheme early in the season when you have the greatest range of plants to choose from. Select plant varieties that will suit the conditions in your garden.

Off-the-peg Look for schemes which include plants that are just coming into bud rather than those in full bloom. Displays that include foliage plants will look good for longer than all-floral displays and will also reduce the need for deadheading. Don't buy overcrowded schemes or those in small pots because they will need a lot of watering.

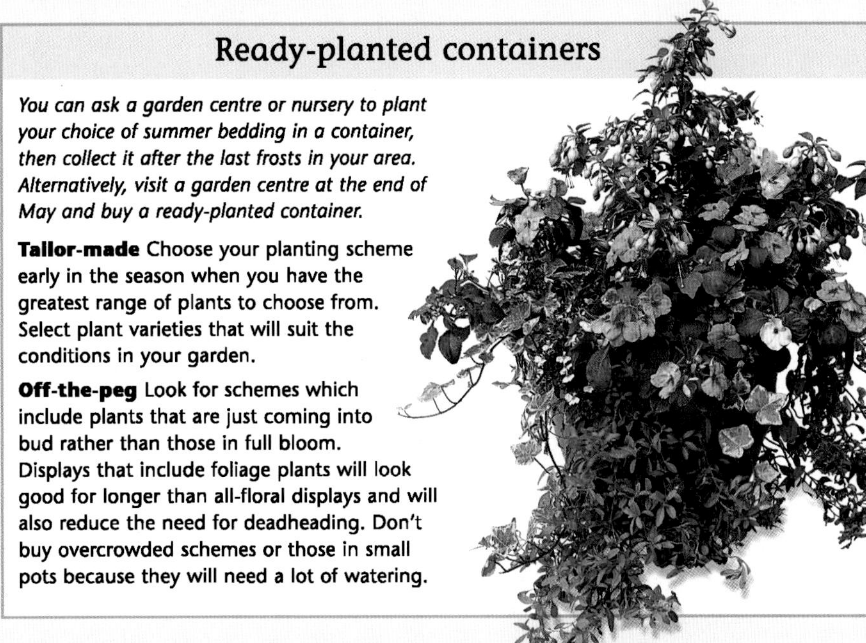

PLANTS TO BUY IN BLOOM

SPRING

Bedding plants: *Bellis perennis*, pansies. Bulbs in flower: *Anemone blanda, Crocus chrysanthus, Eranthis hyemalis (winter aconite),* hyacinths (F), *Iris reticulata* (F), dwarf narcissi, dwarf tulips. Perennials: aubrieta, *Helleborus orientalis,* polyanthus. Shrubs: azalea, camellia, chaenomeles, cytisus (F), forsythia (F), *Magnolia stellata*, rhododendron.

SUMMER

Bedding: a wide range. Bulbs in flower: lily (F). Perennials: dahlia, delphinium, dianthus (F). Shrubs: buddleja (F), hibiscus, hydrangea, *Kolkwitzia amabilis*, lilac (F), philadelphus (F), potentilla, roses (F). Climbers: clematis, lonicera (F), roses (F).

AUTUMN

Bedding: pansies. Bulbs in flower: *Colchicum autumnale, Crocus speciosus, Cyclamen hederifolium, Nerine bowdenii.*

WINTER

Bulbs in flower: *Cyclamen coum.* Shrubs: hamamelis (F), *Lonicera fragrantissima* (F), mahonia (F), sarcococca (F), viburnum (F).

(F) = fragrant

Successful planting

To establish quickly and thrive, new plants must be planted correctly and at the right spacing. It is also important to plant at the correct time which depends on the plants' hardiness, the way they were sold and the local climate

It is essential to get plants off to the best possible start if they are to establish quickly and remain trouble free. You need to plant at the right time (see opposite) when the weather and soil conditions allow. Tender plants cannot be planted out until the last frosts have passed, so growing too many of these will mean you have a lot of planting to do in late spring which is usually the busiest time in the garden. To spread your planting throughout the year, choose a greater proportion of hardy subjects which can be planted in autumn. Planting in autumn has the advantage that the soil is still warm yet moist, which will enable good root growth before the onset of winter. The plants

PLANTING TIPS

All plants are worth planting well, but expensive ones, such as trees, shrubs and climbers, are worth giving the most attention. Before planting, clear away any weeds and other debris and improve the soil with well-rotted organic matter. Dig a generous hole (about twice as large as the rootball) and plant at the same depth as previously. Water each plant thoroughly before and after planting, then apply a mulch (see page 264).

Trees *Small trees establish more quickly than larger ones. Trees over 1.2 m (4 ft) benefit from a stake driven securely into the ground. Use a tree tie to secure the tree to the stake. Protect the young bark from rabbit damage with a tree guard. Bury a piece of drainpipe filled with gravel next to the tree to make watering easier.*

Climbers over other plants *Choose a suitable established* ***support plant and dig a hole at the edge of its leaf canopy. To prevent the roots of surrounding plants competing with the new climber, line the sides of the hole with wood, which will rot away by the time the climber is established. Guide the climber into the canopy of its support plant with a rope.***

Wall climbers

Dig the planting hole 23 cm (9 in) or more away from the wall or fence, where the soil is more fertile and moist. Clematis should be planted so that the bottom 15 cm (6 in) of stem is buried (see page 162). Use a bamboo cane to guide the wall climbers to their supports. Plant woody climbers that are not self-clinging, such as roses, at an angle of 45 degrees, so that they lean towards the wall. All non-clinging climbers need the additional support of wires or trellis.

The quickest way to plant a hedge is to lay a cane marked with the planting distance on the ground to help you space the plants correctly. Plant container-grown plants at any time of year in individual holes, but with bare-root plants (available only during the dormant season) plant in a V-shaped trench made with a spade.

will have become well-established by spring, and should require less-frequent watering in summer than newly planted specimens. It pays to wait until late spring before planting evergreens, especially if your soil is heavy wet clay. Bare-root plants that are available from winter to early spring need to be planted as soon as possible after they are delivered. Container-grown plants can be planted at any time of year, provided that the soil is not frozen or muddy.

Planting distances

Most plants bought at a nursery or garden centre will have advice on the label suggesting the correct planting distances or spacing. These measurements are based on the width that the plant grows to. However, they are only a rough guide, because plants grow larger and faster in some soils and climate conditions than others.

Close planting will cover the ground quickly and smother weeds. However, the plants will crowd each other and will need to be pruned to keep in check. Correct spacing is most important for long-term plantings such as trees and hedging. To calculate the correct spacing for different species, add together the mature height of each species then divide by three. Before you start digging planting holes, place out the plants in their pots on the soil to see how they will look.

INSTANT BORDER DISPLAYS

If you plant a whole border at the recommended spacing using young plants, it produces a rather stark display until the plants fill out and cover the ground. However, you can get a display that looks good at the start by spacing the backbone plants at the correct distance and filling gaps with the temporary addition of low-growing perennials and bulbs for added seasonal colour (see plan).

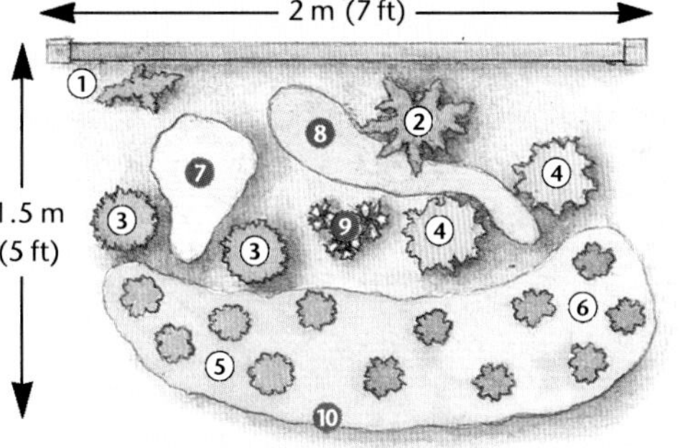

Permanent plants

① *Hedera helix* 'Glacier' (on fence)
② *Magnolia stellata* 'Rosea'
③ *Hebe* 'Autumn Glory' x 2
④ *Weigela florida* 'Foliis Purpureis' x 2
⑤ *Geranium* 'Russell Pritchard' x 5
⑥ *Heuchera* 'Palace Purple' x 7

Temporary fillers

❼ Nicotiana (summer)
❽ Nigella (summer)
❾ *Lilium* 'Regale' (summer)
❿ *Narcissus* 'February Gold' and 'Thalia' (spring)

After five years the permanent plants will have filled the available space smothering most of the temporary additions.

THE BEST TIME TO PLANT

Plant only if soil conditions allow. If the soil sticks to your tools and boots, it is too wet.

TENDER PLANTS
Plant after the last frost. Harden-off well first, then water and allow to drain before planting. Carefully remove the plant from the pot. Hold it by its rootball to avoid damage. Plant in prepared soil. Firm the soil round the rootball. Protect with a double layer of garden fleece if a late frost is forecast.

HARDY PLANTS
Plant hardy trees, shrubs and perennials in spring or autumn. Plant trees and shrubs at the same depth as they were in the pot. Plant the crown of most perennials 2-3 cm (¾-1¼ in) deep to allow for the soil to settle (not peony or bearded iris).

EVERGREENS
Plant in September to give time to establish before winter. In an exposed area, wait until April or protect plants with a temporary barrier of windbreak netting.

ALPINES
Plant in spring. Add grit to the soil and to the planting hole to improve drainage. Plant as for tender plants. Cover soil with a 1 cm (½ in) layer of gravel to improve surface drainage.

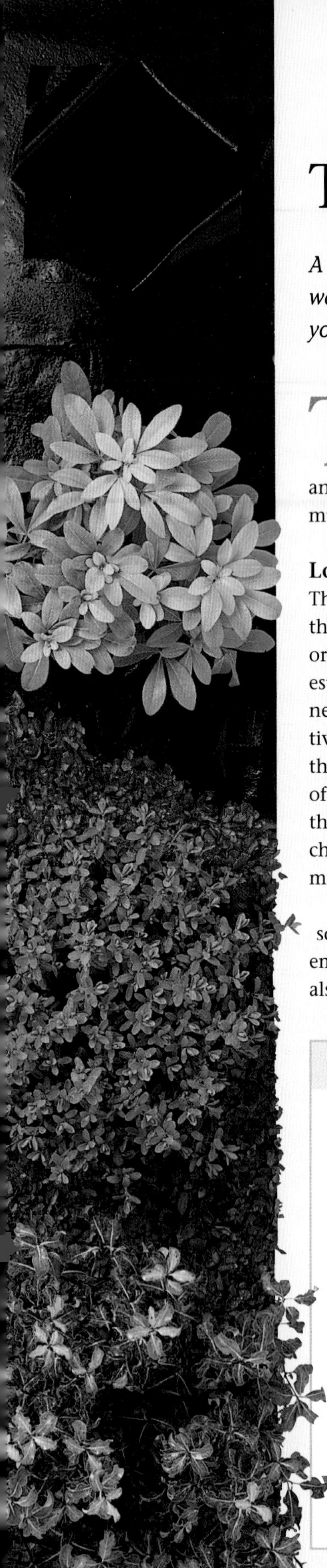

The benefits of mulching

A layer of natural material spread thickly over the soil cuts down the need for watering, reduces weeding and improves the soil – all in one operation. If weeds are your main problem, plant a new bed through mulch matting

There are two main types of mulch: loose organic materials, such as bark chippings, cocoa shells and compost; and sheet mulches, such as proprietary mulch matting, plastic sheeting or old carpet.

Loose mulches

They are more attractive and easier to apply than sheet mulches, and most improve the organic content of the soil. They are used on established and newly planted beds, but they need to be applied annually and to be effective should be at least 5 cm (2 in) thick. For the busy gardener, a mulch 7.5 cm (3 in) thick of good-quality bark chippings will last up to three years – less with sandy soil – but bark chippings are more expensive than most other mulches. A mulch can be applied at any time, but it is best done in late spring when the soil is warm and moist, but before weeds emerge. Garden compost and leaf-mould can also be used as a loose mulch. If your garden does not generate enough waste, try clubbing together with neighbours or join a community scheme. A non-organic mulch, such as gravel, doesn't add organic matter to the soil, but it rarely needs topping up because it doesn't decompose. Apply a gravel mulch at the same thickness as an organic mulch.

Apply a 5 cm (2 in) layer of loose mulch, such as cocoa shells, in early spring when the soil is moist but before weeds grow. Top up each spring.

Six types of loose mulch

1 Bark chippings Attractive, but expensive. Large chunks last a long time and don't blow around, though cheap wood chips rot quickly.

2 Cocoa shells Pricey but more nutrients than most mulches. They bond together when wet so they don't blow around.

3 Garden compost Free, but soon rots away. Can spread weeds unless well broken down.

4 Grass clippings Free, but turn yellow and can introduce weeds. In wet weather, they can become slimy.

5 Composted bark Attractive, but can blow around and may support wind-borne weed seeds. Does not last as long as chipped bark.

6 Gravel Attractive, and long-lasting, but does not add organic matter to the soil. Various grades available.

Covering a new bed with mulch matting

Laying a sheet of mulch matting cuts down the time needed to maintain a newly planted bed. The matting creates a barrier, smothering even perennial weeds, such as nettles and docks. It stops weed seeds from germinating by keeping them in the dark, and protects the soil from wind-borne weed seeds. Like other mulches, matting helps insulate the root area and prevents water loss, so plants will need less watering too.

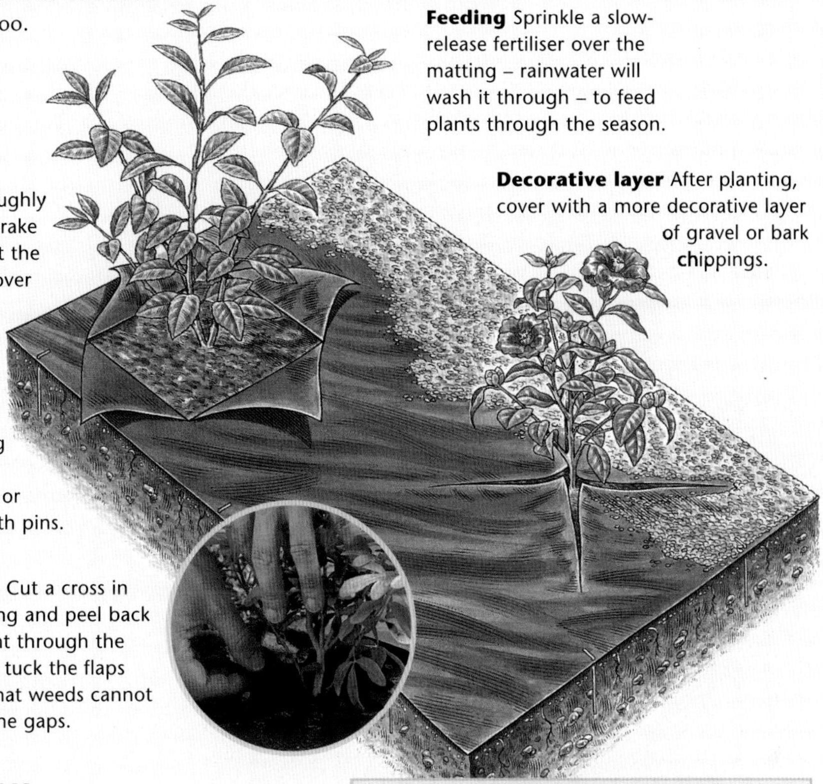

Feeding Sprinkle a slow-release fertiliser over the matting – rainwater will wash it through – to feed plants through the season.

Laying mulch matting Thoroughly dig the soil and rake level. Spread out the mulch matting over the soil.

Decorative layer After planting, cover with a more decorative layer of gravel or bark chippings.

Secure the matting To stop the matting blowing about, bury the edges, or anchor them with pins.

Planting Cut a cross in the matting and peel back flaps. Plant through the hole then tuck the flaps back so that weeds cannot grow in the gaps.

Sheet mulches

These are used to cover a new bed before planting and do not need reapplying or topping up annually (see above). They act as a solid barrier so are more effective than loose mulches at smothering perennial weeds and stopping wind-borne weed seeds from getting a foothold than loose mulches. The main drawback of sheet mulches is that they don't improve the soil and they look unsightly, although a thin layer of gravel or bark chippings will disguise them. Sheet mulches can be recycled materials, such as old carpet or newspaper, or purpose-made products such as woven polypropylene, black polythene or bonded materials and can be purchased at garden centres and DIY shops. The best materials are permeable to water. Special circular sheet mulches can be bought for planting individual specimens.

Effective mulching

Apply at the right time Mulches need to be in place by mid spring when the soil is at its wettest but is no longer cold. There is no point applying a mulch in dry, summer conditions because it will stop moisture from getting to the plants and they will require even more watering than usual.

Apply the right thickness To ensure effective weed control, apply a minimum thickness of loose mulch or gravel of 5 cm (2 in) straight onto the soil surface.

Feed and water plants Add fertiliser before applying a mulch. Lay a seep hose under mulch matting so that you can supply water easily if needed.

Mulch in rows When planting vegetables or bedding plants in rows, lay strips of mulch matting along the bed between the plants rather than planting through the matting.

MULCHES AROUND THE GARDEN

IN A MIXED BORDER

In an existing border, treat perennial weeds with a systemic weedkiller, taking care not to spray surrounding ornamental plants. Hoe off annual weeds. Apply a 5 cm (2 in) layer of cocoa shells or bark chippings to suppress further flushes of annual weeds and to make removing weed seedlings easier. If you are planting a new border, use mulch matting *(see left).*

TREES AND SHRUBS

Shrub borders can be mulched as for a mixed border *(above).* For an individual tree or shrub set in a lawn, remove the grass around the tree and lay a mulch matting designed for new trees with a diameter of 1-1.2 m (3-4 ft). Or just cut the normal sheets of mulch matting to fit.

IN THE FRUIT GARDEN

Individual trees and bushes can be mulched as for trees and shrubs. On each side of rows of soft fruit lay a 45 cm (18 in) wide sheet of mulch matting.

AROUND ALPINES

Improve drainage by applying a 2.5 cm (1 in) layer of gravel or stone chippings. If weeds are a problem around shrubby alpines, lay mulch matting underneath.

Watering and feeding

Watering is the most time-consuming chore in late spring and summer, especially if you have well-drained soil or a lot of container plants. Reduce the need for watering by choosing drought-tolerant plants and installing an automatic watering system

Devote your attention to only the plants that need watering and water efficiently so that no effort is wasted. Containers need most frequent watering, but there are ways to get around this (see page 188). New plants also need to be kept moist until they are established.

Some vegetables benefit from watering at key stages of development. Water peas and beans when the pods begin to swell, and tomatoes and courgettes when the fruit begins to swell. Tubers, such as potatoes, need water throughout the growing season and leafy crops, such as lettuce, will produce more lush growth and are less likely to run to seed if they are kept moist. Established fruit trees and bushes do not need watering, but will produce bigger yields if watered when the fruit is swelling (usually May or June).

When watering, thoroughly soak the soil around each plant once a week rather than sprinkling little and often, because light watering moistens just the surface layer of the soil which encourages shallow rooting, and more water is lost through evaporation. During hot weather, water in the evening to reduce evaporation. Any water on the foliage is wasted, so direct a steady flow of water round the base of the stem. Target water at the roots of trees by inserting a section of drainpipe filled with gravel. For shrubs, make a ridge of soil around each plant to hold the water in place as it soaks in. For small plants or plants in rows, install a seep hose.

WATERING EQUIPMENT

To be efficient at watering, the busy gardener should invest in up-to-date equipment. Where a lot of watering is needed, such as containers on a patio, consider installing an automatic system.

Outside tap *Install an outside tap, and use modern snap fittings to connect hoses and accessories. Lag the tap in winter.*

Water butt *Collects rainwater that is useful for acid-loving plants. Raise the butt so that it is easy to fill a watering can or attach a hosepipe. Keep covered.*

Watering systems *Micro-irrigation systems work well for containers (see page 188) and greenhouses (see page 257).*

Hosereel *Invest in a modern hose in a cassette reel or lay a system of hoses around the garden. Many attachments are available. Devices that guide the hose around bends to prevent kinking will also save time.*

Water computer *These can be programmed to turn the water on and off at pre-set times.*

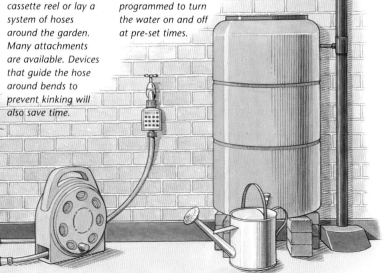

Feeding

It is essential to feed lawns, container plants and fruit and vegetables. Plants grown for their flowers, such as roses, will also benefit from feeding though it is not essential. A garden filled with shrubs, trees, perennials, wild flowers or herbs does not need feeding if the soil is of a reasonable quality. All nutrients required for plant growth are present in most soils, but heavy winter rains on a well-drained soil can deplete the topsoil of nitrogen. In this case, either add well-rotted organic matter to improve soil structure or apply a general fertiliser.

Many fertilisers are suitable for more than one type of plant, so make feeding simple by using a few easy and adaptable products:

General fertiliser This contains balanced amounts of nitrogen, potassium and phosphorus. Growmore is the most widely available general fertiliser, and is useful for feeding vegetables, ornamental plants and lawns that are free of weeds and moss. Balanced blood, fish and bone fertiliser is an organic alternative.

Slow-release fertiliser Some fertilisers, such as Osmocote, release nutrients over weeks or months, depending on the type. They are coated with a resin that releases the nutrients steadily as temperature and moisture increases. The timing of release should coincide with plant growth. This approach is well suited to container plants that can be fed only once, at the start of the season.

Rose fertiliser Despite its name this type of fertiliser is suitable for all flowering shrubs and fruit trees. It contains extra potassium to boost flowering and usually extra magnesium too. There is no organic alternative.

Liquid fertilisers These are fast-acting and give quick results. Use a balanced type – often sold as liquid growmore – for leaf growth, or a tomato feed to promote flowers and fruit. Foliar feeds are used to combat nutrient deficiencies in plants. Instead of the feed being taken up by roots, it is applied to the leaves. Use a sprayer containing a liquid fertiliser made from seaweed extract – an organic option – to combat trace element deficiencies during the growing season.

Time-saving tips

Container plants Use a slow-release fertiliser, such as Osmocote, before planting. Formulations are available lasting from three to nine months. Plugs (shown above) are easier to apply than granules which have to be mixed with the compost. Towards the end of the growing season apply a liquid feed once a fortnight if the plants are running short of nutrients – when the leaves pale or start to turn yellow.

Beds and borders Weigh out enough granular fertiliser for a square metre, and put it in a polystyrene cup. Mark the level, then use the cup as a quick way to measure out further applications.

The organic approach

When applying organic matter, such as garden compost or animal manure, the long-term aim is to feed the soil rather than to supply nutrients directly to individual plants. In the short term, organic alternatives exist to most fertilisers, although those of animal origin will not necessarily come from farms certified as farming organically. For reasons of hygiene, gloves should be worn when handling organic materials.

FEEDING CALENDAR

SPRING

When plants start to grow, fork or hoe into moist soil a general fertiliser, such as growmore or balanced blood, fish and bone. Feed flowering shrubs, including roses, with a rose feed after pruning. When planting up containers add a slow-release fertiliser. When grass starts to grow feed it with a spring lawn feed for heavily used lawns or an autumn formulation for lawns that get little wear (see page 59). Start feeding container plants six weeks after potting if no slow-release fertiliser was added at planting time.

SUMMER

Fast-growing vegetable crops benefit from extra fertiliser during the growing season. Sprinkle it on moist soil between rows or around plants. Don't apply granular fertiliser in a drought because it is not dissolved and can scorch roots. Instead, switch to liquid feeding during dry weather.

AUTUMN & WINTER

Do not feed at the end of the growing season because it can encourage lush growth that is likely to be damaged by frost. Do not apply fertiliser in winter because it will be wasted and could get washed into nearby water supplies.

Ground-cover plants

Keep a garden free of weeds by covering any bare soil with decorative ground-cover plants. Although primarily grown for their weed-suppressing foliage, many ground-cover plants produce attractive flowers, so they are worth choosing carefully

Densely planted areas of the garden will have fewer weeds because the ornamental plants keep weed seeds in the dark which prevents them from germinating. Ground-cover plants work on the same principle and should be hardy and, if possible, evergreen. The site should be free of perennial weeds before planting because these are difficult to eradicate once ground-cover plants are established. The planting distance is crucial to make sure that the area will be covered successfully without requiring a lot of work. Often a range of planting distances is given for a plant. The closer spacings will give quicker cover.

Choose ground-cover plants that will suit the soil and site conditions, and that complement the existing display. Remember that deciduous ground-cover plants lose their leaves in autumn, so if they are used in drifts they may leave ugly gaps in a border during the winter months.

TROUBLE-FREE GROUND-COVER PLANTS

NAME	FOLIAGE	FLOWERS	POSITION	SIZE	SPACING
Ajuga reptans	D/E	May–June	○ ◑ ●	15x60 cm	35 cm
Alchemilla mollis	D	June–July	○ ◑	60x75 cm	45 cm
Arum italicum ssp. *italicum* 'Marmoratum'	new in winter, marbled	April, berries (P) in autumn	◑ ●	30x15 cm	30 cm
Astilbe	D, deeply cut	June–Aug, some later	○ (moist) ◑	60-90x45 cm	40 cm
Berberis thunbergii 'Atropurpurea Nana'	D, some coloured, autumn tints	April	○	60x60 cm	50 cm
Bergenia (eg 'Sunningdale')	E, glossy, rounded	April–May	○ ◑ ●	40x45-60 cm	45 cm
Brunnera macrophylla	D, heart shaped	April–May	◑ ●	45x60 cm	45 cm
Calluna vulgaris	E, some have autumn tints	Aug–Sep	○ (acid)	10-60x75 cm	30-40 cm
Ceanothus thyrsiflorus var. 'Repens'	E	May–June	○	90x120 cm	100 cm
Convallaria majalis	D (P)	April–May	◑ ●	25x30 cm	15 cm
Cotoneaster dammeri or C. x *suecicus* 'Coral Beauty'	E	May	○ ◑	20x180 cm, 90x180 cm	60 cm
Epimedium perralderianum	E, heart-shaped, reddish tints later in the year	April–May	◑	40x50 cm	45 cm
Erica carnea	E	Dec–March	○	15x45 cm	30-40 cm
Euonymus fortunei 'Emerald Gaiety'	E, variegated	n/a	○ ◑ ●	90x150 cm	45-60 cm
Gaultheria procumbens	E, red tints in winter	July, berries in autumn	◑ (acid)	15x90 cm	45 cm

QUICK-GROWING GROUND-COVER PLANTS

To carpet large areas, vigorous ground-cover plants will give the quickest results for least cost. They are ideal between established permanent plantings, such as a shrubbery, or in difficult areas such as over a sunny bank. Bear in mind that these quick-growing plants can smother less vigorous types if they are allowed to spread out of control.

Persicaria affinis *(sun or light shade). 60 cm (24 in) deep evergreen carpet, flowers July-Sep. Plant 40 cm (16 in) apart.*

***Helianthemum* 'Praecox'** *(sun). 15 cm (6 in) deep evergreen carpet of grey-green leaves. Flowers June-Aug. Plant 50 cm (20 in) apart.*

Geranium macrorrhizum *(sun or light shade). Forms a 30 cm (12 in) deep carpet, flowers May-July. Plant 60 cm (24 in) apart.*

Key – **Foliage** D = deciduous E = evergreen P = poisonous; **Position** ○ = Sun ◑ = Part shade ● = Shade

NAME	FOLIAGE	FLOWERS	POSITION	SIZE	SPACING
Geranium	D/E	June–July	○ ◑ ●	30x60 cm	60 cm
Heuchera	D/E, many are coloured	June–Aug	○ ◑	35 cm	30-45 cm
Hosta sieboldiana var. 'Elegans'	D, large, blue-grey	June–July	◑ ●	90x120 cm	60 cm
Lamium maculatum	D/E, some variegated	May–July	○ ◑ ●	20x90 cm	30 cm
Leucothoe walteri	E	April	◑ ●	1x3 m	2 m
Mahonia aquifolium	E, red tints in winter	Feb–May Berries	○ ◑ ●	90x60 cm	90 cm
Nepeta 'Six Hills Giant'	D	June-Sep	○ ◑	90x60-90 cm	60-75 cm
Pachysandra terminalis	E	March	◑ ●	20x40 cm	20 cm
Prunella grandiflora	D/E	June-Oct	◑ ●	15x90 cm	45 cm
Prunus laurocerasus 'Otto Luyken'	E	April	○ ◑ ●	1.2x1.5 m	90 cm
Pulmonaria saccharata	E, with silver spots	March–April	◑ ●	30x60 cm	30 cm
Roses, ground cover	D	June-Sep	○	75x120 cm	60 cm
Saxifraga x *urbium*	E, rosette habit	May	◑ ●	20-30x60 cm	30 cm
Stachys byzantina	D/E, silver	n/a	○	45x60 cm	30 cm
Symphytum 'Goldsmith'	E, green with cream	May	◑ ●	30x45 cm	45 cm
Tellima grandiflora	D/E	April–June	○ ◑ ●	80x30 cm	45 cm
Tiarella cordifolia	E, red tints	May–July	◑	10-25x30 cm	30 cm
Vinca minor	E	March–May	○ ◑ ●	15-20x75 cm	45-60 cm

GROUND COVER FOR ALL SITUATIONS

OVER BANKS
In sun: *Calluna vulgaris* (E), *Ceanothus thyrsiflorus* var. *repens* (E), *Cotoneaster dammeri* (E), *Erica carnea* (E), *Geranium* (D/E), *Stachys byzantina* (D/E).
In shade: *Bergenia* 'Sunningdale' (E), *Convallaria majalis* (D), *Euonymus fortunei* 'Emerald Gaiety' (E).

BORDER GAPS
In sun: *Geranium* (D/E), *Nepeta* (D), *Berberis thunbergii* (D).
In shade: *Brunnera macrophylla* (D), *Geranium* (D/E), *Hosta* (D), *Pulmonaria saccharata* (E).

UNDER SHRUBS
Alchemilla mollis (D), *Arum italicum* ssp. *italicum* 'Marmoratum', *Bergenia* 'Sunningdale' (E), *Brunnera macrophylla* (D), *Convallaria majalis* (D), *Epimedium perralderianum* (E), *Geranium* (D/E), *Lamium maculatum* (D/E), *Persicaria affinis* (E), *Saxifraga* x *urbium* (E).

UNDER TREES
Cotoneaster dammeri (E), *Euonymus fortunei* 'Emerald Gaiety' (E), *Leucothoe walteri* (E), *Mahonia aquifolium* (E), *Prunus laurocerasus* 'Otto Luyken' (E).

D = deciduous
E = evergreen

Identifying weeds early

Remove annual weeds before they set seed because seeds can stay in the soil for years and may germinate whenever the soil is dug over. Perennial weeds need to be caught early and removed before their root systems have a chance to spread

Removing weeds while they are still at the seedling stage saves time later on, but it can be tempting to leave the seedlings until you can recognise them. Use the following illustrations to help you. Hoeing is the most effective way to get rid of most seedlings, but some weeds set seed quickly or regrow from underground parts, so it is preferable to remove them by hand. Otherwise you'll just spread the problem. A contact weedkiller can be used if a flush of weed seedlings appears, but to reach perennial weeds with tough underground roots use a systemic, glyphosate-based weedkiller.

COMMON ANNUAL WEEDS

Chickweed A low-mat up to 30 cm (12 in) across. Hoe or hand weed to remove stems which can re-root.

Cleavers Hoe in early spring before it seeds in summer. Stems reach several feet and are covered with sticky hairs. Adult plants are difficult to disentangle from other plants.

Groundsel Hoe in dry weather when small. Seeds will germinate throughout the year. Adult weed produces small, yellow, dandelion-like flowers and grows 23-40 cm (9-16 in).

Hairy bittercress Can flower and set seed very quickly so hoe seedlings immediately – from late spring to autumn. Flower spikes reach about 20 cm (8 in) from small leaf rosettes.

Chickweed

Cleavers

Groundsel

Hairy bittercress

Dead nettle, red Hoe seedlings that appear in spring and autumn. Mature plants grow to 45 cm (18 in) and produce red or purple flowers all summer.

Fat hen Hoe seedlings that appear throughout the growing season. Hand weed older plants which have triangular leaves and reach 90 cm (36 in) tall. Seed is long-lived.

Ivy-leaved speedwell Hoe seedlings that appear overwinter starting in October. By April sprawling stems are covered in tiny pale blue flowers. Seed dispersed by ants.

Knotgrass Hoe or hand weed seedlings in spring and early summer. If left, plants will grow to 60 cm (24 in) and flower any time between July and October.

Dead nettle, red

Fat hen

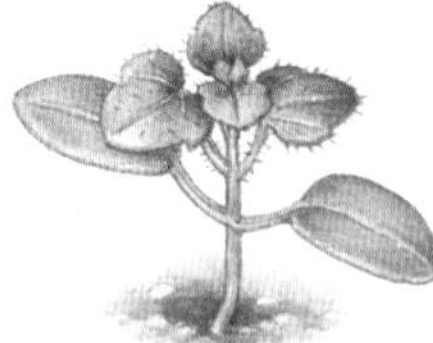

Ivy-leaved speedwell

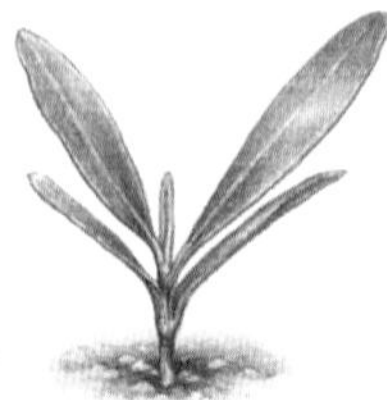

Knotgrass

THREE WAYS TO KILL WEEDS

Between well-established shrubs and trees (not on fruit trees and bushes, though), you can use a chemical weed preventer that inhibits germination of weed seeds *(see column, far right)*. Among other garden plants you are restricted to hoeing, use contact weedkillers and systemic weedkillers. These affect weeds in different ways so are suitable for killing specific weeds.

Contact weedkiller *As it is absorbed by the parts it contacts, thorough wetting is essential. It kills the top growth only. Effective on annual weeds and top growth of perennials.*

Systemic weedkiller *The chemical is transported throughout the plant and kills both top growth and roots. Effective on all actively growing weeds. The best way of killing perennial roots.*

COMMON PERENNIAL WEEDS

Bindweed Hoe often or use a systemic weedkiller in spring before plants climb and wind around other plants. White or pink flowers in summer.

Bindweed

Dandelion Hoe seedlings that appear in April/June. Large plants need to be dug out or killed with a spot weedkiller. Take action before the plant sets seed.

Dandelion

Dock, broad leaved Seedlings appear throughout the growing season. Hoe them or dig them out when they are bigger. Otherwise spot treat with a systemic weedkiller. Older plants can reach up to 90 cm (36 in) tall.

Dock, broad leaved

Greater plantain Hoe out seedlings when they appear in spring and autumn. Flowers in its first year. Plants can reach 30 cm (12 in). Seed is long-lived.

Greater plantain

Couch grass Hoe out seedlings when they appear in summer. Once plants are established use systemic weedkiller. Plants can reach 75 cm (30 in) tall.

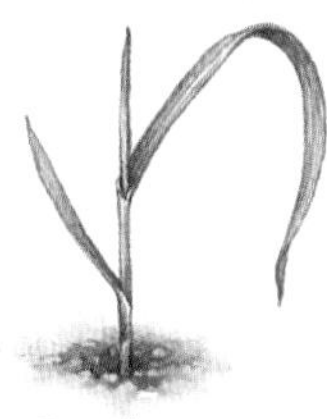

Couch grass

Japanese knotweed A real problem weed once it is established. In the early stages it can be dug out. Use a systemic weedkiller on mature plants. Repeat as necessary.

Japanese knotweed

Creeping buttercup Hoe seedlings from spring to autumn. Once established, dig out by hand, or spot treat with systemic weedkiller.

Creeping buttercup

Stinging nettle Hoe out young seedlings which appear throughout the growing season. Dig out older plants, or spot treat with systemic weedkiller. Leave some to attract wildlife. Seed is long-lived.

Stinging nettle

FIGHTING WEEDS IN DIFFERENT PLACES

Use all weedkillers with care because they will damage any plants they come into contact with.

ON PATHS AND PATIOS
Use an old knife to remove individual weeds or treat with a spot weedkiller. If the problem is widespread apply a path weedkiller, which will kill the weeds and prevent new ones from germinating for a year.

IN A MIXED BORDER
Hand weed or hoe between plants. Dab on a spot treatment or apply a ready-to-use spray based on glyphosate. Protect plants with polythene before spraying, and only remove it when the spray is dry.

BETWEEN SHRUBS
Use mulch matting to control weeds and retain soil moisture. Use a dichlobenil-based weed preventer (not on fruit trees or bushes) to inhibit weed-seed germination where the soil is not disturbed.

ON VACANT GROUND
Hoe, hand weed or apply a weedkiller based on glyphosate. It is deactivated on contact with the soil allowing planting after one or two weeks. Clear neglected plots with sodium chlorate, but you must wait six months before planting.

Beneficial creatures

In the wild, all pests have natural enemies that keep them in check. Encourage these creatures to take up residence in the garden by providing the right sort of habitat and avoiding the use of chemicals that harm them

Working with nature has a lot of benefits for the busy gardener. By handing over the control of garden pests to their natural predators you will save yourself having to tackle the problem. If you adopt this approach, you will rarely need to use sprays. But you must encourage the right mix of wildlife in your garden by providing conditions to suit them. A low level of pests have to be tolerated to provide a food source for the predators.

Ladybirds are commonly known as the 'gardener's friend' because of their appetite for aphids but many insects or their larvae – lacewings, parasitic wasps and hoverflies, for example – also eat vast quantities of aphids. Any nectar producing and pollen-rich plants are useful for attracting predators; *Convolvulus tricolor* and the poached-egg plant (*Limnanthes douglasii*), for example, are good for attracting hoverflies, which eat pollen before laying their eggs among aphid colonies.

Ground beetles feed at night on aphids, the eggs of carrot fly and cabbage root fly, and slugs. Encourage them by providing ground cover to hide in during the day. Use only selective insecticides, such as pirimicarb, and do not use slug pellets containing methiocarb, which is toxic to ground beetles.

Frogs and toads eat slugs and other insects – some of which are beneficial. To encourage them, build a pond with gently sloping sides surrounded by vegetation. The hedgehog's

Biological controls

The introduction of creatures to control pests is being used increasingly in greenhouses. Some biological controls are available for use in the garden too. Fight vine weevil, for example, with tiny worm-like nematodes that are mixed with water and applied with a watering can. The nematodes need warm temperatures to work, so order the control just before you need it. Caterpillars can be controlled by a bacterium called *Bacillus thuringiensis* which is harmless to other creatures. See page 306 for suppliers.

Ground beetles Scurrying, big black beetles that are more often seen at night. Both adults and their larvae are useful predators of slugs, caterpillars and aphids.

Hoverflies A group of true flies that look like bees and wasps. Their greeny brown larvae, 12 mm (½ in) long, feed on aphids and can eat up to 100 a day.

Hedgehogs They eat caterpillars, beetles and slugs at night. If they visit your garden, put out tinned dog food rather than milk. A log pile might provide suitable shelter and a place to hibernate.

Rove beetles This group includes the distinctive looking devil's coach horse beetle. Both adults and their larvae are active predators of soil grubs, insects and slugs.

Ground beetle

Hoverfly

Hedgehog

Devil's coach horse beetle

diet consists of caterpillars, slugs and some beneficial creatures. Hedgehogs are difficult to encourage, but a log pile will provide a suitable place for winter hibernation or you can buy a special hedgehog house. Before lighting a bonfire, it is particularly important to check for overwintering hedgehogs.

Many garden birds eat pests. For example, blue tits eat caterpillars and aphids; starlings prey on grubs; sparrows, great tits and wrens consume insects; while song thrushes eat snails and slugs. They are attracted to gardens on the edges of woodlands and where there is water. If you have a cat, put a bell around its neck so the birds can hear it coming.

Earthworms are perhaps the most beneficial creature to the busy gardener, helping to improve the soil by incorporating organic matter and opening it up with their tunnels. Chemicals were once used to clear lawns of wormcasts, but modern gardeners should just sweep off casts with a broom before mowing. Brandling worms are found in compost heaps where they break down organic material.

New Zealand flatworms, which eat earthworms, have been found in some parts of the UK, and could threaten soil fertility if they become established. They are about 15 cm (6 in) long and very flat, and are found under stones. Squash any you find.

BENEFICIAL CREATURES

Ladybirds A single larva can eat 500 aphids so they are worth encouraging. Two-spot and seven-spot ladybirds are the most common.

Wasps Many solitary wasps are beneficial against aphids and caterpillars. Provide egg-laying sites by drilling 5-10 mm (¼-⅜ in) holes in posts.

Centipedes These fast-moving creatures eat all types of small insects. But do not confuse them with the slower millipedes which feed on plant roots. Centipedes have one pair of legs per body segment.

Earthworms They pull organic matter down into the soil, which saves you having to dig it in. They open up the physical structure of the soil, making it easier for plant roots to establish and provide drainage by making tunnels.

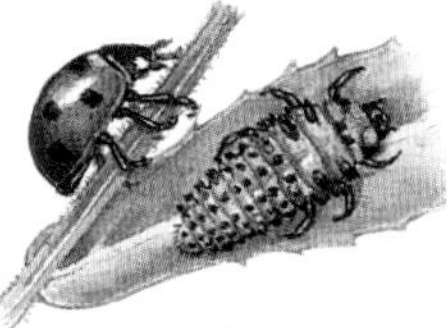

Ladybird and larva

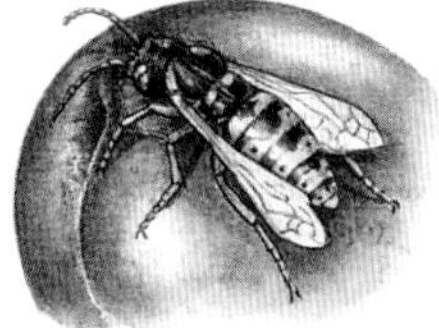

Wasp

Centipede

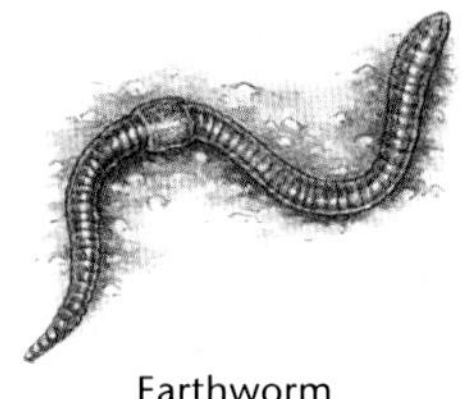

Earthworm

Bats Night feeders of nocturnal insects on the wing. You can encourage them by putting up bat boxes where they can roost. They are under threat, mainly due to the poisonous effects of chemical treatment of roof timbers.

Frogs, toads and newts They prey on slugs, flies and other insects. They need a pond in which to breed (see page 220) and where they will return year after year.

Lacewings Adults are bright green and have large, see-through wings and long antennae. Both adults and their larvae feed on aphids. You can buy chambers to protect them, and lacewing eggs.

Slow-worms These legless lizards up to 30 cm (12 in) long eat the small greyish slugs that feed on the soft growth of young plants and vegetables.

Bat

Newt

Lacewing

Slow-worm

BRINGING BIRDS TO THE GARDEN

The best way to attract birds into the garden is to supply water, feed them in winter and put up nestboxes. You can also encourage them by growing plants with berries and seed heads.

PLANTS WITH BERRIES
Plant any of the following: berberis, cotoneaster, elderberry, honeysuckle, ivy, pyracantha, *Skimmia japonica,* callicarpa, pernettya, viburnum.

PLANTS WITH SEEDS
Seed eaters, including greenfinches and goldfinches, will be attracted by seed-bearing plants such as ornamental grasses and sunflowers.

ATTRACTING INSECTS
Insect-eating birds, such as sparrows and great tits, will come to the garden if you grow nectar-producing plants that attract insects such as alyssum, buddleja, honesty, lavender, nicotiana, sedum, sweet rocket and thyme.

FEEDING BIRDS
Use a commercial wild-bird food or put out scraps of breakfast cereals, flaked oats, dried fruit, bacon rind, cheese, stale cake or cooked potato. But do not put out salty food, dry bread, uncooked rice or desiccated coconut.

Preventing pests and diseases

Avoid problems by choosing disease-resistant varieties, protecting plants with insect-proof mesh and practising good garden hygiene to ensure there is nowhere for pests to hide. Stay vigilant and take action promptly

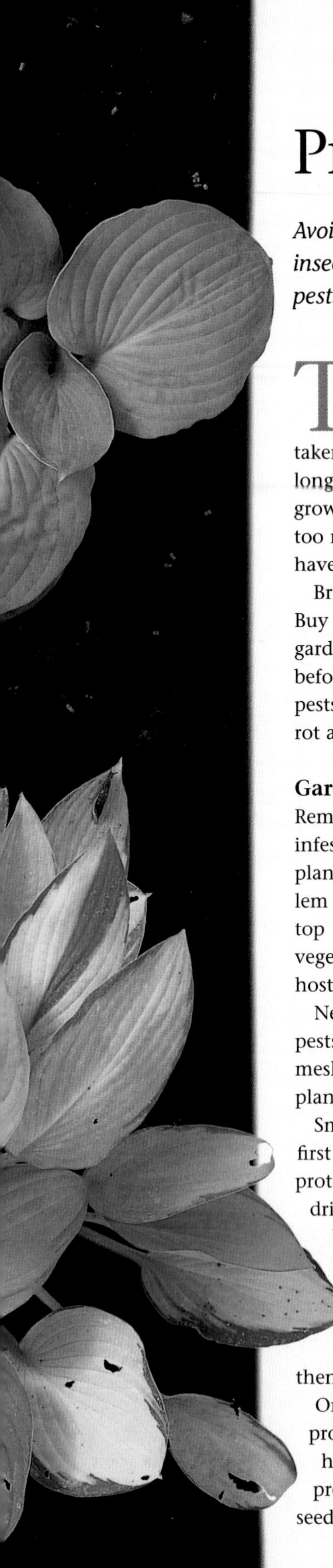

Taking action to prevent pests and diseases is more time-effective than controlling them once they have taken hold. Good garden hygiene will go a long way to avoiding most problems. So will growing a wide diversity of plants, because too much of one type of plant can provide a haven for its predators.

Bring only healthy stock into your garden. Buy from tidy, weed-free nurseries and garden centres. Inspect plants and bulbs before buying them. Check top growth for pests and diseases, and roots in compost for rot and grubs. Bulbs should be firm and dry.

Garden hygiene

Remove the remains of old, rotting or infested plants promptly. Dig up and destroy plants with virus symptoms so that the problem does not spread to other plants. Keep on top of weed control, particularly near the vegetable plot, because weeds often act as a host for pests.

Netting is a useful defence against larger pests, such as rabbits and birds. Insect-proof mesh and garden fleece stop pests reaching plants in the first place.

Small plants are vulnerable to slugs when first planted out. Individual plants can be protected with small bell cloches or plastic drinks bottles cut to size. Slug pellets can be invaluable; sprinkle sparingly around young perennials, bedding plants and vegetable seedlings, so there is a pellet every 7.5 cm (3 in) or so. Do not place pellets in piles because they are then more of a danger to other animals.

Once plant tissues start to rot, secondary problems with fungi and bacteria can take hold. Careful planting and watering can prevent rotting. For example, certain large seeds and some tubers are best planted on their side. Some alpines can be protected from rot with a collar of fine gravel, which allows water to drain away quickly.

Plants growing too close together compete for light, water and nutrients, and cannot grow to their potential. Overcrowding also prevents good air circulation, allowing fungal diseases to take hold. Overcrowded plants are difficult to inspect and care for, so problems can become serious before they are noticed.

Lesions and cuts on plant tissue can provide an entry point for pests and diseases.

Anti-insect compost

Potting compost is available that not only supplies plants with a growing medium and nutrients, but also protects them from pests for up to a year. The compost contains a systemic insecticide which protects the whole plant from pests. Once planted, the plant absorbs the insecticide through its roots and transports it to all parts. If an insect takes a bite or sucks the sap it will be killed. The compost protects plants from caterpillars and vine weevil grubs, and all sap-sucking insects, such as aphids, whitefly and spider mite.

Prevent carrying over diseases by washing pots and seed trays with a garden disinfectant. Rinse them thoroughly and allow to dry before use.

FIRST-AID KIT FOR YOUR PLANTS

You don't need a shed full of chemicals to control most common pests and diseases, but it is worth having a kit of ready-to-use sprays for tackling problems early. Also, keep a magnifying glass, notepad and pencil handy to jot down the name of pests identified, the treatment given and whether it worked, so that you learn as you go along.

1 Insecticides *Choose a good general insecticide based on permethrin or dimethoate that has a 'systemic' action. This means that it will be transported throughout the plant so it doesn't have to be sprayed directly onto the pest. Organic gardeners should use products based on pyrethrum instead.*

2 Slug pellets *If your plants suffer from slug damage every year, prevent attacks by applying slug pellets around susceptible plants before the new leaves emerge in spring.*

3 Fungicides *If you grow roses choose a chemical 'cocktail' that will control rust, mildew and blackspot. If you grow edible crops, check that the product is suitable. Organic gardeners can use fungicides based on copper or sulphur, but they are not so effective.*

4 Aphicides *Aphids are so troublesome that it is worth having a ready-to-use insecticide to control outbreaks when you see them. Choose a selective chemical such as pirimicarb which is harmless to bees, ladybirds and lacewings.*

Take care not to damage plants when hoeing, mowing or using a nylon-line trimmer. Use sharp tools when pruning and make clean cuts just above a bud to prevent die back. Make sure that ties on trees and climbers are secure, but do not cut into the plants.

In the warm conditions inside a greenhouse, young plants are particularly vulnerable to attack by pests and diseases. Raise seeds, young plants and cuttings in clean pots. Use fresh compost and tap water rather than water collected from a water butt because many problems are spread by infected water. While plants growing in the ground or in containers can be watered from stored water in butts, it is important the butt is covered and cleaned out once a year.

Honey fungus

If honey fungus is present in the soil, it can be serious and time-consuming. Golden brown toadstools at the base of an old tree may indicate an infection, but to make sure take a sharp knife and lift up an area of bark near the base of the tree. Look for white, paper-like growths or black growths that look like bootlaces, either under the bark or in the surrounding soil. Early leaf fall from deciduous plants and die-back of branches can also be a sign of fungi. If you suspect a honey-fungus infection in your garden, seek specialist advice (see page 302).

Several garden plants are especially susceptible to honey fungus. These include birch, buddleja, cotoneaster, flowering currant, hop, Lawson cypress, Leyland cypress, lilac, maple, privet, rhododendron, rose, viburnum, willow, most fruit trees and soft fruit bushes. Avoid planting these plants if there has been a honey-fungus infection in your garden. There are also a number of plants thought to show some resistance to honey fungus. These include bamboo, beech, cherry, laurel, holly, juniper, larch and yew.

PEST AND DISEASE WATCH

SPRING

Buy varieties of plants that are resistant to pests and diseases, and keep them growing well. Apply slug pellets. If the winter has been mild, watch out for aphid attacks. If you spot them early, rub out colonies between finger and thumb or apply a ready-to-use spray insecticide. Use a sticky trap to monitor flying insect pests in the greenhouse. Send off for biological controls as soon as pests are seen (see page 306).

SUMMER

Be vigilant. If the weather is warm, pest populations can soar in a few days. Use ready-to-use pesticides at the first sign of attack. Diseases often take hold when plants are overcrowded, so space correctly and ensure good air circulation. Remove and destroy plants suffering from viruses immediately.

AUTUMN & WINTER

Clear fallen leaves showing symptoms of disease. Put up grease bands around fruit trees if winter moths are a problem (see page 251). In the greenhouse, maintain good ventilation to avoid grey mould. Clean greenhouse and equipment with garden disinfectant.

Getting rid of rubbish

Recycling is good for you, your garden and the environment. What is more, it need not be time-consuming if you go about it in a modern way. You can turn most organic garden and kitchen waste into a rich soil improver in just a few months

Making your own compost can be easier than getting rid of garden waste in other ways. If you have a 'working' compost heap, simply adding organic compostable waste is a lot more convenient than bagging it up for the dustbin or taking it down to your local tip.

The decomposition of organic matter in a compost heap depends on bacteria and micro-organisms to break down the material. These require food, moisture and warmth to work efficiently. Buy a big bin if your garden produces enough organic waste material to fill it, because it will keep the material better insulated than a smaller bin. If not, get together with neighbours and share a bin. If you want quick compost you will have to make sure the compost in the bin contains plenty of air, stays warm and does not get too wet and soggy or become dry. This is easier if you add the right mixture of organic matter (see 'making quick compost', opposite).

Sappy green plant debris The season's old bedding plants, debris from cutting back herbaceous plants and vegetable waste are ideal materials for making compost. On the vegetable plot, waste plant material can be buried in a trench while you are clearing up in the autumn and beans can be planted over it the following spring.

Grass cuttings can be left on the lawn to act as a mulch, particularly if you use a mulching mower to chop the cuttings finely. If you prefer not to leave them on the lawn, mix them with the woody materials suggested below so they don't rot into a slimy mess and compost them to use as a mulch.

Woody debris Pruning waste is best shredded to make it manageable. It can then be used as a mulch or in compost (see right).

Weeds The top growth from most weeds as well as the roots of annual weeds are suitable as an ingredient of compost, but avoid weeds in flower or those seeding. Bag up perennial weeds in a black bin liner and leave them for a year. They can then safely be composted.

Fallen leaves Small amounts can be used as an ingredient of quick compost but large volumes are best made into leaf-mould separately because leaves take longer to decompose and they will slow down the compost heap. Composting uses the action of bacteria to break down material, but leaves are broken down by fungi. Because fungi do not need heat, an enclosed compost bin is not needed. To prevent the leaves blowing around, fork them into a simple wire enclosure or a punctured black plastic bin liner. There is no need to mix or turn the material, but water it

Shredders

A shredder is a machine that can turn tree and shrub prunings into wood chips. It reduces the bulk greatly and the result can be used as a mulch or added to the compost bin. Shredders are fairly expensive and bulky pieces of equipment so make sure your garden will generate enough material to get full use out of one. It will need to be stored under cover when not in use. Hiring or sharing with friends might be a better option for small gardens. Brands vary in the speed of their performance and their noise, and some are easier to unclog than others, so try a few out before you buy one.

Making quick compost

To make compost quickly – four months in summer, six months in winter – buy a plastic compost bin to keep the material moist and warm. Add the right ingredients in the right proportions, fill the bin to the top and then leave to rot.

Mix ingredients Combine a variety of materials (see box, right), water lightly if dry and put into the bin. Grass cuttings are best mixed with other material, such as shredded newspaper or wood chips, before adding to the bin because grass cuttings alone will form a solid airless mass that won't rot down.

Compost activator There is no need to add a compost activator or garden soil to provide bacteria. There is enough bacteria on plant debris and roots. You can also help to inoculate the heap using well-rotted compost from the centre of a previous heap.

Reap the rewards The compost is ready to use as a soil improver or mulch when it is dark brown, crumb-like and sweet smelling.

A balanced diet

A compost heap works best if supplied with a balance of soft sappy material, such as grass cuttings, old bedding plants or leafy waste from the vegetable garden or kitchen, together with shredded tougher material such as chopped prunings, shredded newspaper, dead leaves and dry stems of perennials. As a rule of thumb, use two-thirds sappy to one-third tougher waste. Mix well before adding the waste to the heap.

lightly if the leaves are dry. Leave for one to two years then dig the rotted-down material into the soil to improve it. You can speed up the rate of breakdown by adding grass cuttings in spring. Deciduous leaves make the best leaf-mould, particularly beech and oak leaves. Evergreens are best avoided.

Rubbish that cannot be recycled

Not all rubbish will compost or lend itself to recycling in some other way, so you may have to consider a trip to you local tip. However, find out what your local council's arrangements are for garden refuse disposal since some will collect it for a small charge.

Loading waste into your car and queuing at the tip is inconvenient and should be a last resort. If you have to go, try to make the trip during the week because they can be very busy at weekends and bank holidays. Check opening times before you go, especially over bank holidays.

Old chemicals Do not put unwanted chemicals down the drain. Small amounts (less than 150 ml (5 fl oz) can be diluted as per instructions and poured on an unused part of the garden as long as it is away from a water source, such as a pond. Ring your local council for advice on disposing of large quantities of chemicals.

Wood Try to recycle as much sound wood as you can. Use large pieces of timber to build a coldframe, compost bin or other structures. Do not burn wood treated with preservatives because it will give off toxic fumes.

Rubble You can reuse rubble as hardcore for a path or a patio or as part of the foundations for a wall. It can also be used for drainage when you build a raised bed.

Plastic pots If you don't wish to reuse them, a local garden society or charity might be able to make use of them. In theory they can be recycled, but some recycling centres don't take plastic waste.

WHERE TO FIND COMPOST

ANIMAL MANURE
Check out local farms for cow or pig manure. Choose manure with straw rather than sawdust or wood shavings. If the manure is not well composted – a rich brown with little signs of straw, and an earthy smell – allow it to stand for two or three months. Cover the manure with polythene to keep in moisture and to prevent nutrients being washed out. Horse manure can be found at local riding stables, but has a lower nutrient content.

MUSHROOM COMPOST
This is available from mushroom farms and is already composted. It tends to be alkaline, so is ideal for most vegetables, but not suitable for use around acid-loving plants, such as camellias.

HOP MANURE
Small, local breweries often have available spent hops, which make good compost.

USED GROWING BAGS
Tomato growers may sell off used growing bags cheaply at the end of the season.

COUNCIL COMPOST
Green-minded local councils are turning to composting garden waste collected from their areas and selling it as compost.

Raising plants from seed

Growing your own plants from seed is extremely satisfying and allows you to grow unusual varieties that are hard to find at garden centres. Being well organised and using the right techniques and equipment will help you use your time efficiently

An easy and quick way to start off raising plants from seed is to buy packets of annual plants and sow them either in the ground or in pots indoors. Seed packets give full instructions on when and how to sow. The later sowing dates are normally easier because seedlings grow faster when the weather is warmer and the days are longer. Modern varieties can often be sown later than older ones because they mature faster.

Sowing in the ground

If you sow hardy annuals (those that cope with frost) outside where you want them to grow, nature will do most of the work. For the best results, sow when the minimum soil temperature is 7°C (45°F). A sunny site is generally best, but some hardy annuals are shade tolerant. The soil will need to be free of weed seeds, which may germinate and smother the young annuals.

To use a single variety to fill in a gap in an existing border, clear the ground of weeds, rake the soil until it has a fine crumb-like texture, water the ground if it is dry and sprinkle the seed thinly and evenly. Do not mulch this area of the border.

To create a whole bed of hardy annual flowers, select half a dozen or more varieties. Plan which subjects will look attractive

SIX WAYS TO SAVE TIME SOWING SEED

If you decide to raise your own plants from seed there are several ways the busy gardener can save time or avoid wasting it when sowing indoors or out.

Get organised *Make a seed organiser out of a cardboard box sub-divided into months using index cards. Place the seed in the right month for sowing. With seed that is sown several times in succession, salad crops for example, move the seed packet to the next sowing date after sowing. That way you will never forget to sow anything.*

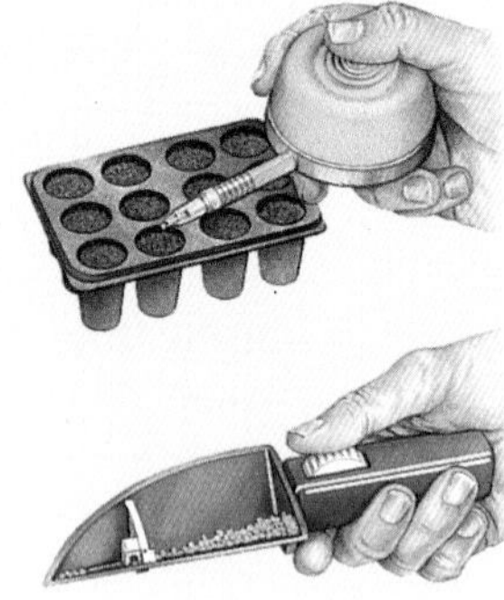

Sow thinly *There are tools to help you sow thinly. The Pro-Seeder has a suction bladder which allows you to pick up and place seeds individually – making spacing exact. The Seedmaster is like a V-shaped trowel with a friction wheel that creates a vibration. The seeds gradually judder to the tip of the trowel and fall off one by one.*

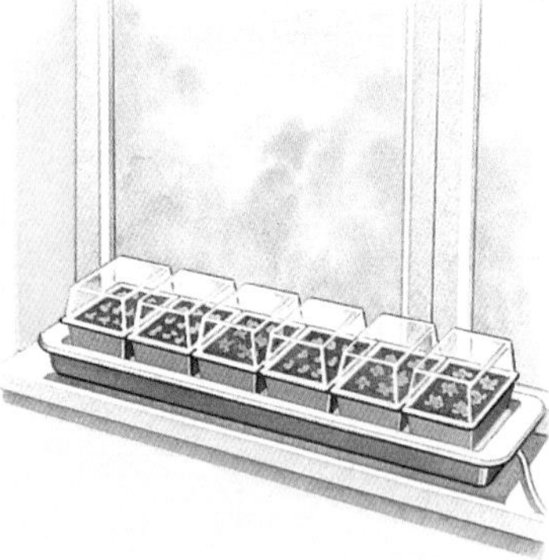

Ideal conditions *It is essential that seeds are given the right conditions if they are going to germinate quickly. A thermostatically controlled windowsill propagator is the most convenient option. For added flexibility, choose one which is large enough to take several half seed trays at once. Choose plastic covers with vents in the lid.*

together taking the final heights and colours into account. Then mark out the planting areas in the soil. To make subsequent weeding easier, sow the seed in short rows within each planting area. Pull out the weakest seedlings, leaving the healthiest and strongest behind spaced at the distance recommended on the seed packet.

Sowing indoors

Annuals that are frost-tender (half-hardy) need to be started off indoors in warmth then planted out after the last frosts have passed. A heated greenhouse is ideal if you want to raise a lot of plants from seed, but a windowsill propagator indoors is an adequate small-scale alternative. These are widely available from garden centres.

Seed packets give germination temperature required, often as a range. For example the temperature for sowing may be 12-18°C (54-64°F). You can grow at the lower temperatures as long as you keep everything clean to prevent disease. The plants will grow slower and will need less watering than at the top temperature. A thermometer that shows both maximum and minimum temperatures is useful for checking the temperature in a propagator. Use clean containers, and fresh compost and labels. Use 9 cm (3½ in) plastic pots or half seed trays. This allows you to try a number of different plants in limited space and reduces the risk of damping-off disease spreading through a whole seed tray. Sow small seeds very thinly on the surface and then cover with vermiculite. For large, single seeds, sow them in modular trays, subdivided into small cells to avoid the need to prick out and so preventing root disturbance.

Use seed compost or multipurpose compost of the current season's stock. Soil-based, peat-based or peat-free types are all suitable for pots and trays. For modular trays, use a peat-based compost, which has fine particles.

Once seedlings appear and their true leaves are present, you will need to prick them out (to avoid doing this, see illustration, below). Hold the leaves and ease the roots out of the pot with a pencil or the point of a plant label. In a tray or pot full of new compost, make a hole with a pencil and plant the seedlings at the distance recommended on the seed packet, firming them gently into place up to their lowest leaves.

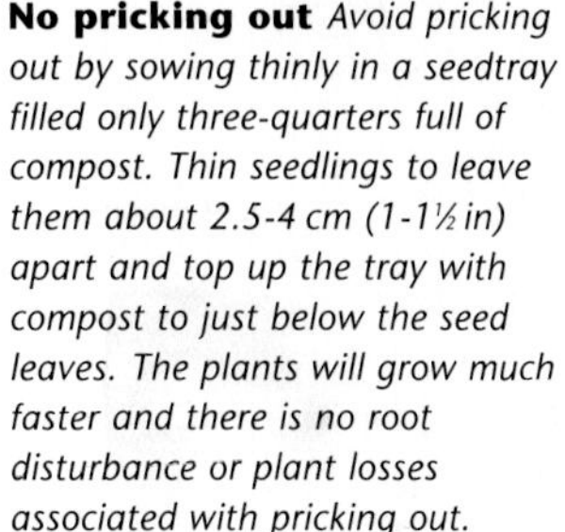

No pricking out *Avoid pricking out by sowing thinly in a seedtray filled only three-quarters full of compost. Thin seedlings to leave them about 2.5-4 cm (1-1½ in) apart and top up the tray with compost to just below the seed leaves. The plants will grow much faster and there is no root disturbance or plant losses associated with pricking out.*

Grow 'instant' plants *Grow quick bedding plants by sowing a pinch of seed in each 7.5 cm (3 in) pot filled with compost. Thin to leave 3-5 seedlings per pot when they are still small but big enough to handle safely. Grow the remaining seedlings on and plant out the whole potful as a clump after the last frost to get 'instant' mature plants.*

Sowing direct outdoors *Make sure the soil is free of weed seeds. Mark out the shape of the drifts with a light-coloured sand or stick. Allocate a plant type to each drift. Within the drifts, use a bamboo cane to make straight, shallow furrows 10 cm (4 in) apart for the seed. If the soil is dry, water it before sowing. Sow seed thinly, cover with soil and firm lightly.*

CALENDAR FOR SOWING INDOORS

MID-MARCH
Bedding: african marigold, antirrhinum (*), *Begonia semperflorens* (*), calceolaria, canna, *Cineraria maritima* (*), dahlia, gazania, lobelia (*), mesembryanthemum, and mimulus.

LATE MARCH
Bedding: ageratum (*), alyssum, cosmos, dianthus, heliotrope, impatiens (*), kochia, lavatera, nemesia, nicotiana, pansy, petunia, *Salvia splendens* and verbena. Vegetables: beetroot, carrot, lettuce and radish. Perennials: achillea, catananche, coreopsis, gaillardia, geum, helenium, lavatera, liatris, lupinus, and lychnis.

APRIL
Bedding: canterbury bell, godetia, French marigold, verbascum and zinnia. Vegetables: courgette, french bean, and runner bean.

MAY
Bedding: *Bellis perennis*, forget-me-not, brompton stock, polyanthus, sweet william, wallflower.

JUNE
Bedding: eryngium, evening primrose, honesty, teasel, and winter pansies.

* = needs light to germinate

New plants from cuttings

Many perennials and shrubs will root readily from cuttings. For the busy gardener who may forget to protect tender plants over winter, taking cuttings in the summer is a good insurance against subsequent losses

Taking cuttings is an easy way to propagate many plants, including perennials and shrubs. But make sure you have the space and time to look after them once rooted (see opposite).

Propagating perennials

In spring, take basal cuttings from perennials where new shoots arise from the base of the plant by pulling them off with some root, or cutting them off close to the ground. Insert into small pots of compost and cover with a polythene bag. Place in a shaded coldframe.

Early summer to late summer provides another opportunity for taking cuttings from perennials. By this time the plant will be producing more top growth, so pinch off young, healthy, non-flowering shoots. Each should be about 10 cm (4 in) long. Strip off the lower leaves to reduce water loss, and insert them into small pots of multi-purpose compost. Cover the pots with a polythene bag and place them in a shaded coldframe.

Shrubs from cuttings

Many shrubs can be propagated easily from softwood cuttings. These are taken using young growth in late spring to summer. Select a healthy young shoot and cut 7.5 cm (3 in) off the tip. Use a sharp knife to remove the lower leaves. Another suitable time is late summer, when the wood is stiffer; hence the name semi-ripe cuttings. Plant both types of cuttings as explained above.

In early autumn, hardwood cuttings can be taken of shrubs. Use secateurs to cut off 23 cm (9 in) long shoots about the thickness of a pencil. Trim each shoot by cutting just below a leaf joint and again just above one 20 cm (8 in) along the stem, so that each cutting has a leaf joint at each end. Deciduous shrubs will have shed their leaves by autumn

Six tips for success

Use healthy material Propagate only from healthy plants and prepare cuttings with sharp, clean tools.

Take extra cuttings Take more cuttings than you need because not all will root.

Use root hormone powder The chances of cuttings taking root is increased, but the powder must be fresh.

Don't let them dry out Cuttings will easily dry out because they have no roots. A polythene bag over a pot provides a humid atmosphere.

Use a fungicide Apply a copper-based fungicide to prevent cuttings from rotting.

Protect from direct sun Put the cuttings in a lightly shaded cloche or coldframe.

Grow your own 'living' garden divider in a single season from extra-long (up to 1.8 m (6 ft)) willow cuttings. Root the living screen in a trough if you want the screen to be mobile – to provide added privacy on the patio, for example. You could even weave the rooted cuttings together to make a more ornamental 'living' fence.

SUCCESSFUL CUTTINGS WITHOUT COMPOST

Cramming cuttings together makes them more difficult to look after because it is harder to see when individual cuttings wilt, and outbreaks of disease are more difficult to control. Use the following methods to improve your chances of success without having to bother with compost.

In water *You can root basal, softwood cuttings successfully without compost by poking the tips of individual cuttings through holes in a polystyrene tile and floating the tile on water. The tile will hold them at just the right depth in the water. Change the water each week for best results.*

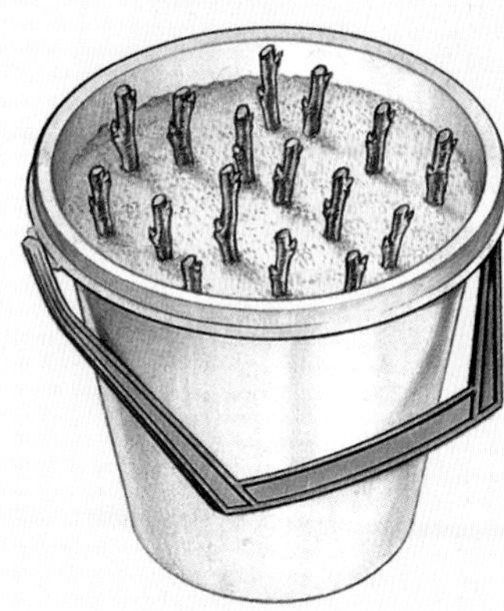

In sand *Hardwood cuttings are easier to root and look after if you push them into an old bucket filled with moist sand. Take 30–45 cm (12–18 in) cuttings and insert individually or in bundles. Keep the bucket in a cool, but frost-free place over winter. Plant out cuttings once rooted.*

but remove all but the top four leaves from evergreens. Insert the cuttings into a trench filled with sharp sand or large pot or bucket outdoors (see above).

Many shrubs that have low-lying stems, such as periwinkle (vinca), naturally produce new roots where their stems touch the ground. Other plants can be encouraged to root this way by lightly scraping a small bit of stem and pegging it into the soil. Leave attached to the parent for six months to two years then use a sharp knife to cut them off from the parent (see page 91).

Aftercare

Create a 'cuttings nursery' by sinking pots of cuttings into a 5-7.5 cm (2-3 in) layer of damp sand covering the base of the coldframe in a shady place. Unroll a sheet of shade fabric over the top and fix down to keep out birds and create more shade. Check the cuttings every week and remove any that are wilting or diseased. Water healthy cuttings with a copper-based fungicide. Rooted cuttings are too small to be planted straight into the garden, so must be potted up individually to grow on into sturdy plants.

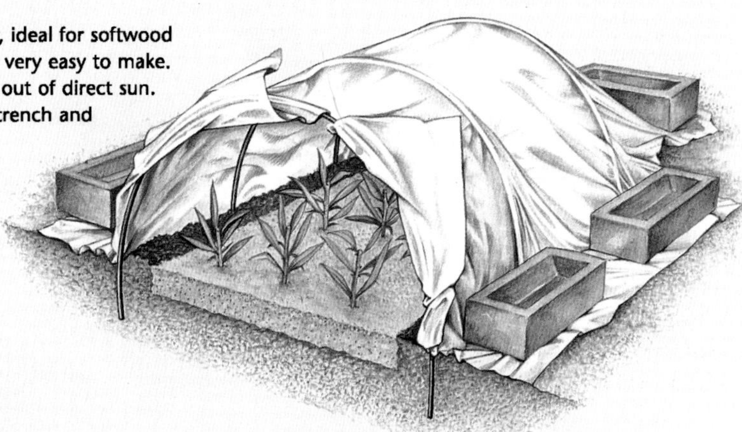

This garden propagator, ideal for softwood or semi-ripe cuttings, is very easy to make. Choose a sheltered site out of direct sun. Dig a 5 cm (2 in) deep trench and fill it with sharp sand. Insert cuttings and water well. Push in wire hoops and cover with white polythene (a large carrier bag is ideal) weighted down at the edges with bricks.

PLANTS TO TAKE CUTTINGS FROM

PERENNIALS

Basal cuttings: achillea, anaphalis, arabis, aster, aubrieta, campanula, centaurea, cheiranthus, chrysanthemum, coreopsis, delphinium, dianthus, diascia, dicentra, euphorbia, gaillardia, *Gentiana asclepiadea*, *Gypsophila paniculata*, *Hesperis matronalis*, heuchera, kniphofia, lupinus, lychnis, lythrum, nepeta, penstemon, persicaria, polygonum, potentilla, pyrethrum, stachys, tiarella, veronica and viola.

For layering: dianthus, tolmiea.

SHRUBS

Softwood cuttings: artemisia, buddleja, callicarpa, callistemon, caryopteris, ceanothus, choisya, chaenomeles, cistus, escallonia, fatsia, forsythia, genista, hebe, helianthemum, hibiscus, hydrangea, lavandula, lavatera, ligustrum, mahonia, philadelphus, potentilla, pyracantha, salvia, skimmia, spiraea, viburnum and weigela.

Semi-ripe cuttings: conifers.

Hardwood cuttings: abelia, berberis, buddleja, buxus, cornus, cotoneaster, deutzia, elaeagnus, escallonia, forsythia, garrya, kerria, ligustrum, olearia, ribes, rosa, skimmia, spirea, viburnum.

Garden Organiser

YOU WILL BE AMAZED BY WHAT CAN BE ACHIEVED IN THE GARDEN IF YOU SET ASIDE SOME TIME FOR PLANNING AHEAD

To get the most enjoyment out of the garden the busy gardener needs to be in control. This means spending what time you have efficiently and being able to step back and plan ahead for the future. The Garden Organiser section of the book will give you a head start by helping you to organise your garden and give priority to the most important tasks, as well as telling you how to save time doing them.

Just like a well-designed kitchen, an efficient garden is one where the working and storage areas are organised so that time is spent completing the task rather than carrying out unnecessary journeys to and fro. This means not only having the right tools for the job, but also keeping them as near as possible to where they are used most frequently.

To be in control, you must know which tasks need doing at specific times and which can be completed at a time when you can fit them in. Use the workload planner on page 288 and the seasonal time-saving tasks listed on the pages that follow to focus on the most important time savers in your garden and to help you to avoid bottlenecks.

Some time-hungry tasks can be made a lot less daunting by buying or hiring specialist equipment. By hiring infrequently used tools, you avoid the initial cost and you don't have to find space for storage or time to carry out routine maintenance. Some garden projects, such as building retaining walls or removing large trees, require specialist skills, while others, such as building a pond, take a lot of time at the outset. In these circumstances, it may be worth hiring a contractor to do the job for you. Don't forget, however, that good contractors will often need booking well in advance (see page 302).

How to save time

Planning ahead and being well organised will save you a lot of time, but it is important to remain flexible so that you can adapt your plans to take into account unexpected events and the vagaries of the weather

The first step to becoming an efficient gardener is to carry out a time-and-motion study of your garden. Anyone who has planned a kitchen will be familiar with organising work and storage areas so that darting around is kept to a minimum. The same principle applies in the garden. Using the illustration (right) as a guide, draw up a plan of your plot; mark on the main features, the tools you use for maintenance and where you store them. As a general rule, store things that are used together in the same place. Then make a rough estimate of how long you spend gardening on each area over the whole year. This will help you to build up a picture of where and how you can save time. One simple strategy that can avoid time-wasting is to pick out all the tools and equipment you need before starting a task and put them in a holdall or wheelbarrow. Then you can start and finish the work with everything you need nearby. Take a rag or scraper with you so you can wipe tools before putting them away.

If you are planning a garden from scratch or want to add a new feature to an existing design, use the chart below to help you to estimate how the feature will affect your existing workload. The chart on page 288 will help you to select garden features which have maintenance needs to fit in with the time you have available throughout the year.

Making plans

Winter is the best time to plan ahead. By reviewing the year's successes and failures you can learn from past mistakes and avoid problems in the future. It is worth remembering that some tasks need to be performed at specific times of the year, but others are flexible. For example, repairing the lawn, clearing perennial beds, planting hardy

How much time? Different elements of a garden take up vastly different amounts of time. This chart compares the time each element takes to maintain each year in an average-sized garden. Once you have decided what elements you want, use the charts on the following pages to plan your workload.

Vegetable plot	100 hours
Greenhouse	80 hours
Lawn	65 hours
Containers	60 hours
Fruit garden	55 hours
Herbaceous borders	35 hours
Mixed borders	20 hours
Pond	20 hours
Wild-flower meadow	15 hours
Ground-cover plants	10 hours
Gravel garden	10 hours
Patio/paving	5 hours

PLANNING WORK AREAS

The most efficient garden is where tools and materials are positioned in the most convenient place. Make sure you have a specific storage area to which tools are always returned and where they can be kept safe and in good condition.

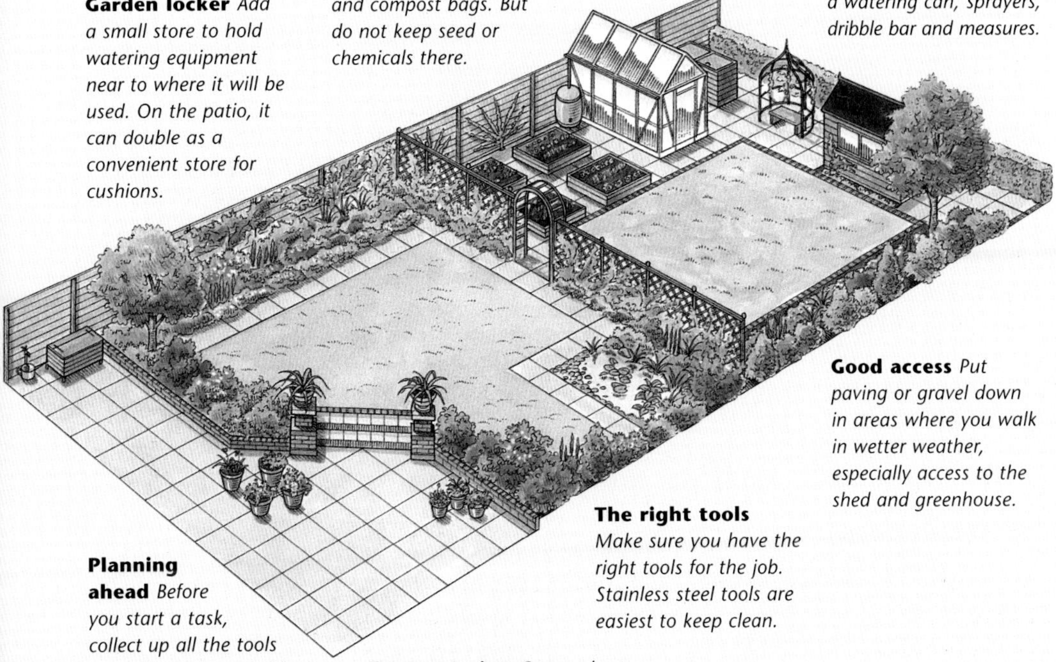

Tidy shed *Add a storage system to the garden shed for tools (see page 299). Keep garden chemicals with a watering can, sprayers, dribble bar and measures.*

Compost bin *Position where access is easy with a wheelbarrow.*

Greenhouse *Keep a tray of labels, pencils, split canes, string, pots and compost bags. But do not keep seed or chemicals there.*

Garden locker *Add a small store to hold watering equipment near to where it will be used. On the patio, it can double as a convenient store for cushions.*

Good access *Put paving or gravel down in areas where you walk in wetter weather, especially access to the shed and greenhouse.*

The right tools *Make sure you have the right tools for the job. Stainless steel tools are easiest to keep clean.*

Planning ahead *Before you start a task, collect up all the tools you will need in a hold all or wheelbarrow to transport to the site.*

Easy watering *Group plants in containers and use hose guides to ease the hosepipe around awkward corners.*

plants, and lifting and dividing hardy perennials can be carried out either in autumn or early spring. Advance planning can help you to decide what jobs to do when, so you can spread the load from one season to another.

A few jobs, such as servicing powered equipment, can be done at any time during the dormant season, from late autumn to early spring. These should be planned in to your gardening schedule like everything else so that they are not continually put off until the spring rush starts with a vengeance.

Taking account of the weather

Each garden has its own microclimates with different temperatures and soil conditions. Through observation and experience, you will discover that even cold, windy gardens offer warm, sheltered pockets. Build this into your planner by, for example, planting up beds that are quicker to warm up in spring, or by adding extra organic matter to improve the soil in the driest beds first.

The weather, as well as the microclimate, varies, so do not garden by the calendar alone. If frost is forecast early in the autumn, bring in tender plants that you want to overwinter and harvest produce likely to suffer frost damage. If late spring frosts are forecast, delay buying and planting out tender plants. Also postpone any outdoor sowing if cold weather is forecast in spring, especially if it is going to be wetter or drier than usual. Instead, raise a few plants in pots under cover and transplant them when the weather is more favourable.

SAVE TIME AT THE GARDEN CENTRE

Shopping for the garden should be one of the most pleasurable activities, but it can also be one of the most frustrating. Use the following tips to keep time-wasting to a minimum.

BULK BUYS

The same garden staples, such as feed, mulches and compost, are used every year. Rather than buying in small amounts throughout the year, save time and money by buying in bulk. Get them at the start of the season, though, because you will have to find sufficient storage space and some items, including compost and fertiliser, are best used within one year of buying. Also keep a stock of sundries, such as string, netting and fleece, to avoid having to go out and buy them later.

PLANTS

Ask when the garden centre receives their deliveries so you can select your plants when stocks are newly arrived and numerous. Make a list of the plants you want before you visit and, if possible, include substitutes in case the garden centre doesn't have the variety you are looking for.

Instant improvements

Even quite simple changes can transform a garden and dramatically reduce the amount of work it takes to maintain it. Use the tips and techniques featured here to improve your garden and help to reduce the workload

Instant mature gardens are prohibitively expensive, but there are several tricks of the trade that can give you quick results at reasonable cost. For maximum impact, concentrate your efforts on specific areas that will benefit most rather than trying to tackle the whole garden at once. Which area you choose may depend on the season. A patio, for example, is best finished before the start of summer, when it will be most used. In the autumn or winter, work may centre on improving the view from a window, with spring colour in mind. Front gardens, or the area by the front door, are good places to start at any time of year. Before you start it is important to spend time thinking about what you want from your garden and the sort of changes that you would like. See page 288 to help you formulate your plans and gardening priorities.

If you have a new garden that has not been planted, you can create the illusion of maturity by including large specimens in your plans. Some nurseries now sell semi-mature trees and shrubs, and will deliver and plant them for you (see opposite). However, do check the access to your garden beforehand. Large specimens are very expensive and may not establish as quickly as a smaller specimen; they also need more aftercare, such as regular watering. If you can afford just one or two mature specimens, choose ones that will have maximum impact on the overall garden design. For example, plants that will make focal points, such as a weeping tree or evergreen topiary. Or plant three smaller trees close together, even in the same planting hole, to form an instant glade. If you want to redesign the whole garden or are planning to make major changes, consider hiring contractors to carry out the bulk of the work (see page 302).

Quick fixes

If routine tasks get neglected because of an unexpected absence from the garden, regain control using the following steps.

Get in trim When the lawn is neat and tidy the whole garden looks better for it, so cut and edge the grass. Also trim fast-growing hedges if they are looking shaggy.

Small weeds When the sun shines, run a hoe roughly up and down between vegetable rows or between bedding plants so that the weeds wilt and die. To prevent a row of seedlings from being swamped by small weeds, use one hand to 'shield' the row and the other to pull out weeds. Weed again once you can see the row of seedlings clearly, thinning the seedlings to the correct spacing as you go.

Big weeds Remove the most obvious, large weeds first, especially those in the most visible areas, such as the front of borders. Also remove those that are flowering or starting to set seed. To tackle tough perennial weeds, such as ground elder, cut off the top growth and remove it. Spot treat regrowth with a glyphosate-based weedkiller.

Improving existing features

Brickwork can often be repointed to give it a new lease of life, paving can be cleaned using a pressure washer and weeds eliminated for a whole season by applying a path weedkiller. Giving your lawn a definite shape can enhance the look of the whole garden and make mowing easier. Mark out your ideas with sand or a garden hose, check the look from an upstairs window, and then use a half-moon cutter or garden spade to cut the turf to its new shape.

When adding new items, keep them in the scale and style of the surroundings. In general, you will save valuable time by keeping displays simple and avoiding clutter.

EASY WAYS TO IMPROVE YOUR GARDEN

Simple ideas are often the best, and this is certainly true of the most effective design improvements. Use or adapt any of the following ideas to turn a dull corner into a seasonal highlight or a year-round focal point.

Plants for paving *Use creeping plants, such as heathers, aubrieta and small grasses, to soften hard landscaping edges. Aromatic plants, such as thyme and camomile, will also perfume the air each time the path is used. By filling the cracks between paving stones with ornamental plants you can effectively prevent weeds getting a foothold.*

Grouping containers *A group of pots of the same plant creates impact and has a unifying effect. Place at the bottom of a flight of wide steps or to highlight a patio corner. Alternatively, group together three identical pots with varied planting schemes but with a common theme, such as colour or style. Grouping also lends itself to easy watering.*

Use wood stains *Brighten up wooden structures, such as fences, sheds, seats, trellis and containers by applying a wood stain. Available in many colours, stains are easy to apply and need less upkeep than paint. For a cohesive design, use only one colour, but use a brighter shade of that colour to highlight a special feature, such as this novel tree seat.*

Architectural and evergreen plants
Eye-catching evergreens, including phormium, yucca, cordyline, clipped box and grasses, give a long season of interest. They make ideal focal points around the garden; for instance, on a patio or at the centre of a garden room. However, you will need to make sure they are sufficiently hardy in your area.

BUYING MATURE TREES AND SHRUBS

PREPARE THE SITE
Preparing the ground for a large specimen is a lot of work because such a large hole needs to be excavated, but only needs doing once. First, clear the ground of weeds and dig over the soil, improving it if necessary. Dig a hole as deep and twice as wide as the plant's rootball. Loosen the soil in the bottom of the hole and add well-rotted organic matter. Then fill the hole with water, and let it seep into the ground.

VISIT THE NURSERY
If possible, visit the nursery so that you can choose a plant with a well-balanced canopy and healthy foliage. Make sure it is hardy.

CHECK DELIVERY
Make sure the nursery can deliver the tree and will help to manoeuvre it into the planting site. Measure the narrowest point of access to the site before you go and note down any obstacles, such as steps.

PLANT IMMEDIATELY
Water and plant the tree or shrub as soon as it arrives, embedding a flexible plastic pipe or cut-off plastic bottle close to the rootball for easy watering. Mulch well. Prevent wind-rock by staking securely and use windbreak netting for shelter. Water well for the first season.

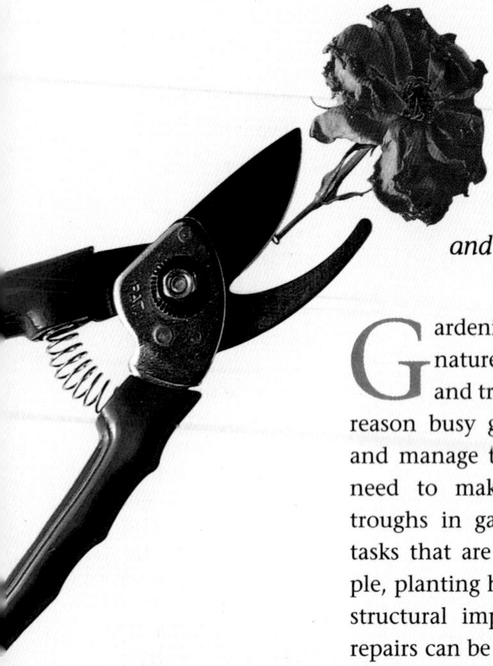

Spreading the workload

To make the most efficient use of time it is essential to spread the workload throughout the year. Use the chart below to help you to choose and to organise your gardening activities to fit in with your time

Gardening is seasonal by its very nature, so there are distinct peaks and troughs in the workload. For this reason busy gardeners need to plan ahead and manage their time very carefully. They need to make maximum use of natural troughs in gardening activity to carry out tasks that are not time-sensitive. For example, planting hardy container plants, making structural improvements and carrying out repairs can be completed at any time of year.

Whether you are planning a new garden or adding features to an existing one, the chart below will help you to select elements so that your time spent gardening is spread out more evenly over the whole year. When planning, the chart will help you to allocate garden space with maintenance time in mind. It can also act as an at-a-glance reminder of which areas of the garden need dealing with in any particular month, so you can organise your activities more effectively.

PLANNING THE WORKLOAD IN YOUR GARDEN

	JANUARY	FEBRUARY	MARCH	APRIL	MAY	JUNE
LAWN	○ ○ ○ ○	○ ○ ○ ○	❶ ❶ ❶ ❶	❷ ❸ ❷ ❸	❷ ❷ ❷ ❷	❷ ❷ ❷ ❷
WILD-FLOWER MEADOW	○ ○ ○ ○	○ ○ ○ ○	❷ ❷ ○ ○	❷ ❷ ● ○	● ● ○ ○	● ● ○ ○
GROUND COVER	○ ○ ○ ○	○ ○ ○ ○	❷ ❷ ❶ ○	● ○ ○ ○	● ○ ○ ○	● ○ ○ ○
PATIO	○ ○ ○ ○	○ ○ ○ ○	❶ ❶ ○ ○	○ ○ ○ ○	● ● ○ ○	○ ○ ○ ○
GRAVEL GARDEN	○ ○ ○ ○	○ ○ ○ ○	● ● ○ ○	❷ ❶ ❶ ●	❶ ❶ ● ●	● ● ○ ○
MIXED BORDERS	○ ○ ○ ○	● ○ ○ ○	● ● ❶ ❷	❷ ❶ ● ○	❶ ○ ○ ○	❶ ❶ ● ○
GREENHOUSE	● ○ ○ ○	❶ ❷ ❶ ○	❷ ❸ ❷ ❸	❸ ❸ ❸ ❸	❸ ❸ ❸ ❸	❷ ❷ ❷ ❷
TRADITIONAL VEGETABLE PLOT	● ○ ○ ○	● ● ❶ ❷	❷ ❷ ❷ ❸	❸ ❸ ❸ ❸	❸ ❸ ❸ ❸	❸ ❸ ❸ ❸
NO-DIG VEGETABLE PLOT	● ○ ○ ○	● ○ ○ ○	❶ ● ❶ ●	❸ ❸ ❸ ❸	❸ ❸ ❸ ❸	❸ ❸ ❸ ❸
FRUIT	● ○ ○ ○	● ○ ○ ○	● ❶ ❷ ❶	❷ ❷ ❷ ❷	❶ ❶ ❶ ❶	❶ ● ❶ ●
CONTAINERS	● ○ ○ ○	● ○ ○ ○	● ❶ ● ○	❶ ❷ ❶ ❷	❸ ❸ ❸ ❸	❷ ❷ ❷ ❷
RAISED BEDS	○ ○ ○ ○	● ● ○ ○	● ● ● ○	● ● ○ ○	● ● ○ ○	● ● ○ ○
CONSERVATORY	● ○ ○ ○	● ● ○ ○	● ● ● ●	● ● ● ●	● ● ● ●	● ● ● ●
POND	● ○ ○ ○	● ● ○ ○	● ● ● ○	❶ ❷ ❶ ❶	❶ ❶ ❶ ❶	❶ ❶ ❶ ❶

The chart is based on average-sized features which have been adapted to take into account time-saving principles. The monthly entries for each area of the garden have four symbols, one for each week of that month. Four solid (●) symbols mean that work is carried out each week of that particular month, while two solid symbols mean that maintenance work only needs to be done once a fortnight. If the symbol has the number one inside, this indicates that maintenance work should take less than an hour to do; the number two shows that the maintenance time will be between one and two hours; and the number three between two and three hours. If there are no symbols, only minimal, if any, maintenance needs to be carried out during that week. You may find it helpful to draw up a chart for your garden based on your own experiences. You will then be able to estimate with confidence how holidays and other events that prevent you from gardening will impact on your activities. Try to set aside time over spring and summer bank holidays, because they fall at peak gardening times and are a useful way of catching up on routine work.

Good planning will also allow you to indulge yourself in the aspects of gardening that you enjoy most. For example, if you have a greenhouse and are keen on raising your own plants from seed and cuttings, but can never find the time to grow the resulting plants on, use the time-saving tips outlined on the following pages to cut down on the chores in the other parts of the garden. You will then be able to spend the bulk of your gardening time enjoying your speciality.

Key - time per week ○ = none ● = a few mins ❶ = less than 1 hr ❷ = 1-2 hrs ❸ = 2-3 hrs

	JULY	AUGUST	SEPTEMBER	OCTOBER	NOVEMBER	DECEMBER
	❷❷❷❷	❷❷❷❷	❷❷❷❷	❷❸❷●	●●○○	●○○○
	●●○○	●●○○	●●○○	❷❷●●	○○○○	○○○○
	●○○○	●○○○	●○○○	❷❷❶●	●○○○	○○○○
	●●○○	○○○○	●●○○	●●○○	●●○○	○○○○
	❶●○○	●●○○	●●○○	❷❶●●	●●○○	●●○○
	❶❶●○	❶❶●○	❶❶●○	●❷❷●	❶●○○	●○○○
	❷❷❷❷	❷❷❷❷	❷❸❷❷	❷❷❸●	●❷●○	●●○○
	❸❸❸❸	❷❸❷❷	❸❸❸❸	❷❷❷❷	❶❶❶❶	❶❶●●
	❸❸❸❸	❷❸❷❷	❷❷❷❷	❶❷❶❷	❶●❶●	●●○○
	❶●❶●	❷❷❷❷	❷❷❷❷	❷❷❷❷	●❶●○	❷❷○○
	❷❷❷❷	❷❷❷❷	❷❷❷❷	❶❶❷❷	❶❶○○	●○○○
	●●○○	●●○○	●●○○	●○○○	●○○○	○○○○
	●●●●	●●●●	●●●●	●●●●	●●○○	●●○○
	●●○○	●❷❶○	●●❷○	●❷●○	●●●○	●○○○

GETTING A HELPING HAND

You can still include time-hungry elements in your garden by getting contractors to carry out routine maintenance.

LAWNS
If you employ a contractor to mow and edge your lawn each week you will also avoid having to buy and store large machinery.

HEDGES
Vigorous hedges may need trimming every six weeks during the growing season. Large hedges also require special equipment. Contractors will get rid of prunings too.

BEDS AND BORDERS
Get them to blitz mulching and weeding tasks in spring.

CONTAINERS
Specialists and some garden centres will plan planting schemes and plant up containers for spring, summer and autumn displays.

PRUNING
Use experts to carry out specialist pruning of shrubs, fruit trees and bushes.

GENERAL REPAIRS
Use a contractor for routine maintenance of wooden structures and walls as well as for sweeping up leaves, and clearing ditches and ponds in autumn.

Saving time in spring

As the garden comes to life again after winter, many key time-saving tasks such as mulching and weeding need to be carried out. Bad weather can postpone planting out and sowing

With the first mild spell in spring, it is tempting to rush out and fill up with new plants. This could be a waste of time and money because the weather at this time can be very changeable, and a cold, sodden soil or a late frost can kill or set back new plants. So, in the first half of the spring, concentrate on maintaining the planting and features already in the garden, and get the soil in prime condition to receive new plants. Weeding (see column opposite) and mulching (see page 264) save time all round the garden, so are not individually mentioned under each heading below. Once

KEY SPRING TIME-SAVERS AROUND THE GARDEN

CLIMBERS AND BOUNDARY PLANTS

Hedge care Shape formal hedges with tapering sides to make the hedge stronger. Lowering the height of a hedge can save time at every cutting. Apply a growth regulator to existing hedges to restrict growth.

Buy plants Before buying plants, research the pruning and training that will be required. Match the vigour of the plant to the area to be covered to save having to prune to keep within bounds.

New climbers Choose climbers that need no regular training – either those that are self-clinging or that need no tying in to trellis or wires.
Pair together climbers that have the same pruning requirements so that they can be dealt with as one.

FLOWER BORDERS

Quick cover Instead of lifting bulbs, such as daffodils or tulips, after flowering, plant day lilies behind them to cover up unattractive, dying foliage.

Add instant colour To brighten up dull borders, buy and plant bulbs in pots or hardy polyanthus that are just coming into flower.

New plants When buying plants, avoid those that need staking or are over-vigorous for the site.

Gap fillers Use large, empty ornamental pots to fill gaps within established borders – the impact created will need much less maintenance than if plants were added.

Scatter slug pellets Protect new plantings from slugs: slug pellets are the quickest control.

FRUIT GARDEN

Prevent problems Set traps for codling moths in apple trees in late spring. Inspect bushes and trees regularly for pests and diseases, and treat promptly. Destroy plants with viral symptoms immediately.

Protect fruit Cover with netting to protect against birds. For greatest time-saving, put up a walk-in fruit cage for year-round protection as well as some shelter.

Prevent weeds Apply dichlobenil granules around the edge of a fruit cage to prevent weeds growing and tangling with the net.

Paths Invest in all-weather paths around the fruit garden that are easy to keep weed-free.

CONSERVATORY AND GREENHOUSE

Shading Apply a wash on the outside of the greenhouse using a roller. Blinds look better in conservatories; if they are too costly, use muslin with loops sewn in the corners and attach to hooks in the window frame.

Watering Set up automatic watering systems. Push slow-release fertiliser plugs into pot plants to feed for a whole season.

Temperature Buy a large outdoor thermometer that you can see easily from the house to check the temperature. A frost alarm is also useful.

New plants If your conservatory is heated in winter, reduce bills by choosing Mediterranean plant types which survive at 6° C (43° F).

LAWN

Clear lawn Before mowing, remove stones. Also sweep off worm casts, otherwise the mower will smear them and they will become colonised by weeds.

Start mowing In mild, dry weather, give the lawn the first cut. Set the blades at their maximum height for the first couple of cuts. Reduce cutting height to 4 cm (1½ in) thereafter.

Lawn treatments Moss starts to grow before weeds, so first apply a moss killer and then a weedkiller when other weeds begin to grow, except on lawns with wild flowers or bulbs.

Trim meadows Cut summer-flowering wild-flower lawns with a nylon-line trimmer in early spring.

weeds have been cleared, aim to have mulches in place by the end of March, because this is when the soil temperature rises and the next crop of weed seedlings starts to germinate.

Avoid walking and dragging heavy equipment over lawn and borders when the ground is wet because you will ruin the soil structure, making it harder for plant roots to penetrate. So give priority to lawns, borders, vegetable and fruit plots when the ground is drier. During wet weather work on the patio or in the greenhouse (a rainy day is also a good time to visit the garden centre because it will be less crowded).

Raising or buying tender plants starts this season, but don't be in too much of a hurry because the sooner you start the longer you will have to look after them before planting out. Pruning trees, shrubs and climbers is easier to do at this time of year because there aren't other plants in the way. Plant hardy plants now rather than in summer because they will need less watering.

Once the grass starts growing and the ground is not soaking wet, set time aside for spring lawn care. Even if it's just a first cut and a weed and feed it will pay dividends all through the summer. Lawn repairs often produce the quickest results in spring.

PATIOS AND CONTAINERS

Make plans Plan your planting schemes and send for mail-order plants early to avoid disappointment.

Tidy up Clean the patio before the area becomes too crowded with pots, plants and furniture. For effective cleaning, use a pressure washer.

Prepare containers Line porous containers with polythene to reduce water loss. Use slow-release fertiliser and moisture-retaining crystals to save time feeding and watering later on. Plan and erect automatic irrigation systems for hanging baskets and pots.

Position pots Put out planted summer containers after the last frosts. Try to use fewer but larger pots to save time watering later.

SHRUBS, TREES AND ROSES

Feed borders Apply a fertiliser to borders in April.

Prune Most pruning takes place in this season (see page 88 for shrubs, and page 104 for roses).

Inspect plants Cut out dead, diseased or damaged wood with clean, sharp secateurs. If a shrub appears dead after a cold winter, wait until July before digging it up because shrubs often shoot up from the base later on.

Planting Evergreens and deciduous shrubs not planted in autumn can go in now. Water all new plants until they are established.

Trim heathers For speed, use shears rather than secateurs to deadhead winter-flowering heathers.

VEGETABLE BEDS

Prepare the soil Before planting, use cloches or sheets of black polythene to warm the soil.

Plant Use a soil thermometer as a guide to planting time rather than going by the time of the month. For seeds, sow a short row each week rather than a single early sowing.

Late frost If a late frost is forecast delaying planting out, liquid feed young plants raised in pots to prevent them becoming potbound. Cover plants already planted with a double layer of fleece at night, secure edges well down, but remove the fleece during the day to prevent overheating.

Prevent problems Check regularly for pests and diseases. Treat promptly if necessary.

WATER GARDENING

Add pump Replace pool heater with submersible pond pump.

Marginal plants Lift and divide any marginal plants that are getting too big.

New plants Add any replacement floating and submerged aquatics needed, because they are important for keeping down algae and the nitrogen level.

Plant Add new marginal and deep-water plants to the pool using special pond compost with slow-release fertiliser and special planting baskets. Cover compost with a layer of gravel to prevent it muddying the water and to stop fish from dislodging your plants.

TOP SPRING TIME-SAVER: WEEDING

STAYING ON TOP

It is essential to keep on top of weeding, even if you have time for nothing else. The old adage, 'one year's seed means seven years' weed' paints a very accurate picture of what happens if you let weeds flower and seed themselves into the soil.

KILLING WEEDS

Clear away existing weeds before they flower to stop them spreading by seed. Spot treat established perennial weeds or use a ready-to-use spray based on glyphosate. On vacant ground, clear all weeds with a total weedkiller based on glyphosate or burn off annual weeds with a flame gun. Kill weeds growing between slabs and in gravel with a path weedkiller.

PREVENTION

Prevent further flushes of weed seeds from germinating by applying a 5-8 cm (2-3 in) loose organic mulch of bark chippings or cocoa shells over beds and borders. Apply a chemical weed preventer based on dichlobenil between established shrubs and trees. Apply a path weedkiller on gravel paths and between paving slabs to prevent new weed seeds germinating.

Saving time in summer

Early summer is a busy time for those who like to find a place in their garden for summer bedding and vegetables. But there are ways to cut down the workload. As the season advances, the number of essential tasks diminishes

Once all danger of frost has passed in early summer, the main job is to plant out tender plants. However, it is still important to keep on top of routine tasks, such as watering and weeding.

Lawn mowing will make demands on time, as will hedge trimming, unless you bring in an outside contractor. Climbers will need tying in regularly to prevent unruly tangles later on, and taller perennials will need to be staked. Prune climbing and rambler roses after flowering to keep them tidy.

Bedding and repeat-flowering perennials, especially those in containers, need to be fed

KEY SUMMER TIME-SAVERS AROUND THE GARDEN

CLIMBERS AND BOUNDARY PLANTS

Train climbers Tie in new growth to prevent severe tangles later on. For climbing roses, tie in horizontally to encourage flowering.

Deadhead Remove faded flowers from climbing and rambler roses, and pull out suckers.

Prune climbers Prune early flowering types soon after flowering if necessary by long deadheading or by clipping back.

Trim hedges Cut back hedges to keep them manageable, reducing the height of unruly ones in several stages (see page 169). Consider investing in a movable aluminium platform or a special ladder support to make hedge timming quicker.

FLOWER BORDERS

Cut back Shear off self-seeders such as alchemilla and geranium (cranesbill) after flowering to prevent unwanted seedlings and to encourage new leaves.

Cover up Plant colourful aubrieta, pansies and double daisies to hide fading spring bulbs.

Fill gaps Use summer bedding, tender perennials and easy-to-grow annuals, such as cosmos, nigella and pot marigold.

Instant colour Buy potted lilies in bud and plant them in the border for quick colour and fragrance. Stagger purchases for a succession of blooms.

Deadhead Remove fading flowers regularly. Use shears to trim back massed displays.

FRUIT GARDEN

Water To save time, water only those plants that need it most, for example, those with fruit starting to swell.

Stay vigilant Watch out for pests and diseases, and treat outbreaks promptly.

Protect Cover strawberries with netting as they come into fruit to protect them from birds.

Harvest Pick fruit little and often. Strawberry plants should be fed after harvesting.

Tie in New canes of blackberries and hybrid berries need tying back in June. In July, tie in raspberries and cut out ones that have fruited.

Prune Cut back new growth to five leaves of cordon-trained apples, gooseberries, and red and white currants.

CONSERVATORY AND GREENHOUSE

Permanent plants Top-dress or pot on permanent plants. Add a slow-release fertiliser to cut down on time spent feeding.

After last frost Place outside conservatory plants, such as acacia, albizia and jacaranda, to lend an exotic touch and to save on having to plant bedding.

Clean conservatory Take advantage of the plants' summer outing to give the conservatory a thorough clean.

Stay cool Keep the greenhouse and conservatory cool by shading and ventilation. If practical, dampen greenhouse floors to keep humidity high.

Pest alert Watch out for pest and disease outbreaks, and tackle them promptly.

LAWNS

Trim lawns Mow and edge lawns as necessary, usually once a week. Use a powered edger or nylon-line trimmer to save time.

Don't water There's no need to water the lawn, even in a drought, because the grass will recover when the rain arrives.

Long grass A lawn that has been left uncut for too long, perhaps because you have been away on holiday, will need to have its first cut with the blades set high. Reduce the blade height gradually over the next few cuts, otherwise the lawn will turn brown.

Quick edging Edges of rough grassy areas can be 'knocked back' using a carefully directed narrow spray of contact weedkiller to kill the grass.

throughout summer with a liquid feed and deadheaded regularly to ensure a longer flowering period. But, in general, the tasks diminish as summer advances. The amount of weeding, for example, should be less because mulches and the developing cover of foliage stop weed seeds from germinating.

The amount of work in late summer will depend on the nature of the growing season. After a long, dry summer, many plants look past their best, and you may decide to cut your losses on temporary fillers, such as summer bedding, by stopping watering and getting rid of them. In other years, flowering can last until the first frosts, with plants needing no care apart from a liquid feed to extend their period of bloom. If you want to keep tender plants, such as penstemons and tender fuchsias, for the next season, it is often easier to take cuttings now and overwinter them under cover.

In early summer in the kitchen garden, water fruiting plants as their fruits start to swell and place netting over fruit to protect against raiding birds. Towards the end of summer, harvesting is likely to reach its peak. Also remember to prune trained forms of tree fruit and to plant strawberries. After picking, dry onions and squashes in the sun before storing, but make sure they don't get wet.

PATIOS AND CONTAINERS

Watering systems Check and adjust automatic watering systems so that each container receives the right amount of water. Extend the system to include new pots.

Plant Set out summer bedding once the risk of frost is over. Pot up any left-over plants and use to fill gaps in the borders.

More flowers Deadhead and feed annuals and repeat-flowering perennials regularly to prolong the flowering season.

Prevent problems Look out for signs of pests and diseases, and take remedial action.

Mulch Use pebbles or grit to cover the surface of containers to reduce water loss and show off the plants.

SHRUBS, ROSES AND TREES

Deadhead From early summer remove dead flowerheads of roses and other flowering shrubs. For shrub roses, remove 15 cm (6 in) of stem with the old flowerheads, cutting just above a leaf joint.

Prune In July, cut back overlong shoots of shrub roses to keep growth tidy, and sprinkle a high-potash feed on all roses to promote flowering the following year. Pull out any rose suckers as near as possible to the base of the parent plant.

Kill weeds Apply a glyphosate-based weedkiller around the base of shrubs once or twice during the growing season.

Cut out Remove green shoots on any variegated plants promptly.

VEGETABLE BEDS

Harvest Pick crops as necessary, especially vegetables, such as runner beans, that need regular harvesting to keep up production.

Water Concentrate your efforts on leaf crops, fruiting crops, such as beans and courgettes, and tomatoes when in flower and when the fruit is swelling. To make watering easier, install seep hoses fitted to a water timer.

Stay vigilant Keep an eye open for pests and diseases. Treat outbreaks promptly.

Store After harvesting, dry onions and squashes in the sun before storing. In wet weather, cover them with a cloche, keeping the ends open to encourage air flow.

WATER GARDENING

Tidy up Deadhead plants as necessary in early summer. Look out for pests and diseases.

Displays If a patio pool looks stark, arrange groups of plants in pots in front of it. Put in upright and trailing plants, so they appear to be an extension of the pond planting.

Top up In hot weather, the pond will need topping up to compensate for water lost by evaporation.

Hot weather If fish gulp at the surface for air, use a hosepipe to aerate the water.

Blanket weed Scoop out blanket weed by twisting it round a bamboo cane. Leave next to the pond to give pond creatures time to return to the water, then put it on the compost heap.

TOP SUMMER TIME-SAVER: WATERING

PRIORITISING

Most gardens don't need a lot of watering once established, but new plants, those grown in containers and under cover, will need to be kept well watered if they are to survive.

NEW PLANTS

If planted in late spring or summer, new additions need watering right through the first growing season. In a drought, newly planted trees and shrubs may need watering during the second summer, too. Make watering easier by pushing hose guides into the ground.

POTS AND BASKETS

Plants grown in hanging baskets may require watering twice a day in summer. If you have a lot of pots, group them together and set up an automatic watering system (see page 188). Individual pots could be moved into semi-shade or stood on bare earth and allowed to root through to reduce the need for watering.

GREENHOUSE

Capillary matting or gravity-fed drip systems can be set up to water container plants automatically. Seep hose is best for plants growing in the border soil.

Autumn and winter tasks

As the growing season draws to a close, time needs to be set aside to clean and tidy the garden. The weather is often good at this time of year, providing an opportunity to start a new feature or the right conditions for adding hardy plants

Summer activity in the garden begins to wane, giving time to assess gardening achievements through the year and to re-establish order. Well-rotted material can be emptied from compost bins and spread as a mulch on borders and the vegetable plot to improve soil condition and structure. Refill the bins with the faded growth of summer bedding and herbaceous plants.

Check that fences, arches and other structures are secure and in good repair as windy weather can strike over autumn and winter. Fallen leaves need to be removed from the lawn, walkways and ponds. Rake lawns

KEY AUTUMN AND WINTER TIME-SAVERS AROUND THE GARDEN

CLIMBERS

Natural mulch Fallen leaves can be left to act as a mulch unless plants have suffered from a fungal disease.

Rampant roses Apart from very vigorous varieties, rejuvenate overgrown ramblers in winter by cutting back to 1.2 m (4 ft).

Prune In February, cut back clematis that need pruning to ground level. Trim wall-trained pyracantha with shears in February in order to keep narrow.

Trellis When putting up trellis against a wall, leave a gap for air to circulate behind it to reduce the incidence of diseases.

Maintenance Use a paint sprayer to apply preservative to areas of fence. Otherwise use a large brush.

FLOWER BORDERS

Lift and divide Tougher, overgrown perennials can be lifted and split in September or early October.

Winter protection Tender plants should be moved inside before the first frost. However, in mild spots with well-drained soil, dahlia tubers and gladiolus corms can be left in the ground with a 5 cm (2 in) covering of bark chippings. In other areas, dig them up, dry them off and store in a frost-free place to replant the following spring.

Mulching Semi-tender plants such as hardy fuchsias and phygelius should also be protected by a 15 cm (6 in) thick layer of organic mulch, such as bark chippings, to insulate the crowns.

FRUIT GARDEN

Collect windfalls Use a garden vacuum to collect fallen fruit and pick up diseased leaves of fruit trees. This will prevent fungal spores overwintering on them.

Harvest Pick and store apples. Attach sticky grease bands to trees to prevent pests climbing up.

Prune Prune apple and pear trees. Cut down canes of autumn-fruiting raspberries in February.

Plant New trees, bushes and cane fruits can be planted in prepared ground in late autumn.

Prevent problems Apply a winter wash to dormant fruit bushes and trees where pests have been a problem during the growing season. This will kill overwintering pests.

CONSERVATORY AND GREENHOUSE

Clean greenhouse Prevent the carry over of pest and disease problems by cleaning the greenhouse thoroughly (see opposite).

Protection Before the first frosts, bring in any indoor or tender plants that have spent the summer outside.

Prune Cut back long shoots of shrubs and climbers after flowering.

Cold snap If there is a danger of temperatures dropping below the 6°C (43°F) that Mediterranean plants tolerate, keep plants nearly dry to prevent roots from freezing and cover them with fleece at night, taking it off during the day to prevent overheating.

LAWN

Trim Keep mowing as necessary, with mower blades slightly raised.

Improve Aerate compacted ground with a powered spiker. Use a powered rake to take up dead stems and moss. To combat moss, brush in two buckets of sharp sand per square metre every few years. Apply autumn lawn feed on well-used areas.

Bare patches Reseed bare lawn areas at the beginning of autumn. Lay turf at any time, provided the soil is not frozen or waterlogged.

Clear leaves Use a powered leaf blower or garden vacuum.

Spring colour Plant bulbs in autumn, in drifts or under trees.

Wild flowers Cut meadows once plants have shed their seed.

before winter to remove 'thatch' – the mat of dead vegetative fibre that builds up naturally.

Autumn is a good time to sow new lawns, lay turf, or carry out lawn renovation work, such as reshaping or repairing edges. This gives the grass a chance to establish itself before the following summer.

While the soil is warm and moist in September and early October, plant hardy perennials, shrubs and trees. This is a better planting time than spring, when new plants need extra water to become established: in winter they need watering only if the weather is dry, although evergreens may need protecting with a windbreak.

Hardy perennials can be lifted and divided, if soil conditions allow. Tender perennials, such as pelargoniums, tender fuchsias and verbena, need to be brought in under cover if cuttings have not already been taken. Semi-tender plants will survive the winter if they are protected by a mulch of straw or bark chippings (see right).

Containers full of summer bedding can be emptied, cleaned and put away. Those containing permanent plantings may need shifting to a more sheltered spot to prevent the rootballs becoming frozen in cold weather. Plant up containers and borders near the house with winter bedding and spring bulbs.

PATIOS AND CONTAINERS

Clear rubbish Compost faded summer bedding plants.

Protection Move tender perennials under cover, keeping them frost free. Shift containers to a more sheltered spot or under cover to prevent the rootballs becoming frozen in wet weather.

Winter colour Plant containers, especially those near the house, with hardy plants, such as ornamental cabbages and winter pansies, that will give winter colour.

Plant spring bulbs Plant as soon as you buy them, apart from tulips and hyacinths, which are liable to rot if planted earlier than late October.

Clear fallen leaves For speed use a garden vacuum.

SHRUBS, ROSES AND TREES

Clear fallen leaves If roses have suffered from a fungal attack (see right), give priority to areas around them.

New plants Plant deciduous trees and shrubs. Evergreens can also be planted in early autumn, but in exposed areas they are best left until late spring.

Prune Cut out any damaged branches and prune back branches that overhang paths.

Plant out Bare-root specimens, such as roses, can be planted out between November and March.

Tidy up Make sure borders are weed-free before spring. Apply a glyphosate weedkiller to perennial weeds to reduce problems the following spring.

VEGETABLE BEDS

Longer season Cover late crops, such as lettuce and french beans, with cloches to extend their season.

Harvest Frost-tender vegetables, such as beans, courgettes and tomatoes, need to be harvested before the first frosts. As crops finish, dig over the ground adding well-rotted organic matter.

Clear up Remove plant debris, such as leaves, from plots so that pests and diseases have no places to overwinter.

Order seed Place orders for next season's vegetable seeds and plug plants.

Easy storage Crops such as beetroot can be covered with earth (earthed up) and in a well-drained soil will keep in the ground over winter.

WATER GARDENING

Before leaf fall Net the pond to prevent leaves falling in or erect a temporary fence of fine mesh netting 60 cm (24 in) high around the pond. Clear away leaves as they accumulate.

Tidy up Remove dead vegetation that could rot in the pond. Feed fish with a high protein diet to build them up for the winter. Do not feed them in winter.

Prevent damage Replace the pump with a pool heater, or float a ball on the pool to protect the liner from damage.
When the pond freezes, stand a pan of hot water on the ice to melt a hole and release accumulated noxious gases that may otherwise build up and kill the fish.

TOP AUTUMN TIME-SAVER: CLEANING UP

LESS RUBBISH

A tidy garden offers a number of advantages to the busy gardener. Besides keeping the garden looking good, there is less chance of rogue weeds growing to maturity and setting seed. Debris around the garden is also a good hiding place for pests such as slugs, and many diseases spread to new spring growth from infected leaves left on the ground over the winter.

GREENHOUSE

On a mild, breezy day, remove any remaining plants from the greenhouse. Use a garden disinfectant to scrub down the greenhouse structure, paths and staging. Also clean pots, trays and equipment to prevent carry-over of diseases to the next season.

SHRUB BORDERS

Clear up any leaves that have shown signs of fungal infection, especially around susceptible plants, such as roses. Elsewhere the leaves can be left to form a useful mulch.

PERENNIALS

Cut back perennials as the foliage starts to brown. Leave statuesque plants, such as globe thistle, for winter decoration.

Helpful hints for holidays

If you go on holiday in summer, it is perfectly possible to return to a beautiful garden – all it takes is organisation. Sadly, though, garden security has become an issue for all the year, not just while you are away

Before going on holiday allow time to organise your garden. Make a checklist of things to do. Friends and neighbours may be willing to help with watering and other simple tasks, but you cannot expect them to do more laborious chores, such as weeding. If you have set up an automatic watering system, make sure that it is working properly and that the helper understands where everything is and how it works.

You may decide to hire a jobbing gardener to do general tasks, such as mowing the lawn and clipping the hedges. Or you could consider a housesitter to look after the house, pets and plants (see page 302).

To make watering as easy as possible, reduce your collection of containers to those with permanent plants, and temporary plants that will still have a good display on your return. Fading bedding plants should be put in the compost bin. If practical, group the containers together in light shade in order to reduce the frequency of watering. Remove all open flowers from healthy bedding plants so they produce a flush of new blooms on your return. Feed with liquid fertiliser, but do not be tempted to give any extra feed – follow the instructions on the packet. Cover containers and bedding plants with greenhouse shade netting to reduce water loss through transpiration – but not in the front garden, because it will act as a message to passers-by that you are away from your home.

Encourage the people who are keeping an eye on your home to help themselves to crops that need regular picking, such as beans and courgettes, so that the plants will still be cropping well when you get home.

On your return, if the grass is long, do not cut it short immediately, otherwise it will turn yellowy brown. Instead, raise the mower's blades for the first cut and gradually lower them over the next two or three. If the garden has become unkempt while you were away and needs urgent treatment, see page 286 for the quickest way to regain control.

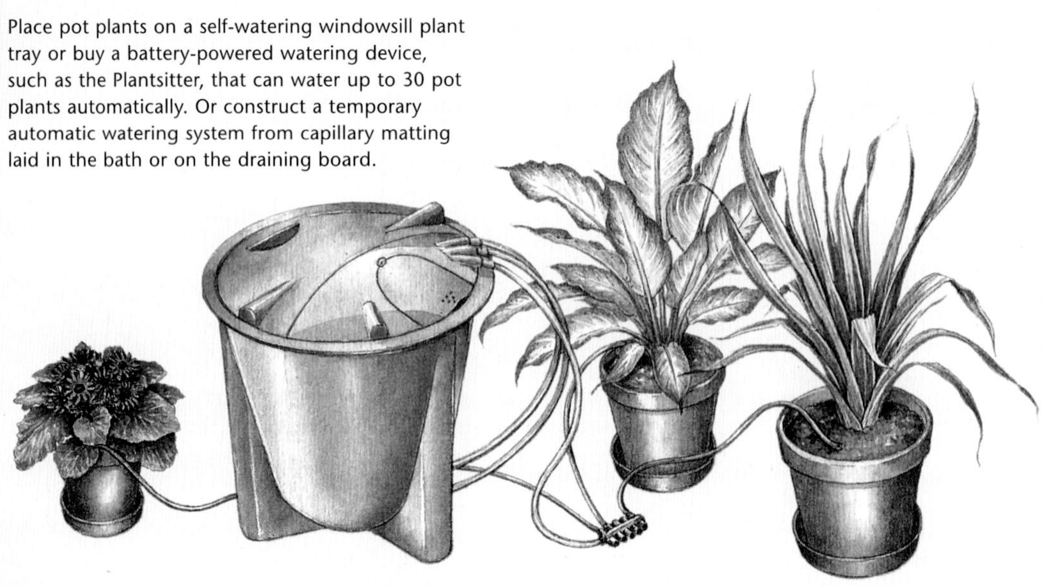

Place pot plants on a self-watering windowsill plant tray or buy a battery-powered watering device, such as the Plantsitter, that can water up to 30 pot plants automatically. Or construct a temporary automatic watering system from capillary matting laid in the bath or on the draining board.

SECURING YOUR ASSETS

Valuable items in the garden, such as garden furniture and statues, can be protected with a wide range of security devices. Before planting up, secure valuable containers to paving using expansion bolts.

Secure baskets *Use baskets that can be locked onto their brackets in order to protect wall-mounted planting displays in susceptible places, such as the front garden.*

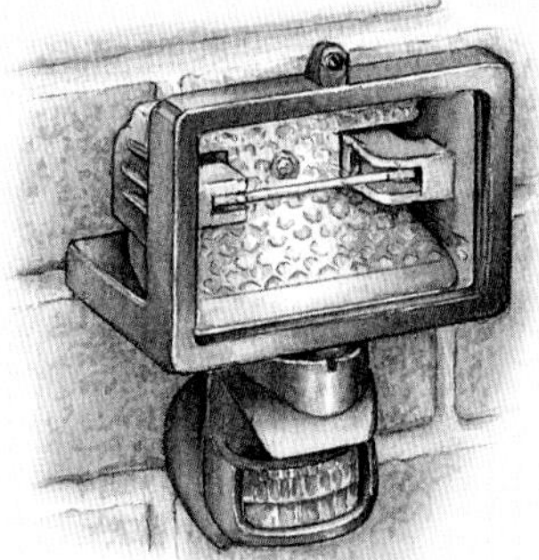

Security lighting *Automatic security lights which turn on if anyone walks past are now widely available from DIY stores and specialist lighting companies.*

Ground anchors *Use ground anchors to protect valuable trees and shrubs as well as garden furniture and tools that are left out overnight.*

Garden security

Security may be uppermost in people's minds before a holiday, but items can be stolen from the garden at any time of the year. Most burglars enter property through the back garden, so check your boundary for weak spots, such as gaps in the hedge, weak locks on gates or broken fencing. In the front garden, fences or hedges should be no more than 90 cm (36 in) high so that a potential thief is not screened from public view. Correctly positioned lighting can also deter intruders, while gravel paths and drives will alert you to people coming and going from your property.

To prevent baskets from being taken from front gardens, fit security brackets (see illustration above). Tubs and large containers can be bolted down to paving using expansion bolts, and concrete and stone ornaments can be cemented into position. Avoid using containers in front gardens if you take holidays in the summer, because if you move them to the back garden when you go away, it is all too obvious to potential thieves that you are absent. As houses are made more secure, the contents of sheds, garages and gardens are being targeted. Most garden sheds are not secure enough to store valuables, such as powered tools, which are popular targets for thieves. Ideally, a shed should have door and window locks, internal hinges and an alarm audible in the house. Screw steel mesh over vulnerable windows to help to secure them.

If you use an alarm, it should be serviced regularly, and a trusted neighbour should have a key. Any ladders and equipment, including spades and forks, that could be used to break into the house or shed should be locked away in a garage. If there is no room for a tall ladder to be put away, chain or padlock it to a secure bracket on an outside wall. Or bolt it down with a U-shaped bicycle lock which is harder to cut through.

Marking and photographing property By marking powered tools, furniture and ornaments, you will make it harder for thieves to sell them. You will also increase the chances of getting your property back if the police recover it. Use an etching tool or an ultra-violet marker to put your postcode and house number on the item. It is worth taking colour photographs or a video of particularly valuable objects – not only will this help the police, but it could also help with any insurance claim. The photographs should give an idea of the size of the object, and include close-ups of any unique marks and serial or model numbers.

HOW TO SECURE YOUR GARDEN

SHED

Make sure the shed is locked at all times. Replace external hinges (those with screws on the outside) with internal ones. Install locks for windows that open and use putty to make sure that window panes are not easy to lift out of their frames. Secure the different sections of the building, including the roof, using screws or bolts from the inside. Consider installing a battery-powered alarm.

OPEN GARDEN

Use wall and ground anchors to secure heavy furniture left out over winter. Bolt down valuable containers and statues. Install security lighting that comes on automatically when someone walks past. Lay gravel paths so that intruders make a noise when they enter.

BOUNDARIES

Increase the height of your boundary fence with trellis. Use prickly shrubs such as a thorny rose or berberis on the perimeter.

PLANTS

Don't put valuable plants in the front garden. Take off plant labels to avoid 'advertising' recent additions, which are easy to remove. Use ground anchors for really valuable plants.

Time-saving tools

Before you buy a tool which is advertised as 'time saving', consider which garden jobs take up most of your time and then look for the best tool for the job. Many tools are heavy and unwieldy, so try them out before you buy

A host of tools and equipment advertised in catalogues and magazines claim to save you time, but there is little point in cluttering up your space with gimmicks you never use. A product has to save time on a task that is time-consuming in your particular garden – and all gardens are different. In addition, the user has to find the tool easy and comfortable to use. Some powered tools are noisy, heavy or difficult to control, so try them out before buying. If possible, try out handtools too, or at least handle them in the shop and compare brands for weight and handle length.

Handtools

Investing in stainless-steel tools, including forks, spades and trowels, saves time. Stainless steel cuts through the soil quickly, and stays sharp and rust-free for years with minimal care. Go for good quality stainless-steel tools; cheap ones often break.

The range of handtools displayed in most garden centres is limited. Often the tool companies make many other variations that can be ordered through the garden centre, such as long-handled spades for tall people, and pruners and trimmers with telescopic handles for cutting extra-tall branches and hedges. Small blades on tools can make cultivating between plants easier: look for border spades and small-bladed trowels and hoes.

Carrying and holding equipment

A wheelbarrow or a plastic sheet is valuable for transporting bulky material around the garden. A holdall, plastic tray, bucket or garden trolley can be used for tools.

When clearing a neglected garden, tipping the rubbish straight into a skip will save time, but hire costs are high. An alternative if you have a tow bar is to hire a trailer from a car hire company to take uncompostable material to the tip. It can also be used when buying DIY materials or loose organic matter – and will certainly save having to clean out the car boot. Trailers come in various types: some have covers and others have crossbars at the front for tying down long items. Don't transport plants in an open trailer, though, because they can be damaged by the wind.

Powered tools

For big tasks, such as cutting a long hedge, powered tools can save time, but most are noisy and potentially dangerous. You will

Powering up You can save a lot of time by using powered tools for routine tasks, such as edging a lawn or cutting a hedge. For one-off heavy tasks, such as digging out a hole for a pond, consider hiring a specialist tool, such as an excavator, instead (see page 300).

Cutting hedge	with shears	3 hrs
	with hedge trimmer	30 mins
Digging	with spade	4 hrs
	with cultivator	50 mins
Lawn edging	with shears	2 hrs
	with powered edger	25 mins
Chop prunings	with secateurs	2 hrs
	with garden shredder	15 mins
Leaf collecting	with a rake	3 hrs
	with garden vacuum	45 mins

need to follow the safety instructions and store the tools carefully under cover after use. Some cleaning and maintenance is necessary.

Most powered tools are either electric or petrol. Electric tools should be protected with a residual current device (RCD) to prevent the user from getting an electric shock if the cable is cut. Many fuse boxes are fitted with RCDs, or you can buy a portable one that plugs into an electric socket. The extension cable must be suitable for outdoor use.

Petrol tools are usually more expensive, and certainly noisier and heavier, than electric versions, but they are more powerful and last longer if serviced regularly.

When choosing a powered tool, aim to match the tool to the task rather than buying on price alone. For example, most electric trimmers will cope with trimming grass, but it is unrealistic to expect their plastic line cutter to clear a neglected garden, which is better done by a metal-bladed brush cutter.

If you have a formal hedge, buy a hedge trimmer to make light work of regular maintenance

The newest devices that are now available are battery-operated or solar-powered, robotic mowers which guide themselves around the lawn. However, these are still undergoing trials and are very expensive. In the meantime, choose a mower suitable for your type of lawn (see page 60).

EFFICIENT STORAGE AREAS

Not being able to find your tools and equipment is a frustrating and time-wasting start to any task. Every gardener needs a storage area – shed, garage or cellar – and it needs to be organised.

Garden chemicals *Keep chemicals cool, dark and dry, in a locked cupboard or high shelf away from children.*
Toolbox *Secateurs, twine, gloves and trowels need to be instantly accessible in a portable plastic organiser box.*
Wheeled hose-reel *Makes moving a hose easier and keeps it out of the way so that people don't trip over it.*
Wheeled storage trolley *For carrying tools and easy collection of garden rubbish.*
Bags of compost *Compost and organic mulch should be kept in a dry place under cover. Use clothespegs to reseal opened bags.*
Storage rack *Long-handled tools, such as spades, and electrical equipment are best hung on the wall on a metal rack or individual hooks.*

POWERED TOOLS WORTH BUYING

Most of these tools are either electric, for smaller areas, or petrol-driven.

LEAF BLOWERS
A garden vacuum or leaf blower is useful in a garden that collects a lot of leaves in autumn or a front garden where litter is a problem.

LAWN EQUIPMENT
Electric or petrol-driven mowers are standard these days, but a powered lawn edger is also worth buying if you have a lot of edges. Ride-on mowers and mini-tractors that can be fitted with other accessories and pull a trailer are worth investing in if you have a very large garden.

SHREDDERS
Electric models shred small prunings, which can go in the compost bin. If there are a lot of thick prunings, hire a more powerful, petrol-driven model.

TRIMMERS
If you have a formal hedge that needs regular trimming, buy a hedge trimmer. Electric models are easier to use and useful for hedges near to a power supply. For very long hedges, especially if they are more remote, buy a more powerful, petrol model instead. For long grass or awkward areas use an electric nylon-line trimmer.

Hiring tools for big jobs

By hiring, you can gain access to an array of powerful and expensive tools that make easier work of major, one-off jobs or tasks that are done only once a year. Whether you hire or buy a powered tool, make sure you always follow safety advice

Powered tools available for hire can give you that extra power to tackle time-consuming tasks quickly. In addition, you don't have to worry about where you are going to store them safely, or about maintaining them or having them serviced.

When to hire

Hiring specialist tools is a good way to gain control of a neglected garden. Use a powerful hedge trimmer for overgrown hedges, a shredder for prunings and a brushwood cutter for undergrowth. It is also worth hiring specialised tools for one-off projects, such as preparing the ground for a new lawn or digging post holes when erecting a fence.

In a large garden, hiring tools could be part of a yearly routine at the start of the autumn tidy-up. Hiring tools for individual jobs can be expensive, so you may find it more efficient and more fun to club together with neighbours to get maximum value out of each day's hire. Alternatively, consider hiring a contractor (see page 302), in particular for specialist jobs or for routine maintenance.

Many seasonal jobs can be made easier using hire tools. For instance, a powered lawn rake makes light work of scarifying – removing the dead grass, which makes the grass more able to withstand invasion from moss and weeds. Where grass growth is poor and the soil has become compacted, the soil structure can be opened up every three years using a hired lawn aerator. This is a much heavier tool than a scarifier, so check that you will be able to get it to the lawn easily.

Specialist hire equipment can make light work of many other gardening tasks. For

SPECIALIST POWERED TOOLS TO HIRE

Many one-off, time-consuming tasks can be made a lot less daunting if you hire the right equipment. Make sure you can arrange delivery and that there is unobstructed access to the site before you hire.

Moving materials *For large jobs, such as digging out a pond, hire a powered wheelbarrow to move the spoil. First check that you have a clear access to the site, if restricted consider hiring a conveyor instead.*

Digging large areas *A powered cultivator or tiller will cultivate ground quickly. These machines are available in a range of sizes, but most are heavy to use and manoeuvre in a small garden.*

example, you can hire a pond vacuum to clean out your pond, a pressure washer to remove lichen and grime from your patio, a cultivator to dig the soil, a powered wheelbarrow for moving soil or rubble and an Alligator saw for chopping up logs. This is like a hand saw but with reciprocating blades and is safer and easier to use than a chainsaw.

All sorts of building tools can be hired, too. It is worth getting a catalogue from a hire company to see what sort of tools are available before tackling any particularly labour-intensive project. Keep a copy of the catalogue on file to help you when planning your garden projects.

Tools can be hired by the half-day, day, weekend or week. As a week costs about the same as two separate days, it is worth hiring tools for the week for tasks that take more than two days to complete. If you are worried about the weather, ask if you can get a daily extension before you hire the tool. The cost of the hire is related loosely to the price of the tool; for example, a tool costing £100 to buy would cost about £20 to hire for a week, whereas one that costs £250 to £300 to buy would cost about £40 to hire for the week.

Before you hire

Explain what you want If you are not sure what hire tool to choose, don't be afraid of asking the hire shop assistant for advice. Be clear about what you want.

Check the tool Do not accept any damaged equipment. Check the tool for wear, damage and cleanliness before you hire. This will indicate how well the tool has been serviced.

Ask for a demonstration Make sure you know how the equipment works and how to use it properly. Ask the hire shop to show you how to start and stop the machine, and to demonstrate any safety features.

Before you hire, work out the number of times you might use the tool in a year. If you will want it more than twice, you would probably be better off buying rather than hiring. However, take into account the cost of any safety gear and the need for storage and servicing, too. Buying your own tools can sometimes be more convenient, too. Machinery needed at a particular time of the year will be in demand at that time, so you may have to book in advance to be sure of getting it when you need it.

Erecting a fence *Hire a post-hole borer like a giant corkscrew to make digging post holes easy. Manual and petrol-driven models are available.*

Cleaning paving *Pressure washers take the hard work out of restoring paving. Electric and petrol models are available with a selection of cleaning fluids.*

Removing tree stumps *Hire a stump grinder to remove tree stumps that cannot be dug up or winched out. Wheeled, petrol-driven models are easiest to use.*

HIRE-TOOL SAFETY

Hire tools are generally heavy and powerful. This means that they can also be dangerous. Make sure you feel confident about using the equipment before leaving the shop and always use as directed.

SAFETY GEAR
Always ask for the right safety gear. For cutting and chopping tools, wear strong gloves and stout shoes or boots with steel toecaps and a good grip. With noisy machines ask for ear defenders to protect your hearing. With equipment that throws up dust or particles protect your eyes with safety goggles, or a face shield, and a dust mask. A safety helmet is a wise precaution when cutting overhead branches. If using chemicals ask for gloves and waterproof overalls.

CLEAR THE WORK AREA
Always make sure the work area is clear of debris and bystanders. Keep children and pets well away. Don't allow others to distract you when using powered tools, and cutting tools in particular.

AFTER USE
Always switch off powered tools, and unplug electric ones, after use. Never leave them running when unattended or when making adjustments or changing blades.

Using hired help

Hired help in the garden, whether it is professional advice or just a strong pair of hands, will certainly make the job of the busy gardener easier. However, pitfalls can lie ahead for the unwary, so it is best to prepare yourself properly first

> ### Before hiring a contractor
>
> **Know what you want** Look at magazines and books and make garden visits to decide exactly want you want the contractor to do.
>
> **Draw up plans** Make a rough sketch of your ideas to help you explain what you want. Instructions must be clear and unambiguous.
>
> **Check credentials** Contact local landscape contractors/designers and visit jobs they have completed recently.
>
> **Get a written quote** Do not settle for an 'estimate', which is only a guide to the cost of the job. Insist on a 'quote' which is a definite price. Match skills to the job, and expect to pay more for trained hands. Arrange to pay the final instalment once the job is complete.

Whatever type of help you need, personal recommendation from someone you know and respect counts for a lot. Otherwise, for local help, look out for contractors' boards outside gardens in your area, or advertisements in garden centres or local papers. Gardening magazines carry advertisements for people operating mainly on a national basis – especially garden designers – but costs will be high if you have to pay for travelling time.

A good, reliable person, whether a tree surgeon or a general contractor, will be busy for several weeks ahead, so book well in advance. Gardening is seasonal, especially maintenance work, so aim to build up a long-term working relationship with a contractor by drawing up a schedule of work for quieter times. The contractor should then be more willing to fit you in during the busy spells.

Match a person's skills to the job. Do not give pruning or landscaping work to an unskilled labourer. Even weeding needs someone who can distinguish a weed from an ornamental plant. Do not assume that someone employed by a contractor is trained in horticulture – and expect to pay considerably more for someone who is.

Make sure that your instructions are clear and unambiguous. With large projects it is important to discuss and agree in advance a programme of work, and how and when you are going to pay. You must also check whether the contractor has third party and public liability insurance, especially if they are using powered tools.

When asking for a quote, do not necessarily choose the cheapest. Some companies end up by charging a lot more and taking a lot longer than they originally specified in their quote. Check whether the company has completed similar work elsewhere satisfactorily that you can see for yourself. However, be prepared for unforeseen problems, which may mean the quote has to be revised.

Garden design

There is no shortage of garden designers, but their qualifications vary. Do not be seduced by fancy plans and drawings; see evidence that they have had their designs successfully built and used. Decide what you want done and how much you can afford. Typically, a designer will pay you a visit, discuss the job and survey the garden. He or she will then send you a layout and planting plan. From there, you can either employ your own contractor or ask the designer to work with one, which may cost a little more but it is the quickest way to turn the design into reality.

Landscaping contractor

Try to pick a company that has a track record in the feature that you want. A contractor should be able to get you materials, such as topsoil, turf or rocks, but discuss the specifications beforehand.

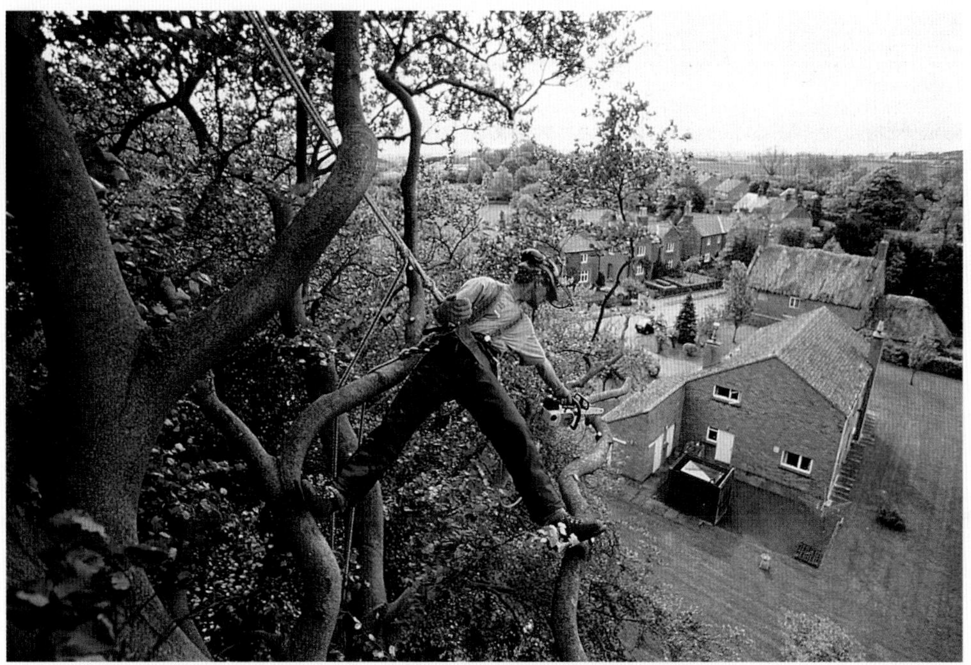

Tree surgery is a dangerous and skilled occupation, so choose a qualified contractor who has adequate insurance *(see column, right).*

Advice on trees

Seek out a qualified tree surgeon if you want a large tree removed or pruned, or if you need legal or insurance advice about trees. Ask the Arboricultural Association or your local authority for suitably qualified tree surgeons in your area (see right).

Housesitters

Your house, pets and garden can be looked after by a housesitter for not much more than the cost of kennels, which works well for people with animals. Again, personal recommendation is a good way to find a reliable local person to housesit. Otherwise look in garden magazines for agency advertisements. You will need to book well in advance; listing everything that needs doing and then arranging to meet the sitter at your house. Before going away let your insurance company know you are using a housesitter.

Routine maintenance

For maintenance you can employ either a jobbing gardener or a gardening or landscape contractor. If you rely on the garden being cleaned up regularly, it may be worth paying more and hiring a contractor. Possibly team up with neighbours to offer a full day's work. Spend time during the winter contacting contractors to find out who will do odd days when needed or just visit to cut lawns weekly.

You should also agree in advance whose tools will be used. And even if you are not a keen gardener, keep an eye on what they are doing – tasks they shirk could get neglected.

Mower servicing

Servicing a mower is like servicing a car: if it's not done regularly the machine won't work efficiently. Service a mower in winter, when the service departments are not so busy. Get a quote in writing before the job is started.

Electric machines A basic service should include a complete check of electrical safety, including connectors, switches, cables and insulation, plus a motor check and blade sharpening or replacement if needed.

Petrol machines These should be given an oil change and new spark plugs. The engine should be checked and adjusted for efficient running and ease of starting. All safety mechanisms should be tested. The blades should be sharpened or replaced.

WHERE TO GO FOR ADVICE

There are useful sources of reliable, independent specialist advice. See page 306 for addresses.

TREE SURGEONS
Your local authority may provide a list of the tree surgeons they use in your area. The Arboricultural Association produces directories of consultants and contractors that meet its standards, and will supply free copies on request. Otherwise try your local *Yellow Pages* and advertisements in the local press.

GARDEN DESIGNERS
The Society of Garden Designers can provide you with a list of full members in your area.

CONTRACTORS
For landscaping jobs, such as clearing a garden or laying a patio, contact BALI (British Association of Landscape Industries). Contractors listed in your local *Yellow Pages* usually specify if they are BALI-accredited, but it is best to check directly with the Association.

PRODUCT ADVICE
Garden product manufacturers often have free helplines for advice about their products.

Buying unusual plants

If you have a passion for a particular type of plant, such as herbs, roses, fuchsias or clematis, you will soon tire of what is available in your local garden centre and want to grow rarer varieties. Specialist nurseries can offer the answer

Searching for unusual varieties of plants from specialist nurseries may bring rewarding results, but it can be time-consuming. Many of these nurseries are small concerns, off the beaten track and with varying opening times. Not only do they offer more unusual varieties, but some also specialise in plants for particular site or soil conditions, such as shade or chalk.

If you do not have any personal recommendations, the first step in choosing the right nursery is to look up the plant in *The RHS Plant Finder*, which is published annually. It is a quick starting-point to track down desired plants, although you will need to know the Latin name since this is how they are listed alphabetically. The *RHS Plant Finder* is also available in a more user-friendly form on CD-ROM.

If you are interested in a particular group of plants, you may find the *RHS Gardener's Yearbook* more helpful. Published annually, it lists specialist nurseries and garden centres according to their speciality. You could also contact specialist societies or try the National Council for the Conservation of Plants and Gardens (NCCPG), which encourages the conservation of plants and gardens. It has an

Buying by mail order

Placing an order Ring to check availability of the varieties that you want before ordering. State on the form whether you will accept substitutes or not. Let the nursery know of any specific delivery instructions, such as where to leave plants if you are out or away. And keep a copy of your order.

When your order arrives Open the packages immediately and check the contents against your original order. If you are not satisfied with the plants, contact the nursery immediately.

Survival kit for garden shows

Shows can be exhausting unless you go prepared. If you are buying plants, you may be able to leave them at the nursery's stand and collect them before going home. Alternatively, make use of plant crèches that most shows offer. Before going to the show, make sure you have the following:

Lists of plants you want, including substitutes and a list of nurseries to visit.

Address labels that are sticky-backed to put into order books, and on mailing lists and plant purchases.

Notebook, pencils and highlighter pen.

Change to pay for catalogues.

Lunch and refreshments.

Polythene bags to use as a makeshift waterproof hat, to sit on and to carry plants.

Shopping trolley for large purchases.

Many shows are ideal places to see a wide range of nurseries and to order plants. Restrict plant purchases at shows to small specimens, because you will have to carry them home.

FINDING OUT ABOUT PARTICULAR PLANTS

Specialist societies are an ideal way to find out more about a specific group of plants. Most produce journals and bulletins, and organise shows, outings and lectures at various venues up and down the country. If you want to find out more, see page 306 for addresses of societies and specialist nurseries.

Roses *The Royal National Rose Society has gardens at St Albans, publishes* The Rose *quarterly and organises shows, visits, lectures.*

Fuchsias *The British Fuchsia Society organises several regional shows and produces a journal and bulletins for members.*

Sweet peas *The National Sweet Pea Society produces an annual journal and several newsletters. It also organises shows and lectures.*

Alpines *The Alpine Garden Society organises lectures and a seed exchange scheme. It also produces a quarterly journal.*

Clematis *The British Clematis Society produces a journal and organises shows, lectures, outings and a seed exchange programme.*

Herbs *The Herb Society produces a magazine and quarterly newsletter, and organises lectures, seminars and workshops.*

address list of plant collections, often held by nurseries. It also organises special plant fairs where you can see and buy unusual varieties. Also look out for advertisements in gardening publications.

If you are interested in roses, the British Rose Growers Association produces a booklet called *Find That Rose*, which lists outlets where you can buy different rose varieties.

Once you have decided on the nurseries that interest you, contact them for a catalogue. When the catalogue arrives, read the terms and conditions first because some have hefty minimum orders or other restrictive conditions. Watch out for nurseries sending substitute plants: check information on availability and delivery before ordering. Many nurseries can be contacted by email.

If you are not looking for anything in particular, but simply want to collect unusual varieties of plants, then there are many other sources, such as local plant fairs and car-boot sales. Visiting specialist nurseries at garden shows is particularly useful for the busy gardener because you can see many of them in a single afternoon. Many nurseries will bring along orders placed before the show, which can be a convenient way of picking up your plants. Alternatively, you can make an order at the show – but stick to the list of plants that you need (see opposite), otherwise you are likely to get caught up by impulse buying.

BRINGING PLANTS HOME FROM HOLIDAY

It is easier than ever for a private individual to buy plants and seeds from abroad. Check plants, though, for pests and diseases.

FROM THE EU

With the Single Market, private individuals can buy plants for their own use in another EU country and bring them back to the UK, so long as they are in your personal baggage or car. The few exceptions are: seed potatoes, conifers, poinsettias and fireblight carriers, such as pyracantha.

REST OF THE WORLD

Small quantities of plants and seeds can be brought into the UK if for personal use and carried with you at the time. Potatoes are the exception: they are not allowed in. 'Small quantities' are defined as: up to 2 kg of fruit or raw vegetables; one bouquet of cut flowers; and up to five packets of seeds of non-flowering plants (you can bring in as much flower seed as you want). You can also bring in up to 2 kg of bulbs and up to five plants from non-EU countries bordering the Mediterranean.

Contact the UK Ministry of Agriculture, Fisheries and Food for further advice (see page 306).

Useful addresses

SUPPLIERS

AUTOMATIC WATERING

Access Garden Products
Yelvertoft Road, Crick,
Northants. NN6 7XS

Autoflow Systems
Auto House, Ashtree Works,
Mill Rd, Barnham Broom,
Norfolk NR9 4DE

City Irrigation
Bencewell Granary, Oakley Rd,
Bromley Common,
Kent BR2 8HG

Erin/Gardena
Dunhas Lane, Letchworth
Garden City, Herts. SG6 1BD

Garden Irrigation Supplies
217 Bath Road, Cheltenham,
Gloucs. GL53 7NA

Hozelock
Haddenham, Aylesbury,
Bucks. HP17 8JD

Leaky Pipe Systems
Frith Farm, Dean Street, East
Farleigh, Maidstone
Kent ME15 OPR

Porous Pipe
PO Box 2, Colne
Lancs. BB8 7BY

Two Wests and Elliott
Unit 4, Carrwood Road,
Sheepbridge Industrial Estate,
Chesterfield, Derbys. S41 9RH

BIOLOGICAL CONTROLS

Agralan
The Old Brickyard, Ashton
Keynes, Swindon,
Wilts. SN6 6QR

Defenders
Occupation Road, Wye, Ashford,
Kent TN25 5EN

English Woodlands Biocontrol
Hoyle Depot, Graffham,
Petworth, West Sussex
GU23 OLR

Fargro
Toddington Lane,
Littlehampton, West Sussex
BN17 7PP

Green Gardener
41 Strumpshore Road, Brundall,
Norwich, Norfolk NR13 5PG
(Dawn-to-dusk helpline)

CROP COVERS/FLEECE

Agralan
The Old Brickyard, Ashton
Keynes, Swindon,
Wilts. SN6 6QR

LBS Horticulture
Cottontree, Near Colne,
Lancs. BB8 7BW

Link Stakes
30 Warwick Road,
Upper Boddington, Daventy,
Northants. NN11 6DH

Power Garden Products
3 Daytoner Drive, Allesley,
Coventry CVS 9QG

GARDEN TRANSPORTERS

Beldray Limited
PO Box 20, Beldray Road,
Bilston, West Midlands
WV14 7NF

Bosmere Products Ltd
St Clairs Farm, Wickham Road,
Droxford, Hants. SO32 3PW

Chillington Manufacturing
Camden Street, Walsall Wood,
West Midlands WS9 9BJ

Haemmerlin
The Washington Centre,
Halesowen Road, Netherton,
West Midlands DY2 9RE

H & E Knowles (Lye)
Britannia Works, Talbots Lane,
off Mount Pleasant, Quarry
Bank, Brierley Hill,
West Midlands DY5 2YX

Interval Systems Ltd
PO Box 40, Woking,
Surrey GU22 7YU

J B Corrie & Co
Frenchmans Road, Petersfield,
Hants. GU32 3AP

Kettler (GB) Ltd
Kettler House, Merse Road,
North Moons Moat, Redditch,
Worcestershire B98 9HL

The Trailer Barrow Company
Bellbrook Park, Uckfield,
East Sussex TN22 1QF

LEAF VACUUMS

AL-KO Britain
(see Shredders)

Black & Decker
(see Shredders)

Flymo
Preston Road, Aycliffe Industrial
Estate, Newton, Aycliffe,
Durham DL5 6UP

Goblin McCulloch
New Yorkshire House,
Don Pedro Avenue, Normanton
Industrial Estate, Normanton,
West Yorks. WF6 1TT

Husqvarna Forest & Garden
Oldends Lane Industrial
Estate, Stonehouse, Gloucs.
GL10 3SY

PLM Power Products
Units 5 & 6, The Shires
Industrial Estate, Essington
Close, Birmingham Road,
Lichfield, Staffs. WS14 9AZ

MATURE PLANTS

Architectural Plants
Cooks Farm, Nuthurst,
Horsham, West Sussex
RH13 6LH

**Plantiles Plant & Garden
Centre** Almners Road, Lyne,
Chertsey, Surrey KT16 0BJ

Tendercare
Southlands Road, Denham,
Uxbridge, Middx. UB9 4HD

MULCH SUPPLIERS

Garden Glow
Bundles, Clay Lane,
South Nutfield, Redhill,
Surrey RH1 4EG

Gem Gardening
Brookside Lane, Oswaldtwistle,
Accrington, Lancs. BB5 3NY

Levington Horticulture
(see The Scott's Company)

Miracle Garden Care
(see The Scott's Company)

The Scott's Company
Paper Mill Lane, Bramford,
Ipswich, Suffolk IP8 4BZ

Shamrock Horticulture
(see The Scott's Company)

6X Organic Concentrates
3 Broadway Court, Chesham,
Bucks. HP5 1EN

Wessex Horticulture Products
Units 1-3 Hilltop Business Park,
Devizes Road, Salisbury,
Wilts. SP3 4UF

Westland Horticulture
14 Granville Industrial Estate,
Granville Road,
Dungannon, Co. Tyrone,
Northern Ireland BT70 1NJ

William Sinclair Horticulture
Firth Road, Lincoln LN6 7AH

POND SUPPLIERS

Blagdon Garden Products
Bristol Road, Bridgwater,
Somerset TA6 4AW

Bradshaws
Nicolson Link, Clifton Moor,
North Yorkshire YO1 155

Cyprio
Hards Road, Frognall,
Deeping St James, Peterborough,
Cambs. PE6 8RR

Honeysome Aquatic Nursery
The Row, Sutton,
Cambs. CB6 2PF

Lotus Water Garden Products
Junction St, Burnley, Lancs.
BB12 ONA

Oase (UK)
3 Telford Gate, West Portway
Industrial Estate, Andover,
Hants. SP10 3SF

Stapeley Water Gardens
London Road, Stapeley,
Nantwich, Cheshire CW5 7LH

**Trident Water Garden
Products**
Carlton Road, Foleshill,
Coventry CV6 7FL

SEEDS AND SMALL PLANTS

Chiltern Seeds
Bortree Stile, Ulverston,
Cumbria LA12 7PB

D T Brown & Co. Ltd.
Station Road, Poulton-le-Fylde,
Lancashire FY6 7HX

E W King
(see Suffolk Herbs)

**John Chambers' Wild Flower
Seeds**
15 Westleigh Road, Barton,
Seagrave, Kettering, Notts.
NN15 5AJ

Mr Fothergill's Seeds
Gazeley Road, Kentford,
Newmarket, Suffolk CB8 7QB

Samuel Dobie and Son Ltd
Woodview Road, Paignton,
Devon PQ4 7NG

S E Marshall & Co
Wisbech, Cambs. PE13 2RF

Suffolk Herbs
Monks Farm, Coggeshall Road, Kelvedon, Essex CO5 9PG

Suttons Seeds
Hele Road, Torquay, Devon TQ2 7QJ

Thompson & Morgan
Poplar Lane, Ipswich, Suffolk IP8 3BU

Unwins Seeds
Admail 324, Cambridge CB4 4ZZ

SHREDDERS

AL-KO Britain
Queensway, Leamington Spa, Warwickshire CV31 3JP

Andreas Stihl Ltd
Stihl House, Stanhope Road, Camberley, Surrey GU15 3YT

Black & Decker
210 Bath Road, Slough, Berks. SL1 3YD

Bob Andrews
Lovelace Road, Bracknell, Berks. RG12 8YT

Makita (UK)
Michigan Drive, Tongwell, Milton Keynes, Bucks. MK15 8JD

Robert Bosch Ltd
Broadwater Park, North Orbital Road, Denham, Uxbridge UB9 SHJ

MISCELLANEOUS

Acorn Planting Products
Little Money Road, Loddon, Norwich, Norfolk NR14 6JD (tree shelters)

Bradstone Home & Country
Hulland Ward, Ashbourne, Derbyshire DE6 3ET (multi-blocks on page 192)

Forest Fencing Ltd
Stanford Court, Stanford Bridge, Worcester WR6 6SR (mini-sleepers and logs on page 192)

Husqvarna Forest & Garden
(see Leaf vacuums) (robotic mower on page 299)

Marshalls
Southowram, Halifax HX3 9SY (wall planter on page 151)

Netlon
New Wellington Street, Blackburn, Lancs. BB2 4PJ (windbreak netting)

SERVICES

PLANT MINDERS

Animal Aunts
'Smugglers', Green Lane, Rogate, Petersfield, Hants. GU31 5DA

Holiday Homewatch
Nursery Cottage, Penybont, Llandrindrod Wells, Powys LD1 5SP

Home & Pet Care
PO Box 19, Penrith, Cumbria CA11 7AA

Homesitters
Buckland Wharf, Buckland, Aylesbury, Bucks. HP22 5LQ

Housewatch
Little London, Berden, Bishops Stortford, Herts. CM23 1BE

Minderskeepers
Riverside Cottage, High Street, Shepreth, Royston, Herts.

Universal Aunts
PO Box 304, London SW4 ONN

ORGANISATIONS

Arboricultural Association
Ampfield House, Ampfield, Romsey, Hants. SO51 9PA (For directories of tree consultants and contractors.)

British Agrochemicals Association
4 Lincoln Court, Lincoln Road, Peterborough, Cambs. PE1 2RP (Useful booklet on using chemicals in the garden.)

British Association of Landscape Industries (BALI)
Landscape House, 9 Henry Street, Keighley, West Yorks. BD21 3DR (Professional body of landscape contractors. It will supply names of members in your area.)

British Rose Growers Association
4 Peewit Road, Hampton, Evesham, Worcestershire WR11 6NH (Produces the booklet *Find that Rose!*, which tells you where you can buy around 2000 different rose varieties.)

Henry Doubleday Research Association
Ryton Organic Gardens, Ryton-on-Dunsmore, Coventry, West Midlands CV8 3LG (Publications; courses; show gardens; mail order.)

Horticultural Therapy
Geoffrey Udall Building, Trunkwell Park, Beech Hill, Reading RG7 2AT (Offers advice for gardeners with physical disabilities.)

Ministry of Agriculture, Fisheries and Food (For advice on importing plants and seeds.) General enquiries 0645 335577 (Telephone 0645 556000 for a copy of *Travellers: Plants brought back to Britain from abroad could carry serious pests and diseases.*)

Museum of Garden History
Lambeth Palace Road, London SE1 7LB (Museum courses and talks on the history of gardening, as well as a show garden.)

National Council for the Conservation of Plants and Gardens (NCCPG)
The Pines, RHS Garden, Wisley, Woking, Surrey GU23 6PQ (Coordinates national collections of plant types.)

National Gardens Scheme Charitable Scheme
Hatchlands Park, East Clandon, Guildford, Surrey GU4 7RT (Runs the 'yellow book' scheme, whereby private gardens open to the public for charities.)

The Royal Horticultural Society
80 Vincent Square, London SW1P 2PE (Organises shows, talks, visits and other events, as well as having a library, and running several gardens in the UK, including Wisley in Surrey.)

Society of Garden Designers
c/o Institute of Horticulture, 16 Belgrave Square, London SW1X 8PS (Will provide a list of affiliated garden designers in your area.)

SHOWS

RHS:

BBC Gardener's World Live (June) Venue: National Exhibition Centre, Birmingham.

Chelsea Flower Show (May) Venue: Royal Hospital, London.

Hampton Court Palace Flower Show (July) Venue: Hampton Court Palace.

Scotland's National Gardening Show (May) Venue: Strathclyde Country Park.

OTHER:

Harrogate Great Spring and Autumn Flower Shows (April and September) Venue: Great Yorkshire Showground, Harrogate.
Organiser: The North of England Horicultural Society, 4a South Park Road, Harrogate, North Yorkshire HG1 5QU

Malvern Spring and Autumn Flower Shows (May and September)
Venue: Three Counties Showground, Malvern.
Show secretary: Three Counties Agricultural Society, The Showground, Malvern, Hereford & Worcester WR13 6NW

Shrewsbury Flower Show (August)
Venue: The Quarry, Shrewsbury
Show secretary: Quarry Lodge, Shrewsbury, Shrops. SY1 1RN

SPECIALIST SOCIETIES

The Alpine Garden Society
AGS Centre, Avon Bank, Pershore, Worcestershire WR10 3JP

British Clematis Society
4 Springfield, Lightwater, Surrey GU18 5XP

British Fuchsia Society
PO Box 1068, Kidderminster DY11 7GZ

Federation of British Aquatic Societies
9 Upton Road, Hounslow, Middx. TW3 3HP

The Herb Society
The National Herb Centre, Banbury Road, Warmington, Banbury, Oxon. OX17 1DF

National Sweet Pea Society
St Anne's, The Hollow, Broughton, Stockbridge, Hampshire, SO20 8BB

The Royal National Rose Society
The Gardens of the Rose, Chiswell Green, St Albans, Herts. AL2 3NR

Glossary

Annual A plant, such as nigella, that takes a year to complete its life cycle, from seed to flower, to setting seed and dying. Some perennials are grown for convenience as annuals.

Bare-root plants A way of buying plants, usually roses or hedging plants. They are grown in a field and dug up for planting in the dormant season, between November and March.

Bedding plants Plants that are planted out temporarily to provide a seasonal display.

Biennial A plant, such as foxglove, that takes two years to complete its life cycle. In the first year it forms leaves, in the second the flowers and seed, and then it dies.

Biological control A way of controlling pests by introducing their natural enemy. For example, nematode predators to control vine weevil larvae.

Capillary mat An absorbent mat that holds a lot of water. Plants placed on it can draw up moisture by capillary action.

Cloche A small, portable structure, usually made of clear glass, rigid plastic or plastic film, and used to warm the soil and provide plants with protection from the weather.

Compost A mixture used for growing plants in containers. Either soil-less, such as peat or coir (best for temporary displays because of its light weight and free drainage), or soil-based, such as John Innes (best for permanent displays because it supplies nutrients over a longer period). Garden compost is an organic material made from decomposing plant remains and used as a soil improver or loose organic mulch.

Crop covers There are two main types: **horticultural fleece**, a lightweight, porous material laid loosely over newly sown seeds or young plants to protect them from frosts and flying insects; and **insect-proof mesh**, which is better ventilated than fleece so it can be left on all summer, but offers no frost protection.

Deadheading Nipping off dead or faded flowerheads from a plant to prevent seeding and to encourage new flowers. Roses and many bedding plants need regular deadheading

Fertiliser Liquid or granular. A general fertiliser, such as **growmore**, has balanced amounts of nitrogen (for leaf growth), phosphates (root growth) and potash (flowering and fruiting). **Blood, fish and bone** is an organic alternative to growmore. **Rose** and **tomato fertiliser** are high in potash.

Foliar feed A quick-acting liquid fertiliser absorbed through the leaves as well as the roots.

Ground-cover plants Plants that cover the ground with dense growth, suppressing weeds.

Hard core A layer of broken-up, hard material, such as builders' rubble or stone chippings, used as the base for the foundations of a hard surface, such as paving. Hard core needs to be well compacted. Its depth depends on the loads carried.

Hardening off The practice of gradually acclimatising plants raised indoors or under glass to outside conditions.

Hardiness Plants that are **hardy** tolerate severe frost. **Tender** and **half-hardy** plants will not tolerate frost.

Herbaceous Plants that produce soft, non-woody growth. They die down in winter, but grow again the following spring from basal shoots.

Humus The organic residue of decayed vegetable matter.

Leaf mould Leaves that have decomposed; usually used as a garden compost.

Manure Bulky organic animal and plant waste incorporated into the soil to improve structure and add essential nutrients.

Mowing strip A narrow 'path' of paving laid round the edge of a lawn to eliminate the need for frequent edging.

Mulch An **organic** mulch, such as cocoa shells, bark chippings, garden compost or shredded prunings, or an **inorganic** mulch, such as mulch matting, pebbles or gravel. They serve to suppress weeds and insulate the soil, and, in the case of organic mulches, also provide plants with nutrients.

Mulch matting A purpose-made product or a permeable, recycled material which is laid over the soil to suppress weeds. Holes can be made in the material to allow for planting, and the material then hidden under a mulch of, for example, bark chippings.

Organic Any chemical compound containing carbon. Organic fertilisers, such as blood, fish and bone, are of natural rather than artificial origin. Inorganic fertilisers are artificially synthesised.

Perennial Generally, a perennial is any plant that lives for an indefinite period of time, but the term is usually applied to a hardy, non-woody plant. They are most often herbaceous, but sometimes evergreen. A **tender perennial** is one not able to withstand frost.

Pesticide A chemical compound used to kill pests. A pesticide is either: **systemic**, entering the sap of the plant and killing pests that eat any part of the plant; or **contact**, killing pests that crawl over a treated surface as well as those that are sprayed directly.

Potting The general term for describing the act of putting a plant into a pot. **Potting up** is the initial act of putting a plant (such as a cutting or seedling) into its own individual pot. **Potting on**: moving a plant into a larger pot than it is in already.

Repotting Either loosely used to describe 'potting on' or for replanting into the same-sized pot with fresh compost.

Pressure-treated softwood Wood of a coniferous tree that has been treated to withstand contact with moisture. It does not need to be treated annually with a wood preservative, as with non-treated softwood.

Rootball The mass of roots and compost visible when a plant is removed from its container.

Seep hose A pliable, plastic or rubber hose with holes perforated along its entire length, used for irrigation. A **porous pipe** works on the same principle, but the holes are smaller and the water trickles out: it can either lie on the surface, for easy moving, or be buried 10-15 cm (4-6 in) deep.

Slow-release fertiliser One in which nutrients are released only when the soil temperature rises to a certain level, and so lasts for several months or even a whole growing season.

Specimen plant A plant grown on its own as a focal point. A specimen plant usually has a particularly striking feature, such as a good shape, sculptural foliage, attractive flowers, or colourful berries or bark, that makes it stand out.

Sucker Either a shoot that arises from below ground, at the base of the plant, or a shoot growing from the rootstock on grafted plants. Roses frequently produce suckers.

Windbreak A hedge, fence or wall which lessens the force of strong winds. A **shelter belt** is one or more rows of trees used as a windbreak.

Winter wash Any insecticide or fungicide applied to plants during the dormant season. The term mainly applies to tar oils and other chemicals sprayed on fruit trees in late winter to destroy overwintering insects and their eggs.

Common and botanical names

Common name	Botanical name
arum lily	Zantedeschia
bear's breeches	Acanthus
beech	Fagus
bellflower	Campanula
bird of paradise	*Strelitzia reginae*
black-eyed Susan	*Rudbeckia hirta*
bleeding heart	*Dicentra spectabilis*
bluebell	Hyacinthoides
blue oat grass	*Helictotrichon sempervirens*
Bowles' golden sedge	*Carex elata* 'Aurea'
box	*Buxus*
box-leaved honeysuckle	*Lonicera nitida*
broom	Cytisus/Genista
busy lizzie	Impatiens
catmint	*Nepeta catatia*
cherry laurel	*Prunus laurocerasus*
chocolate vine	*Akebia quinata*
Chusan fan	*Trachycarpus fortunei*
club-rush	Scirpus
common daisy	*Bellis perennis*
coneflower	Rudbeckia
coral bark maple	*Acer palmatum* 'Sango-kaku'
curly rush	*Juncus effusus* 'Spiralis'
cornflower	*Centaurea cyanus*
crab apple	Malus
cranesbill	Geranium
creeping Jenny	*Lysimachia nummularia*
crown imperial	*Fritillaria imperialis*
day lily	Hemerocallis
dead nettle	Lamium
dog's tooth violet	*Erythronium dens-canis*
dogwood	Cornus
dwarf pine	*Pinus mugo* var. *pumilia*
elder	Sambucus
fairy moss	*Azolla caroliniana*
false acacia	*Robinia pseudoacacia*
feverfew	*Tanacetum parthenium*
firethorn	Pyracantha
flowering currant	*Ribes sanguineum*
flowering quince	Chaenomeles
forget-me-not	Myosotis
foxglove	Digitalis
frogbit	*Hydrocharis morsus-ranae*
geranium	Pelargonium
globe thistle	Echinops
golden hop	*Humulus lupulus* 'Aureus'
guelder rose	*Viburnum opulus*
hawthorn	Crataegus
hazel	*Corylus*
holly	Ilex
honesty	Lunaria
honeysuckle	Lonicera
houseleek	Sempervivum
ivy	Hedera
Japanese anemone	*Anemone* x *hybrida*
Japanese maple	*Acer palmatum*
kaffir lily	Schizostylis
kingcup	*Caltha palustris*
kiwi fruit	*Actinidia deliciosa*
lady's mantle	*Alchemilla mollis*
lamb's ears	*Stachys byzantina*
lily-of-the-valley	*Convallaria majalis*
lily turf	*Liriope muscari*
London pride	*Saxifraga* x *urbium*
lords and ladies	*Arum maculatum*
love-in-a-mist	*Nigella damascena*
lungwort	Pulmonaria
Mexican orange blossom	*Choisya ternata*
michaelmas daisy	Aster
mind-your-own-business	Soleirolia
mock orange	Phildadelphus
mountain ash	*Sorbus aucuparia*
mullein	Verbascum
Oregon grape	*Mahonia aquifolium*
oxeye daisy	*Leucanthemum vulgare*
pampas grass	*Cortaderia selloana*
paper-bark maple	*Acer griseum*
passion flower	*Passiflora*
periwinkle	Vinca
Portugal laurel	*Prunus lusitanica*
pot marigold	*Calendula officinalis*
primrose	*Primula vulgaris*
privet	Ligustrum
red-hot poker	Kniphofia
regal lily	*Lilium regale*
rock rose	Helianthemum
rosemary	*Rosmarinus officinalis*
rose of Sharon	*Hypericum calycinum*
sacred bamboo	*Nandina domestica*
sea buckthorn	*Hippophaë rhamnoides*
sea holly	Eryngium
shasta daisy	*Leucanthemum* x *superbum*
silver birch	*Betula pendula*
snake's-head fritillary	*Fritillaria meleagris*
snowdrop	Galanthus
Solomon's seal	Polygonatum
spotted laurel	*Aucuba japonica*
sun rose	Cistus
sweet bay	*Laurus nobilis*
sweet box	Sarcococca
sweet pea	*Lathyrus odoratus*
sweet rocket	*Hesperis matronalis*
sweet violet	*Viola odorata*
sweet william	*Dianthus barbatus*
virginia creeper	Parthenocissus
wall daisy	*Erigeron karvinskianus*
wallflower	*Erysimum*
water fringe	*Nymphoides peltata*
water chestnut	*Trapa natans*
water forget-me-not	*Myosotis scorpioides*
water hawthorn	*Aponogeton distachyos*
water hyacinth	*Eichhornia crassipes*
water lettuce	*Pistia stratiotes*
water lily	Nymphaea
water soldier	*Stratiotes aloides*
water violet	*Hottonia palustris*
wedding-cake tree	*Cornus controversa* 'Variegata'
whitebeam	*Sorbus aria*
wild daffodil	*Narcissus pseudonarcissus*
winter jasmine	*Jasminum nudiflorum*
winter aconite	*Eranthis hyemalis*
winter heath	*Erica carnea*
witch hazel	Hamamelis
wood anemone	*Anemone nemorosa*
wood spurge	*Euphorbia amygdaloides*
yellow flag	*Iris pseudacorus*
yellow water lily	*Nuphar lutea*
yew	*Taxus baccata*
zebra rush	*Scirpus* 'Zebrinus' (syn. *Schoenoplectus* ssp. *tabernaemontani* 'Zebrinus')

Index

Page numbers in **bold** refer to the main descriptive plant entries.

R

Acknowledgments

Carroll & Brown Limited would like to thank the following for

allowing us to photograph their gardens: Mhairi and Simon Clutson whose garden is open under the National Gardens Scheme in aid of the Brittle Bone Society; Karen and Phill Lloyd; Louise and Phil Pankhurst; Liz Powling; Joanna and Richard Robinson (garden designed by Philip Enticknap of Landscapes by Design Ltd); Erica and Art Timothy.

providing tools and equipment: Atco Qualcast, Bob Andrews; Black & Decker; Clifton Nurseries; Sonja Edwards; Hozelock; The Rushden Granulating Company.

providing plants or locations: Hampstead Garden Centre; Phoebe's Pet and Garden Centre Ltd; The Secret Garden; Suttons Seeds; Van Hague's Garden Centre; West Ham Park.

Photography credits

t = top; *c* = centre; *b* = bottom; *l* = left; *r* = right.
GPL = Garden Picture Library;
HSC = Harry Smith Collection;
HSI = Holt Studio International;
OSF = Oxford Scientific Films;
RD = these pictures are taken from The Reader's Digest Plant Library – some previously appeared in *The Reader's Digest New Encyclopedia of Garden Plants and Flowers*. RD/RS are by Richard Surman for Reader's Digest and RD/JW are by Justyn Wilsmore.

Title page and introduction
2-3 Henk Dijkman/GPL; ***5*** *(br)* Derek St Romaine; ***12*** *(bl)* Jerry Pavia/GPL; ***13*** *(tl)* HSC, *(cl/cr)* John Glover/GPL, *(bl)* Derek St Romaine, *(br)* Ron Evans/GPL; ***14-15*** Juliette Wade; ***16*** Andrew Lawson; ***17*** Ruth Chivers; ***18-19*** Eric Crichton; ***21*** *(t)* John Glover/GPL, *(b)* Derek St Romaine/ Mrs Abbot; ***23*** Ron Sutherland/ designer Anthony Paul/GPL; ***25*** Rosalind Simon; ***26-27*** Howard Rice/GPL; ***29*** Steven Wooster/Beth Chatto Garden; ***31*** Steven Wooster/ Liz Morrow/Waimarino, Auck., NZ.

Front Gardens
32 Jonathan Buckley; ***34*** *(t)* Eric Crichton; ***34-35*** Jerry Harpur/designer Martin Sacks; ***35*** Elizabeth Whiting & Associates; ***36*** *(t)* Derek St Romaine; *(b)* Daphne Ledward; ***38*** *(l/r)* HSC; ***39*** *(l)* Juliette Wade, *(panel, except first)* RD/RS, RD/Jonathan Buckley, RD/RS; ***40-41*** HSC; ***41*** *(bl)* Jerry Harpur/ designer Roderick Griffin, *(panel)* RD/JW, RD, RD, RD, RD/JW; ***43*** *(panel)* all RD; ***44*** Ron Evans/GPL; ***46*** *(l)* Jerry Harpur/designer Jane Fearnley-Whittingstall; ***46-47*** Clive Nichols; ***47*** Marianne Majerus/GPL.

Covering the Ground
48 David Askham/GPL; ***51*** *(t)* Ron Sutherland/GPL, *(r)* John Glover/ Heathfield, Surrey; ***52*** *(l)* Angela Hampton/Family Life Pictures; ***52-53*** Kim Blaxland/GPL; ***54*** *(l)* John Glover/The Anchorage; ***54-55*** Derek St Romaine; ***55*** *(panel)* RD, Gilda Pacitti, Jonathan Weaver/ GPL, Clive Nichols; ***56*** HSC; ***62*** *(b)* John Glover/GPL; ***62-63*** Steven Wooster/ Chiffchaffs; ***63*** *(tr)* Steven Wooster; ***65*** *(panel)* RD, RD/RS, RD; ***66*** Marianne Majerus/GPL; ***67*** John Glover/designer Julie Toll, RHS Chelsea; ***69*** *(t)* Ron Sutherland/GPL, *(b)* Derek St Romaine/designer Julie Toll, RHS Chelsea.

Shrubs, Roses and Trees
70 Jerry Harpur/designer Tessa King-Farlow; ***72*** *(b)* Jonathan Buckley/ designer Diana Yakeley; ***72-73*** Steven Wooster; ***74*** Rosalind Simon; ***75*** Ron Evans/GPL; ***76-77*** Derek St Romaine/ designer Arabella Lennox Boyd, RHS Chelsea; ***79*** (panel) RD/RS, RD, RD/RS, RD/JW, RD/RS; ***81*** RD/JW; ***82*** *(t)* Derek St Romaine/designer Roger Platts, RHS Chelsea, *(b)* Vaughan Fleming/GPL; ***83*** *(panel)* RD, RD/RS, RD/RS, RD/RS, RD; ***84*** *(panel)* RD, RD/JW, RD/RS, RD/ Jonathan Buckley, RD/JW; ***85*** John Glover; ***86-87*** John Glover/GPL; ***88*** Howard Rice/GPL; ***90*** *(bl)* Andy Moran/HSI, *(bc/br)* Nigel Cattlin/HSI; ***92*** *(t)* Clive Nichols/ designer Jill Billington, *(b)* John Glover/GPL; ***93*** *(panel)* RD/RS, RD/RS, RD/RS, RD/RS; ***94*** *(l)* Derek St Romaine; ***94-95*** Steve Wooster/GPL; ***95*** *(panel)* RD, RD/RS, RD/RS, RD; ***96*** John Glover; ***98-99*** Clive Nichols/ Hazelbury Manor; ***100*** *(l)* Lynne Brotchie/GPL; ***100-1*** Karin Craddock/GPL; ***101*** *(panel)* David Askham/GPL, John Glover, RD/RS, HSC, RD/RS; ***102*** John Glover/GPL; ***103*** *(l)* Clive Nichols/ Meadow Plants, *(panel)* RD/RS, David Murray, J S Sira/GPL, Howard Rice/GPL, Lamontagne/GPL; ***104-5*** John Glover/ Blockley; ***105*** Nigel Cattlin/HSI; ***106*** Clive Nichols/ Coates Manor Garden; ***107*** *(t)* Brigitte Thomas/GPL, *(b)* Steven Wooster/Beth Chatto Garden; ***108*** Jonathan Buckley/designer Diana Yakeley; ***110*** *(panel)* RD, RD/RS, RD/RS, RD, *(t)* Howard Rice/GPL.

Flowers and Foliage
112 Andrew Lawson; ***114-15*** Steven Wooster; ***115*** *(tr)* Eric Crichton; ***116*** *(bl)* Steven Wooster/Beth Chatto Garden; ***116-17*** Marcus Harpur/The Dower House, Essex; ***117*** *(panel)* all RD, except third, RD/RS; ***119*** *(tl)* Clive Nichols/Chenies Manor, *(panel)* Sunniva Harte/GPL, RD, RD/RS, RD/RS, RD; ***120*** *(l)* Picturesmiths Ltd, *(r)* Juliette Wade/Overstroud Cottage, Bucks; ***121*** *(panel)* Didier Willery/GPL, RD/RS, RD/RS, RD/RS, RD/RS; ***122*** HSC; ***123*** Richard Soar; ***124*** Eric Crichton; ***125*** Steven Wooster/Tonter Linden; ***126*** Derek St Romaine/Mrs Thompson; ***127*** Nigel Cattlin/HSI; ***128*** J S Sira/GPL; ***129*** *(l)* Clive Nichols, *(panel)* RD, RD/RS, RD/JW, Steven Wooster/GPL; ***130-1*** Derek St Romaine/designer Lady Xa Tollenmache RHS Chelsea; ***132*** *(panel)* RD, RD/RS, RD, RD, *(r)* John Glover/ Great Dixter; ***134*** Rosalind Simon/ designer Paul Findlay; ***137*** *(panel)* John Glover/GPL, RD/RS, RD/RS, RD, RD/RS; ***138*** *(t)* Karin Craddock, *(b)* David Murray; ***140*** *(l)* John Glover; ***140-1*** Clive Nichols/GPL; ***141*** John Glover; ***143*** *(t)* Jonathan Buckley/ Great Dixter, *(b)* Rosalind Simon.

Boundaries and Walls
144 Derek St Romaine/Mrs Thompson; ***146*** *(l)* Densey Clyne/ GPL, *(r)* John Glover; ***147*** *(t)* Jerry Pavia/GPL, *(br)* Steven Wooster; ***148-9*** Eric Crichton; ***150*** *(t)* Rosalind Simon; ***150-1*** Jerry Harpur/Fudlers Hall, Essex; ***153*** *(t)* Lamontagne/GPL, *(b)* Karin Craddock; ***155*** Steven Wooster/GPL; ***156*** *(l/r)* Picturesmiths Ltd; ***157*** *(t)* Clive Nichols/Herterton House; ***158*** *(l)* Andrew Lawson, *(r)* Brigitte Thomas/GPL; ***159*** *(l/r)* Steven Wooster; ***160*** Eric Crichton/ GPL; ***161*** *(panel)* Andrew Lawson, RD/RS, RD/RS, RD/JW; ***163*** *(l)* Derek St Romaine/Mrs Thompson, *(panel)* RD/RS, RD/RS, RD, Juliette Wade/RD; ***164-5*** Karin Craddock; ***166*** Howard Rice/GPL; ***167*** Gordon Roberts/HSI.

Patios and Containers
170 Brigitte Thomas/GPL; ***172*** *(t)* Henk Dijkman/GPL, *(b)* Juliette Wade; ***173*** *(t)* Jules Selmes, *(b)* Steven Wooster/GPL; ***175*** Ron Sutherland/ designer Anthony Paul/GPL; ***177*** *(tl)* Steven Wooster/Whichfords Pottery, *(tr)* Rosalind Simon/designer Paul Findlay, earthenware pot, Jennifer Lloyd-Jones; ***179*** *(l)* Steven Wooster/ Bourton Hill House, *(panel)* RD, RD/RS, RD/JW, RD/RS; ***180*** Steven Wooster/Martin Summers; ***181*** *(l)* Clive Nichols, *(panel)* all Photos Horticultural, except fourth, Garden/Wildlife Matters; ***182*** Lynne Brotchie/GPL; ***185*** *(l)* John Glover/GPL, *(panel)* RD/JW, RD, RD/JW, RD/RS, RD/RS; ***187*** *(t)* John Glover, *(b)* Jules Selmes; ***188*** Derek St Romaine/Glen Chantry; ***190*** *(t/b)* Andrew Lawson; ***191*** *(t)* Howard Rice/GPL, *(b)* John Glover; ***192*** J S Sira/GPL; ***193*** Derek St Romaine/designed by Sparsholt College, RHS Chelsea; ***194*** *(t)* Clive Nichols, Sleightholme Dale Lodge; ***196*** *(l)* Andrew Lawson; ***196-7*** Clive Nichols/ designer Paula Rainey Crofts; ***197*** Steven Wooster; ***198*** *(l)* Juliette Wade; ***199*** *(l)* Clive Nichols/Lisette Pleasance, *(r)* John Glover/Hampton Court; ***201*** *(l)* Steven Wooster/ Rathmichael Lodge, *(r)* John Glover/ designer Barbara Hunt; ***203*** *(panel)* RD, RD/JW, RD/JW, RD/RS, RD/RS.

Water Gardening
204 John Glover/GPL; ***206*** *(l)* Derek St Romaine/designer David Stevens, RHS Hampton Court; ***206-7*** Gary Rogers/GPL; ***207*** *(bl)* Derek St Romaine, *(br)* Clive Nichols/designer Christopher Costin, Hampton Court; ***208-9*** John Glover/GPL; ***209*** *(tl)* John Glover/GPL; ***210*** John Glover/GPL; ***212-13*** Nicola Stocken Tomkins; ***214*** *(l)* John Glover/GPL; ***215*** *(panel)* RD, RD/RS, HSC, HSC; ***216*** *(l)* Clive Nichols/designer Roger Platts, *(r)* Derek St Romaine/designer Clare Palgrove, RHS Hampton Court; ***218*** *(panel)* HSC, HSC, HSC,RD, RD/RS; ***218-19*** Jerry Pavia/GPL; ***220*** *(t)* G I Bernard/OSF, *(b)* Colin Milkins/ OSF; ***221*** *(l)* Paul Franklin/OSF, *(panel)* RD/RS, HSC, HSC, RD/JW, HSC; ***222*** *(t)* Clive Nichols, *(b)* Derek St Romaine; ***223*** Clive Nichols; ***224*** Clive Nichols.

The Kitchen Garden
228 Brigitte Thomas/GPL; ***232*** *(t)* Brian Carter/GPL, *(b)* Jonath[illegible] Buckley/designer Rosemary Lindsay; ***233*** *(panel)* RD, RD, RD, Clive Boursnell/GPL, RD/RS; ***234*** *(panel)* Jerry Pavia/GPL, RD/RS, RD/RS, RD, RD, *(r)* Brian Carter/GPL; ***235*** Liz Dobbs; ***237*** *(tl)* Steven Wooster/ Whichfords Pottery, RHS Chelsea; ***238*** *(t)* John Glover/GPL, *(b)* Lamontagne/ GPL; ***241*** *(panel)* Brigitte Thomas/ GPL, Howard Rice/GPL, Michael Howes/GPL, Brigitte Thomas/ GPL; ***243*** all Nigel Cattlin/HSI, except 'root flies' Len McLeod/HSI; ***244-5*** Primrose Peacock/HSI; ***246*** *(t)* Friedrich Strauss/ GPL, *(b)* Juliette Wade/GPL; ***248*** *(t/b)* Derek St Romaine; ***249*** Derek St Romaine; ***250*** Nigel Cattlin/HSI; ***251*** *(panel)* Nigel Cattlin/HSI; ***252*** Primrose Peacock/HSI; ***254*** *(c)* M H Berlyn, *(r)* Bayliss Precision Components; ***257*** *(panel)* RD, Nigel Cattlin/HSI, RD, RD, RD/RS.

Garden Organiser
282 *(tr)* Derek St Romaine, *(bl)* RD/RS, *(br)* RD; ***287*** *(tr)* Clive Nichols, *(bl)* Clive Boursnell/designer Nick Ryan; ***303*** Tony Stone Images; ***304*** *(r)* David Askham/GPL; ***305*** *(tr)* RD, *(others)* RD/RS.

Jacket photography
Carol Sharp/Flowers & Foliage

Index: Michele Clarke

400-101-1